CW00428770

Dear Friends,
Liebe Freunde

*International friendship
and the First World War*

Rosamund Ridley

www.nomads.vze.com
ridley.nomad@googlemail.com

Liebe Freunde,

Wir hoffen dasz Sie diese Bilde interessanten finden werden.....

Frank Bourne, 19th July, 1910, forwarding photos taken in the Peak District to his friends in Frankfurt's Ferienheimgesellschaft. In WWI, Frank was jailed as a conscientious objector. At Christ's Hospital School, he was the top maths student of his year, excelling too in science, modern languages, shorthand, geography and technical drawing. After the war, he was employed by Lever Brothers, but his career never recovered.

' Poppies made the fields of corn and barley very gay. '

Six Nomads in Normandy, 22nd July, 1912

' In what had once been no-man's-land, the dead lay thick. Caught in a terrible hail of machine gun fire, they lay amongst the tall grasses, where the blue cornflower, scarlet poppy and yellow mustard plant nodded and swayed on the breeze'

' The chief drawback to life in a tunnel, after the lice, is the monotony of living in the bowels of the earth, with only a candlelight, and nothing to do but smoke. But from the bottom of the shaft, one might see the blue sky of heaven, with a brilliant poppy decking the top of the trench on the skyline.'

Alec Westmore, WWI stretcher bearer, 1928 Educated at Liverpool's Collegiate School, Alec had hoped to be a journalist. Discharged in April, 1918, with serious injuries and shellshock, Alec lost the sight of one eye and the other was badly damaged. Even so, in 1919, he published articles in the Liverpool Courier on the work of the RAMC, revised and extended in 1928 as a short history of the 63rd Field Ambulance.

Vergessen werde ich nie, was ich während langer Jahre von ihnen all an treuer Freundschaft und Liebe erfahren habe meh kann icht nicht tun. Sie seien nicht am Krieg und all dem elend Schuld, so sagen sie auf ihrer Insel. Und unsere tapferem Männer, Söhne und Brüder, deren lieben nun trauern haben sie den krieg gewollt ? Trotz allem, grusse Sie bitte, von mir und wenn dies mein letzter Gruss an dich sein sollte... '

Bernhard Seib, 1909 Musterschule exchange student, who worked for three summers at the Newlands hostel, Derwentwater, to his British friends. Stationed near Rheims, Bernhard told his officers that he couldn't shoot his friends. He was transferred to the eastern front and died there.

Foreword

Sitting with people, often at pivotal moments in their lives, I have always considered it a privilege to hear how they or members of their family have tried to make sense of life and to hear some of the aspirations, influences and passions which have shaped them over the years. There is so much to learn from other people's stories. They can give us insights into our own.

Behind the compelling stories of six young people, "The Nomads", told in these pages lie some of the better aspirations, influences and passions of the late nineteenth and early twentieth centuries - international friendship and co-operation - the desire to share with young working people from industrial towns and cities 'regions of loveliness (in the English landscape and beyond) to seek out and preserve, for the highest uses of the human spirit'

It's the story too of Arthur Leonard, a young, radical, congregationalist minister and eventual Quaker, who sought to develop international friendships and appreciation of landscape through founding The Co-operative Holidays Association, recruiting as allies many of the most inspirational men and women in Britain at the time.

The Nomads, four twenty-something lads and two girls, go to Normandy and Brittany on a backpacking holiday in the summer of 1912 and themselves tell the story of their "adventures and misadventures". Seeing "1912" maybe we reach for an obvious point of reference - the year of the Titanic. They would have known that. It sank only months before their trip and its registered home port was Liverpool, the city from which they set out. We also know what the Nomads did not as they walked the woods and fields of Northern France together. Only two summers later their lives would be changed forever by the outbreak of the Great War. International friendships and co-operation would be marked out by front lines, trenches and barbed wire; regions of loveliness were shelled into seas of mud and the human spirit of a generation lay mutilated on the battlefields of the Western Front.

As Rosamund was researching their stories, I would hear the latest news from time to time. A vital piece of evidence was proving elusive, family members couldn't be traced, a promising lead had become a dead end. The detective work continued, and what might have remained an echo in the history of only a few families has become through their generosity of time and spirit a story which we can all be privileged to hear and share.

Coincidentally, sixty summers to the year after the Nomads set out on their holiday, the homes in which three of them had grown up stood literally one and two streets away from my own in the Friends Meeting House in the same part of Liverpool. A former student of Edge Hill College, like one of them, I passed those houses very often. I knew nothing of their stories then. I know better now and I am the better for knowing.

Geoff Watson
Staveley Vicarage
Cumbria   September 2009

Contents

The backpackers' book 'Six Nomads in Normandy', summer 1912
' Long life and happy days ! ' text, photos and interpretation.

Introduction

Arnside beach can be deadly. Killer tides rip across Morecambe Bay in minutes. On a bleak Sunday in January, we'd come to the coast hoping for better weather. But the siren had rung for high tide, and the storm clouds grew darker still. No matter... At Arnside, whatever the weather, there's always the legendary junk shop, full of forgotten lives. It's where I come to find presents for my brother. Once, living somewhere far eastern, he sent me a set of opium scales.

Six Nomads in Normandy had drifted to the top of a pile. There are always piles of books, gathering dust and spiders. Shelf space is reserved for bone-fide classics by real authors. The book I'd picked up seemed to be an old photo album. Its worn leather spine smeared my hands orange. Decaying leather does this, those white gloves worn by archivists give two-way protection. On a dank Sunday afternoon in mid-January, there was very little light anywhere, inside or out. The hand-drawn map was exquisitely accurate, every major town neatly marked, black ink for the many kilometres on foot, red, for journeys by public transport. The south coast of England, the north coast of France. D-Day, surely ? Then I read the date, MCMXII. Flicking through the yellowed pages I saw, dimly, Edwardian fashions, young men in straw boaters, a couple of waspwaisted young women in ankle length skirts. Older adults wore very different styles, and there was nothing waspwaisted about the smiling women with their broad white aprons. One arresting photo showed a row of men, women and youngsters, who seemed to be brandishing pitchforks and scythes. It was captioned ' Our Friends the Peasants'.

The battered album wouldn't do at all. Why should my brother be interested in Edwardian photos ? Returning the 'Nomads' to the unsteady pile of also-ran stock, I headed upstairs, where the larger mathoms are stored, train-sets, shop dummies from the Twenties and Thirties, moth-eaten Monarchs of the Glen, faded samplers, and those vast Victorian reproductions of mountain scenery and Highland cattle. Somewhere in this gallimaufry, there must be something for David.

Then the shop was closing. I never leave empty-handed. Nobody does. Picking up the album again, I began to read the typed text. Interleaved between the photos, it was faded but perfectly legible, here and there slipping into French, a word or two of Latin. Someone had taken the trouble to insert accents, in all the right places. £10? Maybe... What else could I buy him, for ten pounds ? Sometimes, old photos have a charm and market value of their own. There seemed to be plenty of them. Scanned, restored, fitted into a decent frame, something unique is achieved. One, of a sturdy washerwoman by a river, had the look of a Vermeer, light and shade perfectly observed. What did cameras cost in 1912 ? The title page alone was intriguing :

" SIX NOMADS IN NORMANDY "

Being a true and authentic account

of their Adventures and

Mis-Adventures

By THEMSELVES

MCMXII

1912....

So it was just before the First World War ? This book was important. Carefree in the French countryside, six young people had a story to tell, adventures to remember for a lifetime, couldn't know that their whole world was about to end. Between dozens of photos and postcards, the Nomads' story is recorded in sixty-nine carefully typed pages, arranged in eight chapters. Beyond the formality of Edwardian fashion, the faces were young. At a guess, the Nomads were twenty-somethings, six young people, enjoying an idyllic holiday. Enterprising of them to make a book of it, organise the maps, the photos, the binding. This was desktop publishing, vintage MCMXII. The date is surely authentic. There's no reason to think it was written any later. It was the year Titanic sank. Britain was beleaguered by strikes, including the miners and the dock workers. As usual, there was trouble in the Balkans, and, far nearer home, in Ireland. Two men from Birmingham wrote a music hall song, called ' It's a Long Way to Tipperary. '   And six adventurous young people had created this unique memoir. At the end of the second chapter, one line cried out from the faded page :

' Poppies made the fields of corn and barley very gay...

In 1912, poppies were just another wild flower. But in the old language of flowers, the one the young Nomads would know, poppies meant compassion and relief from pain. Very soon, poppies would symbolize the grief of a world in mourning for its sons. Two years later, did those four young men return to France ? Die there, on the Western Front ?

In Flanders fields, the poppies blow

Between the poppies, row on row

That mark our graves.

Contacting the county record office, I arranged to meet a local archivist, warned her that, despite the title, ' Six Nomads in Normandy' was nothing like Three Men in a Boat. Captivating, yes, but hardly a work of comic genius. Irrelevant, she said. The book would be important if the young Nomads could barely spell. Then inevitably, she reached for the nearest cliché... This was 'a letter from the lost generation'. So often, clichés serve as shorthand for painful truths. In one short typescript, the Nomads celebrate youth, confidence and hope. Copyright searches confirmed that it had never been published, but there might be other handmade copies. One for every member of the party ? Possibly... Making this book, they'd wasted nothing, developing even the broken pieces of one photographic plate. Another, broken into three pieces, had to be discarded.

One of the earliest photos in the book is captioned 'sac à dos'. In single file, through the tall grass of July, five of them are walking along a path, all carrying rucksacks. One of the women has hers slung low, exactly like a bumbag. So they're backpackers, just like any young travellers today ? A mixed party too, four men, two women, off on holiday together, like twenty-first century friends. In expert hands, the photos might reveal far more. Clothes, especially, can say so much about the wearer, and in 1912, holidaying ' sac à dos ' with partners was definitely unusual.

In Bradford, photographic experts suggested an approach to the V & A. After studying photographs of the Nomads, two costume historians had intriguing news. The clothes worn by one of the young men aren't typical of English leisure wear from this period. Working independently, in Bath and in Manchester, both experts noticed the distinctive slant of this man's pockets and the curve of his jacket. Unusually high-waisted, his trousers were reminiscent of lederhosen.[1] His hat closely resembles a style marketed at the time as ' The Tyrol '. In Northampton, shoe historians confirmed that the round toes of the shoes he's wearing suggest a style which originated in Austria . Could this mean that the fair, sturdy young man was actually German or Austrian ? Perhaps - and perhaps not... Confidently backpacking across Northern France, willing to do his best in French, had he travelled to Germany too ?

The story of their idyll in France offers 'a glimpse of the twentieth century as it might have been',[2] the final words unbearably poignant : ' And once again raise the glass, refill it to the brim, and with clinkings and deep draughts each pledge each, to better friendship, long life, and happy, happy days, as full of good as was Our Holiday in France.' Long life ? Happy days ? But it was 1912...

In 1912, why not ? A year ago, the dog-days crisis over Morocco had passed. Europe wasn't at war. In April, 1911, Britain and the United States had agreed that in future, all disputes between them would be settled by peaceful arbitration. During a debate in the House of Commons, in April, 1911, Captain J. Bagot, the M.P. for Westmorland, expressed his hopes for the future :

' The twentieth century might go down in history as the period when the heavy yoke of great armaments was taken from the shoulders of the world. '

For the young backpackers, 1912 would be like 1963, the year after the Cuban missile crisis didn't lead to a nuclear holocaust. Armageddon had been cancelled. Their adventures in France could go ahead.

Chapter One

' We dreamt of showing the earth to the company of youth. '

'And once again raise the glass, refill it to the brim... '

The backpackers' 1912 adventures end with their confident toast to 'Friendship, long life and happy days'. In the twenty-first century, every word is stained with sadness.

Long life ? Happy days ? In 1912, why not ? A year ago, the dog-days crisis over Morocco had passed. Europe wasn't at war. 1912 was their 1963, the year after the Cuba crisis didn't lead to a nuclear holocaust. Sanity had prevailed, there'd be no Armageddon. The adventure in France could go ahead. In the still-new century, all disputes between nations would be settled by peaceful arbitration. Now almost forgotten, little more than a footnote in history, Britain's 1911 peace treaty with the USA had been welcomed with enthusiasm on both sides of the Atlantic. Addressing his constituents in April 1911, one Conservative M.P suggested that 'The twentieth century might go down in history as the period when the heavy yoke of great armaments was taken from the shoulders of the world.'[1]

In the twenty-first century, defence chiefs plead, as always, that they need more and better equipment. Hoping, allegedly, for peace, Europe continued to prepare for war. Tranquil as it may seem at first glance, the backpackers' idyll in France is steeped in politics. Six young people with the intelligence and initiative to plan this adventure couldn't fail to be aware of the international situation. On holiday, they bought an English newspaper, discussed Lloyd George's latest budget, knew that warships patrolled the seas. They knew, to their advantage, that the franc was weak. Crossing La Manche, they'd left their own country besieged by strikes, sectarian riots, and even, during a miserable summer, real fears of food shortages. Britain relied far too heavily on foodstuffs imported from all over the Empire, but in the wet and alarmingly cold summer of 1912, only rural newspapers expressed much concern for the harvest. France had serious troubles on the home front. The sporadic food riots of 1911 were a grim echo of 1871, when Paris itself had been starving.[2]

Backpacking through Normandy and Brittany, the Nomads were celebrating the still unfamiliar entente cordiale, defined by John Foster Fraser, for those who hadn't caught up with this novel arrangement : 'The French are our friends. They drink our whisky, and we drink their cheap wine. This is called the entente cordial. '[3] Old habits die hard. The entente was by no means universally popular. Driving through the Lake District in July 1911, Prinz Heinrich of Hesse was greeted by a banner ' Herzlich Wilkommen in Windermere... Blood is thicker than water.' The prince was a competitor in the friendly post-Coronation Anglo-German car rally.[4] In Windermere, he was staying at the country house of the British managing director of Daimler. Blood is thicker than water needs no translation and wine lists of the period can be startling. In the Edwardian era, a case of Liebfraumilch often cost more than Mouton Rothschild, sparkling hock more than Veuve Clicquot, and a cruise on the Rhine was, naturally, far superior to a budget journey along the Rance, in Brittany.

Burying the hatchet with France broke with centuries of tradition. In the summer of 1911, the entente cordiale allies, France and Britain, had been on the brink of war with Britain's old friend, her 'cousin nation', Germany. France and Germany had squabbled over ' a piece of North African sand ', all because, most unreasonably, Germany wanted a port in the Mediterranean. Clearly, this couldn't be allowed. Why not is never discussed. It's self-evident. Britannia ruled the waves and a quarter of the globe, colonising countries for their own good. She would, of course, support her new friend in any dispute over African sand. Why Britain, France, Germany or any other country should claim to own African sand or an African port is another question not worth asking. The flashpoint came, naturally, in the dog-days, ' when most of us were lying on our backs in the shade, and watching the ripple of the soft sea waves. There was going to be a terrible conflict in the North Sea, our great statesmen were much perturbed, and warships were being equipped. This was all over Morocco (where the bedroom slippers come from) with which we had little concern.' [5] In the summer of 1911, when Germany's Panther gunboat challenged the French-owned port of Agadir, Morocco was still a far away country of which we knew nothing.

Then the moment of madness passed. They didn't blow each other sky-high with long distance guns. Germany agreed to settle for part of the Congo. The great battleships really were, as the statesmen of Britain and Germany insisted, merely a deterrent. Like all weapons of mass destruction, they were of course designed to keep the peace. Lloyd George's tax reforms would benefit the poor, a little, but they also raised vast sums for the armed services. At Westminster and in the Reichstag, the need for massive expenditure on armaments was perfectly clear. The Crown Prince was sometimes disgracefully rude about his English cousins, but the Kaiser could surely be trusted to keep his son in order.[6]

At the year's end, the last editorials of 1911 bear an uncanny family likeness to those written fifty years later, in December 1962. Most writers rejoice over peace in their time. The Manchester Guardian found the narrow escape from war alarming :

' a little more misunderstanding might have set England at war with Germany, without anyone outside the Government knowing why.' [7]

Fortunately, all was well. On the shores of Derwentwater, speakers at the 1912 Keswick Convention spoke enthusiastically of peace, of the many Germans they'd met as friends, who were nothing like the monsters of fiction.[8] In July, 1912, spotting a warship off the coast of Jersey, six young backpackers could laugh about German spies, the popular and dastardly villains of political thrillers by John Buchan, Erskine Childers, William Le Queaux and their many imitators. The spies were, of course, wasting their time, Britain, with her fleet of invincible and massively expensive Dreadnoughts had won the arms race. Now that little matter was settled, a reforming government could at last turn its attention to the home front, and a very different war. The stunted and sickly Boer volunteers had made poverty news. The wretched physical condition of so many industrial workers had been known for decades, recorded, not just in campaigning fiction, but in government reports. The poor weren't even decent cannon-fodder. Visitors in another country, the six 'Nomads' recognised the different but very real poverty of rural France. In 1912, moneyed holidaymakers from southern England came to Brittany to gamble. The backpackers were far from rich and definitely not gamblers. Their idea of a holiday was radically different. They'd come, not as casual tourists, but to discover France, meet her people, enjoy the French countryside, observe the abundant wildlife, explore ruins, reflect on a shared history and centuries of conflict.

Analysing their journal, word by word, I failed at first to recognise the most important clue of all. According to the writers, their adventures in France began in a railway carriage on July 20th, 1912. As ' Mr Pulford' s party ', they were heading for London. Some of them travelled by Tube for the first time. After a hectic afternoon of galleries and sightseeing, including the Tate, the Abbey and Trafalgar Square, they caught the London and South Western Railways train from Waterloo to Southampton, to board Hantonia, the overnight ferry for Le Havre. But the inspiration for their French idyll had its origins more than twenty years earlier, at the independent Congregational Church in the Lancashire milltown of Colne, then a hotbed of radical politics and equally radical faith. In the final chapter of their story the Nomads are in Dinan, searching for somewhere called 'the C. H. A. centre' Dusty and dishevelled after their twenty mile walk from Dol, the six travellers welcome a rare chance of speaking English, but the imposing villa, with its 'babble of many tongues' isn't for them. They find somewhere else to stay. Invited to join the C. H. A. guests for an evening of music, they politely decline. After a fortnight living out of rucksacks, their 'trampish' clothes aren't fit for company.[9]

The initials suggested some kind of hostel. Country Hostels Association ? In French, surely Association would come first... When at last they track the place down, the host and hostess are clearly English, a Mr and Mrs Hinchcliff. The centre was apparently some kind of youth hostel. Among the casinos of Dinan, it wouldn't be a spartan Alpine hut. Further research identified the Countrywide Holidays Association, now absorbed by the better known Ramblers. Eventually, the original title, Cooperative Holidays Association led to business records and many other documents deposited in the Greater Manchester archives. The Villa Ste Charles in Dinan was one of the earliest overseas houses leased by the C.H.A. During WWI, it would become a Red Cross hospital.[10]

The Association proved to be a walking club and a great deal more, founded in 1894 by Arthur Leonard, described in the archives as a 'former Congregationalist minister'. Traditionally, the young men and plenty of women in the Lancashire mill towns would spend their 'wakes' holidays get wasted in Blackpool. In an exasperated sermon, Leonard's word is 'vitiated', but he'd understand the current colloquialism only too well. Blackpool in the legendarily dissolute 1890's was a match for any 21st century drunken antics in Prague or Phuket.[11] But why was Leonard a 'former minister' ? Had he been unfrocked ? Had he quarrelled with God ? Young men who've studied and prepared hard for a life of ministry don't, as a rule, set up holiday companies, let alone one targeting the eighteen to thirty set. Arthur Leonard's remarkable career move was inspired by faith, politics, and the tragedy of stunted lives. In his first period of ministry,based in the raw new town of Barrow in Furness, he found the disaffected young, physically and spiritually wasted, both by wretched working conditions and, in his forthright opinion, the tragic misuse of leisure.

For the twenty-three year old Leonard, Barrow in 1887 would be the ultimate culture-shock. Londoners, if they'd read the right books, knew it was grim up North, but Mrs Gaskell's Drumble (Manchester), had a solid bourgeoisie, an Athenaeum, a strong university, a handsome collegiate church, superb music and over two thousand years of history. Dicken's relentlessly grim Coketown (Preston), had been a prosperous community long before the Conquest. For centuries, Preston, not Liverpool was Lancashire's major port. As the 'priest's town', it was a centre of learning too. Barrow was an industrial orphan, stranded on the distant Furness coast. As the new town exploded into unplanned existence, young workers made their own amusements, usually involving too much alcohol. Industrialists and wealthy landowners gave little or no thought to the well-being of their workers. Intermittently, steel and shipbuilding prospered. In 1887, Leonard arrived just as the impressive Town Hall opened. Barrow's new police force posed carefully on a narrow strip of paving stones. Very carefully.... In the foreground, just beyond their toes of their boots, there's only mud and bare earth. In such a narrowly focused economy, the latest recession had forced many out of work. During the Golden Jubilee year, soup kitchens opened on Barrow island and free dinners were provided for hungry school children.[12]   Prosperous Victorian Britain wanted the things Barrow made. The residents themselves were expendable, paid well enough when business was good, but badly hit during recessions. The closest modern parallel might be the new industrial centres of the far east, vulnerable to the fluctuating demands of the West.

By 1887, almost eighty thousand people inhabited the strange and often disturbing wasteland of Victorian Barrow. Very few were local. Like economic migrants now, Barrow's immigrant workers, many of them young and single, were sending over £1,000 a week to their families all over Britain and beyond.[13] Hostility between different migrant communities and faith groups was rife. Stripping out the political and sociological jargon of town planners, Barrow, 'rough, tough and insanitary ' had been allowed to happen. It existed for steel, shipping and the railways. In 1845, it had been a remote Furness village with barely two hundred residents. By the 1870's, Barrow had become, on a simple head-count, a major Northern town. Size isn't everything. Barrow was a town with no heart or history. Contemporary accounts suggest an urban wilderness of unfinished streets, crowded rooms, unlicensed 'hush' alcohol sold from terraced houses, obscene graffiti everywhere, scrawled by all ages and both sexes, and, according to the Registrar General, 'a startling increase in zymotic disease'. Efficient sewers and clean water were very much an afterthought. Until the cemetery opened in 1873, Barrow couldn't even bury her dead. Bodies had to be taken to Dalton in Furness, four miles away.[14]

Faith and philanthropy faced an enormous task. As a young man in his first ministry, Leonard discovered squalor, savagery, intellectual and spiritual poverty. The 'Reverend' title is distracting. It could suggest a sanctimonious Victorian patriarch. Still in his early twenties, Leonard was offering young people excitement and beauty instead of drunken oblivion. Congregational church records reveal an impassioned novice, struggling to reconcile his faith and ideals with the reality of life in the unpaved and disease ridden streets of Barrow. The impact on his faith, and very soon, the direction of his whole career was dramatic. A young man questioning the tenets of Christianity made dangerous enemies. Leonard, far too often for his own good, suggested that many churchgoers ignored all the inconvenient details of Christ's teaching. Young people welcomed Leonard's leadership, enjoying, for the first time in their lives, rambles on the Furness fells. Older members of the community distrusted his politics, and, as they saw it, his increasingly unorthodox faith. It was agreed that a move to the already notoriously radical town of Colne might be appropriate for all concerned. In Colne, Leonard discovered once again that, in his outspoken opinion, the young workers didn't understand how to use their leisure time.

Backpacking through Normandy, the francophile 'Nomads' can seem astonishingly familiar. On holiday, late Victorian factory workers are equally recognisable. Like cheap flights, cheap rail fares carried the working class young to resorts where alcohol flowed. Young people of both sexes shared seaside lodging houses, ten or more to a room, swam together naked, spent to the hilt, returning home hungover and penniless. All too often, the girls would be pregnant. In one August sermon, Leonard expressed his dismay in robustly clerical language.[15] Translated into modern English, he means they got drunk, often, and the rest tended to follow.

Moving from Barrow to Colne, Leonard understood only too well why factory workers headed straight for the pub. The Factory Acts and Coal Mines Regulation Act had achieved a some improvements, but for many, working conditions remained deadly. Briefly and within the strict limits of Health and Safety law, visitors to cotton mills reborn as heritage centres can experience the literally deafening conditions. When museum staff switch on just one loom in a room built for fifty, the noise is ear-shattering to the point of pain. The choking cotton-waste, thick and white as falling snow, can't be replicated, nor can the suffocating heat and humidity. Cotton fibres benefited from that humidity. Stifled and choking workers suffered from constant respiratory illness.[16]

Choosing the passionate young Arthur Leonard as their new minister, the deacons of Colne knew the appointment might be controversial. Born in Stoke Newington, Leonard's childhood world was intriguingly international. In 1871, the seven year old was living in Hackney with his widowed mother, four year old sister, and the six members of a Dutch-Belgian family, of whom only the baby was British born. After schooldays in Heidelberg and studying for the Congregational Ministry at Nottingham, he was now twenty-six years old, married, with a baby son. Reports from Barrow had hinted at unorthodox beliefs, including the suspicion that he was no longer Christian but a Unitarian. In the intensely political Colne of the 1890's, all kinds of unorthodox beliefs flourished. Too many of the clergy and fiery young politicians insisted that the teachings of Christ should be taken literally.[17] The outspoken Leonard was accused of wanting to create a Labour Church in the town. Church elders wrote to him sternly, complaining that he was using his position to promote socialism, a doctrine they entirely rejected.[18] In 1894, many people in Colne would probably welcome a Labour Church. But, as Leonard had already learned to his cost, a powerful minority opposed any suggestion of socialism, Christian, ethical, international, or any other brand.

Founded in Manchester only three years earlier by John Trevor, a former Unitarian minister, the Labour Church movement was spreading like wildfire through the industrial towns and cities of Britain. Critics complained that God was rarely mentioned.[19] From Plymouth to Dundee, Labour Churches were attracting leading socialists, including Keir Hardie, Ben Tillett, and, in nearby Keighley, Leonard's friend and exact contemporary, Philip Snowden. Like the churches, Victorian trades unions carried elaborate embroidered banners. Like the churches, the faithful walked in processions, singing rousing hymns. Leonard's response to his accusers was surely unanswerable. He had never sought to make Colne a Labour Church, and if everyone followed the teachings of Christ, there'd be no Labour churches and no need for them.[20]

Leonard saw his work for the 'holiday movement' as a development in faith and ministry, not an indulgence for the rich, but an absolute necessity for everyone. ' the clerk, chained to his desk all day, the mother, out of sorts with the fretting worries of home, the father and son, weakened by the impure air of the mill, all these require recreation of the body God has given them'.[21] In Northern England, over a century before 'right to roam', much of the wild and beautiful countryside was already accessible by footpath and along traditional ' corpse roads'. Bridleways used now by armies of hillwalkers and cyclists link scattered farmsteads to upland churches and market towns. Until Leonard arrived in Barrow, very few industrial workers explored the Lakeland or Furness fells. In Colne, he began to lead young people out of the hilly and narrow streets around the mills and up into a world few of them had seen, though it was all around them. He introduced them to the Pendle hills, the Ribble valley, and the high moorland around Keighley and Haworth. Dr John Paton of Nottingham, who had prepared Leonard for ministry, supported and guided Leonard's change of direction. Linking the hillwalking and music of Colne to the educational programme of the National Home Reading Union, it was Dr Paton who recognised the national and indeed international potential of the movement. Soon, Leonard and the many friends he inspired 'dreamt of showing the earth to the company of youth' - and not just the youth of Britain.

In his foreword to Leonard's only book, Dr Paton's son Lewis, High Master of Manchester Grammar School, 1903 - 24, defines Leonard's inspiration as ' a great piece of social engineering.'[22] 'Social engineering' sounds ponderous and unappealing. Delivered by government, it can be an insensitive and unwieldy process, often managing to alienate all the parties involved. Leonard's own version of his vision is both more poetic and more immediately practical. He wanted to show young people ' regions of loveliness to seek out and preserve, for the highest uses of the human spirit'.[23] In the caste-ridden Britain of 1890, this was a dangerous ambition. Regions of loveliness were reserved for the elite. Many of the intelligentsia believed that working class people were incapable of recognising beauty. Never afraid of controversy, Leonard decided to take a party of young millworkers to the Lake District. In literary Lakeland, millworkers from Lancashire were about as welcome as the latest killer virus now. They couldn't possibly appreciate the scenery.

The Kendal to Windermere line coralled low-budget day trippers around Bowness and the new railway town of Windermere. Beyond Windermere, economics and expert nimbyism had ensured that the Lake District remained carriage-trade only. Blessed with many friends in high places, the residents of Ambleside had recently defeated the 1887 Railway Bill, which would have extended the existing Kendal to Windermere line. ' Trippers ' were not wanted. Their presence would devalue property and drive away the better class of visitor. Ambleside would soon be no better than an inland Blackpool.[24] In countless letters to the Times, the Daily Telegraph, the Pall Mall Review and the Spectator, the factory workers of Lancashire and Yorkshire are singled out as grotesquely undesirable, in language which makes Wordsworth' s cautious attitude towards them seem moderate. Class hatred becomes indistinguishable from racism. The ageing Ruskin was horrified. Ambleside must be reserved for the delectation of the whole country, as 'a specimen of mountain village'. Allowed into the Lake District, factory workers would drink bottled beer. They might even eat sandwiches.[25] Leonard could have reassured his former idol on those points. Officially at least, the young men of Colne were clean-living and sober teetotallers. As for sandwiches... It would be years before the millworkers achieved such middle-class refinement. They made do with dried fruit and ginger biscuits. Oatcakes and 'pots of butter' carried in jacket pockets, were rather less successful.[26]

The first Lake District adventure was a triumph. Arranging cheap lodgings and walking heroic distances, just to reach the start of a climb, Leonard kept the price within the 21/-s he'd promised, though this sum was for many well over a week's wages.[27] On the slopes of Wansfell Pike, Leonard held their Sunday afternoon service. Later, in the Langdales, his address was based on the text 'What is man that thou art mindful of him ?' Next day, they climbed Helvellyn. In the words of one millhand, ' It were champion.' [28] Enough said, and preferable to some poems. The following summer, they travelled to Caernarfon, and in 1893, the local paper informed its readers that Leonard was now the secretary 'of a scheme which embodies a new idea of summer holidays.' The project was, from the very beginning, intensely and deliberately educational, supported by many of Britain's leading academics. As Leonard himself admitted, 'We did not conceal the fact that we were out for education. We believed in conferences and lectures'.[29]

Walking in the Lakes, Snowdonia, the Peak District and southern Scotland, holidaymakers would travel with University guides. Climbing a mountain wasn't enough. Leonard's project helped young people to explore a new world. Their guides were young academics, explaining the landscape, its geology, its wildlife, its history. [30] In France, the Nomads' early C.H.A. experiences had prepared them to discover and understand every facet of life in another country. City-bred, they didn't quite realise why, in a summer of all too-frequent rain, a harvest-time funeral had to be held at five in the morning. But apart from one youthful lapse (singing popular songs, late at night, in the street) they behave as guests, not careless tourists.

In his new role, Leonard sought out as allies many of the most inspirational men and women in Britain, including Professor Patrick Geddes, the writer and peace campaigner Norman Angell, the composer Walford Davies, Ramsay and Margaret MacDonald, Arnold Rowntree, Cecil Sharp, R. H. Tawney, Charles Trevelyan, Hewlett Davies, the so-called ' Red Dean' of Canterbury and the Archbishop of York. The first officers of the C.H.A included Dr Alex Hill, Master of Downing, and for two years, Vice-Chancellor of Cambridge, Canon Rawnsley, founder of the National Trust, and Sir Drummond Fraser, director of the Midland Bank. A letter to Patrick Geddes, written in August 1900, defines the exhilarating, life-changing experiences Leonard sought for young people. Professor Geddes had just welcomed one of the early C.H.A. groups to the Outlook Tower in Edinburgh, where he'd enabled them to stay in a university hall of residence. A 1901 report in the Globe confirms the modest cost of accommodation in Edinburgh, 32s 6d, for a week's board and lodging in halls of residence, with an additional fee of 5s to take part in lectures and excursions. Based at the 'Outlook Tower', C.H.A. students worked with many distinguished academics from Edinburgh and other universities.[32] In 1900, a visit to the Tower, now better known as the Camera Obscura, would certainly 'show the earth to the company of youth.' in a completely new way. Meeting Charlotte Mason in Ambleside that year, Professor Geddes discussed her approach to the education of teachers.[33] Officially a botanist and biologist, Geddes multifaceted career defies definition, but the twenty-first century understanding of our planet is catching up with his vision of life on earth, and mankind's place as one part of that whole. Long before the Apollo programme, Geddes created images of Edinburgh and the whole planet in relation to the universe. As part of his Craiglockhart convalescence, Wilfred Owen would experience Geddes' holistic vision.[34]

In the early days, C.H.A. guests were expected to share household chores. Most were young, many were working class. Pioneer members from all backgrounds worked hard to restore ramshackle and near-derelict buildings, including, at Newlands, near Derwentwater, a disused woollen mill.[35] In 1905, the opening ceremony included a tribute in verse from Canon Rawnsley. The Canon's poem suggests that tedious industry has been replaced with 'brotherhood', but in any household, however transient, some chores are essential. A shoestring budget and spartan, mainly self-service living kept prices low. Leonard's approach to hiring domestic staff reflects his own egalitarian principles. Staff were offered a fair wage, with the same standard of food and accommodation as the guests. Decades before statutory sick-pay and disability rights, Leonard insisted that a sick hostel worker should be supported until she had recovered, and her post must be kept open. Staff were welcome to join guests on excursions and for social evenings. Early C.H.A groups included, in the same party, millhands, carpenters, students and shop assistants. On arrival, guests were reminded that ' the status of our domestic staff is one of social equality and mutual service.' Tipping was strongly discouraged, cheap for employers, but in Leonard's opinion, sustaining a corrupt social system.[36]

With or without tipping, the astute middle-classes spotted a bargain. The fees charged to holidaymakers covered only living costs. Philanthropists who admired and supported Leonard had enabled the association to acquire substantial properties in highly desirable locations all around the British Isles and in France, Switzerland, and Germany. Gentrification was almost inevitable. Staying at the spartan Keld hostel in Yorkshire with his Manchester Grammar School pupils, Lewis Paton had willingly peeled potatoes. In his schooldays at the Halle Gymnasium, Paton, like Leonard, had known the simple mountain huts of Germany.

By 1912, the organisation Leonard founded was seriously compromised. Inspired by their early C.H.A. experiences and acutely aware of the international situation, the adventurous 'Nomads' explored France independently. Their achievement is a tribute to Leonard's original vision of international friendship. The Villa St Charles in Dinan, where the 'trampish' backpackers felt so uneasy, was depressingly far removed from Leonard's original vision. Its hidebound clients even rejected French food as unsuitable for English stomachs. At British centres, many middle-classes C.H.A. members demanded all kinds of creature comforts. Unlike the pioneer millhands and Lewis Paton, they refused to peel potatoes, polish boots or wash dishes. Leonard detested the insidious middle-class preference for ' people of their own sort.' Almost from the beginning, he'd sensed that what had begun in Lancashire should and must become international, challenging all divisions of class, faith, gender, politics and nationality.[37] In August, 1914, recruiting posters throughout Britain would reassure middle class office workers that they could serve with men of their own class. [38]

Trekking across Northern France, admiring cornfields bright with poppies, the Nomads were consciously eccentric, amused by the disbelief of their hosts. In Brittany, only one explanation was possible. The arduous journeys were obviously penitential. Why else would anybody walk so far, often twenty miles a day, carrying heavy rucksacks ? The Nomads' map of Northern France could be a template for Operation Overlord - the D-Day campaign of WWII. The date of their idyllic holiday and their confident final toast, ' to friendship, long life and happy days', prompted the inevitable questions : Who were they, where did they come from, and how did their story really end ? In peaceful old age ? Or on the Western Front ?

Chapter Two

Sac à dos

Backpacking across Northern France with partners and friends, the young Nomads often seem to be in the wrong century. They've read a couple of Rough Guides, looked up the best internet cafés and backpackers' hostels... Almost, but the date is always there, MCMXII, the future casting its ominous shadow. Already, France was mobilised, not yet on a war footing, but definitely wary. The new entente with Britain was rapidly becoming militaire rather than cordiale. Perhaps, in Dinan, the young travellers chose not to see the gun-carriages and military exercises ? They'd be hard to miss. On July 20th, 1911, exactly a year before the Nomads set sail for Le Havre, Britain and France had agreed that, if Germany attacked, Britain would send an expeditionary force to France. The Morocco crisis brought Europe to the brink of war. Politically aware, highly educated, the young travellers must have known they were taking risks, but this was the adventure of a lifetime, not to be missed. This was no Grand Tour or poetic flight from dreary convention. With or without their girlfriends, the Nomads' halcyon days would be brief.

Twenty-something in 1912, they must have been born around the time of Victoria's Golden Jubilee. Most of the party are determined to speak French, if not perfectly, then well enough to be understood. In the villages of Normandy and Brittany, they certainly don't expect their hosts to speak English. Independent travellers, they must have been superb organisers. Somehow, they looked up trains, booked their Channel crossing, worked out how to use French public transport. Nervous twenty-first century tourists complain bitterly about rip-off taxis, rarely think of hopping onto a local bus, because that would mean buying a ticket, speaking a few words of the local language. Tourists, perhaps deservedly, get ripped-off. Travellers learn enough of a language to go native or at the very least, exchange courtesies. Apologising for an accidental jostle in the street is important. Treading on someone's toe without knowing the word for 'sorry' is unforgivable. Travellers do their homework. The Nomads prepared well for their journey. But surely, the Edwardians didn't do things like this ? Especially young women, closely guarded by chaperones... The stereotypes are confusing, a melange of films and novels too often remembered as fact, like The Go-Between, The Wings of the Dove, Howard's End. Adultery, conspiracy, skullduggery of every kind, in fact, all the usual vices, dressed in soft-focus elegance. By 1912, the Nomads are technically no longer Edwardians but Georgians. Apart from a handful of poets, there were no twentieth century Georgians. Kings and queens no longer define a generation. Like so much else, that tradition died on the Western Front. In 1953, the idea of 'New Elizabethans' met with indifference and quickly died.

Wandering across Northern France on foot was definitely and deliberately eccentric. Historians in St Malo and Rennes confirm that in Brittany, the footslogging British Nomads would have been regarded as beggars, gipsies, or insane. The only acceptable excuse for such a punishing journey would be a traditional Breton pilgrimage or pardon. In theory, like the Chaucerian jaunt to Canterbury, this was strictly penitential.[1] In Brittany, to their evident delight, the disreputable young backpackers shocked Bretons and conventional British tourists too.[2] Since the days of the aristocratic Grand Tour, the British upper classes had enjoyed their own privileged version of Europe. As soon as they could afford to, the middle classes travelled in comfort. Thomas Cook began selling package holidays in 1841. In 1912, Liverpool shipping companies offered cruises to the Canaries for fifteen guineas.[3] Determined not to be mere tourists, the Nomads wanted something utterly different, their own France, and, mostly, on their own two feet. To this day, adventure travel is a niche market. Like the Nomads, the discerning traveller looks for achievement, a couture experience, nothing off-the-peg. Trekking to the Everest base camp or cycling through France between chateaux and gourmet meals, it's useful if one can delegate tiresome details to experienced professionals. At a price, obviously.... Adventures are sold on thick and expensive paper to a carefully targeted market. The Nomads were on their own. Somehow, the idea of this holiday was born... Where did it come from ? A painting ? A popular song ? In 1912, 'Appleblossom time in Normandy.' topped the charts on both sides of the Atlantic. A Bonnard painting celebrated summer in Normandy. Another, by Sargent, records fashionable couples holidaying in the Alps, like the scandalous cast of Women in Love. In Liverpool, the Walker Art Gallery has a Breton scene, Cançale, by Forbes Stanhope, bought by Liverpool Corporation in 1885. Cançale is a fishing village near St Malo. Did the Nomads see this as children, dream of a journey to Brittany ?

From the Pennine Way to Compostella, or following in the footsteps of Hannibal, planning a long distance trek is a serious undertaking, even with lightweight 21st century equipment and guidebooks. Did the six of them meet to study maps, work out how far they could walk in a day, carrying a heavy rucksack in midsummer heat ? How did they plan what to pack and work out where to stay ? How much would this whole adventure cost, and how could they afford it ? Had they saved for years ? Second-class train travel and developing even a broken photographic plate suggests a shoestring budget. Where could they look up the exchange rate ? They certainly knew it, complaining when they thought a hotelier had cheated. According to their journal, cheating was unusual. Far more often, the party were delighted to be offered budget rates and a warm welcome. Searching for food at midday, they met with unstinting generosity. Faced with six hungry foot-sloggers, villagers offered whatever they could. Perhaps their hosts, mystified by the punishing distances, thought the Nomads couldn't afford transport and took pity on them.

For any English journey, they'd look up the trains in Bradshaw, just like Trollope's Warden and Archdeacon Grantly, travelling from Barchester to London.[4] If they planned to use French public transport, they'd need timetables, but how would they obtain these ? Planning an inter-rail trip around Europe today, or a gap-year world tour, young travellers need international timetables, websites, and the right kind of guidebook. Backpackers don't usually check in to Raffles or the Ritz. Nor do they buy their cappuccinos at Florian's. In 1912, there were plenty of French and English guide books for well-heeled English holiday makers, The elite had already discovered the Riviera. Frugally backpacking, the Nomads managed all their own accommodation and waited till the very end of their holiday to dine at a famous Breton restaurant. Sometimes, their supper was only bread and milk.

French historians were intrigued by the journal, especially when they realised the six friends were determined francophiles, willing and eager to speak French with their hosts. Despite their temporary Crimean alliance, Britain and France weren't exactly old friends, and Britain's Royal Family were still happy to be known as the House of Saxe-Coburg Gotha. The Oxford Dictionary of Quotations offers a rough but essentially reliable guide to the history of relations between England, France and Germany. The majority of British anti-German insults are twentieth century. The catalogue of abuse directed at France and the French is long, colourful and age-old. France, Sir Philip Sidney's 'sweet enemy', has always been the next door neighbour Britain loves to hate.[6]

With regret, French archivists warned that virtually no timetables had survived ruthlessly efficient Great War paper salvage. At the end of every year, guidebooks and timetables were collected and pulped.[7] In England, it was the same story. During both wars, newspapers, timetables and heaven knows what priceless old books were destroyed. Timber and woodpulp imports were seriously compromised. During WWI, salvaged paper was needed for shellcases. Salvaging material for the war effort became an end in itself, a test of patriotism. One war later, historic gates and railings were sacrificed, ripped out as scrap metal, and, often, left to rust. It seemed unlikely that many travel records would have survived. At the National Railway Museum in York, the archivist wasn't optimistic. Like the French, he explained that most timetables from that period would have become salvage. They did have the Bradshaw for July, 1912, if that would be of any use.[8]

In real terms, the ' Six Nomads ' were far more enterprising than many a cosseted gap year student, catching a plane to Bangkok or Sidney, heading for the beach and an English-speaking backpackers' hostel. Their map of Northern France is impeccable. As a Geography exercise, it surely deserves an A* Full marks too, for organisation and achievement. If only they'd spent a little time supplying their names, addresses, and a hint at what they did for a living. Professional family historians warned that, thanks to data protection, tracing quite ordinary twentieth century people could prove impossible, especially if the women had married. Unless any of them had achieved fame later in life ? But the Nomads weren't looking for literary success. Their memories of happiness are important as a private pleasure, perhaps shown to friends and family, then conserved for future generations of the family to enjoy. There's no published record of their story. Identifying them was likely to be extraordinarily difficult. On the other hand, they valued this experience, chose to analyse and describe their adventures, shape them into a book. No writer intends to remain entirely unread.[9]

According to the title page, the book was written 'By Themselves', indicating that it was a joint effort. The subtitle 'Put it in the Book' suggests sophisticated storytelling, a record of carefully selected vignettes. The 'adventures and misadventures' offer far more than a record of daily events, leaden and factual as a tour itinerary. The story is always told as if by one spectator, describing the activities of the other five. One of the young women remains nameless. Did this mean that she wrote the whole story ? At first, before reading the journal more carefully, this seemed possible, but in that case, why did they all claim authorship? Were they being deliberately mysterious, or were they simply a group of friends, taking it in turn to tell a story that belonged to all of them ? Studying each chapter, the sequence of authorship soon became clear. The nameless young woman's style is classic Edwardian lady, a young lady who knows her own mind and her King James Bible too. She can be acerbic, especially on the subject of Roman Catholicism, with its 'priest-ridden people', crucifixes and statues, but like her friends, she cares about good manners. In France, observing French etiquette is important. Eventually, to her own astonishment, she admits that friendship is possible, even with people 'so different in creed '. Other parts of the story were quite different in style and might be by one or more of the men. Authorship of the fifth chapter appears to change hands halfway through. One impatient writer scatters the text with abbreviations.

But which Nomad was which, and what were their names ? Throughout their adventures, the other young woman is always 'Miss Gleave '. Her forename is never given. Her style is intelligent and rather less ornate than her companion's. She's more liberal too, intrigued, as an Anglican, by the unfamiliar ceremonies of a French service, but certainly not appalled by the excesses of Catholic worship. As for the men... There are four names, Alec, Frank, Fred and Ross. Identifying them became a kind of brain teaser, an exercise in analysis and logic. Nine of the seventy two photographs show different combinations of men and women, but never more than five of them. A larger, postcard-sized photo shows all six together in a pony-trap, by the causeway to Mont St Michel. Presumably this was taken by a professional photographer. None of them are identified, in any of the photos. One of the men is never given a surname. Or a forename ? Throughout the book, he's always simply 'Ross' . A clue ? Possibly... At least it was a relatively uncommon name, Teutonic in origin, and hopefully, would be easier to investigate than another Fred or Frank.

This was, at least on the surface, a very formal age. If a young woman refers to a man only by his first name, the implication is that they must be related, or possibly, an engaged couple. But all the Nomads refer to this man as 'Ross'. He's named a dozen times, more than anyone else in the group. Could this mean he was the link between the friends ? Was the whole adventure his idea ? Throughout the book, it's usually Ross who's given a personality ; ' Ross, with his usual superabundance of energy.' 'Ross was rather perturbed.' 'Ross' (on a choppy crossing to Jersey) 'wisely remained in his bunk.' Used to travelling, or sea-sickness, or both ? The nameless woman seems unconcerned about his interest in 'the fair sex', as he explores the seashore at Carolles. Did this mean she was absolutely sure of him, gently amused ? Or a friend, teasing ? Fiancé, brother, cousin or simply a very close friend, Ross is allowed to admire bathing belles.

Three of the surnames were uncommon, Gleave, Pulford and Westmore; distinctive enough to limit data searches to manageable numbers. Had they been Miss Smith, Mr Jones and Mr Brown, the search would have been hopeless from the outset. Identifying Mr Bourne was bound to prove more difficult, Bourne being a relatively common English surname. First, then, the pencil and paper elimination, not unlike a game of Cluedo, scouring the text and the group photos for answers. How often was each surname mentioned ? Did this tally with the number of times forenames are given ? Miss Gleave and Mr Westmore were definitely a couple, usually closer to each other than strictly necessary. But was 'Mr Westmore' Alec, Fred or Frank ? The nameless woman and one of the men are often together, but their body language can be ambivalent, their relationship less certain. Covering sheet after sheet of paper, the names were juggled, swapped, substituted. Could there be a clue in the opening lines : 'Mr Pulford's party' was now 'en train' ; followed by an account of 'Fred' giving chemical experiments on the capture of the cold germ. Fred Pulford, then ? Possibly... Fred is named nine times, almost as often as Ross. The brain-teaser progressed. Fred was Mr Pulford, probably. Mr Westmore and Miss Gleave obviously enjoyed each other's company. He seemed to be Alec. Unless he was Frank ?

Eventually, the best guess identified the men as Fred Pulford, Alec Westmore and Frank Bourne. The other woman's continued formality towards 'Miss Gleave' appears strange in our first-name-only 21st century. How could two young women spend a fortnight's holiday together, and address each other as 'Miss' the whole time? Could it be that they barely knew each other, roped into this harebrained adventure by the men in their lives ? It happens, but surely, by the end of a fortnight's backpacking, they could relax ? Arguably, our casual use of first names is just as strange and equally deceptive. As recently as the 1950's, the mother of actor Martin Jarvis still addressed her neighbour and good friend of many years as 'Mrs'.[10] Today, hospital staff almost invariably address patients by their first given name, a practice which can be intensely irritating and has nothing whatsoever to do with friendship. Titles matter, but, unlike the overuse of forenames, the rules are subtle. A century before the Nomads, Emma Woodhouse is very clear on this point. She'll address Mr Knightley as 'George' only once, in the marriage service, but he's definitely her Mr Knightley.

Scanned, the book became far easier to analyse. More answers began to emerge. Mr Pulford had made all the bookings, the six travel to London together from an unnamed station. A fortnight later, returning from France, the party splits, and the beginning of their journey is revealed at last. Three of them are returning to Liverpool, three remaining in London. But which three stay in London and why ? The most likely explanation is that they were working in the capital. In that case, why did they all begin their travels in Liverpool ? If three were really Londoners, why travel to France from Liverpool ? Perhaps they were all originally Liverpudlians, but three now worked in London ? Or vice versa ? And why would any of their descendants part with such an intriguing story ?

' Find out where this came from', urged the county archivist. Provenance is important for any document. When a lost Beethoven manuscript or a missing Rembrandt turns up, people want to know where it's been. How did a story linked to Liverpool and London reach a junkshop in Cumbria ? The shop manager advertises a house-clearing service, but he doesn't record the source of all the jumbled stock. It's hardly Chippendale or First Folio Shakespeare. Real antiques are sent to different destinations. After a routine clearance, the bill is paid, anything saleable goes in the shop, and the rest is discarded. Perhaps the diary's owner had left Liverpool to work in Cumbria, or enjoy a Lake District retirement. The Westmorland Gazette often publishes appeals for information about Lakeland ancestry. The editor had scant interest in young people from Liverpool, who might turn out to be Londoners. Local newspapers used to cover national and international issues. Now, their news and features focus almost exclusively on the immediate area. Contacting thirteen Bournes, eleven Gleaves and three Pulfords in the local phone book produced no results at all, or at least, no obvious link with the Nomads. Some of the Gleaves and one of the three Pulfords claimed Liverpool ancestry. None of them recognised the young travellers or their story. Altogether, though, fourteen people out of twenty-seven took the trouble to reply. Any mail-shot advertiser would be astonished and gratified by such a strong response. They were all fascinated by the backpacking adventure, especially in a mixed party. Some supplied e-mail addresses, outlines of family history, eager to know how the search would develop.

Offered six French-speaking 1912 backpackers from Liverpool, the editor of the Liverpool Echo appeared to be moderately interested, promising that the news desk would be in touch. They weren't. A stronger link with Liverpool would be useful. So far, all the Nomads had done to connect them with the city was catching a train at Lime Street. Only three returned. Perhaps the three who remained in the south were Londoners ? National editors expressed polite disinterest. The travel journal and photos might be interesting, but who were these people ? The Nomads needed a local habitation and, preferably, six definite names. Frustratingly, the best chance of overriding twentieth century data protection would be a newspaper appeal, with photos from the journal. In Liverpool or London, somebody might recognise a great-grandparent, a great-uncle or aunt. The Nomads were still six missing people, in search of a history. The BBC were disappointed that they hadn't used a cine camera. One editor asked if any of the Normandy coast photos had been used to plan the D-Day landings ? But there were no gaps in the text, no signs of missing photos, and the War Office didn't return any of the holiday snaps used to identify the D-Day beaches.

Like their own epic journey, the real Nomad hunt had to begin in Liverpool. Virtual Liverpool first... Many investigations could be carried out before travelling to the city. One day, perhaps, every document will be available online. Nobody will need to visit distant archives. Websites are certainly convenient, saving petrol and train fares, but convenience has a price tag. Paying a fee to pursue fruitless searches, red-herrings can become seriously expensive fish. Searching online or in archives, it's important to focus, define how much is already known. Already, in their own writings and photographs, there was important information about these young people. Linked, however tenuously, to Liverpool, their mindset is intriguingly international.

The Six were characters in their own drama, starring in adventures they'd experienced and described together. Every village, every guest house, every débit de bossons and estaminet becomes a carefully planned location shot. They'd be together for almost every waking moment and for a whole fortnight. The structure of this group was important. To achieve their goal, they had to cooperate, and, as far as possible, support group decisions. From my own experience of long-distance treks in Britain and climbing in the Alps, I know that wise backpackers choose their companions with extreme care. Travelling solo or with total strangers can be safer than sullen miles of disintegrating friendship, or the end of a relationship. The young women's experience was relatively unusual. Rare eccentrics like Lady Hester Stanhope and Mary Kingsley didn't set a precedent. In Arab dress or a stout skirt, they were behaving like men. Decades later, so was Freya Stark. The Nomad women are completely different, startlingly contemporary. Backpacking with men they're close to, they're claiming this brief idyll as equals.

Had they known each other since childhood ? Had they met at work, at university, or through sport ? The warnings from professional historians were accurate. The twentieth century isn't an easy place to look for strangers. Twenty-first century personal data is lost by Government bodies with tedious regularity. For archive material, data protection and official secrets rule. All kinds of recent documents, including individual school and medical records are closed to the general public for up to a hundred years. The 1911 census might hold the answer to many questions, but it wasn't yet available. If I'd judged their ages correctly, the Nomads would be in their early to mid teens for the 1901 census, starting point for so many family historians.[11] The timing was intensely frustrating. If any of the Nomads had children, those children could now be in their eighties or even nineties; their memories a precious and irreplaceable link with the past. Tracing the Nomads became a race against time. Enterprising, confident, and politically aware, the backpackers were unusual young people. Identifying them would lead, perhaps, to their still-living children, and information otherwise lost to history.

Online, the 1901 site is simple enough, besieged daily by eager ancestor hunters all over the world. Tracing the story of their own families, ancestor-hunters have a considerable advantage. Most people know, at least approximately, when their grandparents married, where they lived, and what they did for a living. There are family bibles, deed boxes, wills, even legends of scandal. Official biographers chart already famous lives. Searching for total strangers, armed with nothing but three admittedly less than common surnames is a very different matter. It's rather like fly-fishing blindfold, using a barbless and unbaited hook. Not that the Nomads were total strangers... Carelessly, they'd omitted to mention who they were and where they lived, but like a crime scene, their book was chock-full of clues. Studying candidates with the right surname, some could be eliminated immediately.

On paper, a clear Nomad profile had developed. Most of them were French speaking. It might be French of Liverpool or London rather than Paris, but they knew the language well enough to enjoy jokes. Enjoying their first, and, for the conscience-stricken chapel contingent, highly illicit Normandy cider and vin rouge, they can twist a familiar quotation, play word-games with a classic faux ami. In Le Havre, enjoying boiled eggs for breakfast, they knew perfectly well that oeufs à la coque (boiled, 'in the shell') hadn't been laid by un coq. Some of them could read Latin well enough to deliberately mistranslate the text of the Bayeux tapestry, always a more demanding test than mere accuracy. Articulate, literate, knowledgeable about French history, about botany and architecture, whoever wrote this book also knew the King James Bible and the Prayer Book. Their generation would, but the Nomads were also aware of developments in psychology and contemporary politics, including the social engineering central to Lloyd George's tax measures. Travelling second class, they had enough money to pay their fares to France, and, enjoying the weak franc, stay in hotels and inns for a fortnight. They were privileged enough to take a fortnight's holiday, when ordinary manual workers would be extraordinarily lucky to get one week, without pay. Many workers still saved all year to pay for their holiday at Blackpool or other resorts. When a factory or mill shut down for 'Wakes', the enforced unpaid 'holiday' could mean serious hardship.[12]

In 1912, Britain's economy still depended on child labour. Scrawny hollow-eyed girls and boys were allowed, or more accurately, like Third World children now, were compelled by family poverty to work as half-timers in mills and factories. Half their days were spent risking their lives, scrambling under lethal machinery, the other half in school, too exhausted to learn anything. Ironically, the brightest children, academically ahead of their classmates, could be released to half-time work early, at only eleven.[13] Most working people existed merely as statistics. Unless they'd been chosen as textbook examples of crime, or grinding poverty, or both, their personal stories were unimportant. Sociologists and reformers such as Henry Mayhew, Charles Booth, himself a Liverpudlian by birth, and Seebohm Rowntree published their own studies of poverty, exposing an obscene world of suffering, equal to anything in what we now call the developing world.[14] No government could really claim ignorance. In 1845, Engels, who knew both kinds of Manchester, had described English working class poverty with chilling candour. In the 1850's, Mayhew's London Life and the London Poor was intended to shock. It did, but little changed. Later, street by street, Booth carefully mapped the wealth and poverty of London. Seebohm Rowntree did the same in York. Official Blue Books had produced abundant evidence of disease and lethal working conditions in Britain's industrial cities.[15] Dickens, of course, did it better. So, shockingly, did Mrs Gaskell. In real life, as millhands, farmhands, deckhands, the working classes were machines with inconvenient bodies attached. Victorian servants were forbidden to make eye contact with their upper-class masters.[16]

The actual prices of a century ago are meaningless until they're matched to real lives and real budgets, not so much the cost of living, but the price of staying alive For clarity, I will use one classic contemporary study as a reference point. Just a year before the Nomads set off for France, Maud Pember Reeves, of the pioneering Fabian Society, asked real working class women to record their family budgets and daily routine. Deliberately, she didn't study the unemployed underclass of beggars and casual labourers. Her case studies are of ordinary stable families, husbands, wives and children, with the father usually in work. A working man might struggle to support his wife and several children on far less than a pound a week.[17] Typically, working class families spent about 60% of their income on a pitifully inadequate poverty diet. In recent years, the proportion has been closer to 10%. Now, after decades of cheap food, grocery bills have soared, but even the poorest are very far from the food poverty of 1911.

Overcrowding was quite as damaging as poverty. Families with six children lived in two rooms. The poorest could afford only one. Women, often nursing mothers themselves, would battle to feed perhaps eight people, including an adult man doing heavy manual work and young children, trying to grow, on ten shillings (50p) a week.[18] Governments still claim that up to a third of British children live in poverty, but any 21st century British poverty is strictly relative. Mrs Pember Reeves meant near-starvation. The ordinary working poor, mainly in full time employment, could be sharing one bed. Women and children often went barefoot. Money could only be spared for the breadwinner's shoes.

During the First World War, New Zealand born Mrs Reeves was appointed Director of the Educational and Propaganda Department of the Ministry of Food. Pember Reeves' catalogue of wretched poverty didn't seem to be the Nomads' world, but by their mid-twenties, education and good luck might have taken them far from humble origins. Some of the leading figures of the emerging Labour Party had been born in poverty. At grammar schools, even children from the poorest families could win scholarships, achieve an excellent education. In the city archives of Liverpool, there might be records of that education.

Chapter Three

I can trace my ancestry back to a protoplasmal primordial atomic globule.

W. S. Gilbert, The Mikado, 1885

Ancestors are a luxury. Before the internet, most people couldn't afford them, especially if their families had migrated to a distant city or arrived as refugees.[1] Serious family trees were a luxury reserved for those with Norman blood, stately homes, or plenty of new money. New members of the Royal Family and the peerage could have their history traced by genealogists at the College of Arms. Anybody else who wanted to know their family history needed all the time in the world and enough money to make countless cross-country journeys. Some parish registers were in print, though often incomplete and inaccurately transcribed. Many more could only be consulted in the original churches, in freezing vestries. Census returns from the 19th century were almost as inconvenient, available only during the limited opening hours of county record offices and major libraries. Tracing Nonconformist, Roman Catholic or immigrant ancestors could be fiendishly difficult. Anglicised approximations mangle many Irish and East European names. Ironically, despite their notoriously limited surnames, imposed for the convenience of English rulers, the democratic Welsh always had ancestors of both sexes.

Microfilm, microfiches, and, above all, the internet, have changed all that. Ancestors are big business now and everybody is allowed a family tree. Newspapers publish regular articles on genealogy, programmes such as ' Who Do You Think You Are ? ' have become prime-time viewing.[2] In 1964, it was a Liverpool MP, the self-styled 'Fourteenth Mr Wilson', who defeated the Fourteenth Earl of Home and walked into Downing St, claiming, en route, everybody's right to a pedigree. Now, digitised records and the internet have brought ancestor-hunting out of the freezing vestry, into the local library or home office. If they were British citizens, the Nomads' births, marriages and deaths would be easily available. And if they really did come from Liverpool, there would, surely, be some evidence in the city archives ? Perhaps they'd attended one of Liverpool's famous schools, such as Merchant Taylors', the Collegiate, or the Liverpool Institute ? Given their long holidays and love of France, some of them might be school or university teachers.

Alphabetical order, then, beginning with Gleave. The census online search would like a forename, and a place of birth too. If the searcher has very little information, an Advanced Search can be attempted. Was 'Miss Gleave' born in Liverpool ? How old was she ? On the search form, uncertainty is allowed, and a range of approximate spellings. The census site allows a few years either side of a suggested date. The first search identifies only individuals, not their whole household. Gleave is a relatively uncommon name, but in 1901, there were two fifteen year old Miss Gleaves in the Liverpool area. Both were called Gladys - Gladys Gelderd in West Derby and Gladys Gertrude in Birkenhead. The Birkenhead Gladys had to be a candidate, but the West Derby girl looked very promising; Pupil Teacher at a Board School. Pupil Teaching was the Edwardian version of Work Experience, learning on the job, before applying to training college, offering access to higher education for students from modest backgrounds. Some, as 'uncertificated teachers', never completed formal training. The ablest and luckiest graduated with honours, qualifying for the better paid secondary school posts. The Board School pupil teacher was the right age, and, at fifteen, already preparing for a career in teaching. English schools still break up in late July, just as they did when all hands were needed for the harvest. The Nomads set off for France on Saturday, July 20th. Could it be that hours of guesswork and deduction had led to the right girl ?

Sifting through any archives, it pays to be cautious. Even the most official records aren't necessarily accurate and some misinformation was deliberate. Long before the threat of ID cards and biometric data, our ancestors were shrewd enough to regard government demands for information with suspicion. Since Domesday and Richard II 's poll tax that sparked the Peasants' Revolt, questions about homes, hearths and incomes have led, inexorably, to demands for money. Responding to such enquiries, otherwise law-abiding Victorians can be engagingly economical with the truth. Women, especially those married to a younger husband, always did knock a few years off their age. Checking census records against parish registers, discrepancies of ten years or even longer are common enough. As in the Old Testament, Victorian women could give birth at strangely advanced ages. Almost invariably, these remarkable pre-IVF mothers turn out to have unmarried daughters in their late teens or early twenties, still living at home.[3] But inaccuracies aren't always deliberate. Some nineteenth century census enumerators have terrible handwriting. Their almost illegible scrawl is easily mistranscribed. Even if the original document is neatly written, modern transcribers make mistakes.[4] Most frustrating of all is what the census doesn't reveal. If any member of the household happened to be away on census night, they won't be listed at their home address, and there's no reference to absent members of the family. Census forms weren't created for family historians. If any of the six young people were away from home on census night, tracking them down might prove impossible. Depending on the family income, teenagers could be in service, at boarding school or university, in barracks, or possibly on board a ship. Miscreants might be in prison. In 1901, many women campaigning for the vote deliberately refused to be counted.[5]

But ' Miss Gleave ' the pupil-teacher surely had to be right. Perhaps the other Nomads were neighbours ? From the 1901 census website, her friends began to emerge, as if from hiding. Fifteen year old Gladys was the second of four children born to Charles G Gleave, Solicitor's Manager, 49, and his wife Eunice, 47, of 34, Onslow Road, Fairfield, West Derby. No occupation is recorded for Gladys's twenty year old sister Ada. The eleven year old, incorrectly listed as 'Eunice' would be at school, and the youngest, Charles, was only three.[6] Next door, at number 32, there were the Westmores. At 61, Alexander senior was a commercial bookkeeper, twelve years older than his wife, Eliza. Fourteen year old Alec was their middle child and eldest boy. Frances, the Westmores' sixteen year old daughter was, like Gladys Gleave, a pupil teacher.

Next came the Pulfords, and they too were in West Derby. Fourteen year old Fred - Frederick Ivor, had been born in Tottenham. All three Pulford children proved to be Londoners by birth. But Pulford's a local place name, a village just south of Chester. Fred's father, Thomas is listed as ' Fruit Merchant's Clerk' He'd been born in West Derby. In 1891, Thomas Pulford was still in London with his young family, working in the fruit trade. In 1901, no occupation is given for either Fred or Alec. Presumably, at fourteen, the boys were still at school. The same school? Tracing one's own ancestors, it might be worth investigating every birth, marriage and death certificate, reconstructing the whole story of these Liverpool families. But the real interest here was in the Nomads themselves, not their entire family histories.

Classmates or not, the census data was useful, identifying three young Nomads, living in the same area of Liverpool. The lovers, Alec and Gladys were literally the boy and girl next door. Nineteenth century maps confirmed that in Onslow Road, Alec and Gladys were just one street away from the Pulfords, round the corner in Rufford Road. According to earlier censuses, the Gleaves and Westmores had been based in West Derby for decades. On the twenty-first century Liverpool A - Z , the road names were still there. Hopefully, the actual houses would still be standing. And the man they all refer to as Ross ? Perhaps it really was his surname ? Having narrowed three of them down to West Derby, it was worth asking the census for anyone in Liverpool with Ross as a surname or forename. In 1901, eighty-seven males were surnamed ' Ross', including thirteen teenage boys and a twelve year old. Could he be a Mineral Water Cart Driver ? A Herbalist's Assistant ? Or a Chemist's ? Eighty-seven red herrings ? Probably... Public school boys addressed each other by surname, but would an Edwardian lady really refer to her fiancé, or even a young male friend by his surname ? In conversation, it's just about possible, but in a formal written account, highly unlikely. Trying Ross as a forename, the 1901 census offered only twenty-six boys and men in the whole of Lancashire. Many could be easily ruled out, too old or too young, but in West Derby, there was Ross Hankinson, a sixteen year old grocer's assistant. Nearby, in Toxteth Park, there was Ross Owen, also sixteen, and a joiner. Neither of these occupations seemed particularly promising and excellent French certainly wouldn't be a job requirement. Grocer's boys and joiners wouldn't enjoy a fortnight's holiday. But their lives could have changed dramatically by 1912. As a 'Grocer's Assistant', the Hankinson boy was certainly worth considering. In the early twentieth century, young men expected to start at the bottom on extremely modest pay and work their way up.

Online records are a useful starting point, but the adventurous Nomads lived in a real city, a city by the sea. Arriving at Lime Street station, they seemed immediately much closer, their backpacking adventure entirely natural. Would they have travelled to France so confidently from landlocked Birmingham, Manchester or Sheffield ? At Pier Head, the Maritime Museum celebrates a city of ships and seafarers. Today, Liverpool acknowledges its role in the slave trade. A poignant sculpture pays tribute to the thousands of destitute families, mostly from Ireland, who arrived here seeking refuge, some remaining in Liverpool and other industrial cities, others, if they could raise the money, crossing the Atlantic. Liverpool has always been an impressive city, even in the difficult later years of the last century. If they could return now, the adventurous Nomads would recognise a city closer to the vibrant Liverpool of their youth.

Arriving too early for the archives, there was time to catch the metro to Edge Hill, visit the streets where three teenage friends had been neighbours. In Onslow Road, the Westmore and Gleave houses were still standing, and still, despite the surrounding litter and signs of multiple occupation, essentially solid and decent. Only one street away, Fred's Rufford Road home was markedly humbler than his friends'. In the early twenty-first century, much of West Derby is sadly down at heel. It shouldn't be. Streets of perfectly sound houses stand semi-derelict. Boarded up, some are threatened by the wrecking ball. Too many others, tall and handsome Victorian villas with fine ornamental brickwork, bear all the usual hallmarks of decay, rows of doorbells, drifts of freesheets, pizza clams, chip-papers, lager cans, broken glass, and worse. Once, the families who lived here were the aspirational middle-class. The houses vary considerably in size, but some 1901 residents were, like the Gleaves, able to afford one live-in servant. Why an area slips out of fashion is often a mystery, even to property experts, but when the Nomads were young, this was a popular residential area.

Once hushed and reverent, archive search rooms buzz with suppressed excitement. Competing fiercely for desk space and microfiche readers, ancestor-hunters unearth family scandals equal to any tabloid headlines. Old hands come armed with magnifying glasses, nineteenth century newsprint being hard on the eyes.[7] Online, it had been easy enough to establish the bare facts, where the Nomads lived, what their fathers did for a living, Fred's London birth, the Pulfords' return to Liverpool. In the real city, there was much more to discover. Three Nomads had the beginnings of a history, but how did they become friends ? Street directories quickly confirmed that in 1901, the Gleaves, coming up in the world, had only just moved from the less prosperous Rufford Road. Directories and contemporary maps suggested that Ross Hankinson was still worth investigating. He was the right age and in the right location too. True, he'd left school, but in 1901, so had nearly all sixteen year olds.[8] Ross's father, Ralph Hankinson, was a police inspector. The eldest son, also Ralph, was a nineteen year old pupil teacher, a credible elder brother for a Nomad. A register of trainee teachers confirmed the census entry, but hours of frustrating and fruitless searches proved how very difficult it is to discover anything about teenagers. School records are at best patchy. Many were lost in the WWII bombing of Liverpool, others simply discarded. As for Ross... No school registers list pupils by one name only.

There seemed to be no trace of the Nomads' early schooldays. Living with parents or as lodgers, very few young people would be listed as heads of household, nor could they vote until twenty-one. Many large firms have deposited records in the city archives, but few mention their junior staff.[9] To this day, sober, well-behaved, hardworking teenagers aren't newsworthy, except on two days in August, when their GCSE and A level results are declared. True to form, the early twentieth century Liverpool Courier reported delinquents, including a plus ça change complaint on a 1915 letters page about rowdy secondary school pupils, swearing on the buses. Then as now, columnists lamented the absence of so many adult men, too many women out at work, and the breakdown of family life. In 1915, parents could hardly be blamed for neglecting their children.

What other records might there be ? A newspaper report of their adventures in France ? Any records at all of their day jobs ? In France, Fred had 'tried to teach Ross how to sell timber ! '[10] The exclamation mark suggests that Fred presumed to know Ross's business. But Ross who ? For centuries, Liverpool's timber trade had been hugely important to the city's economy, especially luxurious hardwoods like teak and mahogany, imported from the West Indies, Burma, Java... In the city archives, there are impressively detailed customs records, listing the cargoes of every ship entering or leaving Liverpool, but there are very few records deposited by actual timber firms. There are minutes for board meetings, identifying chairmen, directors, and shareholders, and a handful of trade journals. In 1896, Liverpool's timber dock moved to Birkenhead, but searches in the Birkenhead archives failed too. The National Archives confirmed that the dearth of evidence for the timber trade isn't peculiar to Liverpool. Why this should be is easily explained. In most other trades, customers could be shown samples of the latest products in city centre warehouses and offices. Customers buying timber needed to assess the quality of whole consignment of wood, then bid for it at dockside auctions. Moving heavy and bulky goods into a city centre wouldn't be practical. Traditionally, the offices of timber firms were based in docklands, which were always a prime target for bombing raids. During WWII, London, Liverpool, Hull, Plymouth and other ports all suffered heavy bombing.

A2A, the website linking records nationwide, located only a scatter of timber archives. Searching fragmented records for a man with half a name, working in an industry with remarkably few surviving records was extremely unlikely to succeed. Temporarily, at least, the search for Ross was abandoned. Perhaps it would be better to give up the entire Nomads' search, valuing the journal for what it is, the poignant record of an idyll ? Realistically, the chances of identifying three of the young people were minimal. Even in the twenty-first century, young men are notoriously mobile, and, equally notoriously, they won't fill in forms. Bizarrely, around a million young men are still missing from the latest UK census. Many don't register to vote.[11]

But the search had to continue. In 1912, the young travellers didn't set out merely to enjoy a holiday in France. They wanted to meet French people, newly linked to Britain by the entente cordiale, challenging centuries of prejudice, suspicion and war. The confident final words of their story are poignant only because we can see the 'hell where youth and laughter die'. Discovered by chance, their story was important, couldn't be simply discarded. In Liverpool's archives, it made sense to concentrate on the three certainties. Discovering more about the West Derby trio might just lead to the others. Close neighbours all their lives, Alec and Gladys could have attended the same primary school. Perhaps, as teenagers, all three worshipped at the same church ? Anglican and Nonconformist, in their mid-twenties, they were still practising Christians, choosing to attend church even when on holiday.

For young people born in the mid 1880's, churches were still an important, and for many families, the only social centre. Growing up in their Liverpool suburb, the Nomads were far better placed than many young people. Before scouting and guiding, there were precious few alternatives for youngsters, but nineteenth century West Derby was no backwater. In 1830, the world's first rail passenger train set off from Edge Hill station. Just before Gladys and Alec were born, the pioneering nondenominational Teacher Training College opened in nearby Durning Road. In a city so often wounded by sectarian conflict, this was a courageous step into the future, almost a century before the nondenominational schools and shared holiday adventures of Belfast.[12] The year the Nomads travelled to France, the world's first automatic telephone exchange opened in

Edge Hill. None of the Nomad families had phones, but the Edge Hill exchange served many local customers. As teenagers at the beginning of a new century, the Nomads knew anything was possible, for men and for women. The Gleave parents shared this confidence, supporting two daughters, Ada and Louise, as they worked for science degrees at Edge Hill. Louise continued her studies, achieving an M.Sc. Gladys didn't appear in the Edge Hill College archives, but Liverpool University confirmed that she'd been an external student, working for an arts degree. Alec, Frank and Fred didn't appear in the archives of Oxford, Cambridge, or any of the redbricks, but the quality of their writing indicates that all six 'Nomads' enjoyed a high standard of education.[13]

University educated or not, so far, all the evidence pointed to excellent secondary schools. Despite many WWII losses, Liverpool's Record Office has an impressive collection of school records, including those for the Bluecoat School, the Liverpool Institute, and the Blackburne House Girls' High School. There are infuriating gaps in all the wrong places. The Collegiate School was founded in 1840, but the Record Office has admission registers only from 1904, just too late for the Nomads. For Blackburne House, the years when Gladys Gleave would have been at secondary school are missing. But at the Liverpool Institute, Fred's name was there in the register. Pulford, Frederick Ivor, entered in 1899, leaving at the end of the summer term in 1902, shortly before his sixteenth birthday. According to this Institute register, Fred would become a junior bank clerk. In the early twentieth century this was a career with sound prospects. Young bank clerks might become bank managers, pillars of the community.

On the 1901 census, there were far too many young Frank or Francis Bournes. Although the combination of names was relatively common, no boy of the right age and background seemed to have any links with Liverpool. The right kind of Frank would speak adequate or good French and by 1912, earn enough to spend a fortnight's holiday in France. Reading between the lines of the book, Frank was the expedition photographer, joined, sometimes, by one of the other men. Cameras were still a luxury. The only Bournes in West Derby had no son the right age and an eighteen year old daughter employed as a general servant. Perhaps, by 1912, the three West Derby Nomads had moved house ? Perhaps they'd met Frank, Ross, and the nameless young woman somewhere else, not in Liverpool at all ? The law-abiding young Nomads were proving frustratingly invisible. Their parents might not be. Street directories fill the gaps between censuses, track householders as they move around a city. Sometimes, directories record changing occupations and qualifications. The main drawback is that no other members of the family are listed. Another is that the official householder is usually male or a widow. Despite these limitations, street directories are a great deal better than nothing.

By 1902, Eliza Westmore appeared to be a widow. In the directory for that year, there's no mention of Thomas, in Onslow Road or anywhere else. A search confirmed his death in September, 1901. The Gleaves are still next door. Year after year, through the first decade of the twentieth century, the original trio of families are still in West Derby. The Gleaves and Westmores did move, but not till much later. As a solicitor's manager, Charles Gleave was well placed to keep an eye on the housing market, move when the time was right, to a better area. In Liverpool, the ambitious often moved over the water, crossing the Mersey to live on the Wirral. The ferry and fast underground trains delivered commuters into the city centre. Others would head north to the prosperous coastal communities of the Fylde.

In 1912, and still a solicitor's manager, Charles Gleave was living at 19, Meddowcroft Road, Wallasey, a street of tall Edwardian villas. The other Wallasey Gleaves were clearly cousins. Their son, Harold Gelderd, bore the same unusual middle name as Gladys Westmore. In 1912, Eliza Westmore is listed as head of household at 15, Central Park Avenue, Liscard, just a few streets away from Meddowcroft Road. Only the Pulfords remained in West Derby. There was still no sign of a Frank Bourne or any Ross. In Liscard, a John Howe Bourne, Chartered Accountant, looked promising, but according to the 1901 census, he was only thirty-five. A further check found his marriage, in 1894. Frank or Francis Bourne was proving as elusive as Ross.

According to the cryptic Freedom of Information Act, official information is freely available, unless it's not in the public interest. Information concerning someone else's personal details is not freely available. In archive search rooms, personal details are precisely what most people are hunting for. Data protection guards many secrets.[14] Half the Nomads seemed destined to remain missing persons. Frank Bourne had two names, but they were all too common. Apart from his interest in photography and astronomy, there were no other clues in the book. Even his approximate age was only a guess. He might be years older or younger than the others. After their schooldays, people have friends of all ages. But where was he born ? Where did he live ? In Liverpool ? In London ? Or just about anywhere else in the British Empire ?

In major public libraries, microfiches for every UK birth, marriage and death since 1837 are available. They're a cheap - usually free- alternative to searching on line.[15] The early fiche data is recorded in quarterly periods. As always, there's a fee for obtaining a certificate. Reading a microfiche manually takes barely any longer than an online search. Since there didn't seem to be a West Derby connection, none of the Frank Bournes could be ruled out, anywhere in the country. Reasoning that he was probably about the same age as his friends, I considered all the Frank or Francis Bournes born 1885 - 1887. Could he be Frank Bourne of Droitwich ? Frank Furnival Bourne of Market Drayton ? Francis Ramsey Bourne, of Whitechapel ? Francis Bruce Bourne, of Maidstone ? Frank Bourne of Leek, or of Billericay ? These were just places of birth... London born Fred became a Liverpudlian schoolboy.

And Ross ? Finding Ross was surely important. He was such a vital member of the party. Perhaps Ross Hankinson should be abandoned ? Ross Owen, the sixteen year old Toxteth joiner, was just as likely. A joiner would know about buying and selling timber, and that, the journal implies, was Ross's job. Perhaps Ross had left the country ? After their French idyll, any of those young men could have emigrated. In the summer of 1912, Saskatchewan advertised in the Liverpool Courier for 25,000 young men, needed to work in the harvest fields.[16] Britain's young farmers were keen to emigrate, especially the struggling hill farmers of Scotland, Northern England and Wales. Argentina, Australia, Canada, New Zealand, South Africa and the United States welcomed the right kind of immigrants and all kept records. Checking passenger lists, US, and

Commonwealth immigration records, every search for the missing Nomads failed. There simply wasn't enough information.

Early in the morning of July 20th, 1912 , the six of them were in Liverpool, boarding their train as ' Mr Pulford's party ', heading for London and their backpacking adventures. Three of them returned to Liverpool for the August Bank Holiday weekend, exactly two years before the fateful August Bank Holiday of 1914. Did the inseparable Mr Westmore and Miss Gleave marry and, eventually, live happily ever after ? Or was Alec killed ? Did he return, but so shattered in mind and body, marriage and children were out of the question ? With such distinctive names, the marriage was easy to find. Alexander Wemyss Westmore and Gladys Gelderd Gleave married on August 10th, 1914, at St Hilary's church, Wallasey. The war was barely six days old. But what happened next ?

Chapter Four

' Lord Kitchener has sanctioned my endeavours to raise a battalion

which would be composed entirely of the classes mentioned, and in

which a man could be certain that he would be amongst friends.'

Lord Derby, Liverpool, 26th August, 1914

Britain had invested heavily in Dreadnoughts, but otherwise, the country was unprepared for war. Allegedly, just one British Dreadnought could 'blow the entire German Navy out of the water', but the pre-war British army was small and under-equipped. In August, 1914, the 'Old Contemptibles' of the small peace time army were little more than a police force, scattered across the Empire. When tens of thousands rushed to enlist, the Army couldn't provide them with uniforms or boots, let alone weapons or proper barracks. For weeks, recruits had to manage with armbands, training with staves instead of guns. Many were billeted in makeshift camps with poor drainage and dangerously inadequate sanitation. When the War Office ran out of even makeshift barracks, luckier recruits were billeted at home or in lodgings, for which, at first, a relatively generous allowance of 3s per day was paid. Householders who refused to accept soldiers faced a double penalty, forfeiting the War Office funding, and risking a fine too. Later, the billeting allowance would be very much reduced.[1] In the late summer of 1914, most people really did think it would be over by Christmas. Providing for thousands of excited young men was regarded as a temporary inconvenience. Public libraries, churches and schools willingly offered rooms where off-duty volunteers could meet. The Christmas Truce of 1914 is both legendary and true. In December, civilians, bewildered to find the war continuing, decided to defer such traditional events as church bazaars until after the war. Pessimists concluded that they might have to wait till Easter, 1915.[2]

At the outbreak of war, the four Nomad men were all of military age and surely in excellent health. Two years earlier, they'd been close enough to spend a whole fortnight in each other's company, analyse and record their private entente cordiale. . Investigating how these friends spent the war years was important. Did they serve in France, or were they sent to some other war zone, possibly at sea, or in the Middle East ? Which regiment would they join ? Would Liverpool born Alec choose the King's Liverpool Regiment ? At the Maritime Museum, where many of the KLR archives are held, the news wasn't encouraging, but the regimental data base is still adding new information.[3] Whatever regiment the men joined, if they served as private soldiers, there was less than a one in three chance of finding their records. Collected in a central military archive, over two thirds of the WWI records for 'other ranks ' were destroyed in 1940, by fire and then by water. Now catalogued as the 'Burnt Series' these records can offer detailed accounts of a man's war, including sickness and injuries during the war. At worst, barely twenty per cent of some records survive, depending, as burnt material does, on where the heat had been most intense.[4]

Despite this catastrophe, it's possible to discover a great deal about men who fought in the 1914 - 18 war, especially when families own supporting material. Descendants often have a grandfather or great-grandfather's medals, might know his service number or have some idea of where he fought and when. Medal card records were held separately and often survive though the man's service papers are lost. Both the National Archives and independent websites offer remarkably detailed information about the men who fought, down to minute by minute analyses of a soldier's day. Already, over three million internet sites refer to the 1914 - 18 war. The value of such sites is variable, but The Long, Long Trail site is among the best, excellent in itself, and the links lead the researcher promptly to other key sources.[5] Another outstanding WWI website is managed by the Western Front Association.

Thinking of those four young men in the photos, so carefree in France, the truth might be difficult. Soldiers lost limbs, half their faces, their genitals, their sight, and their minds. Which one would it be ? Newly-wed Alec ? The charismatic and intriguing Ross ? Fred, who'd booked all the tickets, sneezed his way to France and kept his friends awake with mid-channel monologues ? Or Frank, the talented pianist, who taught his friends astronomy, one starlit night in Brittany ? Perhaps they'd be lucky... Allegedly, 73% of men came through the war unscathed. Allegedly... A lifetime of grief and nightmares don't count. The Army explains, in precisely worded paragraphs, how, why and in what condition every soldier was discharged. Grief and terror aren't mentioned. Shell-shock might, depending on the circumstances and the tenacity of an appeal, merit a disability pension. Grief for lost comrades certainly didn't, but friendships are part of our identity. Travelling together in their mid-twenties, the Nomads are defined first as friends, like-minded enough to plan their adventures, and then, immortalise them.

Parking near Lancaster station, catching the train to Liverpool and its archives, I would pass the house where Laurence Binyon was born. The name might be unfamiliar, most of his work little read now, apart from his iconic lament for the fallen.

They shall not grow old, as we that are left grow old

Age shall not weary them, nor the years condemn

At the going down of the sun, and in the morning,

We will remember them.

On September 21st, 1914, when this poem was published in The Times, England could still mourn with proud thanksgiving for her dead across the sea. Some of their children beg to differ. In old age, veterans of World War II speak with astonishing candour. These are the men and women who grew up during the Twenties and Thirties, in families and whole communities scarred with grief and narrowed by poverty. Many children lived with the enduring terrors of shell-shock, their fathers bewilderingly distressed, in a way the adults rarely explained. Instead of reverence, Binyon's too-famous words can fuse blazing anger. Remembering the war that claimed his own youth, one man, who served in the Navy during WWII, suggested a savage rewrite; not the Remembrance Day romance of 'they shall not grow old', but 'they never had a chance to be young'. In the autumn of 1914, the Hun was at the gate, their world had passed away, but the lists of death had only just begun. At the Cenotaph, a more honest tribute might be Sassoon's ' On Passing The New Menin Gate' , with its 'intolerably nameless names' .

Which of those confident young men would die ? All four ? Or none ? Some battalions were lucky. Others were annihilated. Did they live on, blinded, maimed, driven mad by shell-shock, struggling to find any kind of work in the Depression, in a land that never was fit for heroes to live in ? In Lancaster's regimental museum, schoolchildren play on the Great War Wheel of Fortune. No skill required; spin the dial, discover your fate. The figures are brutal. 14 % killed in action, 14% discharged wounded, another 5% died of wounds, twenty thousand British soldiers killed on the first day of the Somme, 564, 715 men killed on the Western Front, and almost as many dying in the East.[6] Perhaps surprisingly, only 0.12 % are described as blinded. The many photos of soldiers covering their eyes with cloth often record tear-gas attacks, hideously painful, but not permanently blinding. Lacking any better neutraliser, many soaked cloth in their own urine to relieve the pain.[7]

Dead soldiers are the easiest to trace. The early stages of most searches are free. If any of the Nomad men were killed, the Commonwealth War Graves Commission website would have the information. The website is austere and spare, an online war cemetery. Key in the last name and forename, choose your war; and the information's delivered almost instantaneously, far faster than the telegrams that brought heartbreak. Fred first... They went to France as 'Mr Pulford's party'. One click, and the report was there on screen :

Pulford, Frederick Ivor, King's Liverpool Regiment, 17th Battalion. Killed in action, 12th October, 1916. Thiepval Memorial.[8]

It was hardly breaking news. Born on August 11th, 1886, Fred Pulford would be long dead by now. In the First World War, almost a million of the Allies were killed. Discovering that Fred's name is on the Thiepval Memorial was unexpectedly painful. The sting of tears was real, my own, my husband's, our son and daughters, their friends. Fred, entertaining and exasperating his friends, hadn't just been killed. He's still missing. It's the ultimate obscenity. Long before nations and history, humanity, including the Neanderthal people, buried the dead with reverence. In the photos, Fred, as yet, hadn't been identified. Alec, yes, always so close to Gladys, but so far, the other three were simply carefree young Edwardians, Frank, Fred and Ross, twenty-somethings, enjoying the holiday of a lifetime. For Fred, it would be the last holiday of his life.

Frederick Pulford, Service No 21996, The King's (Liverpool) Regiment, 17th Battalion, only son of Thomas and Eliza, had died in the last filthy weeks of the Battle of the Somme, one of the many tens of thousands who still have no known grave. Along the borders of France and Belgium, farmers are always finding bones. The telegram delivered to his parents would say that he was 'Missing, presumed killed'. Perhaps this was the worst news of all. Rather than the certainty of death, grieving families and friends faced their own vile no-man's-land. Only after thirty weeks was death assumed to be certain. For the widow and her children, financial help came slowly. The country was ashamed of so much death, grudging with help for the bereaved. In desperation, and facing starvation, some widows placed beloved children in orphanages. War took their husbands, then poverty robbed them of their children. Others divided their families, placing siblings with different relatives. Numbed by grief, mothers could seem indifferent to their children. Older children didn't understand that their missing fathers would never return.[9]

The 17th was the first of the city's ' Pals ' battalions, created as thousands of young men answered the call to fight for King and Country. The massive Thiepval Memorial, designed by Lutyens, commemorates some of the Missing of the Somme. Only some... Even Thiepval couldn't hold so many names. On screen, the Commonwealth War Graves Commission gives the precise location of Fred's name, high up and almost out of sight. War Grave workers, hearing of Fred's 1912 adventure, volunteered to take a photo, making several attempts before conditions were right. In the journal, he's nearly always 'Fred ', rarely 'Mr Pulford' and never just a number. Fred organised their journey to France. Crossing the Channel after midnight, his monologues kept them all awake. Now, his old school, reborn as the Liverpool Institute of Performing Arts, might recognise a promising standup comedian rather than a future HSBC bank manager. Private Pulford was luckier than most of those missing bones on the Somme. Backpacking with his friends, four years before his body vanished into the mud, he shared an idyll.

In museums, in school text books, in films and on TV, there are two kinds of Great War soldiers. Everybody knows the celebrities, Rupert Brooke, Churchill, Robert Graves, General Haig, Kitchener, the Kaiser, the Red Baron, C.S. Lewis, Wilfred Owen, Siegfried Sassoon, Tolkien. They're all History, and frequently Literature too, their stories told so often, the world knows them by heart. The others are like Fred, mere nameless Tommies. In studio portraits, proud in their uniform, many of them seem and probably are little more than children. In regimental histories, they're 'Unidentified Private.' - young boys with no past or future. Throughout the war, local newspapers filled pages with photos of the dead and wounded. On the battlefield, the King's Liverpool Regiment kneel in prayer, backs to camera. Somewhere in Flanders, they lead mud-caked horses, support wounded and dying comrades, offer water to captured Germans, laugh and drink at some field canteen. In a jerking newsreel, the Liverpool Pals march proudly through their city. Their battalions were the 17th, 18th, 19th and 20th, sometimes known as the 1st, 2nd, 3rd and 4th City. At St George's Hall, in Liverpool, there were cheers, and boaters too. Lord Derby had urged thousands of young men to answer their country's call. Did they really believe so fervently in God, King and Country ? By November, 1918, nearly three thousand of the Liverpool Pals were dead. Nobody said ' Give me back my legions.' Grief was allowed, just, so long as the bereaved mourned quietly. Until the war, the Victorian tradition of full mourning backed a flourishing industry. Black was flattering, stylish, popular. Overnight, there were too many glorious dead. Patriotism must come first.[10]

Calculators in hand, military historians reject the idea of a 'lost generation'. It's maudlin, they complain, corny, a journalistic cliché. Inaccurate too, demographically, the losses were quickly made good; at least in Britain. Arithmetically, this is perfectly true. Between 1911 and 1921, the male population actually rose, in part because the male birth rate rose and with targeted care, male infant mortality fell. More than ever, newborn sons were cherished.[11] France had paid a higher price, mobilising twice as many men, and losing one soldier in six from a population already in crisis. Walking or cycling through the French countryside, the lists of death are shocking, far longer, most of them, than the familiar English memorials. The risk of death could be a matter of luck and geography. Following relatively minor illness or injury, many officers were allowed lengthy convalescence. Some battalions, like the Accrington Pals, were almost annihilated. Oxbridge and the public schools sustained the greatest losses of all. By November, 1916, Brasenose College alone had lost fifty-eight men. On average, one in five of their students and recent graduates were killed. The appalling death rate confirms, not the outstanding courage of public schoolboys and Oxbridge students, but how ill-prepared they were for battle. Dulce et decorum est had become an order.[12]

Matching recorded war deaths to the UK population, one historian has calculated that only one family in fourteen actually lost a soldier.[13] Therefore, he seems to imply, only one family in fourteen was devastated by grief. Q. E. D. The arithmetic might be correct enough, the reasoning is peculiarly flawed. Such precise calculation of loss and grief doesn't work. Nor does the crude population rise reflect the true situation. Fred Pulford's death on the Somme shattered one friendship forever. His role in that small group of friends is on record. In photographs, in remembered adventures, Fred was part of their idyllic holiday. Leaving no history at all, every 'unidentified private' had belonged to a whole community. In their narrow and crowded streets, the urban working class still lived close to their kin. For the poor, 'Our' was virtually a title.

Rich or poor, in 1914, few men lived as strangers. One death or thousands diminished everyone who'd ever known them, and at first, the dead had been carefully selected. Privileged Oxbridge students, grammar school educated bank clerks like Fred, solicitors, stockbrokers, policemen, sturdy miners and steelworkers, the young men who enlisted so readily were the pick of a generation. It was the fittest who didn't survive. Romantic patriots called them the 'flower of the flock', especially if they were killed. Prosaically, the brightest and best had passed through quality control, graded A1. In the late summer of 1914, recruiting sergeants could afford to be choosy, selecting the taller volunteers, preferably with 20/20 vision, able to ride and ideally, used to handling a gun. Once again, many of the working classes proved too sick and stunted to serve their King and Country. Some were dismissed from training, identified as a bad influence on their comrades. Some discharge notes stick to the agreed formula, stating that a man is 'unlikely to make an efficient soldier', even when the man in question is a very sick young lead-miner. Others elaborate, specifying such faults as insubordination and bad language.[14] Two years later, many of these 'bad characters' were back in the Army as conscripts. Nobody, least of all the generals, had expected to lose so many.

Trying the other names on the War Graves site achieved little. There was an R. Hankinson. Perhaps... Ross was an unusual forename in England, might confuse whoever retrieved the body, read Hankinson's fire-resistant dog-tag. Days later, the Commonwealth War Graves Commission sent an e-mail. 'R. Hankinson' was actually Robert. No Ross Owen, no Frank or Francis Bourne, no Alec Westmore. A quick scan of UK deaths up to 1920 produced nothing. None of the three surviving men had been invalided home, only to die in a British military hospital. On the Western Front, only 'Mr Pulford' had been killed.

Every battalion of every regiment kept its own record of the Great War. The originals of all war diaries are held in the National Archives, at Kew. In Liverpool, there's a transcript of the 17th battalion's diary, held in the Maritime Museum archives at Pier Head, complete with all the carefully replicated 'xxxx' pre-Tippex and word processor corrections. There was very little information about Fred, only that after he'd left the Institute, he'd worked for the London City and Midland Bank, which is now part of the HSBC.[15] The men of the 17th were all, like Fred, white-collar workers, in ordinary times, potentially officer class. During the extraordinary August days of 1914, the old and powerful ruthlessly ordered the excited young to do their duty. In the right company, naturally... On August 25th, the minutes of the Liverpool Stock Exchange confirm that volunteers would be serving with men of their own caste. Present at this meeting was the editor of the Liverpool Courier, who published the following reassurance:

'We are informed that young men connected with the various markets here are ready to enlist as privates in the regular army, so long as they can be assured of forming a complete body of their own class. The hardships and difficulties of active service have no terrors for such men, so long as they meet them in the company of their own friends and business acquaintances.'[16]

The promise was all-important. Serving as lowly privates was acceptable, just so long as they were guaranteed the company of their own caste. As the war progressed, even officer status wouldn't guarantee social acceptability. In 1917, while both young officers were convalescing at Craiglockhart, Siegfried Sassoon, born to privilege, found Wilfred Owen, 'a rather ordinary young man, perceptibly provincial.' The observation is chilling. Writing almost thirty years later, and with admiration for the poet, Sassoon evidently believed that his provincialism needed to be on record.

On August 31st, 1914, would-be volunteers like Fred queued at St George's Hall, Liverpool, answering Lord Derby's call. Even the venue was suitably patriotic, the architecture classically heroic and inspiring. Three days earlier, addressing a crowd of young men all cheering and throwing their hats into the air, the Earl had promised to refrain from any heroics. Then, in true St Crispin's Day style, he delivered a stirring appeal to the honour of Britain and the honour of Liverpool. The Earl concluded :

' You have given a noble example in thus coming forward. You are certain to give a noble example in the field of battle.'[17] Or, as Lord Derby didn't quite say, 'God for Harry, England and St George ! '

In that strange and painfully hierarchical world, young men were offered the chance to sign up with 'their own sort.' Advertisements emphasising this appeared regularly in the local press. Friends, neighbours and colleagues joined up together. When a battalion of Pals suffered carnage, a whole town would be in mourning. Later in the war, the concept of Pals was abandoned, not because they'd learned to forget class prejudice - most of them certainly hadn't - but because so many deaths in one locality was bad for military and civilian morale. By 1939, the old caste systems were less rigid, though by no means abandoned.[18]

The notice of Fred's death was posted in the Liverpool Courier on October 31st, 1916. In the public search room, the newly restored microfiche copies of the Courier look fresh from the news stand. No longer yellowed, but in sharp black and white, history becomes immediate, horrifically real. Like early newsreels, no longer jerking but adjusted to natural speed, this restoration intensifies the litany of carnage, so many deaths, so many young men lost, all over the city and all over Europe. Some reports are familiar, might be breaking news. In the Courier, the first accounts of Edith Cavell's execution filled two broadsheet pages of a thin wartime paper. Extended reporting on Nurse Cavell continued for days.[19] Private Pulford's death was hardly news at all, only the barest facts, his name, and, though only approximately, where he was killed. Fred had become another dead Tommy, worth two brief lines of small print and no more. There's no photo, no celebration of his life, no comforting story of a heroic death, his career at the bank, or the boyhood friendship that led to adventures in France. If he'd found another girlfriend, she isn't mentioned.

By October, 1916, the death of one more Tommy wasn't news. The media was now carefully managed. In the Liverpool archives, letters in Lord Derby's personal papers reveal how this was done, and how, behind the scenes, Britain's leaders reacted when difficult news leaked out. In the Liverpool press, reports of Allied successes and tributes to heroes appeared in the early pages. The 'officer class' predominates. Ordinary casualties were listed as close to the back of the paper as possible in columns of small print. 'Hun' atrocities were reported in considerable detail. Throughout most of the war, Page 3 was reserved for the exploits of actresses and occasional debutantes. In Liverpool and everywhere else, editors didn't want yet more accounts of slaughter on the Somme. Lloyd George and Lord Derby certainly didn't. It would be dangerously bad for morale. At Watergate House, M I 7 ensured that most press reports were carefully censored and directed. When the news of Fred's death reached them, his parents and sisters would be left to grieve alone.[20]

Military historians have written massively about the origins of the First World War. Many, for all their efforts, their tables of battleships built, the emergence of economic rivalry, shifting allegiances and early twentieth century ententes conclude that none of the so-called causes are convincing. It simply need not have happened. Describing the war as 'a tragic and unnecessary conflict' John Keegan spells out the horrific cost :

' The consequences of the first clash ended the lives of ten million human beings, tortured the emotional lives of millions more, destroyed the benevolent and optimistic culture of the European continent, and left, when the guns fell silent at last, a legacy of political rancour and racial hatred so intense that no explanation of the causes of the Second World War can stand without reference to those roots.' [21]

Keegan analyses the bizarre rush to volunteer, supposedly so instinctive and spontaneous. Thousands of these eager young men were like Fred, fit, healthy, well educated. Somewhere on the middle-class career ladder, they were nothing like the underclass 'other ranks' of the prewar regular army. At the privileged schools where the middle classes were educated, Officer Training Corps had promoted military service with ever-increasing zeal. Lewis Paton, High Master of Manchester Grammar School, who'd encouraged so many boys to share his lifelong love of Germany had become one of the foremost recruiters for the Public Schools Battalion. In Liverpool, firms lined up their bright young staff in battle order : ' Some concerns, like Cunard and The Stock Exchange actually formed up their men first, and then marched them to St George's Hall en masse to enlist.' [22]

Young men were still accustomed to deference. That degree of pressure from their employers would be almost impossible to resist, well before the powerful poster campaigns became ubiquitous. Still living at home or workers' accommodation, as most young men did until marriage, they were expected to obey their elders. Poverty and unemployment would recruit the working class. Allegedly, their country needed them. Nobody else did, and even a Tommy's pay was better than nothing. War fever soon infected the classroom. Aged eleven, the prep-school educated Eric Blair published his first work in 1914, a suitably stirring poem, addressed to the 'young men of England '[23]

Reading Wilfred Owen, most 21st century pupils need text notes to translate the old lie, Dulce et decorum est. Born and schooled in the last years of Victoria, many of those ardent young bank clerks, lawyers and stockbrokers would know Homer's version of this heroic death-wish too, written centuries before Horace. Dying was glorious, especially for King and Country. In Greek or in Latin, public and grammar school text books celebrated war and death in fervid poetry. Elementary pupils learned centuries of British valour. Gilt-edged tales awarded as Sunday School prizes celebrate manly courage and chivalry. Pre-war adult fiction focused on dastardly spies, who were invariably German. Erskine Childers' stirring 1903 tale,' The Riddle of the Sands' is one of the best known of this genre, though in Ireland, Childers himself would become a different kind of patriot. Film versions of Buchan's ' The Thirty-Nine Steps' appear regularly on TV, but there were many other thrilling tales of espionage and high courage. In newspapers, syndicated serials were weekly staples.[24] Late Victorian paintings by artists like Waterhouse, Wheelwright and Topham featured countless handsome, if somewhat effeminate, knights in shining armour, avenging suitably grateful damsels.[25] Inspired by heroic fiction, young men across the Empire suddenly discovered it was their duty to defend Belgium and avenge Hunnish atrocities. Patriotism certainly wasn't enough, they had to hate the right enemy, remembering, carefully, that the French were allies now. Even the officer class could find this difficult. Defining Germany as the great and terrible enemy of Britain needed sustained and careful management. Despite the trickle of propaganda dating back to the 1870's, hating Germans was still something of a novelty.[26] Often, the Hun turned out to be Fritz or Jerry, just as cold, wet and miserable as Tommy. At every level, affectionate nicknames for the French are conspicuously absent. In some remarkably indiscreet letters, Douglas Haig didn't even try to maintain, at least formally, respect for his French colleagues. Personal letters to Lloyd George detail what he regarded as shameless French chicanery in the management of military supplies.[27]

Unlike the sophisticated young Nomads, many volunteers would be unaware of that classic marriage of convenience, the entente cordiale. Ethnically, the Royal Family were almost completely German. This hadn't been a problem, or at least, no more so than usual. British monarchs were hardly ever English. Germans were Anglo-Saxon cousins and friends, German was the language of theology, science, music, philosophy, psychology, economics, and enterprise too. The young Friedrich Engels could write so vividly about destitution in Manchester because he was working in the city, not as a trainee Marxist, but as a young manager in his family's factory. In the late nineteenth century, thousands of economic migrants from the struggling new country called 'Germany' had found work and some prosperity in Britain. Many helped to create that prosperity, for instance, in developing the steel and chemical industries of North West England. Now, these men and their sons faced internment. In 1914, there was no Nazism and no final solution. There had been death camps in the Boer War, but they were British. The skeletal victims weren't Jews but Boers, many of them women and children, their condition described, graphically, by Ramsay Macdonald.[28]

Learned hatred and patriotism can happen overnight, without any threat of 'weapons of mass destruction', invasion, or even the suggestion that British jobs are under threat. For several days during the spring of 1982, the Royal Navy happened to be holding a display on the shores of Windermere. The exercise had been planned long before the unexpected Falklands War. Eerily, breaking news from the South Atlantic was broadcast from Royal Navy loud speakers, echoing across the lake as local schoolchildren queued to explore the deck of a replica submarine. Until April 2nd, 1982, most people at this display probably had no idea where the Falklands were. Nor had they known that these distant islands in the South Atlantic belonged to Britain.[29] By chance, Bristolians and Bristol university students did, because in the Seventies, the rusting hulk of Brunel's SS Great Britain had been towed back to the city docks from the South Atlantic. Bristolians were a well-informed minority. For most people, Argentina meant corned beef, football, and for the upper classes, polo. Overnight, on the street and in the playground, its people became hated 'Argies'. For the honour of Britain, victory was suddenly essential. Bizarrely, in a region of England where the local wool trade was in crisis, buying wool and knitwear from the Falklands was promoted as a patriotic duty. Displays of Falklands knitwear were surrounded by Union Jacks.[30]

In 1939, and, far more recently, in 2003, the British press was well prepared for war. Long before the invasion of Iraq, TV and radio debates on the morality of warfare became staple fare. In July, 1914, the Liverpool Courier certainly knew the country was in trouble, but the conflict they expected was far nearer home, just across the Irish Sea. Newspaper researchers should always turn first to the political cartoons rather than weighty editorials. It saves time. Cartoonists target the real issues of the day. For the first three weeks of July, every single cartoon published in Liverpool focused on Ireland and the battle for Home Rule. Germany simply wasn't newsworthy. Even in late July, 1914, shipping companies were still advertising the short sea route to Belgium. The advertisements say nothing about bagging Ypres before the Germans get there. Belgium was for holidays, and, of course, the traditional gateway for cruises on the Rhine. The change begins on July 25th, when the leading cartoon features the King's cousin, the troubled Tsar. The first cartoon based specifically on the West European crisis doesn't appear till July 29th. Next day, the European news is still tucked away on page six, apparently of far less interest than the Lancashire Agricultural Show. On August 1st, in the daily newspaper of a major city, the prize pigs, sheep and cattle of the Lancashire Show claim more column inches than a report on the German threat to Russia. By August 3rd, armed Europe is front page news, but so is Ernest Shackleton's long-planned expedition to the South Pole. Nobody suggests he shouldn't be going.

On August 4th, 1914, newly arrived in London, Fred Pulford would be swept up in the sudden, unreasoned fervour for war, which swept through the

City. He volunteered almost immediately. Private Pulford had so much to live for, including his steady middle-class job at the bank. He'd joined the Midland as a junior clerk, just before his seventeenth birthday, working at Liverpool's Commutation Row branch. His brief employment records confirm that after leaving the Institute, he'd spent a few months as a cashier for a builder's merchant. Clerks in training were essentially apprentices, certainly not independent. Unable to support himself, Fred would have to live at home. Financially at least, his status would be little different from that of a schoolboy. In 1903, his annual pay was just twenty pounds. Three years later, Fred was still earning under a pound a week, considerably less than many young dockers, miners or factory workers. He'd be expected to study for Bankers' Institute exams and to dress and conduct himself appropriately. Fred could expect an annual increase of ten pounds, but in 1910, the year Maud Pember Reeves studied working class poverty, he was earning only £90, no more than many unskilled labourers. But in their early twenties, Pember Reeves' labourers were already supporting wives and families. Husbands and fathers they wouldn't be backpacking around France, but they could live as adult men. Bank clerks had to be patient. Their rewards might come later. Fred evidently hoped for more than life as a ledger clerk in Bootle on two pounds a week. Returning from France on Saturday August 3rd, 1912, he couldn't stay long in London. By August 6th, he had to be back at his Midland desk in Bootle.

For Fred, opportunity had come at last in the summer of 1914. Moving from Bootle to Threadneedle Street, he enjoyed, briefly, the magnificence of the new banking hall and a salary of £170. There was no time to write anything on the new clerk's work sheet. The line where his duties should be recorded is marked War Service. Fired by London's excitement, Fred headed north, to Liverpool, where Lord Derby was beginning his great recruitment drive. The bank was informed of his death. On his War Service card, nothing else is mentioned. Missing on the Somme, Fred very nearly vanishes from history.[31]

His friends trusted Fred to book their tickets to France. Nobody caught his streaming cold and they survived his cross-channel monologues. Lanky Fred was the best swimmer of the party. On Jersey, caught out by a classic 1912 downpour, his long arms and legs dangled over the sides of a tiny horse trap. Still single, in his late twenties, he was normal enough for the Edwardian age. The least qualified labourers married and produced children early. Like their descendants in the twenty-first century, ambitious young Edwardians were slow to marry. Women like the schoolteacher Gladys Gleave were concentrating on careers. Turning thirty in 1914, 50% of young men were single. Middle-class men were still expected to provide for their wives, women teachers and civil servants were expected to resign on marriage.[32] But Fred would never marry. Moving to London, he would probably live in lodgings, never become a householder. On the Commonwealth War Graves website, his parents are named as his next of kin. Embarking for France on November 6th, 1915, after a year of military training, he had just over eleven months to live. As an ordinary private, he had no plans of attack, no middle-class officer's rank. Perhaps, in the battalion diary, there'd be some mention of Private Pulford ? Unlikely, of course, unless he'd committed some military crime or act of heroism. The so-called 'battalion diary' is merely a terse log book, but it does provide an outline of how No. 21996, 17th Btn, King's Liverpool Regiment, spent the last year of his life.[33]

Chapter Five

In the ranks of death you'll find him...

Thomas Moore, The Minstrel Boy

Nobody would read a battalion diary for pleasure. The KLR 17th battalion's record of the Great War isn't poetic or romantic or even decent prose. Like every other regiment in the British Army, the KLR had a job to do. That job was winning the war for Britain, at whatever cost.[1] Once he'd joined up, Private Pulford's life was no longer his own. Choosing to fight for his country, Fred had made his last decision. From now on, all decisions would be made for him by officers. Recruited straight from public school and the universities, young men who'd trained in their school's OTC had little or no practical experience of military command. In the 17th, 2nd Lieutenant Edgar Wrayford Willmer admitted that :

' My Knowledge of military matters was nil, a condition which was in fact common to nearly all officers in the battalion.' [2] Injured on the Somme, the 'officer class' Willmer would, of course, be cared for in an officer class hospital.

Enlisting as a private, Fred had become a number in a battalion in a regiment. The worst crime he could commit was disobeying an order. Leaving England on November 15th, the 17th sailed on the SS. Princess Victoria. Already, by the time they landed in France, there'd been casualties, one mule and one man. Ominously, the day the 17th left for France, their quartermaster, C.O. Ryder, had been found dying near Stonehenge. Ryder had shot himself in the head. The stark typescript makes no comment.[3] Arriving in Boulogne at five pm, the men were marched to the big purpose-built rest camp at Ostrehove. Three days later, they marched back to Boulogne, arriving at Pont Remy at midnight. It was raining, and they faced yet another march, this time to Bellancourt, where they spent four wet days in billets. On the 14th of November, the weather became colder, fine by day, with light snow overnight. A Lieutenant was evacuated on medical grounds. From Bellancourt, they moved on to Brucamps, where the battalion divided, A and B companies to Vauchelles les Domarts, C and D companies to billets in the nearby village of Surchamps.

And so it goes on, a fatal cocktail of far too much death and very little glory. The leaden record of battalion movements continues right up to the Armistice, as they fight, retreat, come in and out of the line, and, far too often, die in horrific numbers. Military records can be quite astonishingly boring, and even in death, class matters. After every battle, the calculations of officer deaths are, on the whole, correct. Almost all the men with no accurate date of death are listed as 'OR'- other ranks, segregated even in death. Everything about this war was out of kilter. Both sides were armed with hideously effective new weapons, including poison gas. Both could only move at the pace of weary and overburdened infantry. 'Officers' and 'other ranks' suffered hideous injuries, yet throughout the war, their perceived class differences apparently required treatment in separate hospitals.

Somebody had to keep these stolid records. In sweeping arrows across Northern France, maps of army movements look convincing. They suggest plans of attack, policy decisions, a kind of coherence. The battalion diary records endless punishing journeys on foot, never the mens' sodden or sweating exhaustion. They were, as the troops sang, Marching, marching, always ******* marching. Like the Grand Old Duke of York's ten thousand, they move across Flanders, there and back again. Notoriously short of hills, this is where Frederick, Duke of York really did march. The nursery rhyme celebrates futility, and not just Frederick's.[4] It helps to open a map of the French and Belgian borderlands, see exactly where the 17th were so constantly on the move. Only seriously bad weather is worth mentioning. The November of 1915 was bleak. The laconic army typescript refers to severe frost and movement being 'difficult'. By difficult, they didn't mean occasional patches of ungritted ice on smooth tarmac, but deep-rutted mud, frozen hard as concrete, punishing for skidding hooves and heavily laden carts. For largely horse-drawn transport, movement was more than difficult. In very few words, the battalion diary outlines a bleak and wretched life, even when they're not in action. They practice throwing live ammunition, tramp around the eastern edges of France. Vignacourt, Béthencourt, Maricourt... Sometimes, they're close to Agincourt. Five hundred years earlier, conditions were vile there too, mud and dysentery, before and after the glorious victory, Non Nobis and Te Deum. The diary records that early December 1915 was wet, turning colder on the 13th. Someone worked out a plan for improving the billets, decided they needed a butcher's shop and travelling kitchen, but top of the list was the drying room. The butcher's shop was important too. In the 17th, Private Tongue, another young bank clerk, who'd been a year senior to Fred at the Liverpool Institute, suffered severe food poisoning after eating McConachy's tinned meat, imported from America. The illness must have been prolonged; Tongue had to spend time in a convalescent camp.[5] By 1914, tinned meat was normally more reliable than this, but no doubt freshly butchered meat was more palatable. A postcard sent from the Western Front shows Allied soldiers driving oxen to a French slaughterhouse.

The story of Fred's war is grim and all too familiar, the roads frequently atrocious, sometimes a quagmire, sometimes hard frozen, and invariably littered with dying men and animals, shattered vehicles. Even in June, the trenches could be wet, though chalky soils drained better than water-holding clays. It's the First World War, they're near the Somme, the catalogue of weary misery is only an official record. Throughout Fred's eleven months in France, there's no relief, no Blackadder black humour or bawdy marching songs, with or without *******. In the leaden rain of Christmas, 1915, there was nothing to celebrate, no truce, no football, no Silent Night. Stille Nacht ? Possibly... Some German troops did offer a Christmas ceasefire, but this time, the Tommies wouldn't join in. Germany's attempted offer of peace had been rejected, the proposed terms being totally unacceptable.[6] The war to end war had become a war that must be won at any cost. Training for months, eagerly bayoneting sacks stuffed with straw, the volunteers of the New Armies had learned to hate. They certainly hadn't come to France to play football or sing carols. On Christmas Eve, 1915, GHQ in France reported with evident satisfaction that there had been no repeat of the previous year's illicit truce.

' The overtures in the direction of fraternising on the part of the Germans were but slight, and fainthearted, as though their contemptuous rejection by our men were a foregone conclusion. On the whole, there seems to be a general sense of relief among our men that Christmas is over.'[7]

Late on Christmas Day, Fred's battalion were on the move again, as the rain poured down. For many thousands of these young men, it would be their last Christmas. On January 1st, the 17th's diarist reports that the generals had exchanged New Year telegrams, but the date was now 1916. Across half the world, there'd be no happy new year. All over Britain, newspaper editorials are sombre. They know how this year is beginning, seem to guess how it will end.[8]

By January 4th, in yet more heavy rain, they were heading for Maricourt and a return to the firing line, relieving another battalion of Liverpool Pals. The British defences were being shelled and the approach roads too. On the 4th, a private was killed by his own grenade. Then the book records that a mule was killed and a horse wounded. Mules clearly inspired great affection, valued quite as much as horses. On the Bayeux tapestry, Count Guy de Ponthieu is shown riding a mule. Lieutenant Chavasse of the 17th chose as his charger a strange sounding animal 'pink as a cooked salmon'. When one of the 17th's mules developed tetanus, becoming ' stiff as a toy horse', the animal was put in a dark cool cellar, fed on grass and water, pumped with anti-tetanus. He recovered. A post-mortem on a horse that had died of 'cholic' revealed that its intestines had ruptured. The vet found grit and cinders in the horse's colon. When they'd been in France a little longer, trying to count too many lost men, there was less time to grieve for horses and mules.[9]

' January 21st, 1916, Maricourt: Situation Normal '. None of the Liverpool Pals were killed that day. Does that count as normal ? Next day, the 17th encountered 'severe shelling, whizz-bangs, followed by grenades. Gas helmets were tested.' Decoding a military record, a glossary's essential. Whizz-bangs were small calibre shells. British or German, flying pigs, coal boxes, minnies, toffee-apples, shells and mortars of every size were all designed to kill. The nicknames didn't make them any less lethal.[10] On the 28th January, they faced heavy bombardment, and villages behind enemy lines suffered. Suzanne was under heavy fire, and, for the first time, they faced tear-gas too. Maricourt was bombarded by 'about 1,000 shells.' The catalogue continues into February, another week at Maricourt, plenty more shelling. Then they move, first to Bray, then Daours, in the snow, and on to Etinéhem. The 17th would do their fair share of shelling and the Allies were quick to use gas too, not long after expressing their horror over this particular Hun atrocity.

In a strictly military record, stripped of any personal details, there's no time to describe the physical misery of being cold, dirty and lousy, all day and every day. Some years ago, when the BBC recruited volunteers for a scrupulously accurate reenactment, actors playing the part of real soldiers in the Hull Pals had to 'die' at the right time. Authenticity didn't extend to lice, trench foot, or rampant venereal disease.[11] Professors of Archaeology are more ruthless than TV companies, excavation compulsory, deadlines tight, the weather authentically vile. In icy March, on the Northumbrian borders, working in snow, hail and rain, trench life is hell on earth, the bone-numbing cold painful, sometimes actually nauseating. Two or three metres down, anaerobic mud smells foul, even without the stench of putrid bodies. Archaeology students and TV volunteers are spared real shellfire, gas, rats, and corpses who used to be comrades. Despite, or perhaps in response to the appalling conditions, trench esprit de corps becomes powerful, especially when laced with machismo. If my experience on many excavations is typical, nobody, however sick, cold and miserable, wants to be the first to quit. Abandoning team mates becomes unthinkable, commitment to the task transcends common sense and extreme discomfort. It's a deadly perversion of the human instinct to cooperate, pursuing a common goal.[12] Traditionally, we salute the courage of men who served on the Western Front. Endurance and stoicism might be better words. The eager 'volunteers' of the early weeks were hardly making an informed choice. From 1916 onwards, the choice would be stark, conscription, or, for the unusually determined, the disgrace and heavy penalties endured by conscientious objectors.

On March 16th, 1916, Fred's battalion was moved to Franvillers, near Corbie, and billets just outside Etinéhem. Here, thirteen men of the 17th were sentenced to the British Army's most savage punishment, the ordeal known to all ranks as 'Crucifixion'. One man died at the scene. Investigations into the brutal Franvillers incident led to questions in parliament, but 'Field Punishment No 1' wasn't abandoned until 1923. Private Dunn's grim personal account of the events is held in the Liddle collection.[13] At a snap kit inspection, two gas respirators were missing. Addressing the men, the Colonel stressed the importance of respirators. No excuses would be accepted. Citing his traditional paternal role, the Colonel claimed that the men must be punished, in the interests of the battalion. The thirteen men held to be responsible, including Dunn, were sentenced to one day of Field Punishment No.1. Men sentenced to the ordinary form of 'No 1' would be tied to a fence, wheel, or gymnastic equipment and left in this position, exposed to the elements. The punishment could be repeated for days, but they were untied at night. At Franvillers, the thirteen men faced a gruelling ordeal. Examined by Captain Dakin, the 17th's medical officer, all thirteen were pronounced fit. Dakin recognised that the man who died was 'anything but well' but ruled that he was 'quite able to be tied to a wheel.'

In the village square, the men were tied to the wheels of gun-carriages. 'Crucifixion' alternated with periods of double-time forced marching. Released from the second period in this position, the man referred to by Dunn as 'Private Blank' collapsed, shouting 'I cannot go on'. Supported by Dunn, he died almost immediately. For the remaining twelve, including Dunn, alternate fast marching and periods tied to a wheel continued. continued. Finally, as they were leaving Franvillers, the men were ordered to dig a pit, in which to bury the company's surplus food.

If Fred Pulford wrote any letters home in the springtime of 1916, they haven't come to light. He must have known what happened at Franvillers. Perhaps the 17th were grateful when an outbreak of measles forced them into quarantine for almost the whole of April, even though the illness was potentially life-threatening for adult men. The diary doesn't mention any cases and by May Day, they were back in the line, under fire at Maricourt. Inevitably, like any military record, it's a one-sided account, only the British version, more howitzers, more minenwerfers, every action of the enemy, proof of his irredeemable wickedness. In October, 1915, reporting the first British use of gas, the Liverpool Courier explained that it had been captured from the Germans.

Out of line, the 17th were erecting wire to protect their own trenches. Invading German territory, wire-cutters were essential, but they didn't have enough. Writing home, asking for a collapsible mug and tobacco, Lieutenant Wrayford Willmer added a request for wire-cutters, blaming Asquith for the shortage of such essential supplies. Ordered into No-Man's-Land, in pitch darkness, the eighteen year old Lieutenant Lewis Roberts, still, legally, too young for active service overseas, wasn't issued with a compass.[14] Inadequate equipment was matched by punishing schedules. On May 25th, the diary records that Private Lawson was found guilty of sleeping on duty. In theory, Lawson could have faced the death sentence, but this was commuted to penal servitude.[15] Five weeks before the Battle of the Somme, a three year sentence might have saved his life. Predictably, by May 31st, Lawson's sentence had been suspended. Britain and her allies were preparing for the glorious battle that would, supposedly, end the war to end all wars. Exhausted young soldiers often fell asleep on their feet. Lawson was needed, trained men were usually far too valuable to be shot or imprisoned. Out of 449 men sentenced to death for sleeping on duty, only two were actually executed.[16] Lawson himself survived the war.

The 17th were busy digging trenches, going into action on the 11th June, in the all too familiar Maricourt trenches. In another letter, Lieutenant Willmer observed that they ' always seemed to return to Maricourt.' Three men were mentioned in Haig's despatches. On June 24th, the entry reads : 'V' day. Our artillery bombarded the enemy along the whole front.' Three days later, seventeen 'other ranks' were killed and fifty-seven wounded. Next day, heavy rain delayed the great battle. 'trenches v. difficult'. By the 30th, both the weather and trench conditions had improved, in time for the most appalling tragedy of European warfare.

On July 1st, 1916, Fred's battalion were alert by 3.30 a.m. At first, the day 'promised to be fine and hot' At about 7.15 a.m., a thick fog came down and persisted for a greater part of the morning. Zero hour was 7. 30. Private Dunn was sent as a runner to the Colonel, advancing with the Headquarters party. Runners were used when all other means of communication were impossible. Men like Dunn would be right in the firing line.[17] The 17th's diarist reports, optimistically, 'perfect liasion between the French and ourselves' . The comment speaks for itself, betraying the often very far from perfect relationship between French and British officers. At the War Office and in Downing Street, relations with France could be equally fraught.[18] On the Somme, tensions between the allies were all too obvious. Claude Chavasse had met with trouble as his men were waiting for a train. They were turned away, because the French, who were sending messages, objected to the presence of British troops. (It seems unlikely that the average Liverpool Tommy would be fluently eavesdropping.) Soon after this altercation, Chavasse and his men met a party of German prisoners. The men ' booed them at first, then realised how very vulgar it was.' Chavasse himself admired a 'fine looking Hun, who sat, arms folded, and a sort of scornful Napoleon on the Belerophon look.' Later in the war, Chavasse would come upon a beautifully tended grave of an RAF pilot, made and cared for by Germans, paying tribute to 'a very gallant British officer'.[19]

On July 1st, Fred's company escaped lightly enough. The 17th lost only three men. One hundred and sixty-nine of the 18th were killed, almost all of them from Liverpool and Merseyside. At least their rations arrived safely. The detail seems curiously cold-blooded, but this is reality, a raw military record, not fiction. In a film or novel, the survivors of July 1st, 1916 might be too grief-stricken to face food. In real life, exhausted young soldiers were hungry. Britain had just lost twenty thousand young men. Forty thousand more had been wounded, many grievously, but, late that night, as the battalion records confirm, the survivors got their suppers.[20] Over the next two days, the 17th' s losses were still relatively light. Then they were out of action.

Hot baths and clean kit restored men to something like fighting condition, ready for the savagery of woodland fighting in Trones Wood. The Somme woodlands became a wasteland of hideous death. As usual, the dead are carefully divided. In Trones Wood, forty-six 'other ranks' died, and one officer. Fifteen men have no date of death, let alone a known grave, and every one of these are 'other ranks'.[21] Later, awards were presented, the Military Medal for 'other ranks', a DSO and a Military Cross for two officers. Medals for 'other ranks' appear to have been rationed. Private Dunn, one of eight runners, tossed up for a Military Medal. Only four were awarded. Dunn lost.[22] A private from the 17th was awarded the democratic Croix de Guerre.[23] July ended with yet more carnage. In the diary typescript for July, 1916, there's a terse comment, almost a reprimand, handwritten in ink,: ' It is no use soldiers wandering through woods and saying they have taken them.'

August began in bivouacs. Soon, they were on the move again. The catalogue of Somme villages reads like a macabre pre-Beeching timetable. Troops rarely knew where they were being sent. They needed more training, using Lewis guns and mines. Other training came in disguise. The account of Brigade sports seems absurdly parochial. Cross-country runs, football, swimming, boxing, and who came first in the mile belong, surely, to the school magazine, not a logbook from the Somme. The Army, of course, had an ulterior motive. Team sports kept the young men fighting fit. After four days in billets, there's another litany of destinations. Another chance to bath and change heralded a swift return to the front. Training hard, at Vignacourt, Fred and many of his comrades now had less than two weeks to live. On October 11th, at Longueval, British bombardment of the enemies commenced about midday. According to the 17 th's diary, ' hostile shelling ' was intermittent throughout the day. Presumably, the Germans found British shelling hostile too. This is the entry for October 12th, 1916.

Our bombardment continued. Enemy reply weak. 2.5 pm, Zero Hour.

Attack on German front line system commenced. Enemy wire found to be uncut, and the attack was unsuccessful. Hostile machine gun fire was very heavy and caused many casualties. Battalion HQ & Support trench heavily shelled throughout afternoon and evening. Small platoon of 20th Bn only successful in reaching our front line about 5 pm. All communication had to be carried out by runners and Carrier Pigeons, as all wires were being continually cut by enemy shells.

Afterwards, they counted their dead :

Casualties :   Officers Killed 5, Wounded 5.

OR Killed 38. Wounded and missing, about 225.[24]

Among the 'OR' missing was Pulford, Frederick Ivor, Pte, who'd once planned a very different journey through little towns and villages in northern France. Fred's war was over. All that intensive training ended in a classic debacle. As they'd gained about 150 yards of mud, it counts as a kind of victory. The final death toll was far worse than the battalion estimate. This time, they certainly didn't count dead mules. Writing up that first reckoning, nobody could say for sure how many men were missing, and they didn't know who had been killed. Five officers, correct, and another died of wounds, but in reality, ninety-five 'other ranks' died that day, not thirty-eight.[25] The runner, Dunn, managed to deliver a message, but when a heavy shell buried him in a trench, he was evacuated to a casualty clearing station, then invalided home. He'd survived, and wouldn't return to the front. Many of his close friends were dead.[26]

Killed in action, Fred Pulford's story became abominably straightforward, just one more casualty to be added to the reckoning, with as little fuss as possible. Armies always count their dead. They have to decide if their losses are cost-effective, study how they might improve both tactics and equipment. A recent calculation of the financial cost sets the Allies total bill at $125, 690, 477, 000. The Central Powers' bill is given as $60, 643, 160, 000. Germany and her allies were always heavily outnumbered, but they killed far more efficiently.[27] The day Fred died, many other Liverpool families faced a lifetime of mourning. The battalion record doesn't try to dress it up as a glorious victory. They'd made a classic misjudgement. ' The 17th Battalion was particularly badly hit, as its portion of No Man's Land contained a slight rise in the ground, and as the troops emerged onto it, they were silhouetted against the sky, and became an easy target... to be picked off almost at the enemy's will.' [28]

October 12th, 1916, was a grim day for Liverpool, but there were many far worse. On July 30th, 1916, over four hundred and sixty officers and men from the four Pals battalions had been killed. Three hundred and forty eight of them are named at Thiepval. Altogether, there are 73,357 names on the monument, and these are just a few of the Missing of the Somme, only those men killed between July, 1916, and March, 1918.[29] Remembering this battle, fifty years later, Lewis Roberts wrote : The Somme was war as it really is, dreadful, shocking, obscene, wholly evil, an outrage against human nature.' Since the war, this former boy soldier had become an Anglican vicar, devoting his life to peace, and, outrageously, daring to challenge the shibboleth of Remembrance Day. As a young curate, Roberts was dismissed from his first parish because the local squire objected to his pacifism.[30]

Educated for careers in banking, shipping and the law, Fred and all the other Liverpool Pals had trained to throw grenades, fire Lewis guns, dig trenches and latrines, kill as many of the enemy as they could. They marched backwards and forwards around the borders of France and Belgium. Sometimes, according to this spare and dispassionate record, they were drafted to improving conditions in their billets. Sometimes, they could even bath, in brewery vats and dye tubs, change out of lousy uniforms, enjoy a decent hot meal of egg and chips, rather than Army tinned meat and veg. Some would enjoy an hour or so with an obliging mademoiselle. Cheering on a summer's day, tossing straw boaters into the air, what kind of war had they expected ?

Chapter Six

They told me, Heraclitus, they told me you were dead

They brought me bitter news to hear, and bitter tears to shed.

I wept as I remembered how often you and I

had tired the sun with talking, and sent him down the sky.

William Cory, 1823 - 1892

Fred would become a name, carved high on a gargantuan and hideously expensive war memorial, where mourners still lay wreaths of paper poppies.[1] In his late Victorian childhood, he'd learn reams of poetry. Cory, author of the Eton boating song, became a recitation staple. Perhaps, at the Liverpool Institute, Fred studied Heraclitus, remembered now mainly for claiming that we can't step twice into the same river, rather than his attitude to war. We can, sometimes painfully, revisit the scenes of lost happiness. After their summer idyll, Fred Pulford and his five friends set out to record their fortnight in France, At Southampton docks, boarding the troop ship, Fred would think, surely, of July 20th, 1912, crossing to France with his friends. Wandering through the Forest of Cerisy, gathering wild strawberries, admiring brilliant butterflies and dragonflies, the six Nomads would surely tire the sun with talking, live in the perfect moment. In the August heat of Brittany, twenty dusty miles would pass more easily as they laughed and talked together. Long walks in the countryside gave young people the perfect excuse to be together. As teenagers in West Derby, did Fred, Alec and Gladys meet after school, solving the world's problems and a few of their own ? In 1912, they'd sailed along the Seine and then, in Brittany, explored the Rance. Three years later, Private Pulford was heading for the Somme. How would his friends react, publicly and privately, to the news of his death ? Officially, in 1916, they were supposed to salute his courage, applaud a hero's death, agree it was what he would have wanted. In private, surely they'd grieve for their lost friend ?

Fred died single, and, at least officially, childless. But he did have sisters, Mary and Winifred. Both married, Mary in West Derby, in the summer of 1918, and Winifred in the autumn of 1922, in Islington. Would anybody remember a great-uncle, killed on the Somme, a man who'd known France in happier times, backpacking with his friends ? Family legends persist, often grow in the telling. In 1912, backpacking around France was hardly a conventional holiday, especially with partners. Somewhere in Liverpool, people might remember hearing about this escapade ? If his photo was published, would somebody recognise Fred, claim him as their ancestor ?

And the other Nomads ? Married in 1914, did Alec and Gladys have children? Once again, the distinctive surname proved useful. Their first child, Kenneth, was born in Wallasey on September 15th, 1915. Their daughter Margaret was born in January, 1918. But what about Alec himself ? Did he, like Fred, join one of the Pals battalions ? Did he live to see his daughter ? Thousands of war babies were born after their fathers had been killed. Investigating the Westmores would be the easiest research. Not so the other Nomads... Ross still had only one name. Searching military archives online for Frank - (or Francis)- Bourne resulted in the usual bewildering possibilities. In France, the nameless young woman is sometimes, but by no means always, close to one of the men. Was this Frank, Fred, or Ross ? If she'd married Ross, their identity might never be known. By 1914, Ross and Frank could be anywhere in the world. How many young Liverpudlians answered the 1912 Saskatchewan appeal for harvesters ? Such advertisements appeared regularly. In the early twentieth century, some of my own immediate forebears emigrated to Australia and Canada. My husband's family had left the Eden valley to run a sheep station in New Zealand. Movement between countries was easier then, especially within the British Empire.

In the Liverpool archives, more information about the Westmores might yet lead to the others. There was no sign of Alec in any of the city battalions, old or newly formed. Ross remained a mystery. The KLR website offered a list of men with Ross as a forename or surname. Investigated, not one of them seemed to fit the demanding 'Nomad' profile.[2] So where were they ? The possibilities were daunting. During World War One, the British Forces were assembled in five armies. Family ties could link a man to distant regiments. In cities all over England, expatriate Irishmen, Welshmen and Scots had their own battalions. Across the Empire, men rushed to enlist in defence of the mother country. From New Zealand, many former Cumbrians returned to serve in the Border Regiment. Expatriate Irish, Scots and Welshmen enlisted in the countries of their ancestors. But men didn't necessarily remain with the same battalion or even the same regiment. Heavy casualties meant that throughout the war, units were constantly re-forming. Altogether, in the Cavalry, Yeomanry, Artillery, Engineers, Infantry and other divisions, including the new Royal Flying Corps, there were well over three hundred battalions and other units. The Army's historians are unfailingly helpful, but warned that tracing a man with half a name and no other clues seemed highly unlikely. The National Archives gave the same advice.

Online searches confirmed that only one Alexander Wemyss Westmore served in the First World War. Alec's medal card detailed his service in the Royal Army Medical Corps, from February 5th, 1915 until April 23rd, 1918. Almost all RAMC doctors were officers. Private Westmore, service number 39447, served as a stretcher bearer. But why had he waited so many months, and then, why had he chosen the Medical Corps, rather than, like Fred, one of the new City battalions of the KLR ? The delay suggests thought... In the Medical Corps, doctors, orderlies and bearers didn't fight. Serving as a stretcher bearer was, originally, one option for conscientious objectors who were prepared to accept a noncombatant role in the war effort. Later, under conscription, the RAMC became increasingly unwilling to accept determined noncombatants. Obviously, like Alec, many bearers enlisted long before conscription was introduced. From 1917, RAMC men could be ordered to carry arms, but this ruling didn't apply to men who'd enlisted earlier and served abroad. Alec would be entitled to remain unarmed.

The RAMC suffered very heavy losses, facing every horror of the war. Four hundred doctors were killed on the Somme alone. They were phenomenally brave. The only man to gain a double VC in WW1 was Noel Chavasse, of the Liverpool Scottish, the doctor son of the Bishop of Liverpool and brother of another casualty. Noel Chavasse's second VC was awarded posthumously.[3] So often retrieving the wounded from the front line, stretcher bearers and doctors constantly witnessed extreme suffering.[4] In 1914, there were fewer than 14,000 men in the RAMC. By 1918, their numbers had risen to over 144, 000.[5]

The RAMC was responsible for every stage of retrieving and treating casualties. There were regimental bearers, retrieving casualties and giving rudimentary aid on the spot, but RAMC men frequently worked in the thick of battle too. Hospitals and dressing stations had to be contrived somehow, from whatever buildings, ruins and wreckage were available. Existing hospitals and schools, especially boarding schools, could be adapted with relative ease. Life-threatening wounds and the dying were treated as close to the front line as possible. A wounded man would first be treated at a Regimental Aid Post, a small and often temporary position, in or near the front line. Morphine dulled the pain of men whose injuries meant death was inevitable. If the injuries were merely superficial cuts, casualties might be patched up, ready to return to the battlefield. First-aid was given for more serious injuries. Then they were passed on to the Field Ambulance. This wasn't a vehicle, but a division of men responsible for medical care. The Ambulance was responsible for a number of points along the evacuation chain for the casualty, from the Bearer Relay Posts, up to six hundred yards behind the Regimental Aid Posts, through the Advanced Dressing Station (ADS) to the Main Dressing Station (MDS) Perhaps the Army invented acronyms? There seem to be far too many. As the death toll soared, and conditions deteriorated, both RAMC and regimental bearers struggled to cope with the onslaught of casualties.[6]

Why did Alec wait for so many months before enlisting ? Across the whole country, patriotic fervour had been frenzied. Too old or tragically young, men and boys lied in their eagerness to serve. Most people, including some of the generals, really had believed it would all be over by Christmas, but surely that was a powerful reason for enlisting at once. Could Alec's sight be problem ? In all of the photos taken in France, he's wearing glasses. Most men who were determined to enlist managed to pass the sight test, often eavesdropping, memorising letters on the sight charts. Recruiting officers were willingly deceived. The delay and then his chosen service suggests that Alec had thought long and hard about this war, and what part he should play in it. Would Alec have known when he enlisted that Gladys was in the early stages of pregnancy ? Almost certainly not, even if she'd guessed. But why did he volunteer at all ? When Alec enlisted, married men were still, technically, exempted from 'volunteering'. Later in the war, more married men than single were promising to serve. Many had 'attested', that is, they'd expressed their willingness to serve, on the understanding that they'd be summoned only when the supply of single men had been exhausted. Yet Alec, the noncombatant, had chosen one of the most dangerous roles of all. He'd made this choice long before social pressure and new legislation made it difficult to refuse some kind of military service or 'work of national importance'.[7]

Alec's Medal Card states that he was discharged on April 23rd, 1918. The cramped form reports that he was unfit for further service.[8] The German spring offensive of 1918 was devastating. Many British officers thought the war was over, defeat certain. In just five days, 21st - 26th March, 1918, Britain suffered over 75,000 casualties.[9] In one sense, Alec was fortunate to be seriously injured only at this late stage of the war. Army doctors had honed their skills dramatically. Advances in hygiene saved many lives. Before the discovery of antibiotics, the RAMC were checking infection with dressings made from naturally antiseptic sphagnum moss, onions and garlic.[10] Upland areas all over the UK supplied sphagnum for absorbent and antiseptic dressings. Schoolchildren were recruited to collect the moss. All three remedies were still in use during the early stages of WWII. Penicillin wasn't available at all until 1941, and it was reserved almost entirely for military use until 1945.[11] In both wars, cooks on the Home Front were frustrated by the lack of onions. In WWI, much of the crop, which grows perfectly well in Britain, had been commandeered to save the lives of fighting men. Ancient herbal medicine really did save lives. The antiseptic properties of sphagnum had been recognised for thousands of years, including its use by the Vikings, Inuits and many others in the original disposable nappies and wound dressings. Terrible as it was, the Great War death toll would have been far greater without the RAMC's pioneering work. Saline drips were used to treat clinical shock from severe injuries and blood transfusions were used at clearing stations.[12]

Nothing else could be learned from Alec's brief medal card record. If they'd survived, his papers might reveal more. The WWI service records known as the 'Burnt Series' are now available online from the National Archives. Unfortunately, like the majority of the records for 'other ranks' Alec's service papers were destroyed. Burning leads to erratic concentrations of missing data. For private soldiers, all records between ' Westman ' and ' Westmoreland' are missing.[13] Records for the majority of officers have survived. At least Alec himself had survived the war, but discharged sick, what condition was he in? After such catastrophic losses, the Army needed every man who could walk. There are very few surviving hospital records. Many were strictly temporary, operated by the Red Cross, and long since demolished or restored to their civilian role. St Dunstan's, the charity founded to support soldiers blinded in the war, has records of men who returned to action as soldiers or stretcher bearers, even after losing an eye.[14] In April, 1918, Alec must have been in a very seriously condition.

From the frustration of the 'Burnt Series,' the search for Alec returned to Liverpool. Census and street directory records could go no further. In the city archives, missing clues could be anywhere among the plethora of school, religious, military and business records. When Alec was discharged, Gladys Westmore had a three month old daughter and a two and a half year old son who'd rarely seen his father. And a badly injured husband, unable to work again ? Perhaps, if Alec wasn't fit to work, she'd be allowed to return to teaching ? Scene of Crime Officers carry out fingertip searches. Search long and carefully enough, vital evidence turns up. Faced with an unsolved crime, the police revisit old ground. Sometimes, a clue's been missed, when it was right under their noses. During the war, Alec has no Liverpool address, but since he had survived, he should be listed in postwar directories, always supposing that he was physically and financially in a fit state to be a householder. If Gladys had returned to teaching, her name should appear in surviving elementary school records.

' Pupil Teacher at a Board School ' That was fifteen year old Gladys in 1901. Board schools - elementary schools created following the 1870 Education Act - were listed on maps of the city. Would a fifteen year old girl travel far to work ? Half a dozen or so schools around West Derby seemed possible, but not all records have survived, and those which do rarely mention pupil teachers. In 1912 , Gladys Gleave was a very pretty young woman, slender, with dark wavy hair. Sitting beside Alec, as they enjoy lunch in a Normandy inn, she appears younger than her twenty-six years. She and Alec married when the war was six days old. Then, they endured years of separation, ending only when he was discharged sick. How would their story end ?

Waiting for more Board School log books and street directory microfiches, I searched on through the multi-volume manual index. The only Francis Bourne listed was a Cardinal. There were no Gleaves, no Pulfords. The Westmore entry was astonishing.

' A W Westmore and others... The story of the 63rd Field Ambulance, 2/2 West Lancashire Field Ambulance, 1914 - 1919 '

Alec hadn't just survived the war. He was the principal author of this Ambulance history. The Board School log books arrived. None of them mentioned a Gladys Gleave. Then the Search Room staff delivered a small hardback book, just ninety-eight pages of text and the inevitable photos of young men in uniform. In the introduction, Alec and the two secondary contributors, M. Thomson and J. E. Allison thank the Liverpool Courier for permission to use 'AWW's' articles for that paper. Could this mean that Alec had been a war correspondent ? Or had he written after the war, in the Twenties, when old soldiers began to tell their uncensored and disturbing stories ? Badly injured and discharged in April, 1918, Alec had written only the first seven chapters of the Field Ambulance history. In April, Thomson and Allison took over. The final chapter was written by Sergeant S. J. Kay. The preface to this book includes tributes from Colonel Profeit, former Assistant Director of Medical Services, 21st Infantry, and from Lieutenant Colonel Storrs, RAMC. Ten years after the Armistice, these Field Ambulance men, (from now on, simply 'the 63rd'), wanted to set down the story of their war, the suffering, courage and laughter they'd known on the Western Front.

In extreme old age, the last Tommies have told the final version of their terrible stories. Their great-great- grandchildren have listened. Historians and TV presenters talked to these very old men, broadcasting the unthinkable and unspeakable, translating the Great War into some kind of sense, or rather, compelling and painful television. Privately printed, Alec Westmore's account of one Field Ambulance was never revised or reissued. Perhaps, later in life, he would have said more, offered more details, more of what Richard Holmes has called ' the big, political, strategic and operational issues.' He never did, but the book isn't just his own version of the war. In the late Twenties and early Thirties, many personal histories were published. The 63rd 's story is different. In 1919, as journalism, and again, in the short 1928 book, Alec was writing as the spokesman for many, including his senior medical officers. Alec himself is merely the narrator, glimpsed, occasionally, but never centre stage.

Reporting the same event, eye witness accounts can differ radically. The 63rd's story is utterly convincing, and, though issued in 1928, never dismisses the war purely as ' a sham which had wasted men's lives and squandered their courage'.[15] Whatever their personal view of the war, this isn't a treatise on patriotism or pacifism, or why this particular war was fought. The courage is there, always, but the word is inadequate, even inappropriate, tinged as it always is with the glamour of heroism. Heroism has no place here. The Ambulance had a job to do, caring for desperately injured men. Training at Blackpool, they'd learned to deliver vital first aid, how to lift a casualty onto a stretcher, how to carry that stretcher steadily. They didn't study the immediate or long term effects of poison gas. Traditional text books didn't include the management of shell-shock , or how to treat major wounds fouled with mud and putrefaction. Often, and in the face of unimaginable horrors, Alec's account can seem almost bizarrely pragmatic, and there's very little place for individual emotions. The text can only be appreciated for what it is, a candid, unsparing and never sentimental account of their work. Men blasted out of their minds with shell-shock often suffered for the rest of their lives. On the battlefield, bearers and doctors had to keep their traumatised patients as safe as possible, and prevent further injury, both to their frenzied patient and to all those trying to care for him. The style of Alec's own chapters is distinctive, often painful, occasionally anarchic. Sometimes, particularly on their long marches through rural France, there are echoes of the Nomads' adventure.

Alec explains that other members of the Field Ambulance, including one of their senior doctors, had loaned their own diaries - the diaries they were all strictly forbidden to keep. The notebook kept by Private A.F Rogers of the 63rd Field Ambulance is held in the Liddle Collection at the University of Leeds. Like Alec, the Liverpudlian Rogers served as a stretcher bearer, completing his training in March, 1916. Rogers knew Captain Greig, Corporal Maloney, Major Storrs, and many more of the men named by Alec. He records details of the treatment given to casualties, including the precise dosage of some medication. For bronchitis, men would be given Virium Ipecachuana, or a linctus known as Easton's Syrup. Chrysarobinum P.B was used to treat parasites, but old pharmaceutical texts warn that the side effects could be unpleasant. Simple headaches were treated with phenacetin, and a cold in the head with aspirin, or rather, as Rogers' notebook records, 'Acetyl salicylic acid, x gr ' Quinine was given for fevers, and opium for diarrhoea. The constipating effects of opioids were well known, but the dosage Rogers' quotes suggest that doctors might be prescribing for the hell of the western front, rather than simple diarrhoea. He notes, carefully, that adrenaline decreases blood pressure, and lists several methods of purifying even the most heavily polluted water. Once water had been filtered, they could use tablets capable of purifying up to 100 gallons.[16]

On my desk, currently, there are nine First World War histories. Only two, 'Tommy', by Richard Holmes, and 'The Trench', by Richard van Emden, actually include the work of the RAMC, whose officers and men traditionally planned no battles and carried no weapons. Military historians have a clear agenda. They're supposed to analyse the causes of war, judge generals according to the success or failure of their tactics, their skill in deploying the latest weapons, and how many men they lose. The fewer casualties the better, obviously. Even cannon-fodder infantry had to be trained, equipped, delivered to the front line, patched up, removed when no longer fit for service, and finally, replaced. Poets and novelists are myth-makers, don't even try to be objective or impartial; the Poetry is in the Pity... Oral history is always intensely personal. Ninety years later, Harry Patch still grieved for the friends he lost at Passchendaele. Alec Westmore's story of the 63rd isn't about winning or losing a war. In his account, military tactics are almost incidental. Whatever their reasons for enlisting in the RAMC, the 63rd's war is always against suffering.

Ten years is nowhere near long enough to revise and sanitise the dead weight of stretchers carried for three miles through a wilderness of uprooted trees, or through waist-deep mud and rotting corpses. Attacks from both sides hamper their access to casualties. There are, too, many records of a quiet and unofficial cease-fires, as both sides allow doctors and bearers through. Noel Chavasse was one of many to record just such an experience.[17] For Alec and his colleagues, nationality became irrelevant as they treated men in agony. On Blackpool beach, where the 63rd practiced, perfectly healthy 'casualties' were carried along easy golden sands. At Passchendaele, they had to use some stretchers as duckboards, laid across deep mud and dead men, to give themselves some kind of footing. Later, at Epéhy, in March, 1918, they were forced to use duckboards and muddy blankets as stretchers. So many military histories sprawl for hundreds of pages, daunting the reader with brutal numbers, a few inches of mud gained, tens of thousands dead, page after page of battle plans. The catalogue of death and destruction is supposed to be too immense for tragedy. Untrue, of course, like so many other Great War myths. This was a tragedy suffered by the whole world. Abram slew his son, and half the seed of Europe, one by one... As historians, the 63rd have the advantage of their unique role. Although they served in nearly all the great battles of the Western Front, they weren't actually fighting this war. Describing the butchery of July 1st, 1916 and the desolation of Passchendaele, the brevity is compelling, but in a very different way from any careful sonnet. The pain suffered by so many is laced with understated courage and flashes of anarchic comedy.

Telling their story, Alec Westmore and his friends couldn't have read many of the iconic Great War histories. They hadn't been written yet. All Quiet on the Western Front was published in 1929. The film was a year later. Unlike Alec, Remarque saw very little frontline service. Often regarded as an authentic firsthand account, his book is fiction.[18] Immediately after the war, the scatter of stories had begun, continuing during the Twenties, but many of these were by officers, men like Siegfried Sassoon and Robert Graves, with the leisure to write. Unemployed, often sick, or struggling to bring up families on low wages, most of the 'other ranks' had to wait till old age, after their sons had fought another war, or, as Niall Ferguson argues, the next stage of the same war. 'The Long Carry', by stretcher bearer Frank Dunham wasn't published till 1970.[19] Books written over fifty years after the war are, inevitably, a different kind of history. Taped interviews introduce a third party, directing the conversation, focusing on particular memories. Based on the articles by 'AWW' published in the Liverpool Courier barely six months after the Armistice, the 63rd's story of courage, grief, laughter, music and pretty girls comes - almost - straight from the battlefield, the dressing station, and the egg and chip estaminets of the Western Front.

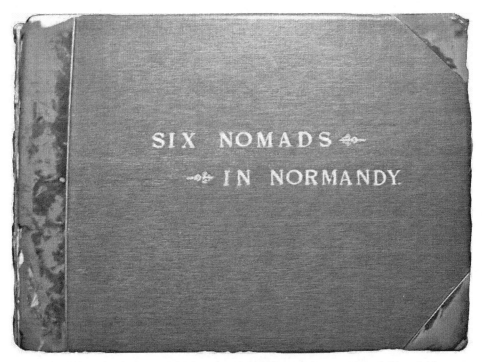

Found in a junkshop, the 1912 book celebrates international friendship.

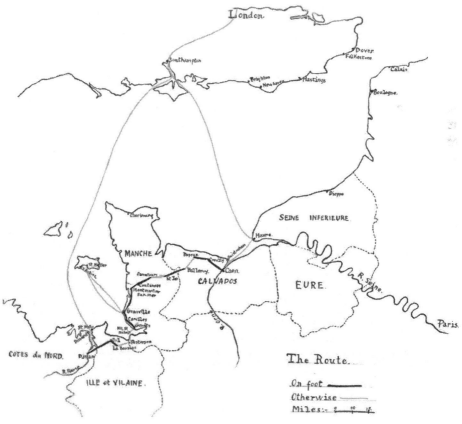

At first glance, the 1912 map suggested D-Day.

o-o-o-o-o-o-o-o-o-o-o-o-o-o-o-o-o-o-o-o-o-o-o-o-o-o-o-o-o-o-o-o-o-o-o-o-o-o-o-o

" S I X   N O M A D S   I N   N O R M A N D Y "

Being a true and authentic account

of their Adventures and

Mis-Adventures.

By THEMSELVES.

" Put it in the Book. "

MCMXII.

o-o-o-o-o-o-o-o-o-o-o-o-o-o-o-o-o-o-o-o-o-o-o-o-o-o-o-o-o-o-o-o-o-o-o-o-o-o-o-o

' The good ship Hantonia '. During WWII, the Hantonia became a troop ship.

Sac à dos, 22nd July 1912. 'Backpacking' first appeared in the O.E.D. in 1916.

Riverside laundry, near Creully.

Harvesters near Bayeux, 23rd July 1912.

' The hotel people were persuaded to face the camera'. Balleroy, 24th July 1912.

' Our way lay through the Forest of Cerisy.'

' Half a Norman loaf would feed a squadron of soldiers'

Auberge, near Belval, 25th July 1912

' We set forth on our adventurous journey, hidden quicksands right in our path.'

During WWI, the C.H.A. centre in Dinan became a Red Cross hospital.

Watching shipbuilding, August 2nd 1912, St Malo.

Riverside washerwomen, St Servan near St Malo.

Chapter Seven

The pity of it !

In France, in that other life, Mr Westmore and Miss Gleave were the lovers, walking through cornfields bright and gay with poppies. Now, all the young men of England were supposed to become killers, suddenly prepared to die for God, King and Country. Fred Pulford had rushed to serve his country, enlisting in the first of Liverpool's new City battalions. Alec had waited. He never explains his own decision to serve but not to fight. He doesn't need to, and, once made, that choice isn't part of the Ambulance story. Before and after conscription, many of those who joined the medical corps and other Ambulance services were devout Christians. Some were Quakers, many more were Nonconformists, a few were Roman Catholic. Many were simply Anglicans, taking the words of Jesus literally, totally opposed to the war itself but choosing to serve the wounded. In Germany too, many, especially in the evangelical churches, opposed the war as unChristian. Faith wasn't the only reason men gave for rejecting war. In 1914, many of those who founded the No Conscription Fellowship belonged to the Socialist Independent Labour Party, rejecting warfare for ethical reasons.[1]

Even before war was declared, men of the West Lancs Field Ambulance were in training under canvas, in Calderstones Park, Liverpool. The army was already critically short of doctors.[2] A second West Lancashire field line was recruited at the depot in Harper Street, Liverpool. Moving to billets in Blackpool, the recruits played and studied hard. Physical training on the beach was strenuous. It had to be. Before very long, these men could be carrying the wounded for miles to the nearest dressing station, often under fire and in atrocious weather. Backpacking across Normandy in 1912, Alec became used to daily drenchings, knew he'd spend the night indoors and in a real bed. Soaked and exhausted on the Western Front, bearers often slept in trenches, huddled in lousy blankets. Sometimes, if they were very lucky, there'd be wire beds and fewer lice. Arduous as it was, their training at Blackpool couldn't possibly prepare them for conditions in France.

On generous Army rations, many of the young men gained weight and strength. They'd need it. Stretcher-bearing was arduous, even when they weren't under fire. In the 1912 photos, Alec himself is very slightly built. Private Rogers recorded his own height and weight. The small field pocket book is stained. His height isn't legible, but at only 8 stone 4 lb, Rogers too must have been slight.[3] In class, Ambulance recruits studied anatomy and first aid. At local hospitals, they trained as nursing orderlies, learning, among other essential skills, the vital role of hygiene in the battle against infection. Matron ruled supreme and her wards were spotless.[4] It could so easily be a game, certainly more exciting than the civilian jobs they'd just left. At Blackpool, their training activities quickly attracted an admiring audience. According to Alec ' The most exciting stunts were the field operations, when splints and stretchers were improvised from hoardings, and an excited crowd watched our heroes bringing in the wounded on the cliffs.'[5]

The Ambulance trainees enjoyed themselves. At night, Blackpool's notorious attractions compensated for the arduous training. But in June, 1915, the Division moved to a training camp at Weeton, near Lytham St Annes. Here, they slept on straw palliasses, and the campsite was soon authentically awash from heavy summer rains. On August 4th, they moved south to join the main RAMC Training Depot at Beachy Head. Alec, writing in 1928, says nothing about conditions here, but according to a postcard from Rogers, his own final RAMC training on Salisbury Plain was 'hell'. Rogers completed his training in March, 1916. By then, officers knew only too well what their recruits would be facing in France. Later that year, on an uncensored postcard sent from Albert, Rogers reported a different hell, 'flooded, raining, life lousy all the time.' At the end of August, 1915, the 63rd were engaged in final training before leaving for France. Embarkation leave was brief for all recruits. The luckiest managed three days, barely time to say goodbye to loved ones. Like Alec, some would be leaving pregnant wives. Gladys was within days of giving birth. Parting, they'd know he might never see this child.

Marching out of camp ' just as the sun was setting in crimson splendour', Alec would arrive at Southampton at midnight, to spend a tedious day on the quay. Like Fred, he would remember, surely, that other journey to France. After boarding ' The Golden Eagle', they set sail at last at about 8 p.m. Three years earlier, six excited Nomads left Southampton on the Hantonia, chattering through the night, and entertained (or not ?) by Fred's monologues. Reaching Le Havre at daybreak, they were captivated by the very smell and taste of France, especially their breakfast of boiled eggs, fresh rolls, and their first French coffee. After a smooth crossing, 'The Golden Eagle' reached France early too, passing the breakwater by 3 am, then dawdling interminably up the harbour, in the way of so many cross channel ferries. This time, there was no coffee, no rolls, no charming French waiters. Disembarking at last, at six, the 63rd faced a weary and disrupted day of marching, bivouacking for a couple of hours, unloading the horse transport, then transferring the animals to the waiting goods trains. True to their reputation ' the mules proved particularly obstinate at the prospect of landing on French soil.' [6] They travelled via Amiens to St Omer in goods trucks marked Hommes 40, Chevaux 12. Unloading the horses and mules till nearly midnight, they still faced a five mile march to Moulle, on the road to Calais. From utter weariness, the men could have fallen asleep standing. On the march, they managed to find beauty in the silent countryside. It was, according to Alec, ' a lovely starlit night, and the road was lined with tall poplar trees, which made the way obscure, but threw the stars above into brighter contrast.' [7]

At Moulle, they had to convert the village school into a temporary hospital. Very soon, illness struck. A stomach bug was suspected, but tests proved that the real culprit was the laxative effect of minerals in the local drinking water. In diaries and letters, men often compared this gentle country to southern England, but they hadn't bargained for a French version of Epsom Salts. After this minor upset, the first few days in France were easy enough, route marches and drill balanced by lively concert parties. A captain of the East Yorkshires sang

And when we meet the Hun

We'll make the blighter run...

Bedad, me lads, we are the pick of the army...

Most of them, of course, had never met a ' Hun '. German sailors, possibly, in Hull.' Hun' was always a curiously inaccurate, officer-class, public school insult. The original Hunnoi certainly weren't German. With no Latin and less Greek, recruits in 'other ranks' had much to learn, not just military routine, but the approved insults. Alec was only quoting the Yorkshire captain's song about the 'Hun'. Throughout his own seven chapters of the 63rd's story, the word 'Hun' is never repeated, nor are the enemy dismissed as Boches. Stretcher-bearing through the terrible battles of this war, Alec always writes about 'the Germans' or 'Jerry'. Backpacking across Normandy and Brittany, the Nomads, all Protestants, living in a city of bitter religious conflict, celebrated the internationalism of the C.H.A, learning to respect and value the people of Catholic France.

The concert parties were soon over. Slowly, and moving by night, the Brigade advanced towards Haut Rieux, near Lillers, guided, in theory, by an elaborate but, according to Alec, ineffective system of coloured lights. Halts were frequent, delays were never explained. The lofts where they were billeted offered soft straw to lie on, but this straw concealed holes in the rickety floor. Several men fell down into the stable below. It was here, too, that the cantankerous mules became unexpected allies. Parked in an orchard, and, on Army rations, starved of fresh fruit, the 63rd were strictly forbidden to scrump apples. Perhaps the mules were carefully encouraged in their vandalism ? Breaking loose, they knocked down young apple trees and the men seized the chance of collecting so-called 'windfalls'. On a diet of bully beef and biscuits, with fruit and vegetables a rarity, men suffered from chronic constipation. Some resorted to desperate measures, taking engine oil as a laxative.[8]

Weather conditions were deteriorating. Tramping for mile after mile, in continuous wind and rain, men rapidly became exhausted. Many of the infantry collapsed by the roadside and had to be transferred to the Horse Ambulances, presumably suffering from hypothermia. Soaked to the skin, bivouacking near Noeux les Mines, the exhausted men slept soundly, despite the sounds of gunfire. They were close to the battlefield of Loos, on the outskirts of Lille, near enough, in fact, for a piece of spent shell to hit part of the transport section. Alec couldn't know that he'd just become a father.

At Philosophe, there was already a war cemetery. The 63rd converted a building near the ruined station into the Headquarters hospital. They had to occupy ruined houses, all roofless, many with yawning cavities where shells had exploded. In a few of the ground floor rooms, they managed to light fires. One of the men sat down in a plush armchair. Since landing at Le Havre, they'd only been edging towards the front. Wet, exhausted, and wretchedly uncomfortable for most of their journey, they had yet to experience the devastation created by modern artillery. Here, in the ruined villages around Loos, they found the deadly wasteland created by twentieth century warfare. Alec, who'd known so many villages in rural Normandy, imagined their thoughts.

' One wondered what the feelings of the peaceful villagers would have been, could they have seen the desolation and ruin which war had brought to their houses.'[9]

Communication with Divisional Headquarters had failed. The 63rd didn't know where each battalion was fighting. Did the generals ? By the autumn of 1915, great tracts of the French and Belgian borderlands were unrecognisable.

Through constant shellfire, bearers went out into the night, searching for the wounded. Alec records the chaos seen in so many photographs :

' Many dead lay around, both British and German. After going about three miles, a number of wounded were discovered lying in shell holes, and these were carried back to the horse ambulance. The road between Philosophe and Loos had been churned up by the heavy transport and men, and was chock a block with a continual stream of ammunition columns, artillery, and A.S.C. At one point, an ammunition column had been blown to pieces, and dead horses and men obstructed the road. Hundreds of motor cycles lay on the roadside, abandoned by dispatch riders, who had found it impossible to continue, and through this quagmire of mud and blood, the bearers carried the wounded some three miles to the horse ambulances.[10]

Then came the news that the dressing station was being gassed. This was the first time the British used their own poison gas, scoring a hideous own goal as the wind blew it back in their faces. Very few Ambulance staff had their own gas masks yet. The few they could use had actually been taken from wounded men who were being sent for further treatment, away from the front. Soon, conditions were so dangerous that the dressing station had to be evacuated. At Loos, there were over 50,000 Allied casualties. Three hundred and eighty four men of the King's Liverpool Regiment died, and almost a hundred and fifty of those East Yorkshires, who'd been so eager to meet the Hun. Twenty thousand missing are named on the Loos memorial, including Kipling's underage and shortsighted son.

Relieved from front line duties, the 63rd moved to Béthune. Grateful again for soft straw, this time on the floor of a church, the men searched out an estaminet, where they devoured the Army staples of fried eggs, rolls, and coffee. In Normandy, Alec had known many cheerful estaminets, but for most of the men, this was their first journey abroad, their first experience of French cuisine. The respite at Béthune was brief. That afternoon, they were on the move once more, but, and this was all too common, there wasn't enough room for all the men to travel by train. Railway Transport Officers - RTOs, - had a thankless task. They couldn't conjure up trains - or railway lines - out of nowhere. As the war continued, hundreds of miles of light railway would be built. Forced to travel on foot, Alec's unit marched on, into still more desolate country. At midnight, they were still marching. Nobody seemed to know where they were or where they were heading. Their officer, Major, later Colonel Storrs, chose to walk alongside his weary men, rather than ride. Relationships between officers and men weren't always so democratic, but in the 63rd, they seem to have been very close indeed, and in some cases, the friendships forged in France became lifelong.[11]

Around four a.m., they arrived at the village of Blessy, where they were billeted for one night at a farm, before moving on to Morbecque, and billets in a school. They were filthy, of course, unwashed and stinking, crawling with lice. Rough wet khaki smelt like wet dog, and the mud of rural France was laced with all the usual excrement. The Ambulance horses and mules added their share. Lifting the wounded onto stretchers, inevitably, bearers were soaked by other men's blood and other body fluids. Issues of clean underwear became a rare luxury. Lice were endemic, crawling along every seam, gnawing at crotches and armpits. Delousing would be a routine experience, as it was for Captain Edmund Blackadder.[12] By the late twentieth century, any kind of reticence was out of fashion, in black comedy or straight histories. Stretcher Bearer Westmore came from a very different world, decent, respectable, bug-free. A 1912 household encyclopaedia, published for the middle-class housewife, discreetly mentions dealing with 'vermin'; defined as mice, rats and cockroaches, but not lice.[13] Used to houses infested with bedbugs, working class men were less squeamish, expected every kind of body wildlife.

Since they were all lousy, officers and ranks alike, what matters is the heroic ingenuity of military engineers, achieving the impossible, hot baths and clean clothes for every lousy man. At Strazeele, where the 63rd was billeted in October, 1915, bathing facilities were primitive but effective : ' A general service wagon was lined with tarpaulin, and a fatigue party carried water from a neighbouring clay pit. The water was heated in a copper boiler, and then poured into the improvised bath. In this, a section at a time bathed, and, though the water was rather thick, it supplied a long felt need.' [14]

In December, at Pont de Nieppe, a local dye-works was converted into military baths.

' It was cheering to see the lads from the trenches, covered with mud, enjoying a hot bath.

Punctually, at eight in the morning, the first batch would arrive. The (dye) vats were filled with water pumped from the river, heated by steam. Each vat was capable of accommodating 16 men. We could bath about 120 men at a time, on a busy day, 2,400 were bathed in all.' [15]

No use getting back into lousy clothes. Providing the troops with clean uniforms was a colossal operation.

' After the bath, each man received a dry towel, a clean shirt, vest, underpants, in return for his discarded dirty underwear. The dirty clothes were first put in a boiler and boiled for half an hour. Then they were taken on a trolley to three wash houses, and washed by French washerwomen, of whom there were 200. The clothes were then ready for the press, and finally hoisted to the drying rooms, where they remained for the night at a high temperature. Should the boiling be deemed insufficient to destroy the vermin, the clothes were passed into a fumigator, and subjected to dry and wet steam.' [16]

A year later, in the last rain-sodden weeks of the Somme, army engineers created baths at Vermelles Brewery, just outside Béthune. Breweries, with their huge vats, made excellent bath houses. The Army's interest in personal hygiene was pragmatic. Dirty men felt, quite literally, lousy. Transmitted by lice, typhus was a serious risk. Clean, they were ready to fight again, but the thought was often present, and especially when we knew that the men were detailed to go over the parapet in the evening, that many of these manly forms would be maimed and shattered. The pity of it ! ' In their brewery and dye-vat baths, the young men sang.

' I want to go home, where the Alleyman can't catch me

Oh ! my! I don't want to die ! I want to go home !' [18]

In November, 1915, at Armentières, the 63rd were able to take over a hospital, L'Institution de St Jude was a former secondary school, ideal, if only they hadn't been right in the line of fire. Here, the dressing station had been created from an old brick kiln. Walls five feet thick were reassuring, though the flagstoned floor proved cold, especially as the ambulance staff had only one thin blanket each. Based around Amentières for over four months, they enjoyed a kind of savage idyll, savage, because the horrors were never far away. Hunting for shrapnel souvenirs, two men were killed, and another lost an eye to a live grenade. Idyllic, because they'd found two Mademoiselles, one blonde, one brunette, both captivating, but, at least according to this account, nothing like the Mademoiselle from Armentières of the famously bawdy song.[19]

' The most celebrated establishment was ' Georgine et Jeanne's' at Pont Nieppe, names that became happy memories whenever troops foregathered.... Here at midday, and in the evenings, a goodly company of every branch of the service sought relief from the monotony of the eternal stew. Madame's delicious 'pommes de terre frites' , with tartines, and café au lait, made an excellent meal.'[20]

Blue-eyed blonde Georgine had a smile for everyone and every occasion. Jeanne was a Belgian refugee, 'a buxom wench with a coal black eye,' good-humoured enough when not teased. Deliberately, the story of these two young women sidelines the war. As if caught in a searchlight, the girls' music and laughter become the story, the war somewhere outside, in the winter darkness. Some of the men had instruments, violins, a cornet. Impromptu singsongs brightened their evenings. The men's relationship with the two girls sounds (and perhaps it was) entirely innocent. Alec's tribute is lavish : ' Gallant Georgine and Jeanne... You carried on with light hearts when misery and desolation were all around you, and only when the terrors of poison gas were added to the devastating shells did you quit your posts of kindly service. Not yours the Croix de Guerre or the Medaille Militaire, but perhaps some gallant soldier returned 'après la guerre', to claim a bonnie bride.'[21]

Is this just a shade too effusive ? Alec's old comrades of the 63rd would know the truth, whatever that was. Wives and mothers could read a perfectly innocent story, two lovely girls, unfailing hospitality, food, and music, Après la guerre' meaning exactly what it says. Even a generous scatter of asterisks couldn't make the bawdy pidgin French of ' Après la Guerre' suitable for singing around a family piano. Georgine and Jeanne might have been angels of virtue. Other Mademoiselles from Armentières offered rather more than music and laughter. The town's brothels were notorious, venereal disease an ever-present problem among the young soldiers.[22]

Unlike Fred Pulford's wet and wretched experience, Alec's 1915 Christmas Day proved strangely happy. The 63rd's intimate and human story is nothing like the terse military account of Fred's war. Music, laughter and good company so often kept the Ambulance men sane. At home on Merseyside that winter, there was Gladys and her new baby, Kenneth, the infant son Alec hadn't yet seen. Communication with families was often severely censored. Men needed all the treats and distractions they could find. Members of the West Lancashire Ambulance held their first Christmas dinner at a local convent, following the meal with a lively concert. Throughout the winter, Georgine and Jeanne's estaminet remained a magnet.

' Mamma was never so pleased as when there was 'plenty musique' The sordid side of war was forgotten in the good -humoured banter with Georgine and Jeanne... Jeanne would sometimes sing with much verve, the song of the Liègois with a very catchy air and a haunting refrain, ending with ' Hola, voila, vive la Patrie, le Roi.' [23]

Leaving Armentières on March 22nd, 1916, they moved via Amiens to Poulainville. According to Alec, the tiers of wire beds looked rather like a hen roost, but at least they were cleaner than lying in straw. At La Neuville, on the banks of the Somme, they were billeted in sheep pens and pigsties; presumably not sharing this accommodation with the usual residents. Sheep and pig faeces would be quite deadly enough. Throughout the war, soldiers in the vast military camps faced the additional hazard of disease. Recent research into H5N1, the virus responsible for the deadliest bird flu, confirmed that the flu pandemic of 1918 mutated from farm animals to humans in precisely the insanitary conditions described by Alec.[24].

At the end of April, most of the 63rd left to take over a rest station at Allonville, near Amiens. In the local chateau, which had been a shooting box for M. Paul Hennessey, of brandy fame, this was strictly for officers. In the grounds, ambulance staff built a convalescent camp for 'other ranks.' Such construction work meant that peacetime skills were always in demand. Adapting existing and often damaged buildings, the army needed bricklayers, bakers, butchers, engineers, electricians, sign-writers, gardeners and painters. At the Chateau, Private Rogers' friend Corporal Jack Maloney of Liverpool created a hospital incinerator and ovens, mainly from old petrol tins. In his book, Alec gives details of maloney's ingenuity.

The weeks at Allonville were peaceful enough, but rumours spread daily of preparation for a crucial battle : ' The early summer months glided by with everybody on the tiptoe of excitement, for the day when the British were to put an end to the stalemate of trench warfare, and drive the German back at the double.' [25] On June 24th, the 63rd left the chateau, led by their new brass band. Canteen profits had paid for the instruments. ' The band had been making the solitude of the woods hideous with discord for some weeks past, during their first attempts at melody, but had made wonderful progress. and were now able to make quite a cheerful noise ' [26] Rogers sent a postcard of the 63rd's band to the girlfriend who became his wife. His postcard messages are affectionate but bland. In his notebook, written in a cramped and barely legible hand, his plans for their 'après la guerre' reunion might not survive censorship.

The Somme woods would soon be hideous with sounds infinitely more ghastly than those made by any novice brass band. Throughout June, preparations for the battle continued. Towards the end of the month, the wet and stormy weather suddenly cleared. News spread that the morning of July 1st was to see the launching of the great offensive. By the 30th June, the men were eager for action and expecting victory.

' Throughout the day, battalion after battalion of cheering whistling men swung past. Tanned by rain and sun, strong, virile, keen eyed, they joked with the stretcher bearers standing on the roadside. One giant of a man laughingly asked if we had a stretcher long enough for him. It is doubtful if such a display of high-spiritedness had ever been seen before. It was never seen again.' [27]

Close to the battle-lines, preparations were being made for the wounded. Stretcher bearers, blankets and surgical dressings were sent to a series of dugouts, water carts had been filled. Soon after the battle began, small parties of RAMC bearers set off for the trench lines.

' Most of the bearers, distressed by the hot sun, threw aside their tunics and worked in shirt sleeves. Many of the trenches were so narrow, it was impossible to get stretchers around the angles. Wounded men were placed on groundsheets, and carried from one traverse to another until it was possible to utilise a proper stretcher.' [28]

The first attack was considered successful. The price of that 'success' has become a hideous legend, the very word 'Somme' stained with carnage. In two stark sentences, Alec records the evening of July 1st, 1916 : ' In what had once been no-man's -land, the dead lay thick. Caught in a terrible hail of machine gun fire, they lay amongst the tall grasses, where the blue cornflower, scarlet poppy and yellow mustard plant nodded and swayed on the breeze'. [29]

History has sidelined those other summer flowers, leaving only wreaths of scarlet laid on grey stone. Alec's battlefield blooms in all the colours of a child's paintbox.

Retrieving casualties, bearers were under constant fire from snipers, struggling across uneven ground : 'The German trenches were like a shambles, heaps of bombs, rifles and helmets made walking difficult. German and British dead, often at hand-grips, lay in grotesque positions, and very often had to be moved, to allow the bearers to pass.' [30]

Towards the end of the second day, news came that a party of wounded had been seen signalling for assistance from some open ground.

'Attempts to get them in had been met with machine gun fire, but it was thought that under the protection of the Red Cross, the RAMC would be treated with more respect. Captain Greig, with a number of bearers, set out on their quest. Crossing open ground, where the wounded men lay, a vicious hail of bullets, and the staccato rattle of a machine gun compelled the men to take cover. A small Red Cross flag was waved but had no effect. Dropping to the ground, the party crawled over the rough terrain, taking shelter wherever possible, till the wounded men were reached. They received speedy attention, and were placed on stretchers, and the return journey to the trench began. At the first movement, the gunner again opened fire, and kept up his barrage until the trench was reached. Fortunately, there were no casualties, a pierced water bottle being the only evidence of a hit.' [31]

Fortunately ? Could it be that the German gunner wasn't trying very hard ? One water bottle from a ' vicious hail of bullets' sounds like a very poor hit rate. On both sides, and in defiance of orders, respect for the Red Cross was strong, certainly among the 'other ranks.'

On July 4th, Alec's division were taken out of the front line, moving by train to Ailly sur Somme, where nothing was too good for 'Tommy'. Local women willingly cooked for the British troops. Perhaps some offered rather more than rabbit stew. Alec doesn't elaborate. Already, the French, and especially, excited French girls, seemed to think the war was over. In high summer, beyond the battlefield, the Somme countryside was gentle. At Glastonbury, for the annual sea-of-mud festival, lazy journalists head straight for the Somme or even Passchendaele, cheap shorthand for celebrity mud and misery. Armies can make a hell of anywhere. The roses in Picardy were real enough, the comparisons with southern England geologically accurate. Late one night, in the spring of 1915, when there were still trees, Noel Chavasse heard a nightingale sing. All this is familiar territory. Everybody knows the story of the Somme, the senseless carnage, the wicked and stupid generals, lions and donkeys. It's in the aftermath of this first unspeakable slaughter that the 63rd's story triumphs, and the effect is almost surreal.

War poets are single-minded in their grief, keening in the same desolate minor key. Reality is different, anarchic and unexpected. Raw comedy breaks through, even in the pitiful July of 1916. At Buire, the dead lay thick among the poppies and stretcher bearers tending the wounded were under sniper fire. Days later, at Ailly, the men were given permission to take a dip, au naturel, in the cool waters of a summer river. Blackadder Goes Forth really should have included the Somme swimming gala : ' Hundreds of hot and perspiring Tommies were soon disporting themselves in the water. Officers arranged races, and soon, white streaks of humanity were cutting through the waters of the Somme. Bathing costumes have no place in the official kit of the British army. Soon, on the fringe of the river bank, French lasses, laden with trays of chocolate and fruit, made their appearance, their keen business instincts aroused by so many potential customers. British sentries had allowed the girls through. Seeing this unexpected chance of obtaining refreshments, the men in the river sprinted for the bank. Peals of laughter and chaff greeted the dripping warriors, who had forgotten their nakedness. The least concerned were the girls themselves.' [32]

Naked and dripping young warriors... What more could the girls want ?

From Ailley, the 63rd travelled by train to Corbie, due east of Amiens. As usual, there wasn't enough transport. As many of the bearers as possible were packed into motor ambulances. The rest had to march, not reaching Bécordel till midnight. From here, some of them moved on to the ADS at Fricourt. This proved to be a captured German dugout, the Vorsprung Durch Technik version of military burrows.

'Some forty feet below the ground, it boasted two or three different entrances. Well made staircases gave an easy entrance and exit... Numerous rooms opened out from the passages. Walls were boarded and even papered, and the whole place lighted by electricity.' [33]

Presumably, the Germans wouldn't be wasting new wallpaper on a dug-out? In 1916, the trench decor might have been an old-fashioned Biedermeier design, rather like a Laura Ashley.

In summer heat, the heavy work of stretcher-bearing became still more exhausting. Almost totally unprepared, Ambulance teams had to learn how to care for men suffering mental torment, a danger both to themselves and to the bearers :

' Time after time, the straining heaving muscles of a difficult patient sent the bearers staggering from side to side of the trench. Ultimately, it was found necessary to strap a man to a stretcher to save him breaking his neck.' [34]

Then the 63rd received a message from Headquarters, warning them that two hundred men lay in Mametz wood, waiting for help. Mametz is another of those names fouled by history, familiar even to those with the sketchiest grasp of the First World War. Combing the ground of Mametz, they found British dead everywhere, 'their faces burned black by sun and exposure. Dark masses of flies buzzed and swayed over the gaping wounds. The place was filthy, loathsome, and terrible to see.'[35]

Along the Fricourt- Mametz road, bearers forced their way into the outskirts of the wood under constant bombardment. The northern area was still under German control. Misled, presumably by an incorrect map reference, one party of bearers found themselves only yards away from the Germans. Tear gas added to their difficulties. When Mametz had been cleared of Germans at last, a party of bearers, led by Captain Greig, set off to bring in any wounded who could be found. All over the wood, wounded men had crawled into any crevice that offered shelter. Once found, they had to be carried through a wilderness of broken trees and trailing branches. In conditions like this, wheeled stretchers couldn't be used. Even when stretcher parties did reach the road, horse ambulances often proved worse than useless. ' Slow, cumbersome, bone-shaking, they seldom, if ever, justified their existence.'

Relieved on July 18th, the Ambulance Unit moved in the usual tortuous way to Longneau, where they caught a troop train to St Pol. Like Fred's journeys with the 17th, a dreary litany of place-names suggests the weary tedium of their march. At St Pol ' everybody wanted breakfast. No-one got it.' [36] At Ternas, the hungry men at last spotted the cooks, but the only available pump had been padlocked. Traditionally, it was the enemy who poisoned wells. Here, a French farmer denied the Allies water. Keeping the men fed and watered was a constant problem, especially on the move or in the trenches. In theory, and carefully researched by army dieticians, they were supposed to receive 4,300 calories a day, far above the 3,859 calories allegedly consumed by the average civilian. Only allegedly... Reality was, of course, nothing like this, in France or on the home front. Soldiers might, if their luck was in, enjoy a lavish 1 ¼ lbs of meat a day. (about 750 grams). Maud Pember Reeves' 1911 survey found working class families with four or more children affording barely a pound of meat a week between them.[37]

Coming to Habarq, on the Arras front, the 63rd took charge of a hospital for seriously wounded patients. Making themselves at home, they created a Lime St, a Harper Street, a Low Hill and a Pall Mall. Across the wasteland of the Western Front, troops named trenches after their home towns. On September 9th, just before Kenneth Westmore's first birthday, a section of the 63rd were directed to Bécordel, now littered with ammunition dumps, forage dumps, water points, cavalry, and light railways, utterly different from the little town they'd known just two months earlier. Here men were drafted into road-making, laying duckboards, erecting marquees and bivouacs, in preparation for the renewed attack on the enemy, at Flers. The 63rd would soon be overwhelmed by casualties.

' In the storming of Flers, the corps station was taking in over 1,000 seriously wounded a day.... Hundreds of men, British and German alike, had to be left on stretchers in the open all night, waiting their turn for the operating table, and dying in droves before such help could come. ' [38]

Bécordel also faced constant shelling, and enemy bombing. On September 15th, the main body of bearers were sent into the line. Some historians like to suggest that the Somme mud and misery has been exaggerated.[39] The 63rd's account sounds measured and even restrained. Undeniably, the legendary battle began on a warm summer's day, but the Somme offensive dragged on for months. With the arrival of autumn, conditions were steadily deteriorating :

'Heavy rains filled disused trenches with mud, Night after night was spent searching for the wounded, under the direction of Captain Pool of the 65th, or Captain Greig of the 63rd. By late September, they were working in Delville Wood, known to the troops as ' Devil's Wood' Men entered Delville with weary fatalism, not expecting to survive. Once, taking refuge in a shell-hole from the constant barrage, a group of bearers occupied themselves with some map training.' [40]

Fred was now nearby, only at Vignacourt, training hard for his last battle. Would he and Alec have known this ? Whether they did or not, the friends would never meet again. On October 4th, the 63rd left Fricourt for Mericourt, then on to Labeuvrière, near Béthune, where they took over the hospital. Eight days later, Fred was killed. How soon would the news of his death, and the loss of so many more Liverpool men reach Alec ? [41]

Chapter Eight

I fell,

Into the bottomless mud, and lost the light

Siegfried Sassoon, Memorial Tablet, 1918

Somewhere near Flers, his body lost forever in the mud, Fred would deliver no more comic monologues. Perhaps, in the last months of life, he'd kept his comrades amused ? In the First World War, there was no official ENSA to entertain the troops, but the men were endlessly resourceful. The celebrated 'Wipers Times' offers a safely irreverent Private Eye view of the war. Concert party costumes are magnificent. In drag, fresh-faced young privates are sweetly feminine, plump carrier pigeons are delicious, all generals bumbling idiots.

In a suburb of Béthune, the 63rd enjoyed their second Christmas in France. The menu suggests a feast; oxtail soup, beef steak pie, turkey, plum pudding, mince pies, figs, oranges, apples, coffee, cigars, beer, and wine. Wishful thinking? Perhaps they didn't all dine quite so well, but British newspapers of December 1916 are full of adverts encouraging those at home to send 'comforts' and gifts of food to men at the front. The lavish dinner was followed by a lively concert, a melange of popular hits, parody, and comedy sketches. The 63rd's Christmas programme includes an advert promoting 'Alexander's Ragtime Band'. In the early twentieth century, Alexander wasn't a common forename. Could their bandleader be Alec himself ? Deprecating comments about their performance suggests that he was involved in the band. In Liverpool, the musical Westmores enjoyed a lively social life, based in the community attending St Cyprian's Church. The Westmore parents organised church dances and concerts, Alec and his siblings all played instruments and sang.[1]

Moving to the prosperous little mining town of Auchel, on December 27th, 1916, the 63rd were billeted at the Mairie, in unfamiliar comfort. Celebrating the New Year, Auchel made its guests very welcome. Back in Britain, Lord Derby, now the Minister for War, was writing to Douglas Haig about Britain's new shells, reportedly bigger and better than ever :

Derby House, 8th January, 1917

' I have gone carefully into the question of production of a 60 pounder shell, of longer range than the present design, with at least another 1,500 yards range. '[2]

Weapons with a range of three miles and more distanced even the soldiers releasing those shells from any contact with the distant enemy. The weapon used in hand to hand trench fighting was a single razor sharp blade, mounted on a hand-grip.

By January 26th, the 63rd were on the move again. Travelling in a windowless train, the men were frozen. At 1 am, they had to march ten kilometres to Droogland, which was no more than a handful of cottages. The winter of 1917 was bitter. Often, the thermometer registered several degrees below zero Fahrenheit. (-18 Celsius.) The men often slept on frozen straw in draughty barns. Troops had been brought up here to prevent any German invasion across the frozen Yser canal. In full view of German observation balloons, the 63rd were sent on route marches, allegedly to impress the Germans with the strength of Allied reinforcements. This was the closest Alec came to military action, though some RAMC bearers, having enlisted as noncombatants, refused to take part in even feigned military action, risking serious punishment, and even jail.

No German invasion was attempted, and by mid-February, they were back in the hospital at Béthune. Some of them operated a dressing station at Cambrin, underneath the ruins of the church. Weather conditions were now atrocious: 'Stretcher bearing was very difficult, owing to the clayey nature of the trenches, which were a veritable quagmire.... Stretchers had to be carried along the top of a trench, a very dangerous procedure.'[3]

In good conditions, along level ground, a First World War stretcher, weighing 30 lb, (about 14 kilos) might be carried by two bearers, or four, if they could be spared. Often, as archive photos confirm, in the thigh-deep mud of Flanders, six men would struggle. The Bell Mark III stretcher, used by today's RAF and Mountain Rescue teams, weighs 24.7 kg. The MacInnes, which can be fitted with wheels, weighs 22 kg. For both types, eight bearers are expected, with a relief eight to take over every mile. Rescuers are often battling in atrocious weather conditions, but never under fire, nor are their casualties frenzied with shell-shock. In winter, training on treacherous ground, stretchering even a perfectly healthy 'casualty' demands far more of the bearers than mere weightlifting.[4]

On March 5th, 1917, the 63rd moved to Robécq, where they stayed for a few days. Then, traveling on to La Cauchie, they took over a hospital, contrived from huts. Here they found more desolation :

' As the Ambulance party proceeded, one could see that not a tree had been left standing for miles. The huge ferro-concrete telegraph poles lay prone on the ground, the scattered concrete and twisted ironwork testifying to their violent destruction. Miles of scarred earth and ugly wire marked the deserted trenches. Craters gaped at the crossroads, and only derelict ruins remained, with gaunt gables and shattered rooftrees, of what had been pretty French villages, once resounding with children's prattle, but now silent and sinister.'[5]

The silence and the miles of deserted trenches express the weary stalemate of unending war. Alec's son Kenneth was now almost eighteen months old, old enough to be walking, and if not exactly prattling yet, a lively toddler. For millions of men, family life would be a distant memory, and the lost years of marriage and fatherhood could never be regained. Women like Gladys were forced to depend on their parents, living as daughters with children, rather than as wives and mothers. America was just about to enter the war. In a letter to Major Philip Sassoon, Douglas Haig's private secretary, Lord Derby expressed the prevailing hope that this would hasten the end of the war. War Office, 3rd April, 1917

I must say, I never expected Wilson would be so determined, having vacillated for two years, so it is most surprising to see him and America in the war up to their necks and it ought to have a great effect in bringing the war to an earlier conclusion than otherwise would be the case.[6]

Lord Derby's confidence in America was misplaced. Alec's increasingly grim and weary account indicates nothing of the kind. Just outside Béthune, the 63rd rigged up dressing station under a railway embankment. Arriving soaked to the skin, in another of that bitter winter's snowstorms, they were forced to bivouac under a rough shelter contrived from stretchers. On April 9th, 1917, a party of bearers picked their way through the ruins of Boiry-Bécquerelle, a village south-east of Arras, where they found the Durham Light Infantry Medical Officer, dug in on the side of a sunken road. They all had to spend a wet night in funk-holes in the side of a trench. Carefree in Normandy, sheltering from downpours, the Nomads thought their backpacking adventure was ' as close to nature as any of us will ever get'.

Next morning, by scrounging among the ruins of Boiry for wood and corrugated iron, the Ambulance men managed to improve this rough aid post. Using wheeled stretchers, and negotiating craters in the road, they managed to take the wounded on to the next relay post, under fire as usual, frequently from both sides. On Good Friday, the Germans put two Allied guns out of action, killing a bombardier, wounding six men and a medical officer by the roadside.

Preparing for the next major battle, at Arras, even the debris salvaged from Bécquerelle was precious. Loading corrugated iron onto wheeled stretchers, they crossed the fields, rigged up another crude shelter, nearer to the battlefield. Here, bearers and medical officers spent the night, huddled together, with no room to lie down. Next morning, they were under fire once more, but around 8 am, they saw the infantry advance over the ridge, aiming for the Hindenberg line, on the far side of Henin. Grimly, but appropriately, regimental bearers would hand over casualties to the RAMC by a cemetery crucifix. The first casualties didn't arrive until mid-afternoon, but from then on, they had to work nonstop : ' Forwards and backwards we toiled over the shell-swept ground between us and the cemetery... Three o'clock in the morning found us still with plenty of cases coming through... In the darkness, we sometimes missed our way, but the flare of a Verey light would suddenly illumine the crucifix, and enable us to take our bearings.' [7]

Relieved next day, the 63rd learned that the famous Hindenberg line had been taken by the Allies. More precisely, they'd occupied a short section of the vast strategic defence, a tunnel cut out of the chalk by Russian and French prisoners. The crucial British assault on the main Hindenberg line wouldn't come till September, 1918, heralding the end of the war.

On April 15th, 1917, the men marched some fifteen miles back to billets for a much-needed rest. A week later, the Ambulance returned to Boisleux au Mont. Soon parties of bearers were actually living in this captured section of the Hindenberg. Not much more than five feet wide at this point, the famous tunnel provided just enough room for the men's wire beds. There was no room for stretchers, which had to be taken along the dangerously exposed nearby trench. When they first reached their underground post, all was quiet. They decided not to sample some jam abandoned by ' Jerry', but agreed that enemy tobacco was 'a tolerably good smoke'. Removing a dead German from the well-cut stairway, they were brewing tea when the trench was hit by a 5.9 shell.

The tunnel had saved their lives. Answering the call for bearers, usually by night, one false step could be fatal for both bearers and casualties. Yet despite all the dangers, bearers preferred to spend as much time as possible in the relatively exposed trench, rather than in the comparative safety of the tunnel. Even the briefest glimpse of the world above lifted their spirits. Alec, who rarely wastes a word, offers an unforgettable flash of memory :

' The chief drawback to life in a tunnel, after the lice, is the monotony of living in the bowels of the earth, with only a candlelight, and nothing to do but smoke. But from the bottom of the shaft, one might see the blue sky of heaven, with a brilliant poppy decking the top of the trench on the skyline.' [8]

To men serving on the western front, one flower meant more than any words could say. Alec Westmore would think, surely, of wandering through summer cornfields in Normandy, 'bright and gay with poppies', sac à dos with his fiancée and closest friends.

Living in the bowels of the earth brought its own problems. Collected from the water carts at dusk, in old petrol cans, water for drinking or washing was precious. Even vital water deliveries could be shelled. Visits to HQ for baths and clean clothes were welcome but necessarily brief. The 63rd lived in the captured Hindenberg section for months. For the latter part of the time, they were attached to the Royal Engineers, excavating in the forward part of the tunnel to create a (relatively) safe aid post. Working in shifts, round the clock, Alec and his comrades achieved more than miracles. The aid post was completed, and their sense of humour survived both lice and shellfire. Startled by a whizz-bang, one bearer dashed for cover, falling down a staircase they hadn't finished digging. The rest fell after him, a laughing medley of arms and legs, picked themselves up, carried on digging, and singing.

Bawdy military versions of popular hits don't feature in the 63rd's story. Nearly forty years before the 1963 Chatterley trial, most of the text would have to be peppered with asterisks. In the trenches, men really did sing sentimental ballads, like Tipperary, There's a Long, Long Trail, and Roses of Picardy, but Tommies didn't always sing the parlour versions. In the Navy, 'Bless them all' began life as ' F*** them all' . Some adaptations were innocent enough, such as 'That's the wrong way to tickle Mary'. The 63rd's version of the sentimental 'My Little Grey Home in the West' is ironic, but safe enough for wives and servants. Instead of the syrupy original, they sang :

' There are dug-outs for all

Full of creepies that crawl

In that little grey home in the West.'

They left their Hindenberg home late in August, 1917, just as electricity was being installed throughout the tunnel. Leaving Izel, the Ambulance marched to Aubigny, then travelled by train to Cassel, en route for Caestre. Here they were back on familiar ground, but there was no time to look up old friends. One party was immediately dispatched to erect a Special Abdominal Hospital. A week later, the rest moved to Meteron, just outside Ypres. Part of their first night was spent under canvas, the remainder in trenches and funk-holes. Alarms were sounded constantly. Weary of moving from tents to trenches, the men decided to stay in the trenches. Bandsmen were ordered to save their instruments at all costs. The detail is arresting. Canteen profits paid for these precious instruments.

Next day, they were at Dickebusch, working under constant fire. Military historians will know that the 63rd have been summoned to the battle of Third

Ypres. Everybody else calls it Passchendaele. Already poor, the weather would soon become far worse, as wind and rain swept across Europe. Writing again to his secretary, Major Sassoon, Lord Derby lamented that he'd been forced to abandon the Scottish grouse moors :

26th August, 1917 ' Appalling gale and rain, more like December than August, I am afraid it will do an infernal amount of damage to the crops here, and if you have got it in France, it must interfere very much with the push.' [9]

Far away from Derby's rainswept moors, Alec Westmore and his RAMC comrades were experiencing the Ypres salient for the first time. Very soon, they understood why the Menin Road and Hell Fire Corner had such a grisly reputation. Through the 'sinister and silent' streets of Ypres, men marched in single file. Officially, Ypres was now behind the Allied lines, but the town was still a target for long distance shelling. For bearers and casualties, conditions were indeed hellish :

' Wounded had to be attended to under constant shell fire, even before men had a chance to reach the bearer posts with their equipment. [10]

One party of the 63rd worked from a tunnel, on the left of the Menin Gate. Another group were based at ' Clapham Junction.' Temporarily, the weather was fine, stretcher work comparatively straightforward, if hideously dangerous. Pack mules and horses laden with shells picked their way along the littered road, right in the firing line of 18-pounder guns. Often, startled animals would run amok, colliding with bearers and knocking them and their patients into shell-holes. Inevitably, some of the constant bombardment came from British artillery, so-called ' friendly fire'. Writing in 1928, the memories were painfully clear, from the increasingly vile weather to the ruined food. It's worth pausing, to think again about what kind of book the little Ambulance record is. Narrated mainly by Alec, it's simply their own story, memories of their war against suffering, written and published privately for the surviving members of the ' 63rd '. Military tactics are only mentioned when they're relevant to the Ambulance task of retrieving and caring for the wounded, in Passchendaele and every other man-made hell :

' The tracks were practically obliterated in a sea of ooze and mud, making the carrying a heavy burden... Stretcher squads were forced to work under heavy shell fire. Owing to the number of wounded coming in, and the lack of any adequate shelter, the only thing to do was to keep on carrying. At Clapham Junction, a shell landing in a shallow dug-out killed fourteen out of sixteen bearers. Here, Privates Ellacott and Martindale were killed instantly, while bringing in the wounded. Every casualty threw additional work upon those who remained. Rations were difficult to get, and no hot food had been available for a week. Cold tea, sent up in petrol tins, was almost indistinguishable from petrol itself. Ration bags, when they did arrive, were saturated with water and mud.' [11]

Private Ellacott was twenty-one, Martindale, whose mother was a widow, twenty-five.

For the wounded, the promptest possible treatment was vital. Bringing them in to aid posts demanded constant and extraordinary heroism, but the Field Ambulance men never claim to be heroes. It's not a word they use. Alec focuses instead on the practicalities. The Medical Officer of the Northumberland Fusiliers was operating from the relative security of a concrete pillbox, which offered protection from both shelling and rain. To reach the box, bearers had to cross what had been a small creek, swollen to a sea of mud by heavy rain. Here,

' Bearers with loaded stretchers became bogged, and had to be pulled out with stretcher slings. Stretchers were sunk to make some kind of footing, and over this precarious bridge, tripping over the bodies of men lying beneath the surface, the men staggered with their burdens.' [12]

In All Quiet on the Western Front, Franz, one of the young friends, is injured in the leg. Gangrene sets in and his leg has to be amputated. Visiting Franz in hospital, his friends Paul, Krapp and Müller know he's dying. Everybody covets his soft yellow leather boots, salvaged from an English airman. If one of his friends doesn't snaffle them, the hospital orderlies certainly will. At Passchendaele, Alec and his Ambulance comrades claimed far more shocking salvage :

' For 24 hours, wallowing in ooze and slime, the work continued with few intervals. Food here consisted of what could be picked up. Here and there, by the side of dead men, one found begrimed rations, which helped to give fresh strength.' [13]

Filthy food, taken from dead men, but it kept them alive... On October 8th, 1917, the 63rd were relieved, but so late at night, they had to stay on till morning. They spent the night singing. Again, Alec doesn't elaborate. Perhaps he'd need too many asterisks... In the morning, lorry drivers gave the cramped, weary, and mudcaked Ambulance men lifts to ' Pop' (Popinghe). Next day, they marched on, without breakfast, to Blaringhem, where they were billeted in barns. During eight or nine days in the front line at Passchendaele, Ambulance casualties had been horrific. Over fifty per cent of the men had been killed or wounded.

After ten days rest, they were heading back to Dickebusch. At sunrise on October 21st, they reached Ypres again. ' Sinister and silent' little over a month ago, Ypres had been ravaged yet again, a city of desolation. Beyond the Ypres-Menin gate, the 63rd took over a dressing station, once an Engineering School. Here, an underground operating theatre was set up, in cellars strengthened by the Royal Engineers. Setting off once more for the aid posts, bearers again faced Hell-Fire Corner, and all the havoc of the Ypres-Menin road. Once again, terrified animals ran amok. Reading this report, the first reaction is déja-vu, surely this is just repetition, poor editing, carelessness ? The repeat action nightmare is merely accurate, the same hideous experiences, without respite. Bleeding, one mule dashed riderless down the track. The bearers pressed on, under constant fire. In a small dugout, they found an artilleryman, with both his arms blown off. In what remained of Glencorse Wood, bearers sheltered in another pillbox, after running the gauntlet of German guns.

So many bearers had been drowned in shell holes, stretchering by night had been abandoned. Retrieving casualties, almost always under fire, speed was vital. Sometimes, both bearers and wounded were struck. One bearer, terribly mutilated, was taken to a dressing station, but died soon afterwards. Here, in a pillbox, thirty bearers, a corporal and two Medical Officers spent the night, sleeping like sardines in a tin. They shared a rum ration, and another sing-song, before turning in, ready to work again at daybreak. The Nomads had enjoyed late-night music too. Sitting on a bridge at Balleroy, in Normandy, Alec, Frank, Fred and Ross serenaded the girls with Goodnight, Ladies. Next morning, leaving Balleroy, and trying to work out which road to take, Alec had seen, not terrified and bleeding mules, but a travelling menagerie.

Passchendaele needs no adjectives, or poetry, or drama. The stark facts are enough. In military histories, the inquests continue. Writing to Haig at the end of October, 1917, from his house in Mayfair, Lord Derby, then under pressure to resign, admitted that the situation was very serious indeed : Derby House, 29th October, 1917:

'I have an extremely difficult role to play, and I do not want to strike, if strike be necessary, until I am perfectly sure that I am in the right. In other words, I do not want to resign simply because your advice is questioned. I foresee therefore a crisis coming to a head in the next few days. It is a most disagreeable position to be in.' [14]

Later, in a remarkably candid letter to Haig, Derby considered the radical shift in the national mood. Already, Siegfried Sassoon had delivered his outrageous attack on the war. Tactfully diagnosed with 'shell-shock' and packed off to Craiglockart, to recover his officer-class senses, the privileged Sassoon was arguably far less dangerous than the steady onslaught of reports from the front. Sassoon's emotions changed readily. Among the 'other ranks', grieving parents, wives and sweethearts needed speedy and determined re-education. Far too many working class women lacked the patriotic Spartan attitude to sons and warfare. Far too many ill-educated working men were still wilfully misunderstanding the New Testament. A series of articles published in the 'Globe' called for immediate intervention. In a letter to Lloyd George, marked 'Confidential and Personal', Derby set out his plans to reinforce control of the press, and also, to stimulate rapidly waning patriotism.

Derby House, 17th October, 1917

' I hope to see Maxse, and I hope I shall be successful in preventing similar articles. I sincerely hope it will not be necessary to take any action against the newspaper, either under the Defence of the Realm Act, or by means of a speech from yourself. I hope I have your support in arranging with Hayes Fisher and through him, with the Local Authorities, that when we achieve any distinct successes, it should be notified to the people and steps should be taken to celebrate it as such by ringing church bells and hanging out flags. I'm also planning to arrange as far as possible that military funerals should be given to civilians who are killed in air raids.' [15]

At Watergate House, MI7 continued to monitor German censorship and German propaganda. Such practices were, of course, deplorable, deliberate manipulation of the truth, yet more confirmation of German tyranny, Prussian imperialism. Across the Irish Sea, a journalist at the Cork Examiner wondered if the English realised how tightly their own supposedly free press was being censored. In North Wales, including Lloyd George's own constituency, Irish newspapers were and still are widely read. Potentially damaging news stories from Wales were certainly suppressed before they could reach newspapers in England. In the intensely patriotic Liverpool press, pages traditionally reserved for Welsh news fail to report serious and persistent dissent, reported regularly in the Welsh newspapers.[16] Among Lord Derby's personal papers, it seems that even the evidence of censorship has been censored. The file of letters and telegrams from Derby to Lloyd George bears a pencil note, stating that 'the contents were read, on 29th April, 1954', and that 'interesting letters were removed and placed in chapter file.'

One apparently unremarkable strip of brown paper was left in the file, possibly unnoticed, between two other documents. No bigger than a compliments slip, it's covered with sums, like a child's old-fashioned roughwork; thousands, hundreds, tens, units. They're the French dead of Passchendaele. On the battlefield, using stretchers as duckboards, Alec and his Ambulance comrades had to walk over drowned and rotting bodies to reach the living. Lord Derby was attempting to calculate the French losses at Passchendaele. Initially, it looked as if the French deaths alone exceeded the total number of British dead, missing and wounded combined But there's a problem, immediately identified by the Management Committee. The Passchendaele calculations are spurious because at the time the French couldn't say with any certainty how many of their men had been killed. Nor could the British.[18] There's no suggestion that these scribbled numbers on brown scrap paper have any connection with many thousands of young men, morte pour la France.

On official paper, a neat spread sheet offers more exact calculations, how many British dead, how many replacements are needed, and another column, for how many the War Office should claim will be needed. It would be prudent to exaggerate the need, rather than underestimate. Long before the internet or even radio, serving soldiers, the majority conscripts now, were reporting on leave what they couldn't say in their heavily censored letters. Writing to Haig again, Derby recognised the serious impact of such reports on morale.

Derby House, 12th December, 1917

Everybody is war weary. The glamour and enthusiasm of the first two years have worn away.... It is not only the letters that come back, but still more, the talk of all ranks when home on leave, which shows that there is a disgruntled feeling in the Army, which is impossible to ignore. [17]

' Disgruntled' hardly seems an appropriate word for the weary survivors of Passchendaele, but Lord Derby was a politician, not a poet, or even a war correspondent.

Released from ' Third Ypres ', the 63rd Ambulance, or rather, the few battered survivors, were transferred to the 5th Army. At Longavesnes, they took over the Divisional Rest Station. Here, though so close to the Somme battlefields, the countryside was relatively green and unscarred. The hospital, consisting of huts and bivouacs, had been built by another Liverpool Field Ambulance. Some bearers were sent to the nearby dressing station at Epéhy. For a time, especially in fair weather, 'life passed very pleasantly' Some of the men found this idyll deeply suspect. They were right. Beyond the hospital, lines had been prepared, where they might, if necessary, retreat. Most Tommies suspected nothing, until the dressing station was ordered to move. Their position was required by a Royal Field Artillery battery. Even so, they were all, including the sick and convalescents, determined to enjoy a good Christmas.

Throughout Alec's story, unimaginable suffering is counterpoised by flashes of laconic humour. Asked to write reports from the trenches, twenty-first century children have read too much poetry, too many heartrending bestsellers and watched far too many films. The tin hats of their Tommies usually come with haloes, conferred by both kinds of war poet. Elegiac National Curriculum war poetry by Wilfred Owen, Siegfried Sassoon, Edward Blundell and Isaac Rosenberg wasn't popular in the First World War. Only five of Owen's poems were published before his death. Recent critics of the English Literature A level curriculum have complained that pupils shouldn't be studying the ardently patriotic (some would say emetic) verses penned by Jessie Pope and her ilk. On the contrary, this is the authentic voice of the Home Front, glorifying the war, determined on victory at any price, and all but canonising 'our brave boys'. In real life, the 'brave boys', conscripts and disillusioned volunteers alike, were more Blackadder and Baldrick than Rupert Brooke and Julian Grenfell.

The men's cautious cynicism is clear in Alec's account of early spring, 1918. After Christmas, the uncertain peace continued. Very few wounded were arriving. This left the men with time on their hands. The authorities quickly remedied such idleness by appointing an Agricultural Officer. Much of the Western Front was, or used to be, prime farming country. Since the previous summer there had been serious difficulties with food supplies. On August 6th, 1917, Lord Derby had complained, in a letter to Lloyd George, that the British were not receiving their share of the harvest. The entente militaire was often extraordinarily churlish.[18] In that strangest of springs, land was ploughed, seeds were sown and a variety of vegetables planted. Fiction would surely romanticise this 'swords into ploughshares' interlude. The troops, according to Alec, thought otherwise :

' The average Tommy was no altruist, and he saw no reason why the fruit of his labour should be garnered by others.... It savoured too much of an indefinite stay in France.' [19]

Hunting parties proved far more popular. Once, the 'Tally-Ho' brigade caught a hare. On an excellent pitch near the hospital, the RAMC enjoyed football. This was the calm before yet another savage storm. In the early hours of March 21st, 1918, the 5th Army experienced ' a bombardment unparalleled in its intensity'. Aided by morning mist, the German advance crushed the British machine gun posts. Large parties of bearers were at once dispatched to Epéhy. Under heavy shell fire, the onslaught of casualties was appalling.

' Epéhy itself became the scene of a bloody struggle. For two days, the divisional troops held up all attempts to take the village. Stationed in dugouts outside the village, stretcher bearers were cut off, by the enemy advance, and killed or captured. One party of bearers were cut off from their ADS, and forced to carry the wounded to the most distant medical units.' [20]

Attempting to describe yet more agony, more churned up trenches, the stench of putrefaction, the writing falters for the first time, lost for words. Perhaps the brief interlude of springtime farming, however reluctant, made the return to savagery even worse. Expecting capture, they were ordered to destroy any papers, which might be of use to the enemy. Eventually, it was decided that the whole party of bearers should 'run the gauntlet'.

' The few stretchers they had were absolutely laden, and for other cases, they were compelled to use trench boards covered with blankets. All wounded men who could possibly walk had to do so, some carrying their comrades. To the credit of the Germans, the bearers were not fired on, though obviously within rifle range.' [21]

Eventually, casualties were transferred to vehicles heading for the Divisional Rest Station, and the very sick were evacuated to the Clearing Station. It became clear that a retreat was intended. All but the worse cases of incoming wounded were moved on by motor ambulance. From daybreak, the advancing German guns continued to shell the roads. On the afternoon of March 22nd, the hospital was abandoned. Once more, casualties among the Field Ambulance men had been devastating. Many retreating troops had lost touch with their regiments, many more fell by the wayside. No ambulances being available, wounded men were placed on service wagons, or carried on wheeled stretchers.

Intense spring heat by day followed by cold nights and biting wind added to the misery. Leaving Longevsnes, the Ambulance had at least managed to retrieve some stores of tinned fruit and sweet biscuits. By the 28th March, the 5th Army had ceased to exist. Aware of the appalling casualties, Haig feared that the heavy losses would sap morale even further. Throughout the war, Haig and Derby exchanged letters and messages constantly. Many are handwritten. In most of these, the script is controlled and legible, Haig's being particularly neat, exactly as one might expect. In public, in the terrible spring of 1918, Haig might still appear to be the icy and unyielding military commander. On the page, like Guy Fawkes' signature after torture, the change in his handwriting is startling, his concern for Lord Derby's son and brothers surely charged with emotion. The wild scrawl of his letter to Derby suggests that even his legendary impassive calm had been shaken. The Stanleys are real. Missing in the Spring Offensive, they're Lord Derby's 'boy', Lord Derby's brothers, and not, like the nameless dead of Passchendaele, mere numbers on a scrap of brown paper. News of their safety brings relief and almost rejoicing.

6th April, 1918

' I was greatly relieved to hear that your boy and your brother were all (sic) safe. This is no time to indulge in criticism or cavilling. Personally, I have a clear conscience.' [22]

In a letter marked ' Confidential & Personal ', Derby also wrote to Lloyd George :

' I got a letter from Rawley last night, to say that both my boy and one of my brothers were alright. Nothing of my other brother as yet. ' [23]

At this point, Alec Westmore's story ends. Discharged sick, on April 23rd, 1918, his war was over. Like the Stanleys, he'd survived, but he was very far from 'alright'. The remaining men of the 63rd continued to serve casualties until November 10th, when they were informed, quite casually, that there would probably be no further hostilities. Men were still dying, right up to the eleventh hour of the eleventh day, but in Paris, where he was based for the final months of the war, Lord Derby's letter to Haig suggests a relaxing day.

Paris, 10th November, 1918,

' After luncheon, Victoria and I picked up Capel, and we played a three ball match, 9 holes. I was two up... Foch very much moved, though I feel his heart of hearts he regrets the armistice coming quite so soon as it did.' [24]

It's barely credible that anyone could want to prolong this war, but Lord Derby's suspicions would be confirmed. Ferdinand Foch, the French Chief of Staff, had to be content with delivering the punishing Armistice terms to the Germans. For him, they could never be savage enough. The humiliation of France's defeat in the Franco-Prussian war had been avenged. In Metz cathedral, Foch celebrated France's victory with a triumphant Te Deum, and the dramatic gift of his sword. [25]

On Armistice Day itself, the 63rd's celebrations were muted. The Germans had been defeated. Their new and deadly enemy was flu, claiming among its victims a 'gallant soldier and conscientious doctor', and a beloved Sergeant Major. In Liverpool, cheering crowds thronged the city centre again. They sang ' Praise God From Whom All Blessings Flow'.   At the Stock Exchange, brokers complained, peevishly, about the damage to trade :

' The city streets were practically impassable, and monetary business was rendered all the more difficult'. [26]

Alec Westmore's history of the 63rd Ambulance is never sensational. The story it tells is carved on every town and village war memorial across Europe. Coming home, to wives, sweethearts, and the strangers who were their children, what could the men say ? The dignity and instinctive stoicism of that generation is easily misunderstood. In the twenty-first century, novelists leave little to the imagination, especially when writing on war and weapons. Grotesque injuries are described in lavish and obscene detail. Alec gives only the sparest facts. The stench and squalor of the trenches is understated. The men who'd served with him knew broken young bodies and the agony of dying men too well. They didn't need a treatise on the life-cycle of the human body louse or details of foul latrines, trench-foot, the sweet stench of death. Those who hadn't been in France wouldn't understand, no matter how remorseless and bloody the details. Perhaps they'd understand the laughter even less.

Leaving the city archives and Alec's Western Front, it was twenty-first century Liverpool that seemed unreal. In the damp city streets, people were selling poppies, like the cornfield poppies admired by six young friends, somewhere in Normandy. Setting off together from Lime Street on a summer's day, the Nomads could celebrate Britain's new friendship with her old enemy. After the triumph of their adventures in France, the years that followed should have been so very different, so ordinary, only weddings, christenings, the mixed joys of family and working life. Instead, the bright future they drank to was destroyed on the battlefields of the ' war to end all wars'. Fred had vanished into the Somme mud. Now, another of those high-spirited young men had become a quiet and awe-inspiring hero. A fine writer too... Alec's image from the Hindenberg line trench is haunting : 'the blue sky of heaven, and the brilliant poppy, decking the top of the trench'

As for the Somme swimming gala... Were those laughing girls only selling fruit and chocolate ? Two lively Mademoiselles from Armentières, one blonde, one brunette, Alec's innocent or tongue in cheek speculation about their fortunes, 'après la guerre '...   A brass band, rehearsing in one of the infamous Somme woods... A lanky Tommy, asking if they had a stretcher long enough for him... The men Alec Westmore served died worse than any cattle, but they accidentally dose themselves with a French brand of Epsom Salts, prefer egg and chips to Army rations, whinge when they're ordered to be farmers, scrump apples with the help of obliging Army mules. Unforgettably, they skinny-dip in the river of death, race naked towards laughing girls.

Chapter Nine

War's annals will cloud into night...

Ere their story die

Thomas Hardy, 'In Time of The Breaking of Nations '

The Field Ambulance history had developed from Alec's features in the Liverpool Courier, telling the story of the RAMC's role during the war. Two war heroes are infinitely more newsworthy than any number of carefree backpackers. One of those heroes had written for a Liverpool newspaper. Days later, the Liverpool Echo published a photo of the young Nomads, sitting around a table, somewhere in Normandy. Did any readers recognise these people ? At first, this bid seemed to have failed. There was no response at all. Perhaps there was nobody left ? Three generations later, all their descendants could have left the area. More than a week later, the editor rang at last. Somebody had contacted the news desk. The stretcher-bearer's son ? There was an address and an outer London phone number. Nobody answered. When Norman Westmore returned my call, it was my youngest daughter who answered the phone. Realising who he was, she seemed awestruck. Born two generations after the Second World War, to her, the Nomads had become utterly real, heading straight from a Morecambe Bay junkshop to the Western Front. She'd watched Blackadder Goes Forth with her brother and sister, laughed, of course, until Captain Blackadder's trench went over the top into a blood-red field of poppies. At school, Blackadder and The Frightful First World War paved the way to the Imperial War Museum and harrowing reality. Study guides teach youngsters how to deconstruct the poetry. In textbooks and military histories, countless ' Unknown Privates' live their brief lives, then die, like Fred, 'somewhere in France'. Alec Westmore's Field Ambulance history was nothing like a textbook or a military history. Alec the stretcher-bearer had been Alec the young Edwardian, planning adventures with his friends. Backpacking across Normandy with his girlfriend, he could be any gap-year student.

A retired civil servant, Norman Westmore knew all about his parents' escapade. He had his own copy of their adventures, knew that Fred Pulford had booked the tickets. Fred was identified as the sturdy, fair-haired young man, often, but not always close to the nameless young woman. Tall, lean and dark, the other young man in every group photo must be Ross. Norman didn't know his surname, nor could he identify Ross as a family friend. Because he was usually the cameraman, only two photos include Frank Bourne. Norman's knowledge of his parents, their friends, and their relationships would prove to be crucial, but at first, we talked about the journey itself, the impressively detailed map, wondered how they'd managed to research French public transport, use it so expertly.

Moving on from trams and buses, Norman said, unexpectedly, ' When we were children, they never told us Fred had been killed.' At first, this doesn't seem credible. Six young men and women, cheerfully flouting convention, sure enough of each other enough to spend a fortnight's holiday together... Surely Norman's parents hadn't been afraid of the truth ? In 1919 and in 1928, Alec had written unflinchingly about the hideous years of war. Why couldn't he talk to his children about Fred's death ? Historically, though, this rings true. In the Twenties, the survivors wanted to forget, or at least, chose not to share grief with their children.

Children learn quickly when to be silent. Fatherless, motherless, orphaned, the children of early 20th century fiction rarely talk about their loss. Adults don't allow them to. Even in 1929, Arthur Ransome's Amazon pirates dismiss their father's death in three words.[1] Sneezing on a train from Lime Street, reciting midnight monologues in mid-channel, limping with a blister in the Forest of Cerisy, shinning up trees to shelter from a classic 1912 downpour, scaling the walls of a castle with Ross, and, allegedly 'nursing a sick heart', Fred Pulford was real and very much alive. Pas devant les enfants... Perhaps they hoped the children need never know about October 12th, 1916, when the Liverpool Pals went over the top into a hail of bullets, targets too easy to miss.

Fred's role in the French adventure was no secret at all. It was only his death they couldn't talk about. Norman, born in 1924, knew exactly how his Gleave grandparents had reacted to the Nomads' journey. Stalwarts of their local Anglican church, Gladys's parents were scandalised by their middle daughter's plans for a backpacking holiday with Alec, and insisted that they must at least be engaged. The presence of another young couple was little comfort, even if, in theory, the women could chaperone each other. Engaged or not, in 1912, respectable unmarried couples weren't supposed to holiday together. Middle-class churchgoing morality was strict and uncompromising, strongest, perhaps, among the lower echelons of that class. The louche Bloomsbury set and upstart lowlife like D. H. Lawrence kept nobody's rules. Artists and their models never had. In high society, adultery was both rife and rigorously discreet. Edwardian house-party guests slept where they liked, on condition that they were back in the right bed by morning. In Pygmalion, dustman Alfred Doolittle couldn't afford morals, but for the suburban middle-classes, propriety was essential.[2] Sudden wealth trapped Doolittle into middle-class morality.

Norman recognised the so far nameless young woman as his mother's friend 'Mrs Taylor'. She'd lived in Wallasey, in the same road as his Gleave grandparents. Widowed fairly young, Mrs Taylor had a daughter, Helen. A year or two older than Norman, Helen had become a doctor, but they'd lost touch long ago. He remembered Mrs Taylor as 'rather a sad lady.' Between the wars, children would know many sad ladies, war widows and 'superfluous women', the men they'd hoped to marry only names on stone or hideously mutilated. Lying on the grass in a field near Carolles, the slender young woman who became the sad Mrs Taylor is laughing with her friends. They've been joined by a stray dog. It's an enchanting déjeuner sur l'herbe. Scrambling up the tower of a ruined abbey with Gladys, she's hardly a demure Edwardian lady. Carefully observing the demands of French etiquette, her frequently removed and decidedly battered hat spent a good deal of the holiday in her rucksack. Norman had known 'Mrs Taylor' during his Twenties and Thirties childhood. The child's empathy is significant. Teenage egotism wouldn't have recognised her sadness. Norman's most reliable memories of her begin some time in the early Thirties, when he would be seven or eight.

In 1912, the Nomads had written their unfinished story together, a private memoir of happiness. Now, and still defined by their pre-war friendship, they were living through indescribable grief, the end of all their youthful hopes and dreams. War-widows and sorrowing parents were counted, after a fashion. Some of them are recognised on war graves. The 'superfluous women' would staff schools, offices and hospital wards for decades, skewing the population with too many spinsters. Unfinished friendships can't be assessed on any census or spreadsheet, but, like any other love, friendships define who we are and can shape careers. The Nomads' expedition to France was a triumph. It could have led, as Arthur Leonard hoped, to so much more, a network of international friendships in a Europe without frontiers. At the end of their story, confidence shines from the page. Mission accomplished, with a glorious sense of achievement. As members of the C.H.A., they were linked to what Sheila Lockhead (Ramsay Macdonald's daughter) has called 'a splendid company of progressive thinking people of varied viewpoints, all trying to solve the problem of how best to bring Utopia to Earth'.[3] Norman Westmore knew that his father chose the RAMC because he would not and could not kill. Serve the wounded, yes, kill, never.

After that first phone-call, on a noisy railway platform, there were months of letters, more phone-calls and more photographs, including one of Alec in his RAMC uniform, just before embarkation. It looked as if there could be up to six copies of the journal. Martin Gleave, of Lancaster University, had the one made for Gladys. Visiting Liverpool University, it was he who'd first spotted the photo. So whose copy had drifted into a Cumbrian junkshop ? And how did the story end ? Who were the other young travellers ? So far, struggling with detection, guesswork, and data-protection, the search had led to many dead-ends and red herrings. Now, perhaps, the Westmores' surviving son would be able to provide more information. Perhaps he could resolve the mystery of Ross, so close to the other five, so extraordinarily elusive.

At what point does a private record become common property ? Senior Royalty, all politicians and every kind of celebrity are fair game, certainly until their lawyers object. So are the long dead. Exploring more recent history is problematic. Trespassing just beyond living memory, investigating people who never were celebrities can be dangerous. Once, as a number-crunching demographer, I published a lighthearted exposé of 'Victorian values', as upheld in 19th century Cumbria. (Women may lie about their ages. Babies can't.) The outraged response was astonishing. Rejecting the perfectly accurate evidence of church and civil records, people preferred the bonnet and crinoline myth of Victorian respectability celebrated in their family albums. Public records confirmed that at least half the local brides were pregnant on their wedding day. As the girls who left the area on marriage weren't investigated, the true figure was certainly far higher. Furious, their descendants besieged the news desk of local papers and radio stations, sent angry letters to a regional magazine. I'd libeled their corseted great-great-grandmothers.[4] Cherished illusions are important. So is what's left of privacy. The Nomads were remarkable and adventurous young people. Twenty-something in that summer of 1912, they're having the time of their lives. Living out of rucksacks, eagerly hunting down the next debit de boissons, their entente cordiale was a triumph. Two years later, they were swept into one of history's greatest tragedies. Fred's pitiful death and Alec's quiet courage were historical facts; Alec's articles and the book an unexpected bonus. Perhaps two answers were quite enough ? Why pursue the story further ?

Printed and written records hadn't led to the three missing Nomads. In the war years, Frank seemed to have disappeared. Even though the name is common enough, no credible Frank Bourne could be found in any military records. He hadn't served in the Army, the Navy, or the Royal Flying Corps. Now, through Norman Westmore, the search had moved into oral history, which has its own strict code of conduct.[5] Teaching oral history, I'd warned eager students to be patient. Bombarding a client with intrusive questions, the truth might be lost for ever. When in doubt, wait. The oldest generation are key witnesses, but they have an absolute right to silence. Norman was a precious link with the past, but how much he revealed about his parents and their friends must be his decision entirely. In Cumbria, a local man who'd kept silent about his wartime experiences for sixty years told his story at last. He'd taken part in the relief of Belsen.

In the safety of a public archive, the truth is unguarded. Released for anybody to read, long-kept secrets are exposed at last, some hideously painful, ancestors imprisoned, hung, transported, mutilated, often only for petty theft. Many, including convicts transported to Australia, stole only the food they needed to survive. Well into the twentieth century, young women were locked in asylums simply because they'd had a child outside marriage. Some things aren't secret at all; young men who could bear no more, shot at dawn as cowards. In a new century, their families have at last achieved justice for these traumatised 'cowards'. Could this be why Ross and Frank had proved impossible to trace ? Almost certainly not... The men executed for so-called cowardice are buried in military cemeteries, like any other casualties of war. Better understanding of mental trauma has, at last, led to compassion and recognition of their suffering, rather than the condemnation of a century ago.[6] If this was what had happened to Frank or Ross, they would have been found via the Commonwealth War Graves site. If they'd deserted, successfully or not, there'd be army records. On the phone, unable to read an expression, it would be unwise to press for too much information. Norman knew nothing at all about Ross. Neither the name nor the face, were familiar. But what about Frank ?

Frank Bourne had been his godfather... He qualified this... Kenneth's godfather really, the boy born in September, 1915, soon after their father landed in France. Norman's own godfather, Jack Allison, had helped to write the 63rd's story. Jack was very kind, but, as a devout Christian, gave suitably spiritual presents, hymn books, bibles, that kind of thing. Nine years younger than Kenneth, Alec had been allowed to share Frank, who kept goats, hens and ducks, loved all animals. Godparents are notoriously unpredictable. The Westmore brothers became close to Frank, who'd built his own house on the Wirral, grew all his own vegetables. More Cobbett than Good Life, he produced his own milk, eggs and meat too. Frank spoke excellent French, better than any of the others. Alec and Gladys spoke French well, but according to their son, couldn't match Frank's fluency. Frank was a fine pianist too, entertaining everyone at their Jersey hotel. They'd all enjoyed music, sang Gilbert and Sullivan.

Norman's failure to recognise Ross was disappointing, but hardly surprising. Ross - whoever he was - could have been killed in the war, or he could have died later in the flu pandemic. In 1918, 'flu killed millions, far more than the war itself. One medical historian has expressed the death rates memorably in graves per square mile. All the 1914 - 18 war dead could be buried in a single cemetery of 1.2 square miles. Victims of the so-called 'Spanish' flu', would fill 62 square miles. As a percentage of the population, only the Black Death killed in greater numbers.[7] As for his father's book... Published when he was only four years old, Norman hadn't read the Ambulance story, remembered seeing copies around the house, something about the war. In his childhood, the war had seemed like ancient history, remote as the Crimean, and anyway, neither his parents nor their friends talked about it.

Another phone call ended, with much food for thought, a few more clues, and even more unanswered questions. Ross remained a mystery. And 'Mrs Taylor'? First, she'd had no name at all. Now, after marrying a man called Taylor, she still had no first name. Norman didn't know it. Nor, understandably, had he known her maiden name. In a child's world, adults come ready-made, only their present self is real. Connecting with a parent's distant childhood is difficult enough. Why would he know the maiden name of his mother's friend ? Even to his mother, she would always be 'Mrs Taylor'. Twenty years after their holiday, the two women never used each other's first names. Online archive searches for the lady would remain impossible. Asking a family history website to produce a female Taylor, age, first name and maiden name unspecified, the reply is swift and forthright. 'Refine your search.'

But Norman had known Frank Bourne well. Frank was important, more so now, because the Westmore brothers admired and loved the man who understood how boys feel about hymn books. We agreed to meet, probably in Liverpool, where the Westmores still had friends. In a letter, Norman sent his own analysis of the text, identifying how the authors had contributed to the story. Chapter Six was his mother's, with, probably, contributions from Alec. The first two chapters were almost certainly written by Gladys too. Soon after they arrive, the writer refers to putting on 'war-paint', which should rule out any of the men. Anglican, she's intrigued rather than horrified by Catholic worship.[8] In the second chapter, she admires the ' fine Calvary '. The sternly Protestant author of the final chapters claims to be physically sickened by the smells, bells, statues and crucifixes of Catholicism. Perhaps the energetic Ross dashed off the uneven fifth chapter, scattered with abbreviations. Or Fred ? Or both of them ? The style is often abrupt, erratic. As a travel writer, Frank Bourne was in a class of his own, vividly evoking the sense of place. The fourth chapter was entirely his, and he'd written other parts of the story too. Alec was certainly a contributor. He and Gladys often worked together. He'd hoped to become a journalist, but after the war, they decided that his health was too delicate for such a stressful job. The Westmore children knew that their father suffered from 'nerves'.

This proved to be classic British understatement. In April, 1918, Alec had been a patient at Netley, the same Red Cross hospital where Wilfred Owen was treated, before the Army sent him up to Scotland and Siegfried Sassoon.[9] D ward at Netley specialised in shell-shock cases. Leaving her infant daughter and toddler son with her parents, Gladys travelled south to be with Alec. How long she stayed at Netley isn't clear. Alec had lost the sight of one eye, and the sight of the other remained poor for the rest of his life, corrected with a thick bottle glass lense. His Netley records haven't survived, but it was Alec's 'bad nerves' rather than his damaged sight, which ruled out a career in journalism. In the Twenties, adults wouldn't talk to small children about shattered minds. Norman did remember his father talking about the terrible weight of those stretchers. There were never enough bearers, especially when so many had been killed and injured.[10]

Some of the new photos from Norman showed the young friends sharing other adventures. An undated early group must have been photographed years before France. Alec's wearing outgrown clothes. He's at the gangling stage, all wrists and ankles. Teenage boys grow too fast, and after his father died, money was difficult. Thomas Westmore's death forced Alec to leave the Collegiate School at fifteen, to start work with an insurance company. Fortunately, there was still enough money to enjoy the shoestring walking holidays they loved. From Liverpool, it's no distance at all to the Welsh mountains. The final Westmore photo of the Nomads shows them together at Easter 1913.

Exchanging information over several months of letters and phone-calls, the story moved constantly between the Nomads' French idyll and the Western Front. Research in Liverpool kept pace with Norman's discovery of more family records and contributions from other relatives. The photos confirmed that most of the Nomads had enjoyed backpacking together for years, but only the adventures in France became a jointly written book. Producing one copy each would be a considerable challenge. Handwritten notes had to be typed, photos had to be developed and mounted. In Normandy, one glass plate had broken in two. Frugally, they still processed the broken pieces. All this additional material supported the 1912 date for their book. Wartime newspapers carry regular adverts, offering good prices for waste paper, twelve shillings per hundredweight in 1916.[11] Regularly, on the same pages, there are other advertisements, reminding readers of the paper shortage, and encouraging them to send supplies of stationery to the men at the front. With Germany blockading the Baltic and the North Sea, Britain's normal sources of Swedish wood pulp had been cut off.[12]

The Nomads' story, with its hand-drawn map and carefully captioned photos is authentic desktop publishing, in a (very) limited edition. Private publication was a luxury for the rich. In 1901, Beatrix Potter, privileged daughter of a man who'd inherited a cotton fortune, could pay for the publication of her rejected manuscript, Peter Rabbit.[13] Living in modest suburbia, the young Nomads were far from wealthy. Even so, most of their contemporaries in Liverpool wouldn't be able to afford the bare ingredients of the journal. Backpacking anywhere would be unthinkable. Working families needed every penny for rent, food, clothes, and the funerals of too many children. In desperation, they might emigrate to Australia or America, but until August 4th, 1914, they wouldn't even think about France.

How much would it have cost to produce six copies of their story ? In the 1907 Army and Navy catalogue, albums remarkably like the Nomads' book cost 4s 3d, about 21p in 21st century money. In real terms, pre-WWI, that's about a fifth of the average working man's weekly pay.[14] To produce one copy each of the journal, they'd need at least a ream, five hundred sheets of paper, costing 1s 11d, or just under 10p. Almost certainly, there'd be some wastage due to typing errors. Sheets of carbon paper were about 1s per dozen. Typewriter ribbons cost 2s 2d. Getting their work typed professionally would be yet another expense. In the Edwardian language of survival, enough coal for a week cost at least shilling, and many ordinary working families had far less than 2s per head to spend on a week's food. Literally on the bread line, many families survived on a diet of bread, potatoes, suet, lard, vegetables, and once a week, a few pennyworths of meat. Producing their own book, the spirited young backpackers weren't poor.

Travelling second class, reusing carbon copies and developing a shattered photographic plate, their budget for this enterprise was slender.

At least 'Mrs Taylor' had a name now, or rather, her husband's name. The best clue yet to her identity was her daughter Helen. Helen's birth certificate would reveal her mother's maiden name. Born in Birkenhead, in June, 1923, Helen was registered as the daughter of Llewellyn Strafford Taylor, and her mother's maiden name was Emma Irving. Irving is a Borders name, located firmly in the old debateable lands of southern Scotland and northern Cumbria. Once, like the Armstrongs and Elliots, Irvings were Reivers, rejecting both English and Scottish law.

Now she had a complete name, Emma Irving needed an address, ideally somewhere in or near Liverpool. She might, of course, turn out to be a Londoner. Llewellyn Strafford Taylor would have to wait. Unless he could be Ross ? Llewellyn Strafford sounds distinguished, his forenames resonant with history, but it doesn't exactly trip off the tongue. Four hundred years ago, Shakespeare resorted to Fluellen. Mere Anglo-Saxons still choke over the Welsh Ll. Perhaps Llewellyn Strafford's friends gave up too, came up with something easier. Could it be that, after all the searching, 'Ross' was simply a nickname ? So often, detested 'real' names only emerge in obituaries. Official records, including the census, never ask for the name informants are known by. Perhaps, and this was equally possible, Ross was Emma Irving's brother or cousin ? This would explain her informality towards him, especially when 'Ross' has been down at the beach in Normandy, admiring the fair sex.

Emma Irving and Llewellyn Strafford Taylor married in the summer of 1914. Emma was thirty-two. In 1923, aged forty-one, she gave birth at home to their only daughter. There were two elder children, both boys. Born in 1924, Norman Westmore remembered only Helen. In 1901, when Emma was nineteen. Fred, Alec and Frank were fourteen year old schoolboys. Friendship with the boys at this stage seems highly unlikely. Young ladies of nineteen usually steer well clear of spotty adolescents of either sex. Toy boys might come later. Despite the convention that a woman should 'take an elder than herself', many Edwardian women did marry younger men. Had Emma really known them in West Derby ? The first search of the 1901 census didn't find her anywhere in Liverpool. A second, advanced search failed too. There are glitches still, even on the official website. A rival site traced her to Liskard, on the Wirral, working as a typist. When the Westmores and Gleaves moved over the water, Emma would become a close neighbour. Born in Scotland, her father Richard is described as a foreman printer, though he had been the manager of a letter press. Emma's Presbyterian Scottish background explains her frosty attitude towards Catholicism. Throughout rural Cumbria, many Anglican churches are similar to Quaker meeting houses, with whitewashed walls and no stained glass or other ornaments. Over the border, in what was once Covenanter country, Lowland Scottish churches of any denomination are equally spartan.

Presumably, as a professional typist, with a father in the printing business, Emma would be able to buy paper and all the other stationery for their book at trade price, typing the story herself. At nineteen, she seemed to be the youngest of the Irving family. By 1914, her brothers, William, born in 1873, and Arthur, two years younger, would have been older than most of the first volunteers.

Urging the young men of England to enlist, Lord Kitchener asked for men aged between eighteen and thirty. Later, as the death toll mounted, this was raised to thirty-five. By the spring of 1916, conscription extended to men under forty-one. Finally, the age-limit was raised to fifty.[15] Some of those who 'attested', i.e. registered as willing to serve their country, were older still. Surviving attestation records include some fifty-five year olds. In 1914, William and Arthur Irving were mature adults, but still of military age. If they'd been killed in action, the Commonwealth War Graves Commission would have details of their deaths. In the 1914 - 18 Medal Rolls, there was a William P. Irving, but he'd served in the Border Regiment. Would Emma's elder brother be so attached to his Scottish ancestry ? Many men were. On the same page, another Irving demanded immediate investigation. IRVING, William Ross, Liverpool Regt.

William Ross Irving served in the King's Liverpool Regiment, initially as a second Lieutenant, then Lieutenant. 'Ross' is written in bold ink, and underlined. Above, and rather cramped, his first name 'William' is smaller, indicating that Ross was the name he normally used. Just above the entry for Ross Irving, there was a Thomas Henry Irving, aged twenty-two and also of the 3rd Battalion, King's Liverpool Regiment, killed in action at Caterpillar Valley, August 19th, 1916 and buried at Longueval.

War Graves entries vary tremendously. Many don't give a soldier's full name, age or regiment. Many headstones bear the inscription suggested by Kipling, whose own son was one of the missing at Loos. 'A Soldier of the Great War, Known Unto God'. The war graves record for 2nd Lieutenant Tom Irving is precise and detailed. He was the son of Canon Thomas Henry Irving, M.A., Vicar of Hawkshead, and his wife Margaret. [16] Hawkshead, then in Lancashire and now part of Cumbria, is just over twenty miles from Arnside, and the junkshop where the book was found. Canon Irving was born near Carlisle, and his wife in St Helen's, near Liverpool. They had three sons, David, Ross, and Thomas. Through their mother, the Irvings had strong connections with the Liverpool area. Ross Irving the vicar's son could be the right man. Contemporary newspapers report a dramatic story. Tom Irving was killed while searching the battlefield for his missing brother, Ross. But in the Westmorland Gazette for September 1st, 1916, 2nd Lieutenant Ross Irving, fair and sturdy, looks nothing like the lean and dark haired Ross the Nomad.

On the 1901 census, Emma' s future husband didn't seem to exist. There was a plain Llewellyn Taylor, but no Llewellyn Strafford. Eventually, after an advanced search of institutions, he was traced to a small boarding school in Richmond, Surrey. On the website transcript, Llewellyn is described, bizzarely as a 'sister' of the headteacher. This is a classic example of mistranscription. The word should be 'sizar'. [17] Later, Llewellyn gained his FIA, becoming a land agent. Llewellyn's surveying skills could have been useful to the War Office, but there's no surviving evidence that he served abroad. After he and Emma married, they lived on Kingsway, Liscard. According to the street directories, he was away from home during 1915, but by 1916, he and Emma are together again. Llewellyn continued to work as a land agent until his early death, shortly after his forty-fifth birthday, in April 1929.

He isn't listed in the Medal Cards, nor is there any surviving record of attestation. Since many attestation and discharge records have not survived, it's entirely possible that Llewellyn did volunteer, but was later discharged, as 'unlikely to make an efficient soldier'. Men who'd enlisted but never served abroad didn't qualify for a medal. The so-called 'Burnt Series' records of army pensions and volunteers discharged during the war on medical grounds tell a grim story. Appalling injuries, mutilations, shell-shock, and the blue-lipped nausea of gas victims are well documented. The physical condition of men who'd been passed fit by over-enthusiastic recruiting officers and doctors is startling. Once the recruits reached their training camps, more exacting army doctors found that thousands were unfit for service. Many were suffering from TB, chronic bronchitis and emphysema. Others, cheating, had 'passed' the recruitment eye-test, but were hopelessly shortsighted. Some had marked deformities, including curvature of the spine and rickets. Already, in their early twenties, many lead miners were fatally ill, slowly dying from lead poisoning. The War Office couldn't use them, and didn't want to pay pensions either.

Norman Westmore was astonished to learn that Mr Taylor had been in his mid-forties, actually a few months younger than his wife. He remembered, distinctly, a very old man, thin and frail. What the child really saw was a very sick man. Llewellyn's death certificate records that he died of haemetemesis - a wretched death, vomiting blood from a gastric ulcer. Emma was with him as he died. He could have been sick for years with recurrent ulcers, pitifully thin, and, though he might have been able to undertake civilian work, would be definitely unfit for military service. Despite the absence of a miltray record, Emma's husband could have been another casualty of the Great War. In 1915, when he isn't listed in the street directories, he may well have been away in camp, training for service in France. During the war, and many decades before the bacterial cause was recognised, unusually high numbers of young men developed gastric ulcers, now linked, retrospectively, to helicobacter infection. .[18] Like Llewellyn, they'd face years of chronic sickness. There would be no effective treatment until 1982. In 1912, Emma Irving hoped for long life and happy, happy days. Visiting the widowed Mrs Taylor in the Thirties, an eight year old boy recognised and remembered her sadness.

THE BEGINNINGS OF THE C.H.A. AMBLESIDE 1891

MINISTER—
T. A. LEONARD,
99, KEIGHLEY ROAD.

SECRETARIES—
B. WATSON,
14, EMIL STREET.
R. W. WATSON,
SALISBURY STREET.

INDEPENDENT CHURCH,
COLNE.

Nov ____ 189 4,

Dear Mr Leonard

At our Deacons meeting last Wednesday night conversation turned on the affairs of our Church Generally and the conclusion come to was that matters were very unsatisfactory The opinion of the Deacons present and whose signatures are appended was that the present dessatisfaction has been mainly brought about by your efforts both in the Pulpit—

and outside to disseminate the Principles of Socialism and with which they have no sympathy—
The Church I think has been brought into a very similar condition to the one described in the Congregation at news Column of this weeks issue of the Christian World (first item) & which I have no doubt you will have seen. If you think any good can be done by meeting & discussing with us on these matters we shall be happy to do so at your convenience—

B Watson
Saml Greenwood
William Gill
Joseph Haighton
Arthur Smith.
R. W. Watson.

101

This photograph of the Barrow Police Force was taken soon after the opening of the Town Hall. Note the unfinished paving.

Newlands Hostel 1905

IN THE EIFEL 1906

' In 1910, a kindred organisation was founded in Frankfurt'

Park Hall, Hayfield, a popular C.H.A. centre, 1902 – 1911.

Alec, Gladys, Ross, Emma and friends in the Peak District

The Visit of the Ferienheimgesellschaft Frankfurt a/Main to some Centres of the Co-operative Holidays Association July 1910

PARTY NO. 3:

HAYFIELD, BANGOR AND LONDON
JULY 1—23

REPRESENTATIVES:
Miss HAMBURGER and Mr. KONZACH.

JULY 2: Arrive in London (Charing Cross Station), 5-40. Here the party will be met by Mr. T. A. Leonard, Gen. Sec. of the C.H.A., and other friends and taken by the underground "Tube" railway to Euston Station, where luggage will be left. Breakfast at the "Gwalia" Hotel. Train from Euston 10-30, arr. Manchester 2-5; dep. Manchester 2-22, arr. Hayfield 3-30. Lunch can be had *en route*, 2s. 6d.

SUNDAY: Rest day. For arrangements see green booklet.

EXCURSIONS: 1st Week

MONDAY: JULY 4: ROYCH CLOUGH,
TUESDAY: BUXTON & CHEEDALE.
WEDNESDAY: LIVERPOOL, for arrangements see under Party No. 2.
THURSDAY: CASTLETON.
FRIDAY: ASHOPTON & THE SNAKE.
SATURDAY: JULY 9: Departure to Bangor. 8-35, dep. Hayfield, arr. Manchester (London Road), 9-20; 9-45. dep. Manchester (Exchange), arr. Chester, 11-0. Visit the Cathedral and other places of interest mentioned in the Bangor programme, page 5. 2-40 (or 4-42) train from Chester, arr. Bangor 4-24 (6-9).

EXCURSIONS: 2nd Week

MONDAY: LLANFAIRFECHAN AND ABER FALLS.
TUESDAY: THE ASCENT OF SNOWDON.
WEDNESDAY: Rest Day.
THURSDAY: BETHESDA, NANT FRANCON & LLYN OGWEN.
FRIDAY: HOLYHEAD & THE STACKS LIGHTHOUSES.
SATURDAY: JULY 16: Departure to Addiscombe. Leave Bangor, 10-15 a.m., arr. London, 4-20 p.m. Take underground (Tube) railway to London Bridge, thence by train to East Croydon. Ashburton House is 20 minutes' walk. Cab fare, 1s. 3d.

EXCURSIONS: 3rd Week

The Excursions from Addiscombe will be those given for Party No. 2, but not including the one to Oxford.

Frank Bourne (circled) was a C.H.A. host, welcoming the Ferienheimgesellschaft.

Summer Holidays in the English Lake District (Newlands), 1911.

Organised by the Co-operative Holidays Association, in connection with the National Home Reading Union.

Headquarters:
NEWLANDS VALE GUEST-HOUSE, near KESWICK.

Manageress: Miss CLARKE

COMPANION GUIDES, LECTURERS, AND HELPERS.

Revs. Canon RAWNSLEY (Keswick), W. TAYLOR HERD (Keswick), Messrs. E. EVANS (Burnley), A. W. RUMNEY, M.A. (Keswick), Rev. F. R. SWAN (London), Mr. B. A. TOMES, B.Sc. (Gloucester), the HOSTESSES, and others.

LOCAL SECRETARIES.

June 3—Mr. JAMES CRAIG, Glasgow.
    10—   ,,   ,,
    17—Mr. J. W. HENLEY, Woking.
    24—   ,,   ,,
July 1—Mr. W. BASHFORTH, Sheffield.
    8—Rev. T. L. BEVERIDGE, Falkirk, N.B.
    15—   ,,   ,,
    22—Mr. W. J. WALSH, Manchester.
    29—   ,,   ,,
Aug. 5—Mr. JONATHAN SHAW, Leeds.
    12—   ,,   ,,
    19—Mr. F. E. DODSON, Skipton.
    26—   ,,   ,,
Sep. 2—Mr. J. W. PRICE, Maidstone.
    9—Mr. T. ARMSTRONG, Manchester.
    16—Mr. J. TINCKLER, London.
    23—   ,,   ,,

Corresponding Secretary.

Mr. J. B. HENDERSON, Central Office of the C.H.A., 223-225, Brunswick St., Manchester, S.E.

Assistant Local Secretaries.

Messrs. A. E. PRINCE, of Leigh, Lancs., BERNHARD SEIB, of Frankfort, A. MALCOLM HALL, of Louth.

Organising Secretary.

Mr. T. ARTHUR LEONARD, College House, Brunswick St., Manchester, S.E.

All communications of immediate importance should be addressed:
THE SECRETARY, GUEST-HOUSE, STAIR, near KESWICK.

Summer Holidays in the Taunus, 1911.
(GERMANY)

Organised by the Co-operative Holidays Association, in connection with the National Home Reading Union.

Headquarters:
HOTEL TAUNUSBLICK, KELKHEIM.

LOCAL HELPERS, LECTURERS, &c.

Director WALTER (of the Musterschule, Frankfort), Direktor DÖRR, Landrat E. VON MARX (Homburg), ED. DE NEUFVILLE, Oberkriegsgerichtsrat CELARIUS, The Burgermeister (Herr KREMER) of Kelkheim, Oberlehrer AUGUST LOREY, Dr. JULIUS HÜLSEN, Consul-General A. D. MÜLLER BEECK, Oberlehrer MAX MEINIG, Mrs. LINDLEY, Frau SCHWARZ, and others.

LOCAL SECRETARIES.

June 3—Mr. G. A. BEACOCK, M.A., of Marburg University.
  ,, 24—   ,,   ,,
July 8—   ,,   ,,
  ,, 22—Dr. SIMPSON, of the Royal Technical Institute, Salford.
Aug. 5—Dr. P. SANDIFORD, of the Manchester University.
  ,, 19—Dr. C. E. HODGSON, of Bootham School, Yorks.
Sep. 2—   ,,   ,,

Corresponding Secretary.

Mr. J. GLAISYER, Central Office of the C.H.A., 223-225, Brunswick St., Manchester, S.E.

Resident Secretaries.

Messrs. R. V. HOLT and AUGUST SIEBERT, of Marburg University, and Mr. ARTHUR KIRK, of Manchester.

Resident Hostesses.

Miss B. PAGE and Miss K. WARD.

Organising Secretary.

Mr. T. ARTHUR LEONARD, College House, Brunswick St., Manchester, S.E.

Postal Address of Centre.

HOTEL TAUNUSBLICK, KELKHEIM, IM TAUNUS, GERMANY.

1913 GERMAN GROUP

English and German school parties enjoyed holidays at Newlands.

Kelkheim friends including Spitz

A Peasant's Hut — Kelkheim.

Frankfurt on Main.

108

THE C.H.A PARTY IN A MOTOR-BOAT AT BINGEN.

WIESBADEN'S "COVENT GARDEN."

Gasthaus in Cronberg

CALVARY AT KELKHEIM.

Chapter Ten

'Let every soldier hew himself a bough'

In the Nomads' adventures, Ross is clearly important, central to this group of friends, yet he never dominates. Norman Westmore hadn't recognised him, nor could he offer a surname. Searches online and in archives nationwide for a man named Ross led only to more vast shoals of red-herrings. Nationally and locally, British military archives are impeccable, allowing researchers to test even the most rudimentary information. Even so, some searches fail. It's still not known for certain how many men from all over the British Empire served in WWI. Like so many others, Alec Westmore's service records were destroyed in 1940. Ross's records too might have been lost. Exhaustive searches of all available WWI data had failed to identify a credible candidate. Even the most promising men had been ruled out, including Lieutenant Ross Irving of Hawkshead, who lived so close to where the Nomads' book was found.[1]

Returning to the Nomads' story, page by page, photo by photo, Ross was redefined. Unusually for those pre-war years, Ross seems to accept informality. Is he already secure in himself, distanced from the constraints of Edwardian life, more worldly-wise than his contemporaries ? Every mention of his name might offer a missed clue. Soon after they land at Le Havre, Ross meets a friend, a young Frenchman, who had spent some years in England. Ross himself can't be French, nor is he fluent. Sometimes, making himself understood is a struggle, but he's spiritedly determined to get it right. Buying stamps on a Sunday or eager for 'miel' at breakast, Ross intends to be understood and doesn't seem to be shy. Effective communication is important to him and he persists. In the fourth chapter, during a classic 1912 downpour, they all scramble up steep banks, to shelter under trees. Here, ' Fred taught Ross how to sell timber !' [2] The Nomads enjoy teasing and wordplay, in English, French, and even the Bayeux tapestry's Latin, allegedly open to 'particularly diverting mistranslation'. In Bayeux, studying the strip-cartoon tapestry, did they notice that, like all invaders of Britain, from Julius Caesar to William of Orange, William of Normandy needed ships? The scenes captioned HIC WILLELM DUX JUSSIT NAVES EDIFICARE show tree felling and shipbuilding in progress. William's shipwrights must be building with green wood. Perhaps a timber-trader would spot this ? [3]

The Nomads didn't want to think about work. Occasionally, routine French bureaucracy required their names and occupations, but the backpackers gloss over this unwelcome intrusion. Timber isn't mentioned again. Dreadnoughts or Ironclads, warships are metal now. Blessed with 'superabundant energy', Ross is enjoying every minute of his holiday. Recklessly trespassing, he and Fred scale the walls of Mont Orgeuil castle, only to find they can't get in. At Granville docks, Ross makes himself useful fetching luggage. In Carolles, while the others relax, he heads off to inspect the beach and its bathing belles. At Pontorson, he returns to the station in the nick of time. They're catching a vital train. Ross, who owns a chronometer, points out that he has two seconds to spare.[4] Ross might be a calmly experienced traveller. Anybody who has travelled with a split-second chancer will sympathise with his friends. In Dinan, after their punishing twenty mile walk, Ross is still fresh enough for an extra journey to the C.H.A. The glimpses are fleeting, but perhaps enough to suggest his personality. Ross is resourceful, determined, energetic, can be reckless, and he's on first name terms with everybody, including Emma, so formal even with her close friend, 'Miss Gleave'. Ross might or might not work in the Liverpool timber trade. Or in London ? Or both ? Both cities had major timber yards.

Well placed for the West Indies and the Americas, Liverpool's timber merchants specialised in luxury hardwoods. From the mid-eighteenth century until the late Victorian economic crisis, Liverpool's trade had prospered. Mahogany, walnut and rosewood furnished gracious drawing rooms, first for the wealthy, and later, the aspiring middle classes. London and the east coast ports traded primarily with the Baltic and Germany. In the years before WWI, timber from Germany was thirty per cent cheaper than UK sourced wood. Exports to the UK were important to Germany's trade balance, and Britain was used to relying on Baltic and German softwoods, considered far superior to homegrown Scottish pine. Victorian master builders rejected knotty softwood.[5] A young man working in the timber trade might well move between London and Liverpool and further afield too. From Burma to the Americas, Liverpool knew good timber.

When war was declared, Germany immediately declared all timber contraband, blocking the Baltic trade in timber and wood pulp. The German government knew, surely, how much of their own timber was normally sold to Britain, and how badly Britain would be missing both their own and the Baltic trade. Overnight, the British timber industry faced major supply problems. For the duration of the war, the state had first call on all timber and controls would remain in force until six months after the Armistice. The word itself was unfamiliar, but in August, 1914, British timber was immediately and effectively nationalised. In 1915, the Timber Committee was formed to manage all timber supplies. With the Northern trade cut off, Britain had to look to the west. Cargo space was at a premium. In 1914, shipping costs for timber were about £4 per ton. By the end of the war, the price had trebled. Wood for civilian use was severely rationed. The Government argued that domestic requirements could be met from home grown trees.[7]

In the early months of this unplanned war, recruiting officers enlisted thousands of the wrong men. Countless photos from 1914 - 1915 confirm that recruits could wait weeks and even months for uniforms and the most basic weapons. The chronically sick and weak could be weeded out and discharged. (preferably without an Army pension.) Some under-age boys were released.[8] Men with specialist skills presented very different problems. Their country needed them, certainly, but not as cannon-fodder. But the Army was in no hurry to hand them back, demanding proof. In a country still powered mainly by coal, the miners' key role was obvious. In the steel industry, skilled men employed on government contracts were discharged only after protracted bureaucratic wrangles with the War Office.[9] The concept of 'reserved occupations' developed unevenly. A few thousand patriotic young stockbrokers and public school boys might not be missed. Timber was an altogether different issue. Warships were no longer made of oak, but the trenches, military railways and vast camps of World War I surely devoured more timber than any other war in history. Workers in the timber trade would be in much the same position as miners or steelworkers. Their work was surely 'of national importance', but at first, the government didn't appear to recognise this. In the Royal Engineers, the first Forestry unit only began to operate between 1915 - 1916. At first, they worked in the forest of Nieppe. A year later, five Forestry companies were formed, to serve in France. The need for timber and timber workers was real and considerable. Admitting to it was a very different matter.

When Dr Noel Chavasse heard his nightingale, some of the Somme woodlands were still green.[10] They quickly vanished, becoming mere names in a wasteland of mud, craters and twisted metal. In desperate need, men on the western front could beg their families to send wirecutters.[11] However willing, families could hardly supply their sons with timber. If Ross really did sell timber, the war would have a profound effect on his career, but, despite the unprecedented demand for both timber and timber workers, the industry didn't become a reserved occupation until 1917. In the same year, the Directorate of Forestry was established in France. Wood cut and milled by the Forestry companies was used to construct roads in the Ypres salient area. In some of the familiar scenes of weary men, churned mud, and wholesale destruction, road construction can be seen in progress.[12]

British dependence on French timber suited nobody. Increasingly desperate for timber and for experienced workers too, Lord Derby, Lloyd George and Douglas Haig exchanged urgent letters, telegrams and memos, all secret, all confidential. Some were encrypted. If necessary, they'd scour the entire Empire for timber workers, but officially, there was no shortage. When conscription became law, many timber workers who had applied for exemption from military service were refused, including men based in the Liverpool yards. Throughout 1916, military tribunals steadfastly refused to exempt British timber workers. On appeal, the case of a young Welshman was heard in Liverpool. Managing the largest timber operation in Wales, he was granted exemption, but only until August 1st, 1916. The owner of the business was already serving at the front.[13] Admitting to a problem would be an admission of weakness. Haig's chronic distrust of the French further complicated the problem. In a telegram to Derby, originally sent in cypher, Haig argued that timber imports for domestic use should be banned.[14] Behind closed doors and in cypher, as supplies in France dwindled, Lord Derby reassured Lloyd George that urgently needed 'coloured labour' (sic) was being shipped in from all over the Empire. Canadian lumberjacks were also being sent to France. Thousands more Canadians were cutting timber in the Scottish forests.[15]

In British archives, national and local, information on timber supplies during WWI is severely limited. The scanty archive record reflects the antiquity of many timber firms, and the dangerously exposed position of the industry. Many offices were based in docklands, a prime target for enemy bombing. Ancient ledgers and account books recording trade during both world wars are still held by the firms themselves. The Imperial War Museum has no copy of the 1917 directive, which made timber a reserved occupation at last. (On the Somme, Captain Blackadder's 1917 dug-out received a surprise delivery of trench-climbing ladders. According to Private Baldrick, these ladders were ' the first solid fuel we've had since we burnt the cat' .[16]

The civilian population wouldn't know, officially, about military shortages. Anyone who lived near woodlands could see for themselves what was happening. Long before the Ypres salient became an infamous quagmire, thousands of Army huts had to be constructed. From the autumn of 1914, newspaper advertisements and trade records in private hands record felling on a massive scale.[17] Many nineteenth and early twentieth century landscape photos record established woodlands. Post 1918, as Ordnance Survey maps confirm, the woodlands have gone. Wood based rural industries such as turning and bobbin making for the textile industry record a dramatic shift in production, as they begin to supply naval and military depots with tons of wood. Soon, one North Lancashire timber firm was sending major deliveries to shipyards in Liverpool, Glasgow and Belfast and to an army base in Yorkshire.[17] After the war, the Forestry Commission was founded to restore a countryside stripped of its trees.

Ross, who surely didn't need lessons in selling timber, had to be traced. Timber might well be the key to his war years. Returning from France in August, 1912, he could be one of the three who remained in London, working in a Baltic timber dock or receiving imports from Germany. Further searches of the 1901 census and City of London archives led nowhere. In Liverpool, closer study of the known facts had led to Alec Westmore's unique record of the war, and eventually, to Alec's son, who had recognised Emma Irving. Perhaps Emma's family would know who he was ? Tracing the Taylors' two sons might be impossible, but their daughter Helen became a doctor, surely the best documented of all professions. The Medical Register recorded Helen Taylor's training in Liverpool, her early career, her marriage, and her move to the Midlands, where she and her husband worked together as GPs. Helen's British Medical Journal obituary reports that, as a seventeen year old first year medical student, she was in the city centre, caring for the severely injured victims of the Liverpool blitz. Serious bombing of the city began in August, 1940. The heaviest raids of all came on September 26th, targeting many docks and warehouses.

Once again, historical research was about to invade private space. Tracing two doctors to the Midlands was simple enough. The Medical. Register and BMJ information was in the public domain. Helen and her husband were both dead, but medicine is often a family career. Helen's obituary mentions her daughters, naming one as a consultant. Identifying a doctor of the right surname, age and background was simple enough. Proceeding further required caution and sensitivity. Alec Westmore's descendants came forward willingly, responding to newspaper appeals. They'd volunteered much more information, including many personal documents and photographs. Gradually, this material, none of which was available in any public archives, augmented the Nomad's own memoir, that tantalising glimpse of another twentieth century, as it might have been.

The approach to Emma's granddaughter was made by phone. At first, her reaction was incredulity... Her grandmother ? Backpacking in France ? With a boyfriend ? In France, Emma was the spirited and 'trampish' Miss Irving, backpacking with her Nomad friends. Forty-one when her daughter Helen was born, she was remembered as a little old lady, old, even for a grandmother. Scrambling up ruined towers, knocking on village doors, scrounging for any food they could buy, quaffing vin rouge and sharing jugs of Normandy cider ? Married to Llewellyn Strafford ? Llewellyn Strafford's names settled the matter, but until this moment, Emma's granddaughter had known nothing about the backpacking adventures in France. Days later, after much searching in family attics, she rang to report that relatives had found Emma's own copy. Among other family papers, they'd found the name Ross, godfather to one of Emma's sons. Ross Telfer...

Once again, routine census searches failed to identify a Ross Telfer. Even at the last hurdle, finding Ross wasn't to be straightforward. He wasn't one of the twenty-seven Lancashire men named Ross who were recorded on the 1901 census. Official records fall down badly on the use of forenames. Authority, doggedly singleminded, insists of identifying us by our first given names.[18] Known always by his second name, he was (Matthew) Ross Telfer, second son of (Matthew) Campbell Telfer and his wife, Flora Ross Gallie. Puzzled by an unfamiliar forename, the census enumerator had recorded his second name as Rose... Elusive for so long, Ross the Nomad had been traced at last. Like Alec, Gladys and Fred, he lived in West Derby. Like Fred Pulford, Ross was educated at the Liverpool Institute. He too had left school at sixteen, enjoying a longer education than most British boys. The second of four brothers, Ross was born in 1886. The family's religious tradition was Scottish Presbyterian and his mother had been born in Rosshire. Ross's grandparents came from the Dumfries area. So did Emma's. Telfer and Irving, the two Liverpool Scots were cousins.[19]

In the cosmopolitan world of nineteenth century Liverpool, members of the Scottish community were recognisably different from many of their neighbours. Many followed their own austere and distinctive version of Presbyterianism. As a group, they tended to be of higher socio-economic status than those locally born, and were, of course, utterly different from the predominantly Catholic and frequently poor Irish migrants. The strict Protestant work ethic came with a stern disapproval of alcoholic excess. In France, searching for the next débit de boissons, it's the lax Anglicans who form the 'wickeder' party. Austere and hard working, Liverpool Scots had their own battalion in the city's regiment. Ambitious civilians could look to the ultimate role model. In 1892, when Ross Telfer of West Derby was six, another Liverpool Scot, the eighty-two year old Gladstone, won the general election and formed his fourth ministry.[20]

Now he had a surname, Ross Telfer's career could be followed in Liverpool's street directories, in the national archives and in the scanty remaining archives of the city's timber firms. Why so few records survive from this period is part of Ross's own story, gleaned, at first, from the official records. In December, 1916, he married a young war-widow, whose first husband, another West Derby neighbour, had been killed in action early in 1915. Years before his marriage, Ross appears briefly in the national archives. The tantalisingly brief 1912 sketches are true enough. Crossing the Channel, most of the party were leaving Britain for the first time. Ross, who measured his time on a chronometer, in split-seconds, was already an experienced transatlantic traveller. In 1909, aged twenty-three, he was in America, representing Vincent Murphy & Co, the timber firm he'd joined at sixteen. Other passenger records list a twenty-seven year old M. R.Telfer, travelling to Boston in 1913, and in 1915, to New York.[21] Landing at Le Havre, he'd arranged to meet his French contact. Determined to be understood, Ross was used to fending for himself, even in unfamiliar surroundings. The characteristic 'superabundant energy' recognised by his friends fired a successful fifty year career in the Liverpool timber trade. At the docks, in Granville, Ross, better than any of the others, knew how to deal with customs. In the Liverpool archives, customs records detail the cargo of every ship, listing every item on board, from immense consignments of timber to delicate porcelain.

Ross's chosen career made him a world traveller. Killed on the Somme, his neighbour and Liverpool Institute contemporary Fred never really left West Derby. When he died, his parents were still 'next of kin', still living in their small terraced house. Moving to London in 1914, working so briefly in Threadneedle Street, Fred barely had time to discover the capital, begin a life of his own. Ross would go far, literally and metaphorically. Street directories record Ross's moves from West Derby to Crosby, then from Crosby to Blundellsands. In 1922, aged thirty-six, he's listed as a 'company director'.Described as a ' tall, thin, bespectacled youth', Ross had joined Vincent Murphy's timber firm straight from school, in August 1902. It was still a very young company, founded only five years earlier, when Murphy himself was twenty-six. In 1900, the enterprising young trader had been the first to instal electric cranes at his timber yard. The usual route for any timber trade recruit was a five year apprenticeship, during which the trainee would be paid a total of £100, only half Fred's five year earnings as a low-paid junior at the Midland bank.[22]

Ross and Fred's barely pocket-money earnings were normal enough for men aspiring to middle-class careers. Financially, trainees were often far more constrained than twenty-first century students. Adult independence would be a distant prospect. Earning even less than a junior bank clerk, a timber apprentice was learning to master a complex global market, and the eventual rewards could be considerable. Once they'd served this exacting apprenticeship, even very young staff were expected to be independent, working on their own initiative. Liverpool's huge timber sales took place at the docks, where cargoes were auctioned. Each agent would arrange his own sales, on his own contract forms. Agents would travel extensively, buying from established sources, and also, obtaining rare woods from all over the world. Importing ceramics, textiles, and luxury goods, other traders could display samples to potential customers in city warehouses. Timber couldn't really be judged from a small sample. To assess the quality, it had to be viewed in situ, at the docks. Potential buyers would be given lunch, but there was no marketing hall. Rare woods would always find their own market.[23]

In 1902, sixteen year old Ross was taking a risk. Fred's choice was, ostensibly, far safer. Business was difficult, not just in the timber trade, but in all Britain's key industries. Not entirely recovered from the late Victorian depression, the economy wasn't strong. A year after Ross began his apprenticeship, one long established Liverpool timber firm collapsed, with liabilities of nearly £78, 000. Timber prices continued to fall, the cost of shipping soared, and the decline in housebuilding affected every area of the timber trade. Ambitious, enterprising, and clearly willing to travel, Ross and his young employer worked hard. Slowly at first, the market recovered. 1914 began well, but when war was declared, many contracts were cancelled. Timber workers, with good reason to fear unemployment, were eager to join the armed forces.[24] In St George's Hall, on August 31st, 1914, one table was allocated to the timber trade. Nobody suggested that the War Office might have different work for them.

A search of the Sefton archives led immediately to Ross's impressively detailed 1952 obituary, and, earlier the same year, a tribute from the timber trade, celebrating his fifty years with Vincent Murphy. He'd also become managing director of another Liverpool timber firm.[25] Obituaries from this period tend to be stereotypical eulogies, obeying very specific rules and avoiding any remotely controversial issues. The time honoured rule for reporters was ' De mortuis, nihil nisi bonum' Delegated, traditionally, to junior staff, a local newspaper obituary would be read almost exclusively by people who'd known the deceased. Praise is expected and unstinting. Coded euphemisms such as 'he was unmarried' were strictly observed. Ross had been, of course, an outstanding member of the timber trade, not only of Merseyside, but of the whole country... His integrity and leadership were widely recognised.'

The record of professional success in one of Liverpool's key trades is clear enough. Ross enjoyed a rewarding and successful career on both sides of the Atlantic. Eulogies aren't supposed to be interesting, let alone revealing. A later tribute, published a week after the funeral, suggests a more complex character, respected for his 'wise counsel' and unstinting generosity. Rather than lend money to someone in need, Ross preferred to give. His WWII career suggests more than competence. From 1940 - 1947, he'd served as Area Officer for Region 9; the North West of England, managing timber supplies for the entire region, despite the serious dockland bombing of 1940. In 1941, more Liverpool timber offices were destroyed. London's docklands suffered too. Vincent Murphy's London base was completely destroyed. Timber yards were moved out of the cities to safer rural areas.[26] With no office and no records, Ross's leadership, organising skills and expert knowledge were vital. In every obituary, his WWII service is recognised and praised. But WWI isn't mentioned, anywhere. Earlier that year, in the tributes to his long career, his role during WWII is recorded in detail. Again, there's not a single word about his role during the 14 - 18 war.

The omission is striking. In 1916, when conscription became law, Ross was a healthy young man of twenty-nine. Blessed with 'superabundant energy' he doesn't seem to have a service record at all. Attestation records are at best patchy, but in the surviving War Office records, there seems to be no sign of Ross or his three brothers. Before the war, all four had been working in the timber industry. Alec Westmore's service records were certainly destroyed. The gap in the National Archives 'Burnt Series' where his data should be is perfectly obvious. The records for many other Telfers have survived, with no immediately obvious gaps. The explanation for this remarkable silence and the equally remarkable lack of information might lie in those encrypted, highly confidential messages exchanged by Lord Derby, Douglas Haig and Lloyd George. In 1914, Ross had thirteen years experience in the timber trade and many contacts in North America.

The encrypted messages have survived, acknowledging both the serious shortage of timber, and the immense efforts made to secure more supplies and more timber workers for the Allies, even from China. So many timber records were destroyed in the WWII bombing of docklands offices, it might be impossible to discover anything more about Ross's role during WWI. Until the summer of 1919, the government would remain in overall control of the timber industry. On the Western Front and at home, Britain's urgent need for timber and experienced men had to be met. Ross's contribution during the utterly different

Second World War was important. His wide experience in sourcing timber linked him to the Austrian born plywood expert, Dr Karl Zuckerman. Zuckerman arrived in the UK from Vienna in the spring of 1939, bringing his expertise in plywood to Merseyside. Throughout WWII, with all timber production once more under Government control, Dr Zuckerman was producing specialised plywood for government aircraft and marine construction. Like Birnam Wood, some of these plywood constructions were intended to deceive the enemy. Camouflage expertise began to be important during WWI, but military hardware was still relatively primitive. Numbers on the ground counted. In 1917, by the hard-frozen Yser, Field Ambulance men like Alec Westmore were disguised as a trained armed unit. A generation later, faking powerful hardware was far more important than pretending to have more infantry. In the desert war, plywood was used to create the dummy tanks and other military simulations used to deceive Rommel's army.[27]

Eventually, through the timber trade, Ross Telfer's descendants were traced. They too owned a copy of the Nomads story. The condition of this version is poor. The binding's badly damaged. So are several photos. Many pages of typescript are carbon copies. Ross seems to have settled for the worst copy, pieced together from leftovers. Battered as it is, his version of the gentle adventures in Normandy does reveal more of his own story. In the spring of 1914, he was in New Orleans again. There and in New York, American friends and colleagues read the Nomads' story, recognised a near-perfect idyll. The final page of Ross's copy is filled with their messages.

In the North of England, newspapers recorded the names of mourners well into the 1970's. The reports of Ross's funeral list well over three hundred mourners and identifies many unnamed groups too. The names of these mourners reveal quite as much about Ross Telfer as the straightforward account of his career. This was a Merseyside funeral in the early Fifties. At worship, at school, in the workplace and on the football pitch, sectarian divisions could still be deadly. How one pronounced the letter H or abbreviated the name William could be dangerous and sometimes life-threatening.[28] The wrong name and wrong creed ruled out many jobs. But the men and women who came to mourn Ross Telfer were Catholic and Protestant. Some names appear to be Jewish. One of the chief mourners represented the Ministry Ross had served throughout WWII. Others came on behalf of American firms. Ross was mourned sincerely, and that mourning was both international and, given the date, impressively ecumenical. Elusive for so long, the energetic young backpacker of 1912 became a distinguished and successful businessman. On Merseyside, he was mourned by people of all faiths. In a city still bitterly divided by sectarian hatreds, they came to his funeral.

But there'd been four young men in Normandy; Fred, Alec, Ross and Frank, the man who hardly ever appears in the photos. Norman Westmore had said, during one phone call, 'Frank wasn't in the war'.

Chapter Eleven

Dishonour not your mothers

Shakespeare, Henry V

Frank wasn't in the war...   But why not ? The cryptic comment explained nothing, begged many questions. In France, two years earlier, the 'indefatigable' Frank could walk twenty miles with ease. He and Ross were the energetic members of the party. In Brittany, he'd talked to the others about the stars. He was a keen photographer too. Astronomy and photography demand excellent eyesight, and in any case, recruitment officers soon stopped insisting on perfect sight. Sight was negotiable, charts easily memorised. Alec Westmore usually wore glasses. In February 1915, he'd been accepted by the RAMC to train as a stretcher-bearer. Fred Pulford's army service and Midland Bank employment records confirm that he volunteered immediately. Frank, a fit, healthy and impressively well educated man in his twenties, hadn't joined the rush into uniform. Why would this be ? Oral history proceeds with caution. Information is given willingly or not at all. Direct, intrusive questions are for door-stepping journalists and ferocious interviewers, grilling politicians. Norman Westmore had identified his mother's friend ' Mrs Taylor', née Emma Irving, the woman who had no name at all in the Nomad's narrative. He could have vital information about Frank Bourne, but so far, he'd said very little.

Everybody knows the myth of how the Great War began. In August, 1914, patriotic frenzy swept the country. Mass communication was barely in its infancy, yet immensely potent. Without radio or TV, let alone mobile phones, the British public was being controlled, directed and deceived as never before. People were told that patriotism was universal, every young man eager to fight, every wife, girlfriend and mother just as eager to wave goodbye. In straw boaters or flat caps, boys were desperate to enlist. Messages targeting women were subtly different. Only a man willing to serve his country was worthy of them. Closely monitored by MI7, the national and regional press became the most effective recruiting officer of all. Dissent was marginalised and opposition to the war underreported.

Selling any message to the public is always a calculated exercise in manipulation. Advertisers exploit the instinct to conform. Dissenters are threatened with terrible consequences, from grey hairs and bad breath to certain death. The state is far more ruthless than any commercial advertiser. After a postgraduate degree, I worked for a government agency. Our job was to collect and analyse medical data, then convert raw statistics into a forceful marketing campaign. We had to name the new enemy, warn the public of serious danger and direct a radical change of behaviour. The brief was to make people scared, but not so scared that they would ignore the message. Assessed as a marketing campaign, early WWI propaganda was an outstanding success. Some tactics worked better than others. The legendary Order of the White Feather was founded by Admiral Charles Fitzgerald when the war was only days old. Women were encouraged to hand out white feathers to all men not in uniform, a tactic which achieved rather too many own goals and was soon abandoned. White feathers were pressed on civil servants, the medically exempt, and on men who had enlisted, but weren't yet in uniform or equipped with arm-bands.[1]

The timing of Fitzgerald's famous campaign is curious. So is the gender of his chief agents. If young men were really so eager and willing to fight, in the fevered August of 1914, why would they need to be shamed into khaki by women? The Kitchener posters and white-feather campaigns are too familiar, clichés of history. Women of Britain say 'Go' is a different and profoundly disturbing image. No clogs, no shawls, no aprons, these are ladies, elegantly well dressed. Like the strange and brutal women of Sparta, they seem to crave death and glory rather than living sons and lovers. (Lysistrata's pioneering Stop the War tactics don't feature in WWI recruiting posters.) Upper class women were conditioned to loss and separation. Across the Empire, they expected to send small children 'home', knowing they would not see those children again for years and perhaps never. Reared mainly by nannies, sent to boarding school at seven, their classically educated sons understood 'Pro Rege et Patria', and knew Wilfred Owen's 'old lie' too.[2]

They sold dreams. Many feature idealised rural landscapes, invariably a southern English idyll. Mills, mines, foundries and industrial slums are conspicuously absent. So are war cemeteries, amputees and the victims of shell-shock. One of the most sinister posters shows a young boy apparently in his early teens. The text suggests ' Shouldn't you be in Khaki ? ' In the original pre-war Baden-Powell Scouting poster, the call to dedication comes, not from a recruiting officer, but from Jesus. Other posters show serving soldiers, inviting recruits to join them, reaching a hand across the Channel. Young men were subjected to relentless pressure. They weren't supposed to wait and they certainly weren't expected to think. The very least they could do was attest, sign up, spend their token day in service, returning as soon as the Army could use them. After attesting, they might be left in peace. The khaki armbands issued to recruits and those who'd 'attested' protected men from verbal and physical abuse. Many of those who had 'attested' soon knew only too well what conditions they'd face in the trenches.[3]

Men of all ages came forward to serve their country. They knew it was their duty. Too old, or, far more often, too young, they lied about their ages. Early in the war, recruiting officers encouraged and even ordered the lies. The latest figures suggest that in WWI, over a quarter of a million Allied soldiers were under-age. Some were still under-age when they became officers. Lewis Roberts enlisted in the Royal Welch Fusiliers at 16. Aged 18, and officially, still too young for service overseas, he was appointed Lieutenant. The North Wales Chronicle reported the case of a soldier on leave who had been charged with theft. Family members came forward to insist that he must be tried in the juvenile courts. Still only fifteen, he'd already served for a year on the Western Front.[4] The recorded height and weight of many underage boys indicates how unconvincing their lies would be. An Edinburgh sixteen year old, his occupation listed as 'scavenger', was barely five foot and weighed under seven stone.[5] At the front, when terrified schoolboys broke down crying for their mothers, they could be shot for cowardice and desertion. Challenged in the Commons by Sir Arthur Markham, Sir Richard Grey insisted that everything possible was being done to stop the recruiting of underage boys. In practice, military regulations made their discharge increasingly complex. Boys were released only after their original birth certificates and supporting proof had been checked with a rigour never applied to the original lies. Military history acknowledges, at last, the vast numbers of schoolboys who served in WWI. At the time, surely everyone knew ? Newspapers regularly published their Rolls of Honour. Page after page of photos record the local dead and wounded. Too many of the 'other ranks' casualties have the unformed and barely adolescent faces of boyhood. Thin, childish necks with no sign of an Adam's apple suggest unbroken voices.

It's often claimed that the appalling health of so many would-be recruits led, eventually, to the Beveridge report and better health care for all. Even if this were true, it's hardly a convincing case for a war that cost, in real terms, so many billions, killed ten million men, triggered a flu pandemic killing up to 50 million and scarred at least three generations. By 1914, working class poverty and sickness had already been exhaustively researched. Maud Pember Reeves' study of family life on a poverty income was one of many such reports. Almost contemporary with Mrs Reeves work was Philip Snowden's ' The Living Wage.' [6] Fifteen years earlier, during the Boer War, the government knew perfectly well that 70% of would-be recruits from the working class were too sick, stunted and half-starved to fight. Even when they were supposed to be young men, many of the working classes were so stunted the army had to lower its standards, creating 'bantam' units of men under 5 ft 3 inches, like the East End war poet, Isaac Rosenberg.[7] In 1917, despite the greatly modified fitness tests, Scottish doctors were rejecting over 50 % of conscripts as unfit. The doctors' judgment would be accurate enough, and probably optimistic. In the twenty-first century, the health of Scots is still notoriously poor. Writing to Lloyd George on September 9th, 1917, Lord Derby complained bitterly about manning problems.[8] He appears to be exasperated equally by the sick Scots, and the many attested 'badged' men, ostensibly willing, but never actually available. Loyally assenting to the Defence of the Realm Act, and later, to conscription, many of these men were fit, healthy middle class professionals or business men. Having sworn loyalty and donned their armbands, many were promptly declared to be invaluable to their local communities. (Class was an infallible guide to a man's value.)[9]

The energetic Frank was an unlikely reject. Could he have been in a reserved occupation ? In the Second World War, there were plenty of those. The army needed less cannon-fodder and more intelligence. In the 14 - 18 war, the army was hungry for men, needing constant replacements. Military technology had created devastating weapons, but in the early years of the war, the infantry were arguably more vulnerable than the deadly archers of Agincourt. Reading anybody's writings, fiction or non-fiction, it's natural enough to imagine the writer, try to form some impression of their personality. Co-authors, the Nomads reveal many things about each other and their relationships. Already engaged, 'Mr Westmore' and 'Miss Gleave' are inseparable. In France, the charismatic Ross predominates, vividly defined by his companions. ' Mr Pulford ', who'd made all the bookings, quickly develops as stand-up comedian with, perhaps, a troubled relationship with Emma Irving. Frank, the adventure's main photographer, is a subtler, altogether more complex character, but there's never any suggestion of weakness.

In the Nomads' story, Frank's chapter is just over two thousand words, little enough to define a man, but there are intriguing clues. Technically and aesthetically, he's assessing each photo, rather than simply taking random snapshots. Evoking the spirit of Balleroy, his vignettes are musical, late-night singing, obviously, and the church bells, but he writes, too, of being in tune with a place, of sympathetic vibrations in the mind, the music of rippling water. Recognising a quotation from Terence, when he breaks a photographic glass plate, ' hinc illae lachrymae' - hence these tears, it was reasonable to suspect privilege. Frank's language skills, music and photography all suggest an excellent education and early career success. In 1912, even a basic Thornton-Pickard quarter-plate camera, advertised as 'suitable for juveniles and beginners' cost 21/-, rather more than the average working man's wage.[10] Perhaps he was a public school boy, more privileged than his friends ?

Frank's real story was utterly different, and it was Iraq that led, eventually, to the truth about this man. Norman had been talking about his grandchildren, much the same age as my own son and daughters. Opposing the invasion of Iraq, actively rather than in hindsight, his grandchildren and my daughters demonstrated confidently, despite the efforts of schoolteachers and other adults to constrain them. IT literate from infancy, their sources of information were at once global and local. The internationalist C.H.A. pioneers had dreamt of 'showing the earth to the company of youth'. Now, the company of youth can talk to each other across the globe and round the clock. Adults running the 2003 'Stop the War' coalition played some part in the young people's intelligent response to the invasion, but they were only mentors, startled by the immediacy of teenage action, teenage communication. Sixthformers who'd grown up inspired by Mandela and Ghandi refused to be censored, walked out of their classrooms, took to the streets, and went online. Unlike the savagely censored peace campaigners of WWI, they couldn't easily be silenced or punished. As a reporter, I observed every stage of one youth-led demonstration, organised by sixth form pupils in a country town in the North of England. Unlike the brutal student rioters of Paris and Grosvenor Square, they were remarkably courteous. Ringleaders reminded their classmates to observe the rules of peaceful non-cooperation, not to swear, and to obey police orders at all times. A woman priest, wearing her dog-collar, rebuked the youngsters, suggesting that they should be loyal to their country. No angels, and few, if any, regular churchgoers, the young demonstrators referred her to their banners and posters, which included several extracts from the Sermon on the Mount. (always a difficult text for the Church militant, and during WWI, frequently classified as 'sedition', likely to prejudice the Defence of the Realm).

Moving on from Iraq, Norman Westmore and I considered this generation's very different understanding of the 20th century wars, best defined as informed sadness. On Remembrance Day, teenagers stand in silence around war memorials. So do the little ones, five, six, seven year olds. Nearly all wear poppies. The crimson paper for all Britain's 36 million poppies is produced in a Cumbrian paper mill, James Cropper plc of Burneside, near Kendal . Bidding for this contract, almost thirty years ago, the firm had expected sales to decline, as memories of the two world wars faded. They were wrong. Seventy years after World War II, poppies are very much in demand, and the two minutes silence is once more observed on Armistice Day itself.[11]   At our local primary school, pupils have researched every man and boy recorded on the war memorial. Fresh flowers are laid there, not just in November, but commemorating the young men's actual anniversaries.

Throughout much of the Sixties and Seventies, the adult code of 'don't mention the war' remained in force. Thermopylae might still be on the public school curriculum, but very rarely ' Third Ypres '. Once they'd finished the obligatory dinosaurs, Romans, Vikings and Victorians, my own children and their contemporaries studied Hitler's rise to power and WWII to the exclusion of almost every other period of history (including the unification of Germany and the Franco-Prussian war). Studying the Third Reich, they analysed the alleged dangers of proportional representation and Hitler's control and manipulation of the media. The Holocaust is compulsory, but school pupils rarely study the much earlier episodes of persecution and expulsion experienced by Britain's Jewish community. Impeccably schooled in 20th century horrors, sixth form history students and many younger pupils know the names of every death camp and how Jews, Romanies and other undesirables were disposed of. They know how many died in Dresden and Coventry, the names and killing power of every weapon. They dare to challenge the sacred legends of D-Day, then ask, shockingly, who really won this war ? Far more than their parents and grandparents ever did, they question the alleged inevitability of Hiroshima and Nagasaki. Almost too late, this generation have approached their great-grandparents, to talk about WWII. On the battlefield and politically, today's history students know far less about the 'war to end all wars', described by John Keegan as ' a tragic and unnecessary conflict.' [12] Appalled by the massacre of a generation, they discover the 1914 -18 war through literature. They know the literary war poets by heart, dissect the patriotic fervour of Jessie Pope and her contemporaries, read the classic and the twenty-first century novels, try to understand why any of this happened, the fervour and the slaughter. [13]

The intensely focused history curriculum has been much criticised, but perhaps, for a time, such single-mindedness was essential. Dutifully chanting 'we will remember them', three generations had tried far too hard to forget, rarely spoke to their children or grandchildren about the wars that shaped their world. Studying the history of WWII since primary school, and the WWI poets, young people have been invited to shift the generations, imagine the vast armies and 'nameless names ' as their fathers, uncles, older brothers and sisters.

Already, much information from the twentieth century wars has been lost, from public records and personally. The Luftwaffe's destruction of many WWI Allied service records was an accident of war. In April, 1945, Allied bombing destroyed the entire Prussian archives. [14] Silence has killed much of the unofficial record, the old unable to speak, the young reluctant to ask. Personal data has been irretrievably lost because for so many years, the wars were rarely discussed. Contradicting the famous campaign poster, children didn't ask what Daddy did in the war and fathers rarely volunteered information. Oral history crosses many boundaries. Sometimes, it invades or hopes to invade the most intense and deeply personal relationships. Routinely now, celebrities explore their family history on prime-time T.V. Confronted with deaths in Auschwitz or the workhouse, the tears are genuine, but they're also part of a carefully programmed and staged performance. Private stories are different, revealed willingly or not at all. Norman

Westmore's relationship with Frank Bourne had been formed in childhood, a childhood between the two world wars, surrounded by the unspoken grief of adults. Frank Bourne's story was important, but it was also secret history. So far, even his true identity remained uncertain. Which Frank Bourne was he ? What was his background ?

Only about four hundred of those who registered as conscientious objectors were granted complete exemption from service or 'work of national importance', because the importance of their own regular work had been accepted.[15] Few conscientious objectors were given absolute exemption on religious grounds, and a third were refused any exemption at all. Their faith itself could be regarded as suspect, or in the official term, 'not genuine'. Some objectors had attracted suspicion before the war, visiting on peace missions and entertaining German friends in England. Stuart Beavis, a German speaking conscientious objector, was doubly suspect. He'd lived and worked in Germany for several years.[16]

Seventy years later, Norman Westmore still remembered his mother's anger over how Frank had been treated, simply for obeying his conscience. But to the patriotic majority, 'conchies' were criminals and even traitors. Even distinguished public figures who opposed the war were subjected to physical abuse.[17] Conchies had refused to fight for God, King and Country. In the First World War, that was most definitely a thought crime. Patriotism was supposed to be automatic. Church windows dedicated to the glorious dead often bear the inscription, ' Pro Rege et Patria'. God's approval is assumed, England expected ' the love that asks no questions.' Only an intriguing minority dared to ask any questions at all. Then, outrageously, they suggested that war wasn't the answer. In the streets, they distributed handbills, quoting the dangerously unpatriotic words of Jesus Christ.[18] For such crimes, contravening the Defence of the Realm Act and the Military Service Act, many were prepared to die, to be tortured and to serve long years in jail.

Norman then recalled vital information about Frank. Though employers had been urged never to employ former 'conchies', Lever Brothers (now Unilever) took a different view. In 1919, all conscientious objectors were released from prisons and work camps. Lever Brothers offered Frank a job.[19] He was lucky to find work with any firm, but Lever Brothers were unusual employers. It's possible that his membership of the C. H. A. was known to the firm. Founded in 1885, by devout Congregationalist brothers, Lever Brothers had a strong tradition of respecting its employees values, translating that respect into the model community of Port Sunlight. Like Saltaire, Bournville, and Robert Owen's idealistic but troubled venture at New Lanark, the Lever brothers' creation provided workers with outstanding living conditions. Writing in 1885, Lever was already defining his ideal community. Port Sunlight was to be a way of living, rather than a mere factory. Even the church was a model of Christian unity, one of the first nondenominational churches to be built in Britain.[20]

According to the Unilever archives, Francis Ramsey Bourne, of Greasby, Wirral was initially employed by Planters of Bristol, one of Lever Brothers' subsidiaries. Their archives give his date of birth as 11/01/1887. The date and middle name identified him conclusively as the Francis Bourne registered in Whitechapel, born a Londoner, like his friend Fred Pulford.[21] Frank's birth certificate describes his father as a 'grocer', at 5, Lamb Street, Spitalfields, right next to Spitalfields market. On Charles Booth's 1889 sociological map of London, incomes in Lamb Street were mixed, some middle-class, others very poor. By the age of four, Frank had lost his father. Like so many children in the Victorian age, he'd known life in a one-parent family.[22] Good or bad, the relationship between the surviving parent and their child or children is intensified. Already a single mother, Emma Bourne would be defined as the mother of a 'conchie'. Whatever her own views, she too would pay a heavy price.[23]

Meeting the Liverpool Nomads must have come later, but Frank and Fred had spent their early childhood in the same area of London. On the 1881 census, Fred's father Thomas is a lodger in Lavender Grove, Hackney, barely a mile away from Lamb Street. According to Booth's map, Lavender Grove was then solidly middle-class, but it was normal enough for a young single man to become a lodger, rather than fend for himself in a bedsit. On the 1901 census, there was no sign of Frank in Spitalfields or anywhere else in London. He wasn't in Liverpool either. The first searches didn't find him. At just fourteen, such a well-educated boy would surely be at school. Records for boarding schools are filed separately.

Frank proved to be a Bluecoat Boy, not in Liverpool, but at Christ's Hospital, with its distinctive uniform and glorious setting. The school moved from London to its present Sussex site in 1902. Born in the parish of Christchurch, Frank was a public school boy, but, unusually for a public school, Christ's Hospital honoured the principles of its founders. Scholarships for boys like Frank offered a first class education to children from very modest backgrounds. In the twenty-first century, over eighty per cent of Christ's Hospital pupils come from ordinary, ethnically mixed backgrounds. Owning the right kind of London property is, of course, extremely useful, but the school could have chosen the route taken by so many foundations created for the poor and now reserved almost exclusively for the rich. Christ's Hospital archives revealed that Frank was an outstandingly able student. In his final year - he left just before his seventeenth birthday - Frank came top in mathematics and second in every other subject, including French, German, science, shorthand, and technical drawing. Linguist, pianist, able mathematician, Frank had enjoyed a privileged education, but it was a different kind of privilege. As a bright mathematician from Christ's, with the bonus of excellent shorthand, Pepys would surely consider him a fine candidate for the Navy office.[24]

However they met, in the 1912 journal, it's clear that Frank and Fred are close friends. Their utterly different response to the war must have been painful for both men. In August 1914, Frank was twenty-seven, just a few months younger than Fred. Any regiment would have welcomed him. Public school educated, he was undoubtedly officer-class. Now Britain and France were allies, his French would be a battlefield asset. A man who spoke fluent German too could be very useful indeed. Somehow, men like Frank, who didn't volunteer in those August days, managed to stand outside the situation. Patriotism was the order of the day. During the first three months of the war, over 900,000 men volunteered to serve their country, but the nature of this incoherent patriotism is questionable. Three years earlier, the dog-days flashpoint of Morocco hadn't triggered a major war, though Britain had promised to defend her new ally against Germany. In 1914, young men - or enough of them - were keyed up for battle, urged, encouraged, and directed by their elders. At leading schools, thousands of boys were being drilled in the Officer Training Corps. In Liverpool, it's on record that young men marched from their city offices to volunteer en masse. It's also on record, though only in the small print of council minutes, that their services had been agreed by their employers several days before Lord Derby's stirring speech and their carefully synchronised enlistment in St George's Hall, where there were separate tables for every profession. [25]

In 1914, Fred's patriotic zeal was the nationally approved response. Conscientious objectors quickly became a target for abuse. Sacked by his employers, Frank had made his views clear from the outset. During the autumn of 1915, demands for conscription mounted, even though the War Office was still seriously under-equipped, and would remain so until Lloyd George took control. In September 1915, he'd announced that Britain's munitions factories needed 80,000 more skilled workers and 200,000 unskilled. On November 1st, newspapers published full page announcements, detailing the increasingly compulsory arrangements for enlisting. Young men were urged to volunteer while they still could, rather than face the stigma of conscription. Miners, dockers, railwaymen, munitions workers and some other trades, though not, as yet, timber, were identified as reserved occupations.[27]

Some statistics are surprising, even to the most cynical misogynist. A higher proportion of married men had enlisted or attested, even though they'd been assured that single men would be called on first. Many single men - over 13,000 in Liverpool alone - hadn't even attested. Initially, so long as men didn't voice opposition to the war, they were safe enough. Then, as the war moved towards its third year, joining the armed forces became compulsory. Ensuring that men would serve became a local authority responsibility, the supervision of a civic duty, like paying rates or putting rubbish in bins. Civic duty requires no thought, no philosophical debate, merely compliance. On October 26th, 1915, over five months before the Military Service Act became law, this statement by the Lord Mayor of London was entered in the minutes of Liverpool City Council.

' The President of the Local Government Board is appealing to the Local Authorities of England, and Wales. to do everything in their power to assist the Recruiting Authorities and asking the Councils to constitute a committee to act as the local tribunal for Liverpool.[28] The Lord Mayor's appeal was sent to every local council in the land.

Liverpool assented loyally. The Lord Mayor of London also invited all citizens to ' take part in a prayer of humble homage to Almighty God.' The first Sunday of the New Year, January 2nd, 1916, was chosen for 'this most solemn occasion.' Liverpool's civic patriotism was the normal and expected response. Across Britain, almost every local authority promised to do everything in its power to promote recruitment. On receiving their copy of the Lord Mayor of London's appeal, most authorities acted swiftly to appoint the tribunals who would assess unwilling conscripts. (and naturally, protect invaluable pillars of the community, such as overseers of the poor.) In the Liverpool press, dissent is sidelined, and, when it is reported, routinely condemned.

Newspapers reflect the views of their editor, and beyond the editor, those of their proprietor. Independently owned papers, especially those published in distant regions of the UK, such as the Cumberland and Westmorland Herald could and did take a very different line. In its first issue of 1916, the Herald published a very positive report of the less than patriotic service of intercession held on January 2nd in Keswick.[29] Nationally, press barons were still promoting war and unthinking loyalty. Working men remained resolutely opposed to conscription, and, especially in the industrial North and in Wales, were in sympathy with fellow workers across Europe. Reports of widespread opposition to conscription couldn't be ignored, though many pro-conscription editors expressed their own opinion of these dissenters. The North Wales Pioneer reported that 'Practically all the Labour organisations in England, Wales, Scotland and Ireland have moved strong resolutions against conscription'.[30] In January, 1916, the Labour council of North Wales didn't salute the coming Military Service Act. Nor did they declare their unstinting loyalty to King and Country. Instead, they passed the following resolutions :

(1) 'That this Council will view any attempt to forcibly billet troops on unwilling households with the gravest disapproval.'

(2) 'That we oppose the efforts that are at present made in this country to deprive the British citizen of the right of free speech. In view of the great cost of the lives and bodies of our young men, that is caused by the present War, we urge upon the Government to consider the impact of this policy.' [31]

The MP for the Caernarfon Boroughs was, of course, David Lloyd George, the Secretary of State for War, who had warned all conscientious objectors what they could expect if they refused to serve their country.[32] At public meetings and in the press, his brother William would denounce conscientious objectors as 'objectionable cowards'.[33] The future Prime Minister knew perfectly well that Wales was seething with Christian dissent and sedition. Not a believer himself, (despite his passion for singing Welsh hymns) Lloyd George was exasperated by his compatriots' reluctance to fight for King and Country.(defining that country as 'England' didn't help) Working men, especially the Nonconformist majority in Wales, read their Bibles, quoting, far too often, seriously inconvenient passages of the New Testament.

A few miles north of Caernarfon, living at the Bryn Corach hostel, Conwy, one of Lloyd George's least patriotic constituents was the former Congregationalist minister, Arthur Leonard, founder of the C.H.A., by now a Quaker and a well-known pacifist.[34] Throughout the war years, Leonard would welcome many of his equally unpatriotic friends and colleagues to the hostel, including several 'rascally, pro-German' members of the Labour Party.

Chapter Twelve

'Blessed are the peacemakers, for they shall be called the children of God...'

New Testament : Matthew, v, 3.

During WWI, 'peacemakers' were called many things. 'Children of God' isn't on the list. 'Conchie' was one of the kinder insults. For the duration, the armies and the navies of the Allies and the Central Powers ruled the world and understood each other far better than they would ever understand men who chose to serve conscience rather than country. Men like Frank Bourne were denounced as traitors, shirkers, 'peace-freaks' and cowards. They deserved to be shot. When some conscientious objectors agreed to undertake ' work of national importance ', decent patriots refused to work with them.[1] Absolutists in the peace movement despised them too. Some regarded stretcher-bearing as support for the war effort. Many determined conscientious objectors held stubbornly and unpatriotically to their Christian faith. A few were Jewish and at least one conscientious objector known to the No Conscription Fellowship was a Buddhist. Sometimes, the principles held by these non-Christians was acknowledged and supported by Christian ministers. At one Liverpool tribunal, an Anglican vicar appeared as a character witness for a Jewish moneylender living in his parish. The man had always dealt fairly with his many Christian customers and they valued his service. But the NCF survey is a small sample (126 individuals) of a pacifist minority, the absolutists who refused to take any part in the war, even the so-called 'work of national importance'. Nationally, the majority of Nonconformists supported the war.[2]

Increasingly fierce debate on the ethics of war raged in the churches and in the trades unions. The Bishop of Manchester denounced all 'conchies'.[3] In September, 1915, the Bishop of Stepney personally recruited fifty-six men in a single day. During an eight day recruiting campaign, seven hundred Stepney men came forward. The Bishop's patriotism was prominently reported and praised. In a letter to Lord Derby, Douglas Haig puts the case for Caesar with some eloquence : ' The needs of the State and the wishes of the Government must take first place, and the interests of the individual must be ignored, so do not consider me.'[4]

In this handwritten letter, the underlining is Haig's own. At Wandsworth, as one young conscientious objector was being led down to the cells after sentencing, the commandant barked out an order : ' Take away his ****** Bible ! That's where he gets his ideas'.[5] Guided by faith or ethics, very ordinary men were branded as criminals, yet until WWI, Britain had taken pride in her volunteer army. The compulsory archery practice of the middle ages was ancient history. Press gangs were for the Navy, Britain's senior service, which had always been hungry for manpower. Men who served in the relatively small pre-1914 army had chosen their career. Officers were gentlemen, other ranks had their own hotchpotch of reasons for enlisting, unemployment, debt, escaping a pregnant girlfriend(s), or the very certain dangers of nineteenth century mines and factories. Army service offered travel, adventure, and enough to eat, but many families continued to regard enlisting in the army as a disgrace. In the rest of Europe, a compulsory period of military service was a rite of passage, and, in fashionable regiments, a considerable expense too. 'Conscript' implies reluctance, but as Ilana R.Bet-El has pointed out, more than half the men who served in the First World War were conscripts. Reluctant or not, they fought.[6] In the late summer and early autumn of 1914, many photos of eager recruits in their first camps suggest a leisurely boy-scout existence. Reservists, including men who'd served in the Boer War, were recalled at once. Already trained soldiers, it was these men who went straight to France and Flanders.

By the spring of 1915, losses had been devastating. In January, as the Westmorland Gazette reported, the popular 26th Battalion of the Border regiment, home to the soldiers of Cumberland and Westmorland, was still attracting around ten recruits a day. Then, and far sooner than the War Office cared to admit, the number of recruits dwindled rapidly nationwide. Nearly a third of all volunteers came forward during the first eight weeks of the war.[7] OTC trained public schoolboys, Oxbridge undergraduates and bored city workers craving excitement had led the way. In August, young stockbrokers expected to be idle. In the real world, young men were needed to work on the land and in industry. Buried in France, many in mass graves, the dead were at least out of sight. Discharged with shattered minds, missing limbs, eyes and genitals, many of the wounded would never work again. Increasingly, on the streets and in the press, men and women dared to challenge not just the 'war to end all wars' and the horrific casualty lists, but the morality of all war. Debating the morality of our current wars, politicians and journalists frequently quote Thomas Aquinas. His tests for identifying a so-called 'just war' applied to thirteenth century hand to hand combat, not twentieth century mass destruction. Aquinas, as the journalists sometimes agree, was merely editing the perennially difficult New Testament to justify the wars of his own time, when the mediaeval Popes had many divisions.

At the end of March, 1915, a new and vigorous nationwide recruiting campaign began. A month later, a Colonel of the Border Regiment's Territorial Army admitted that they had done all they could by persuasion. Now, reluctant young men must be ordered to fight. Freedom of conscience was a peacetime luxury, attractive in theory, but only après la guerre. That autumn, several months before the Military Service Act became law, two young men in Liverpool were arrested and later sentenced to six months imprisonment for distributing seditious material, contravening the Defence of the Realm Act. Their 'sedition' consisted of quotations from the New Testament. A new crime had been defined. Before long, many would receive far harsher sentences, including, naturally, the Field Punishment torment of 'Crucifixion'.

Over a year earlier, in the frenzied August days, white-collar volunteers like Fred Pulford and his bank clerk colleagues had marched in their tens of thousands to enlist. Offered generous Army rations, poverty and unemployment had recruited the fittest of the underclass, and many more who were very far from fit. Now, healthy young men were no longer so eager to defend 'King and Country'. Nobody, in Government or in the armed forces had been prepared for the grotesque catalogues of death. Like culled cattle, nameless bodies were smothered with quicklime, somewhere in France. Resisted so fiercely as unBritish, conscription had become the obvious solution. Church and state united to deny freedom of conscience. The cynical parody of ' Onward Christian soldiers' is all too accurate -

' Onward Christian soldiers, marching as to war/With the cross of Jesus left behind the door'. Across Britain, leading churchmen were defining the war as a sacred duty and using their pulpits to promote the new faith of patriotism. In this internal war against faith and conscience, patriotism and a travesty of Christian teaching were in deadly allegiance. Addressing his congregation in May, 1916, the Reverend D. Evans explained that the sayings of Christ in the Sermon on the Mount were 'not to be taken literally.' They were coloured by the times in which He lived. (not, obviously, in an occupied country, ruled by a military dictatorship.) Mr Evans knew exactly how Christ would respond to Germans. 'I am sure that if He had been living today, He would not have spoken in soft terms to Germany, whose soldiers, under the cover of culture and religion have done such acts of cruelty and barbarism.' [8]

The prevailing 'muscular Christianity' had rebranded Christ himself as a virile carpenter, a paragon of manliness. Church ministers denounced 'cowards and shirkers' from their pulpits. Christ's own words, as recorded by John: 'Greater love hath no man than this, that a man lay down his life for his friends', were given a patriotic spin. For ' friends', substitute 'country' . Patriots carefully glossed over the context of this teaching, delivered at the Last Supper, the day before the Crucifixion, and four remarkably consistent reports of a political prisoner abused by the military. Anyone who suspects that the abuse of WWI conscientious objectors has been exaggerated might consult the first century evangelists, before turning to twenty-first century Iraq. Other passages of the New Testament seem to have gone awol for the duration, especially the subversive ' Love your enemies, do good to them which hate you' , the surely uncomfortable 'Put up thy sword into the sheath. Those who live by the sword will die by the sword', and the totally unacceptable ' Blessed are the peacemakers, for they shall be called the children of God'. All seriously contravened DORA. Taken literally, without the warning that Jesus hadn't met any Germans, they might indeed prejudice recruitment. Found guilty of distributing such sedition, two members of the Brotherhood Church were informed by the magistrate that they had committed 'the greatest possible disservice to their country.' Only a determined minority allowed mere Christianity to prejudice their patriotism. In churches across the land congregations promised:

' To lay upon the altar / the dearest and the best '.

Ministers of any denomination who dared to speak against the war could be ejected from office, and this attitude persisted long after the war. A Congregationalist, the Rev Seward Beddows of Walthamstow, lost his place after he had contacted the No Conscription Fellowship to report on the abuse of prisoners. Others, such as the Reverend Leyton Richards, of Bowden in Cheshire, regarded their position as untenable and chose to resign. Laymen and women resigned from their original church membership, including some of the Colne congregation who had worked with Arthur Leonard when he took the young millworkers to the Lake District. Some, like Leonard, and Bert Brocklesbury, jailed for a time in Richmond Castle, became Quakers.[9] In Oldham, Lancashire, the Rev. M. P. Davies, minister of the Union St Congregational Church openly challenged the machinery of war and denial of conscience. In a long letter, which was published in the Sunday Herald, on November 14th, 1915, he wrote :

' We are a nation organised for war. Freedom of speech, freedom of the press, and liberty of action have already been sacrificed to the War God.... Conscription is the denial of good government, and the last violation of conscience. No-one can deny that there are thousands in our country of the most law-abiding and worthy citizens, to whom war is a thing abhorred and, rightly or wrongly, they are sincerely convinced that to take human life is a crime, a crime against reason, a crime against civilisation, in its hellish waste of life.' [10]

Mr Davies was recklessly outspoken. This public declaration could have cost him his job and his future in the church. In high office or parish ministry, few Christian churchmen now dared to state their opposition to the war so explicitly. The Bishop of Limerick defended, forcefully, the position of young Irish emigrants, attacked in Liverpool for refusing to join the British army.[11] So long as they returned home, the 'poor Irish emigrant lads' would be safe enough. Eclipsed by the long struggle for independence, conscription wasn't enforced in Ireland, but Russian refugees fleeing the revolution were, in theory, subject to conscription.[12]

Though Pope Benedict XV had argued the case for peace, and in 1914, promoted the idea of a Christmas truce, one English RC bishop announced that no Roman Catholic could become a conscientious objector. In England, Catholics, whose loyalty had been questioned since the Reformation, must be seen to be British patriots and not in allegiance with Rome. The NCF survey of June, 1916, identified only two Roman Catholic conscientious objectors.[13] Many of the clergy actively promoted the war. In a statement on ' The War in the Diocese', the Bishop of Liverpool declared that :

' The War should bring us closer to God, and should make us more spiritual... The first impulse of each and all of us when the war broke out was to offer our service to the troops. We honour their zeal. We are sorry we are not with them. They are doing God's service.' [14]

Others were outspokenly belligerent. At the outbreak of war, as his own sons rushed to enlist, the robust Canon Irving of Hawkshead preached the absolute obligation to serve.' We must fight. The young men must obey the call to manly and heroic duty. Every able-bodied man, certainly the unmarried of fighting age, should follow the example of those who are nobly doing their best for their country.' [15] In a 1916 sermon, Irving was insisting that ' This is a holy war '. In victory, as the father of one dead and one wounded hero, the Canon remained intransigent. Soon after the Armistice, he delivered a fierce condemnation of both Germans and pacifists : ' I suppose all you pacifists will be clamouring for peace with dear Germany, urging ' let bygones be bygones' Keep' em in hell, on Christian teaching, until, in penitent sackcloth, they have paid up.' [16] Understandably, the Canon didn't quote chapter and verse to back this curious item of Christian teaching. Summoned before a tribunal and challenged with the usual questions, one Methodist lay minister declared that he could not defend his wife against a theoretical German attack because Jesus Christ had chosen to be crucified rather than strike a blow. Exempted only from combatant service, the lay minister was ordered to undertake 'work of national importance'. [17]

Patriotism certainly wasn't enough. Throughout the war, true patriots had to perfect hatred. The Defence of the Realm Act licensed something disturbingly close to Orwell's Thought Police. Speaking or writing against the war, or even, by distributing Christian texts, promoting peace, became a crime. Those found guilty of conduct likely to prejudice the Defence of the Realm could face the death penalty, imprisonment, or at the very least, a substantial fine. Christianity was revealed as a seriously inconvenient faith. Caesar, in the form of the British Government, was no longer satisfied with taxes alone. In the police state Britain of 1916, Caesar demanded hearts, minds and unquestioning obedience. Administering the new laws, civil and military authorities faced an opponent more enduring than any weapon. On trial for distributing seditious material, one offender was reminded of his duty to 'Render unto Caesar'. The defendant replied: ' And to God the things that are God's. And when the two clash, God must come first, however regretful we may be.' Found guilty, he was fined £100, with £10 costs. For many working men, this would be close to a year's wages, and their families could face starvation.

One rainswept August afternoon, a troupe of lively Gospel singers were entertaining homeward bound Liverpool shoppers. Unusually for current city-centre road shows, they weren't denouncing fat people, smokers or drinkers. Between lively song and dance routines, young men and women proclaimed their faith in Jesus Christ. Some accents were American, others Scouse, the mood more Edinburgh Fringe than Billy Graham. Neither the music nor the message would be to everybody's taste. No-one could doubt their sincerity. Leaflets were handed out, to anyone with a spare hand. Travelling home on the crowded metro and buses, a few shoppers might read a line or two. Most people were far more interested in the football, Everton v Liverpool, broadcast on vast Orwellian TV screens. The young Christians were in no danger. Nobody would arrest them, nobody would fine them a year's wages. They wouldn't be taken in handcuffs to police cells. After a show trial, they wouldn't face years in jail, in a no-go area, sentenced to hard labour, bread and water, and often, solitary confinement. In Liverpool, though not, of course, anywhere near Downing Street, a bit of preaching in the streets isn't (currently) a crime, and 'Love your enemies' isn't classified as sedition.

Refusing to fight and kill, Britain's resolute ' conchies' paid a heavy price. Some were imprisoned despite clear medical evidence of serious illness, including a case of grand mal epilepsy reported to the NCF by Philip Snowden. Soldiers diagnosed with epilepsy were given a complete discharge, clearly unfit for any military service.[18] Seventy-three conscientious objectors died in custody, all of them men of military age, judged fit for active service. Surviving War Office pension records reveal the permanent disability and sickness of men who had served in the armed forces. As so much evidence was destroyed, the long-term mental and physical health of former conscientious objectors isn't adequately documented, certainly not in official records. Several men suffered long term mental illness. The class and pre-war professional status of dissidents was important. Fenner Brockway, Bertrand Russell and George Bernard Shaw commanded respect. Siegfried Sassoon's temporary anti-war outburst could be set aside. For 'other ranks', including men like Frank Bourne, the position was often very different. How many conscientious objectors and their families endured a lifetime of abuse, exclusion and under-achievement is unknowable. There are no figures for broken friendships, damaged careers or bullied children. Even after the Armistice, though all those imprisoned were released by August 1919, they were disenfranchised for five years. In 1918, they shared this stigma with the Royal Family, peers, criminals, ' lunatics', and women under thirty.[19]

The Peace Pledge Union is in the process of creating a database of known conscientious objectors, but for many reasons, this record is likely to remain incomplete. Frank Bourne's lifetime of dignified silence about his war years was by no means unusual. Many former prisoners chose to remain silent about their time in prison and work camps. Friends and family, although personally loyal and distressed by the men's suffering, continued this silence. In Liverpool, the family of one WWI conscientious objector decided that his private memoirs should remain private. In life, he'd been stigmatised enough.[20] The absence of so many official records is frustrating. In Liverpool, the records of Walton prison, where Fenner Brockway was imprisoned and led his famous hunger protest, have not been available to the City Archives. Archive material deposited by other prisons, including Wakefield, is incomplete. Material considered unlikely to be in the public interest has not been deposited. Lord Brockway's autobiography includes a graphic account of his own imprisonment but many of his fellow inmates have left no such record.[21]

By January 1916, 528, 227 men were already dead, missing, or severely wounded. Once the Military Service Act became law, anyone who claimed exemption from service, for any reason, practical, moral or religious, was sent before a tribunal. Some, running family businesses, or the last son remaining to manage a family farm, argued, often successfully, that the work they were doing was vital for the country. Now, after so many terrible losses in France, men who appeared to be of military age but were not in uniform could be arrested. Underage boys were no longer rushing to enlist. In the twenty-first century, the Western world is shocked by images of African boy soldiers, kidnapped by rival militias, brutalised into killing machines. Armies desperate for manpower don't issue call-up papers. The infantry was always for boy soldiers, willing or not. Cherubino was drummed into the army.[22]

Conscription had been very much a last resort, fuelling bitter disputes in parliament, and the withdrawal of Ramsay Macdonald and the ILP from the Coalition government. Patriotism and unquestioning loyalty to King and Country had been expected to fill every battalion and of course, win the war. In what was still an age of deference, this loyalty had been masterminded and manipulated by the older generation. How many of the excited recruits eager for a fight knew that their elders had already met behind closed doors, offering their young men to the nation ? Remastered and played at something close to normal speed, those 1914 newsreels of young volunteers shift from the traditional concept of epidemic patriotism to something markedly different, more sinister and disturbingly familiar. The strange hysteria of crowd behaviour paralyses rational thought. In black and white at Nuremberg, other crowds marched and cheered like this, sang in chorus, bayed approval for uplifting speeches. Hysteria and the madness of crowds fuelled the bizarre Diana days. In Britain, during the first week of September, 1997, anybody who remained calm and rational was seen as abnormal and even callous. Regret for an accident was nowhere near enough. The national mood demanded public outpourings of grief. In 1914, eager patriotism was demanded and delivered. When the eagerness faltered, patriotism became compulsory and the teachings of Jesus were rebranded as sedition.

The men who drafted the Defence of the Realm Act and then imposed conscription had a singular mindset. Britain was at war, Britain must win that war. To do so, she needed men. If men like Frank wouldn't volunteer, they must be ordered to fight, 'combed out' from wherever they were lurking and evading their duty to Britain. In this context, it's remarkable that the majority of the men who came before tribunals were granted some kind of exemption. Very much could depend on a man's willingness to serve the country in some capacity. In Britain, 16,500 men registered as conscientious objectors. About fourteen thousand of these appeared before tribunals. Fewer than four hundred were allowed absolute exemption, including some exempted on grounds of ill health. Over six thousand were granted partial exemption, and directed to 'work of national importance'. Some five thousand were ordered to serve in Noncombatant units. Many of these refused, because they would be under military authority. Nearly 2, 500 were refused exemption of any kind. In all, over six thousand men refused to accept the tribunals' verdicts, refusing both military service, and anything which contributed to warfare.[23] Once a man was conscripted into the army, in combatant and (technically) noncombatant units, the rules changed. Conscientious Objectors were now defined as soldiers. They were given numbers and military ranks. Subject to military discipline, they could be physically compelled to wear uniform. Unwilling bodies were jerked into a semblance of drill.[24]

The typical sentence for 'absolutists', the men refusing to undertake any kind of war work, was two years hard labour. Like the pre-war suffragettes, absolutists reaching the end of a sentence were released, only to be rearrested and returned to prison to serve another sentence. Writing in the Manchester Guardian, George Bernard Shaw offered their jailers a characteristically waspish solution. Such men were ' virtually under a sentence of death by exhaustion... If we wish to kill them, cannot we shoot them out of hand and have done with it, Dublin fashion ?'[25] All freedom was now strictly conditional, and any hint of sedition was suppressed, often with considerable force. Some areas attracted more than their share of attention. Electing a Labour MP immediately suggested the presence of troublemakers. Pre-war, as Arthur Leonard recognised, many of the working class had strong internationalist sympathies. A campaigner in Merthyr Tydfil, Keir Hardie's former constituency, was initially sentenced to a month's hard labour, simply for distributing leaflets. Released on bail, he was later fined £10, plus £5 'security'.[26] Pacifists here were targeted frequently. The valleys of South Wales were in a difficult position. Coal mining was certainly 'work of national importance' and there was little other employment. If men opposed to the war refused to work, their families would suffer, and few if any of their neighbours would be in a position to offer much financial support. Their cramped terraced houses, described by Ramsay Macdonald as 'not fit for pigs', were owned by the coal bosses.[27] Dissidents risked eviction, and policing could be heavy-handed. At Briton Ferry, near Neath, a meeting of the Independent Labour Party was raided by Superintendent, an Inspector, two sergeants, and a constable. It was here, in March 1916, that Macdonald delivered a passionate speech, denouncing the war as 'the result of secret undertakings and secret diplomacy, without the consent of democracy.' Moving seamlessly from Ecclesiastes to the Sermon on the Mount, he identified with the profoundly unpopular peacemakers.[28]

Lord Derby had wanted to believe in Britain's tradition of voluntary service. The original 'Derby Scheme' invited men to come forward, attesting their willingness to serve. Technically, men who attested actually enlisted, immediately becoming members of the Army, but transferring to the volunteer reserve, to be called on when they were needed. Rather than resort to conscription, Lord Derby had threatened to resign. In a speech delivered in Manchester in September 1915, he expressed regret 'that we should have to go about begging and praying our men to defend their country and their homes.' On September 21st, full page newspaper appeals urged men to volunteer now, while they still could, rather than face the stigma of becoming a mere conscript.

Policing the British Empire, all kinds of men had been willing to serve their country. Volunteering to join the tens of thousands who'd already died 'somewhere in France' was a different matter. Throughout the war, in several letters to his Prime Ministers, Derby would struggle with this reality, and, far more dangerously, the unforeseen consequences of the 'conscience clause' he had supported. The merely reluctant could be shamed as cowards. Derby's letters reveal his inner conflict. He argued, forcefully, that men who had been invalided home for the second or even third time shouldn't be returned to the front. Seriously wounded men who'd been discharged from the army were being targeted in the streets (usually by women), accused of cowardice. Their war office files include many letters pleading for the long-promised badges which might protect them from assault.[29] Reluctant to conscript married men, Derby was profoundly unhappy when these too began to be arrested. He made a very strong case for allowing secondary school teachers to remain in their posts, especially if they were teaching boys approaching military age.[30] There was also, as Lord Derby knew only too well, a sound practical reason for delaying conscription. The War Office wasn't just short of khaki badges. More than a year into the war, they were still seriously under-equipped. No matter how many men volunteered, the Army wouldn't be ready for them.

The Nomads' glimpse of a very different twentieth century survived by chance. In 1962, and also by chance, a remarkable collection of papers was rescued when what was then Cumberland County Council needed a new outdoor centre for its schools. On the western shores of Derwentwater, Hawse End was the perfect choice. Formerly a C.H.A. centre and later, a YHA youth hostel, the old country house had been the home of the wealthy Marshall family. Abandoned in the house and ignored by its recent owners was the complete archive of the No Conscription Fellowship. It's the lost history of police state Britain. In more than seventy files, a passionate battle is fought. On every letter, and, as the paper shortage bites, on every page torn from the front of a book, every scrap of cardboard packaging or blue Home Office prison form, the dates are those of World War I. Like Alec Westmore's story of his Field Ambulance, this is another kind of war. It's a battle for freedom of conscience and free speech, a battle for Britain's hard-won liberties, suddenly withdrawn. Signing letter after letter, many names are familiar, Bertrand Russell, Shaw, Lloyd George, Sylvia Pankhurst, Ramsay Macdonald, Philip Snowden and Norman Angell... Frank Bourne's name isn't among the many cases defended by the NCF, but the story told in these documents indicates the kind of conditions he'd experience. The Marshalls had friends in Frankfurt who knew and loved the Lake District. Wartime letters from the Kniepers and from Emma Bartsch reached

Hawse End via neutral Sweden. From Sweden too, Catherine received a report on Women's Peace Sunday, identifying the wartime suffering of women and children.[31]

Catherine Marshall and her mother had been dedicated campaigners for women's suffrage, working with the nonviolent National Union of Suffrage Societies, rather than the Pankhursts' more aggressive W.S.P.U. In November, 1914, when she was first asked to speak against the war, Catherine suggested, cautiously, that she wasn't sufficiently well-qualified.[32] Catherine's key role has often been underestimated; historians and even many of her contemporaries giving most of the credit to her male colleagues. Opposing first the war itself, and then, increasing military coercion, she quickly became the NCF's de facto leader and chief administrator. The men's names remained on the NCF letterhead, but the official chairman, Clifford Allen, and the secretary, Fenner Brockway, spent much of the war in jail. After a lengthy game of cat and mouse, Bertrand Russell was also imprisoned. The value of Russell's contribution has often been questioned, but Jo Vellacott's recent research into his previously unpublished papers has confirmed the strength of his own convictions, and his powerful contribution to the battle for free speech. Defending freedom of conscience, including his own, he became a spirited and devastatingly articulate member of the Fellowship. At Cambridge, Clifford Allen had been one of Russell's students. Both men were willing to learn campaigning tactics from Catherine.[33]

Catherine herself commanded respect from the peace movement, from political leaders, and from serving soldiers of all ranks. Where she found compassion and humanity among the military she wrote to express her thanks.[34] According to Fenner Brockway, she monitored the whereabouts of imprisoned conscientious objectors so efficiently, the War Office used to phone her to ask in which camp men were being held. Apparently, they were unaware that Catherine herself had instigated the question.[35] Burdened with an almost intolerable workload, she juggled camp and prison records, appeals, attempts to support families, and exhaustive letter writing, to political leaders, to senior churchmen, to newspaper editors, and any other potential supporters, throughout Europe and in the USA. Her status and influence was recognised at the highest levels. On April 10th, 1916, she and Clifford Allen were invited to lunch with Lloyd George.[36]

Catherine's efficiency in monitoring the whereabouts of men in detention didn't extend to her management of NCF finances. Among the many hundreds of documents in the NCF archive, there all too many uncashed cheques and postal orders, together with letters marked 'Destroy', and original documents which should have been returned to the families of conscientious objectors more than ninety years ago. In a personal letter to Catherine, the writer, editor, League of Nations pioneer and 1933 Nobel Peace Prize laureate Norman Angell urged that propaganda should be organised on modern business lines, like any commercial operation. Angell's undated letter is filed with other paperwork from the late spring and early summer of 1916.[37] Modern business efficiency, including the dating of all correspondence, would have to wait its turn. There was a war on. Facing matters of life and death, the NCF battled constantly to publicise the abuse of British prisoners of conscience.

The term is, of course, deliberately anachronistic. In 1916, there were no prisoners of conscience, anywhere in the world. The Declaration of Human Rights came in 1948. Amnesty International was founded in 1960, sending observers to the trial of Nelson Mandela the following year. Jailed, tortured, and initially, even sentenced to death, the political prisoners of WWI relied on amateur support. Conscription into the armed services was law, and the police had a duty to enforce that law. For 'deserters', there could be no hiding place. Like sixteenth century Catholics and Protestants, they could be pursued with ruthless and impressive determination. In a chase, which seems pure John Buchan, one Warrington 'conchie' was hunted down in the Ayrshire hills. Allegedly, he was found milking a goat.[38]

Monitoring regular reports of brutality, conditions in camps and the conduct of tribunals Catherine and her network of NCF volunteers battled with punitive censorship and all the attendant hazards of promoting what was, at least officially, a deeply unpopular cause. Civilian patriots could be dangerously hostile. Catherine herself was lamed for a month by New Zealand members of the Anti-German Union. From Birkenhead camp, one man submitted this report :

' The treatment here is vile. I have been held down whilst my hair has been torn off, and I have suffered much physical abuse. I cannot hold this much longer, without outside aid. They refuse to let me object, and I am forced to obey. I have suffered hell today. Relays of men have had me, one on each arm and one at my back, putting me through all the gymnastics and drills. They kicked my ankles, dragged me on the floor, and continued for two hours in Birkenhead Park before the public. Finally, I had to give in and drill.' [39]

At Wandsworth, the objector Fred Crowsley was 'punched around the square, knuckles rapped, and a walking stick rammed up his nose.' [40] A private soldier contacted the NCF to report that the treatment of C.O's here was 'very bad'. Also writing from Wandsworth, the determined absolutist and Bertrand Russell's bête noire, C. N. Norman reported similar abuse, but remained resolute. ' I have never had any fear that I was not on the right side, and have none now. We have the happy reflection that the future is with us.' [41] Informed that two conscientious objectors had been subjected to ' every manner of ferocious brutality that men can be capable of ', Lieut Col Reginald Freehey expressed approval : ' I am delighted to hear it, and sincerely hope the whole of the C.O.s will be treated in the same way.' [42] Occasional compassion is startling. A month before Easter, 1916, a recruiting officer found himself moved by one man's sincerity. The unwilling recruit, a bricklayer from St Helen's, refused to sign any of the necessary papers. The only option left to the officer, Captain C. E. Pearson, was to place the man under arrest. Pearson then submitted a report to his Colonel:

' The man seems perfectly genuine in his belief, and I do not like to resort to extreme measures until every other means have been exhausted.' [43]

The bricklayer's appeal was dismissed. Approaching Easter, perhaps a few readers of this report found the case strangely familiar. Eminent scholars and simple working men, some of them still boys in their teens, tried to explain to their tormentors why such tactics were bound to fail. One man, now officially 'Private' A. T. Thacker wrote to his mother, explaining the moral wasteland of military orders.' In short, there is not a single commandment in the decalogue I must not break, not a single principle advocated and practised by them which I must not violate if I am ordered to do so by an officer.' [44] On prison paper, another C.O., sentenced to ten years penal servitude, put the case more simply: 'Dear Mum, I am a full blown convict, for refusing to kill or help to kill other men.' [45]

In the 21st century British Army, institutional bullying of recruits remains a serious issue. Overseas, British soldiers' abuse of prisoners of war is ascribed to 'inadequate training'. Investigations into cases of abuse and unexplained deaths are made, but the problem appears to be intractable. In any army, this is how some soldiers behave. During WWI, some were undoubtedly allowed and even encouraged by their senior officers to treat conscientious objectors as fair game. Wandsworth became notorious. The Archbishop of Canterbury, Cosmo Lang, believed that serious abuses were being committed. Abuses were reported from Newhaven, and, according to the report made by Seward Beddows, two conscientious objectors at Seaford Camp had been murdered. Precisely what happened at Seaford is unclear, and likely to remain so, but three prisoners were in a serious condition from their injuries. Officers agreed that there had been 'fairly rough horse-play' on the part of the Essex regiment. The admission is enough. That it was made at all is sufficiently unusual. Men detained at the camp were welcomed and supported by local Nonconformist churches.[46]

Probably the best known and best documented examples of extreme abuse began at Richmond Castle in North Yorkshire, where the story is now recorded in an English Heritage exhibition. Seventeen absolutists were first imprisoned in the castle, then enlisted by force into the uniformed Non-Combatant Corps and sent to France. Visiting the castle today, school parties appear awed. According to a report in the Sunday Chronicle, one man was carried face down around the hilly streets of Richmond. Those carrying him continuously twisted his arms and legs, as they threatened to dash his face against the cobblestones. [47]

In Harwich prison, the Quaker Howard Marten and sixteen other resisters were locked in irons, sentenced to 28 days in dark cells, on bread and water. At Le Havre, and now, officially, on 'active service', Marten and five colleagues, T. C. Brombergh, Rendel Wyatt, C. Barrett, H. L. Stanton, A. C. Ricketts, were sentenced first to 28 days of Field Punishment No.1.[48] Some were roped face down to a barbed wire fence. Tried in France, they were sentenced to death, a sentence, which was, after a long deliberate pause, commuted to ten years penal servitude. Twenty-eight successive days of 'Crucifixion' might appear barely credible, but others were sentenced to almost as much. Sylvia Pankhurst wrote to the NCF in support of a prisoner sentenced to twenty-five days. Like the suffragettes, some men went on hunger strike, which led to force feeding. In Hull prison, conscientious objector W. E. Burns choked to death.[49]

Visiting distant prisons remains a serious problem, especially for families living in poverty, harder still, because the location changes constantly. Fenner Brockway spent time in Chester, Lincoln, Pentonville, Walton, Wandsworth and Wormwood Scrubs. To this day, English prisoners, especially those convicted of serious offences, rarely serve their whole sentence in one prison. Many conscientious objectors were held in restricted areas which could only be visited by those articulate and determined enough to obtain the necessary passport. Visiting Clifford Allen, after she'd secured a passport, Catherine Marshall had to catch a train at 5.30 a.m. If a man had been directed to a 'work camp', rather than an actual prison, family contact was, ironically, even more difficult, and the chances of reporting abuse greatly diminished. Though the regimes were certainly penal, camps weren't legally defined as prisons. Noncombatants in such camps were not entitled to receive prison visitors. Evidence of what proved to be very serious abuse emerged only slowly. At Broxburn, 'manure slaves' were sentenced to filling sacks with dung. Unable to wash or change their stinking clothes, they suffered serious health problems. One of these dung shovellers was a brilliant young doctor. At Edinburgh, Dr MacCallum had graduated as the best surgeon of his year, winning the Mowatt prize for surgery. In Wales, workers at Llandreusant reservoir were forced to sleep in wet bedding, and subjected to constant verbal abuse. Some were found to be suffering from TB.[50]

Prisoners of conscience have been jailed and persecuted throughout history, but the catalogue of routine cruelties reported to the NCF never loses its power to shock. The prisons are British. The men are in jail because they refuse to kill. The commandants were, supposedly, only obeying orders and according to British law, the criminals in their charge were traitors. Throughout the war, faith, philosophy and inconvenient debates on the nature of warfare faced uncompromising militarism, an ideology, which fought with completely different weapons and would never speak the same language. Britain's newest criminal class included many scholars, writers, philanthropists and political leaders, and others who would eventually achieve high office and major honours. In May, 1916, the eminent classicist and internationalist Professor Gilbert Murray, who had originally supported the war, was arrested in Oxford and fined £100. Murray became one of the founders of the League of Nations.[51] In Cambridge, Bertrand Russell was stripped of his Trinity fellowship and eventually imprisoned in Wakefield jail.

Refused a passport to lecture at Harvard on mathematical logic and ethics, Russell planned instead to deliver a series of (ostensibly) philosophical lectures in Glasgow. Overnight, the nature of philosophical debate became a cause célèbre, especially in the upper ranks of the army. Russell suggested to General Cockerill of the War Office that it was almost impossible to avoid sedition, and, with deadly courtesy, asked for guidance.[52] In the early autumn of 1916, the letters exchanged between Russell and the exasperated General Cockerill became an elaborate and unequal duel. Negotiating permission to deliver his lectures in landlocked Manchester, rather than the forbidden territory of Glasgow, which was far too close to key naval dockyards, Russell laces mockery with lethal challenges. Did his own great respect for the ethical teaching of Christ break the law ? Would a philosophical lecture on the 'limits of allegiance to the state' be illegal ? The author of German Social Democracy was unusually well prepared for elaborate philosophical and political debates with the agents of DORA. Exchanges between Russell and the military suggest total incomprehension at the War Office. Correctly, they suspected sedition, or at least, an attitude they'd define as seditious. Equally correctly, they suspected that sometimes, Russell was taking the mickey. Both were true, but Russell's mockery was in deadly earnest. He would not ' follow a multitude to do evil.' Grandson of a distinguished prime minister, the brilliant celebrity academic couldn't be intimidated by a mere General or an upstart Welsh lawyer. Lloyd George - so Russell claimed - 'would prosecute a reprint of the Sermon on the Mount if it interfered with the supply of munitions'. (a statement later hotly denied by Lloyd George. Russell's report sounds exactly like LG. Perhaps the Secretary of State for War realised he'd gone too far.)

Outclassed, General Cockerill withdrew. The curt War Office reply to Russell's final request for information was penned by a secretary. Russell was eventually and grudgingly allowed to deliver his lectures at the Union St Chapel in Manchester, safely far away from any naval shipyards. He refused to give any undertaking to avoid contentious issues - including his 'great respect for the ethical teachings of Christ.' [53] On August 4th, 1916, a police raid had seized all copies of Russell's pamphlet, Two Years Hard Labour . Professionally and personally, Russell was philosophical, taking the long view, arguing that the persecution endured by conscientious objectors had enormously increased their moral weight. ' I would say to the persecutors, you can't defeat such men, you cannot make their testimony of no avail. ' Russell used his own day in court to challenge the military regime :

' I would say to my lords - that whether I personally am committed or convicted matters little, but it is not I who am in the dock, it is the whole tradition of liberty which our ancestors built up through centuries of struggles.'[54]

Found guilty, inevitably, he was fined £100, with £10 costs, or 61 days imprisonment. Unlike many working class C.O.'s, he could well afford the fine. Naturally, he chose prison. His absence left Catherine Marshall even more burdened, and, perhaps understandably, furious with Russell for choosing the 'funk-hole' of prison. She needed the leaven of his irreverence, and also, his genuine concern for her exhaustion.[55]

Setting out his secular, socialist faith in the sanctity of all life, Clifford Allen declared simply that

' To me, war is murder'. Claiming absolute exemption from the provisions of the Act, he refused noncombatant or any conditional service, since all these must contribute directly or indirectly to the prosecution of war.'[56] The terms of the Act didn't protect men like Allen. Religious dissent was problematic enough. Christian pacifists did enjoy limited and decidedly cautious support from some senior churchmen. Recognising the grave difficulties experienced by Allen and other determinedly secular objectors, Catherine Marshall hoped to enlist Nonconformist support for them. The Free Churches would, she hoped 'uphold the principle of respect for freedom of conscience, whatever form each individual conscience may take.' [57]

Offered so-called 'Work of National Importance', men were often tempted to compromise, if only for the sake of their families.[58] Such half-measures might satisfy the Government. Patriots or absolutists, nobody else was fooled, and their families suffered anyway, both personally and financially. The No Conscription Fellowship convention voted to reject Government work schemes. Men who accepted such work would certainly be contributing to the war effort. Conditions were harsh, and the so-called 'wages' derisory. On average, men who might have earned £3 per week as civilians received 26s, most of which was deducted for living costs and as a contribution to their families' upkeep. Bertrand Russell feared long-term moral consequences from such compromise, predicting that 'a good many men will be morally broken, and forever degraded in their own eyes, and that the general level of self-respect will probably be lowered for centuries.'[59]

Russell's letter is dated April 11th, 1916. Five days before the Easter Rising, the Western Front was unusually quiet. Britain and her allies were preparing for the battle that would surely end the war. At Etinéhem, quarantined for measles, Fred Pulford and his comrades were enjoying their brief respite. It was less than a month since their 17th battalion comrade had died during Field Punishment No 1. Reflecting on the long term moral consequences faced by cowards and shirkers was yet another peacetime luxury, of no interest whatsoever to most loyal citizens.

In the trenches, the satirical 'Wipers Times' and its various reincarnations could be allowed to flourish. The authors were decent military men, serving at the front. Pacifist sedition was a different matter. Throughout 1916, police raids on offices, printing presses and even private homes were common. Presses were destroyed. The London flat of the Kendalian pacifist Theodora Wilson was raided. Like samizdat in the old eastern bloc, print runs of twenty five different pamphlets were seized, including up to 10,000 copies of the No Conscription forms, and in Manchester, all copies of a play by Fenner Brockway.[60] Financial, practical or literary, any support for the conscientious objectors could be construed as 'sedition'. Their dependents were even more vulnerable than the families of ordinary criminals. The NCF supported many families, paying the wives of some prisoners to distribute campaign literature. Advertising their work presented many problems. Some organisations refused to accept any No Conscription material. The YMCA, who were closely involved with army training camps, explained that : 'The Military Authorities are very strongly down on us if anything is introduced that savours of controversy.'[61] (How the Young Men's Christian Association reedited tricky passages in the gospels isn't recorded.) NCF workers carefully monitored the British press, identifying supportive editors and recording those articles expressing any degree of support for the conscientious objectors. Writing to Catherine, C P Scott, editor of the sympathetic Manchester Guardian, suggested that the Government recognised the need to moderate the 'excessive zeal' of the military authorities.[62]

By March, 1917, nearly 4,000 conscientious objectors were in prison or in a Home Office 'camp' under penal conditions. In the same month, the NCF received a report that conditions at Dartmoor would become harsher. Punishment would intensify. Fenner Brockway, Clifford Allen, and hundreds of other men were repeatedly imprisoned, sentenced, variously, to hard labour, penal servitude, and solitary confinement. By this stage of the war, the RAMC no longer accepted men who intended to be noncombatants. Stretcher bearers and orderlies could now be ordered to bear arms. Some of the men who'd been serving throughout the war couldn't accept even the possibility of being ordered to use a weapon. Private S. D. Moss, of 3/6 London Field Ambulance wrote to the NCF that he had 'decided to do only work for which I volunteered. I would be pleased to give you a full report, which would be a great testimony against war. Yet ever held at heart the laws of God, greater than the powers of the military. Thou shalt not kill. I would choose to be shot, rather than do 12 months in the infantry... The evil of it, the horror of every deed.'[63]

Despite many searches, press reports of Frank Bourne's tribunal haven't been identified. In press reports, certainly in the Liverpool area, defendants are not usually identified by name. This anonymity defines them merely as 'conchies'. Identified, they might be recognised as respected friends, neighbours, or colleagues. The limited survival of official WWI records for conscientious objectors is the result of a government decision. In 1921, all papers relating to individual cases were discarded, except those of the Central Tribunal. For England and Wales, most of the official papers are gone, only those of the Middlesex Appeals Tribunal surviving. The National Archives of Scotland have only the appeals for Lothian and Peebles. There are other records in the national archives, but pursuing individual cases is difficult.[64]

Why were so many of the conscientious objectors official records destroyed? Given the uncompromising severity of DORA, it's tempting to suspect conspiracy, but caution is essential. The majority, including the glorious dead, had served their country. Records of their loyal service had priority. In 1921, Britain's conscientious objectors were regarded by most of their fellow citizens as a cowardly and disloyal minority. It's just possible that before microfiches and digitisation, many documents really were discarded for want of space. Possible, but still questionable... The stark facts, which are on record speak for themselves. In a culture, which celebrated the so-called just war, Britain didn't need an offshore Guantanomo to contain her 'traitors'. Most loyal citizens thought conchies deserved everything they got, and worse. Often, the police had to protect them from potential lynch-mobs. In sickness, they could be refused medical treatment.[65] The punishment known to all as 'Crucifixion' was torture. So was force-feeding. In British prisons, in the twentieth century, young men suffered and died for their beliefs. Substitute 'faith' for belief, and that record becomes even more shocking. Bertrand Russell, though not himself a Christian, identified their courage and faith with the Protestant and Catholic martyrs of the sixteenth century.[66] In the aftermath of the Iraq war, with terrorism a constant threat, one distinguished scholar of religion and ethics has insisted that:

' Pacifism is not a morally sustainable position in the real world '[67]

Norman Westmore knew nothing more about Frank Bourne. Frank and his wife had been guests at his wedding, but after that, with a career move to London and the demands of a young family, they'd lost touch. The bare bones of Frank's life after WWI had to be shaped from a handful of official records, and the Unilever archives. In 1925, aged thirty-eight, Frank married thirty-seven year old Agnes Hodgins, known as 'Peggy', whose father was employed by Lever Brothers. According to Unilever, his occupation was 'Home Sales'.[68] Just before retirement, in December, 1951, a month before his sixty-fifth birthday, Frank was earning a respectable 196/- per week as a ledger clerk. By June, 1952, he had returned to work, this time as a temporary clerk, paid 120/- for such tasks as sorting soap coupons.[69]

Anticipating the twenty-first century, Frank finally retired at sixty-eight. The summary of his career with Lever Brothers describes his punctuality and attendance as 'Excellent', his work and conduct 'Very Good'. In the space for Remarks, a different hand describes him as 'A quiet, steady, and very reliable clerk.'[70] The brightest maths student of his year at Christ's Hospital School, able linguist, talented musician, and, in his early twenties, a promising photographer, his career might have been very different. He lived to be 97, last of the Nomads, dying in 1984, sixty-eight years after his friend Fred was reported missing on the Somme. Perhaps, in the Wirral archives, there'd be some record of his long life ? In the Eighties, schoolchildren armed with tape-recorders began to ask questions. Frustratingly, all attempts to trace Frank failed. On the Wirral, nobody had interviewed him. Even his house and garden in Greasby were gone, vanished beneath a modern housing development. Frank had disappeared again, and there were still many unanswered questions.

His story was important. Refusing to serve his country by killing other young men or taking any part in the war, even Ambulance work, he faced vilification, imprisonment, and risked serious physical hardship. Reading the reports of their show trial 'tribunals' and the abuse suffered by so many, the faith and courage of WWI conscientious objectors is awe-inspiring. No prison sentence or state sanctioned torture could touch that faith.

Chapter Thirteen

The better course ?

Frank had rejected the frenzied patriotism of ' I vow to Thee, my Country'. Like all the Nomads, he was a practicing rather than token Christian. He would know, word for word, the 'ethical teachings of Jesus Christ', and the history of his name saint. Francis of Assissi was no sentimental bunny-hugger. Born to wealth and trained to fight, he came to reject both wealth and violence. In the twelfth century or the twentieth, young men weren't supposed to take Christianity seriously, to the point of defying their Government. Patriotic clergymen of all ranks did their best to explain that the teachings of Jesus Christ didn't apply to the current situation, and, as Bertrand Russell had observed to General Cockerill, the entire New Testament could be classed as 'sedition'.

Returning to Frank's reflective analysis of two happy days in Normandy, it wasn't entirely surprising to discover that this thoughtful young man became a conscientious objector. Everything about his writing suggests a carefully examined life. Perhaps, as a fluent French speaker, Frank had read Candide, and would understood very well how men have always been eager to conscript their God. Satirising the Seven Years War, Voltaire wrote :

'Enfin, tandis que les deux rois faisaient chanter des Te Deum, chacun dans son camp, il prit le parti d'aller raisonner ailleurs des effets et des causes.' [1]

The causes of any war are as old as humanity. The effects of this particular war are still hideously obvious. Almost every village in Europe has its war memorial, the lists of young lives barely lived. Like Fred Pulford, many are commemorated on memorials to the missing. In Candide, Voltaire describes a village reduced to ashes, like the villages of the Somme, and, in 1944, St Lo, in Normandy, where the Nomads stayed after their idyllic journey through the Forest of Cerisy. Like Alec Westmore, more than 182, 000 British soldiers suffered major physical disabilities. Deaths and serious injuries are at least easy to classify. So is the cost of weapons, and even the astronomical cost of rebuilding Caen, Coventry, Dresden, Hiroshima, Liverpool, London, Warsaw, Ypres, Sarajevo, Dubrovnik, Baghdad, Basra... The price paid by Frank and all the WWI prisoners of conscience doesn't fit easily into any kind of cost/benefit analysis. In their eighties and nineties, men and women talk, at last, about the neighbours their parents shunned as despised ' conchies '.[2]

As a 'conchie', Frank could have been rejected by his family, his colleagues, and even his closest friends. Many papers in the No Conscription Fellowship archive record the hostility of family members. How two of Frank's close friends responded to his decision is very clear and a tribute to their enduring friendship. Asking him to be godfather to their first child, Alec and Gladys Westmore demonstrated the greatest possible respect for Frank's faith and courage. When his elder son Kenneth was born, in September, 1915, Alec was approaching the savage battle of Loos.[3] As a stretcher bearer, he would be in constant danger. The young Westmores couldn't know that Alec would survive, or that they would have three more children. Today, only a minority of British children are baptised, but for parents who do ask for baptism, choosing godparents remains an important decision. The ceremony invites strong personal commitment to that child, until he or she reaches adulthood. In 1915, the Westmores' decision wasn't made lightly. The godfather they chose could soon be supporting a fatherless child. By September, 1915, they knew that, with conscription increasingly likely, Frank could soon be imprisoned. Already, men had been jailed merely for distributing extracts from the New Testament. In quiet counterpoint to the battle plans of generals, Alec's Field Ambulance history pays tribute to the extraordinary courage of the medical services. Frank's was a different kind of courage, but no less remarkable. Frank, the tireless walker, never knew weary marches to billets in hen houses and pigsties, the stinking glutinous mud of Passchendaele or the frozen straw of a barn in Flanders. Each man respected the choice his friend had made.

After one extraordinary and defining moment, rejecting that tragic war, Frank had lived on the Wirral, working hard for his family, caring for his animals and cultivating his garden, as the world descended once more into hell. The main archive connection site, A2A, found no other record of Francis Ramsey Bourne. Searches of the Liverpool, Wirral and National archives failed. But the Bournes had children. They'd played with the younger Westmores. Were they still alive ? If so, could they be traced ? Would they respect the choice their father had made? Or would they be ashamed, stigmatised as the children of a 'conchie' ? Even in the twenty-first century, they might be reluctant to talk. The families of other conscientious objectors had chosen to protect their relative's privacy. This uncertainty ruled against a direct approach, and Bourne is a common enough surname. Once more, publishing an article in the local press was a calculated gamble.

The phone call, when it came at last, offered remarkable and complex news. Frank's grandson had inherited all his surviving personal papers, including boxes of photos and records of other backpacking holidays, some with his 'Nomad' friends, others with quite different young people. There were letters too... On a bad line, the voice seemed hesitant... 'I can't read German, but it's his writing'. Frank's copy of this letter began 'Liebe Freunde' The date was 1910. And the key to this story was international friendship, pioneered by Arthur Leonard and his circle.

Frank's grandson suggested that we meet at his nearest metro station. Across most of Northern England, there'd been a heavy late snowfall. Even on the sheltered Wirral, it was bitterly cold, though the snow cover was lighter. Frank and his wife are buried in the churchyard of St John the Divine, Greasby. Standing by the grave, questions became impossible, because this, at last, was the private man, husband, father, grandfather, friend. In WWI, obeying his conscience, Frank had refused to 'serve' his country. His family had their own version of his life. Historians always have their own agenda, editing the written records to fit their own kind of truth. How much would his family reveal, and want to reveal, about the real Francis Ramsey Bourne ?

The imagined Frank had developed slowly. In the beginning, there'd been all too many candidates. Serendipity led to Norman Westmore, and then, slowly, to the truth about Frank's war. Crucially, Norman had known about Lever Brothers. In 1919, they didn't need to employ a ' conchie'. Frank's later career had been precisely documented, apparently quite ordinary, unless, that is, one happened to know the circumstances in which that career began. Itemised pay slips, good conduct records and a retirement tribute reveal little enough about a man, but thanks to this material, the story of the talented Bluecoat Boy from Spitalfields had emerged. National registration records confirmed his father's early death. In Frank's late Victorian childhood, losing one parent was a common experience. But how had the widowed Emma Bourne reacted to the war, and her son's refusal to fight ? On war graves, many mothers, including widows, claim to be proud of their dead sons. Dishonour not your mothers always has been a strong selling point, especially when young men appear reluctant. Pride in a dead son isn't merely traditional. In times of war, it's almost compulsory. From every conflict zone, coffins return to the UK draped in the Union Flag. Grieving parents proclaim that their son or daughter died serving the country they loved, in the cause of 'freedom'. When the families of soldiers killed in Iraq began to denounce that war, a crucial taboo was broken.

The meeting with Frank's family was held in Meols, at the home of his daughter and son in law. In Greasby, Frank and his wife had been given a plot of land, where they lived for years in a gipsy caravan, till they'd built their own house. Just over an acre, the land gift was possible because Peggy Bourne's family were farmers. Frank's mother, Emma, moved to live nearby, in the same village. She remained close to her son, chose to live near to him for the rest of her life. Identifying only those present on one night, census returns are often misleading. Frank wasn't an only child. There'd been a younger boy, George. Like Frank, he wasn't at home for the 1901 census. A diabetic, George died young.[4]

In France, Frank was the indefatigable guide and interpreter, eager to talk about the stars, even after a punishing twenty mile walk across Brittany in August heat. Energetic and hard-working all his life, Frank never owned a car, cycling to work every day, a return journey of twenty-two miles. Past eighty, he could still walk for miles, exhausting his grandchildren. In the garden, he'd worked happily all day. His grandson remembers a spade, the blade worn away from decades of use. In his nineties, Frank was still cycling, still growing his own vegetables, and music, as always, was his passion. He'd play the piano for hours, tune into Radio 3 for concerts. Like so many who prefer the classics, he was mystified by his grandchildren's strange taste in music, but he cared passionately about their education. In a family photo, taken in his nineties, he looks a happy man, at peace with his world.

The conversation shifted, via Frank's own gifts for mathematics, music and languages, back to history and one man's courageous stance in a world at war. At this meeting, three generations of seven families exchanged ordinary tragedies, our grandparents and great-grandparents, British and New Zealanders, dead, missing, maimed, gassed, the next generation blighted, brought up by grieving women and traumatised men, then a second war, bred from the first. Frank's daughter, Elizabeth, remembered that her father would sometimes begin to talk about Fred Pulford, then stop in mid-sentence, unable to say another word. There was so much he didn't talk about. What became of his relationship with Fred is unknowable. Most civilians scorned 'conchies'. Records suggest that serving soldiers, who knew the reality of war, were far more sympathetic. Frank's silence, and his inability ever to speak about Fred suggests intolerable grief.[5] Elizabeth remembered Alec Westmore clearly, blind in one eye, a thick pebble lense for the damaged but still sighted eye, and the younger Westmore children, coming to play in the garden. Just before WWII, a family called Adler came to stay for a long time, a doctor, his wife, and their children. Her father always spoke to them in German. They were refugees, fleeing the Nazis, but she knew nothing more about them. In Liverpool, no police records of this family survive, but this is by no means unusual. In 1938, as bone fide refugees, fleeing persecution, the Adlers wouldn't have been interned initially, until fears of invasion and a fifth column intensified early in 1940. In Liverpool's strong Jewish community, there were other Adlers, but so far, no members of the family who took refuge with Frank have been traced.[6]

Frank's personal records confirmed that he did nothing lightly. Among his papers is the declaration of faith and commitment he made in 1915 at the baptism of Alec's son. In the sunny room, close to the sea, he would have analysed the exceptional quality of the spring light, enhanced by reflected light from the snow. His photographs, notes, letters and diaries celebrate many journeys, some with the 'Nomads', some with other friends. In Derbyshire, long before the legendary mass trespass on Kinder Scout in 1934 and the postwar creation of National Parks, Frank and his friends walked mostly along country lanes. Apart from the traditional bridleways and 'corpse roads', few paths were legally open to ramblers. One of Frank's albums is simply a photographic essay on the Lake District, with no text at all. Anyone familiar with the Cumbrian fells could follow his route today. The accompanying pen and ink maps are meticulous. Like the map of Northern France, every detail is precise. Just before their 1912 adventure, he'd taken a group photo of the Nomads. Ross, as usual, is on his own, slightly apart from the two couples, Emma and Fred, Alec and Gladys. Before leaving for France, Emma and Fred appear to be close. The young women's hats are gloriously My Fair Lady, nothing like the battered objects occasionally worn in France but far more often squashed into their rucksacks.

All Frank's Normandy photos were stored together. He'd numbered and defined every one of them, including failures not included in the 1912 book. His notes outline many incidents in the Nomads' story, and others too, from the cutting room floor. On the reverse of these quarter-plate photos, Frank's own record of their idyll adds the precision of a zoom lens, giving the time of day, describing how they managed to find food, and at least equally important, how they hunted down the next supply of cider. Frank, the perfectionist, explains the context of one rather mundane rural scene. All photographers will understand this, the one that doesn't quite work, technically accurate but devoid of atmosphere. The Nomads' book doesn't mention harbour porpoises, chased by a motorboat at Le Havre, or the cheaper fares paid by standing passengers on Le Havre's trams. There's no account in the book of how the washerwomen of Bayeux set to work. Frank's record of riverbank laundry methods anticipates Alec's grimmer reports of delousing baths for young soldiers.[7] The young men's fascination with washerwomen seems odd, until one remembers that their own laundry would be sent out or managed by female members of the household.

Surprisingly, Frank's personal papers didn't include a copy of the 1912 adventures. There were many other photos, together with notes and lists of names, some of them German, indicating exactly when and where they'd been taken. Shutter speeds too... The photography had been rather more than a hobby. At twenty-three, Frank was almost a professional, selling his work to support the

C.H.A.'s free holiday scheme. Those who were financially able to give were strongly encouraged to support the 'Goodwill' holidays. Donations from people like Frank made it possible for the poor, adults and children, to enjoy their first ever holiday. CHA guests included a ninety year old man and many children from inner-city slums.[8] Every document Frank had kept confirmed his commitment to Leonard's cooperative ideals.

Meeting Frank Bourne's family, studying the private records of one conscientious objector, the whole story began to make a new kind of sense, linking the idyll in France to the choices made by these young people two years later. Once again, the flashpoint came in summer. All the youth of England were on fire and most of them had no idea why. In Liverpool, the young office workers who marched to St George's Hall, then queued patiently to enlist, knew nothing about the boardroom meetings several days earlier, which had promised their services to King and Country. Germany, or so they were told, posed a terrible threat to Britain. Inflamed by speeches like Lord Derby's and the cheering crowds, they volunteered. It was their duty, and conventionally, the hero of this story is Fred. Many would brand Frank a traitor. Killed in action, Fred made the supreme sacrifice. On the vast Memorial to the Missing at Thiepval, and at his old school, Fred and all the ordinary, brave young men deserve their tributes. They died horribly. But two of the young 'Nomads' made very different choices. Unarmed, but facing the greatest possible danger, Alec served the wounded. Disgraced, and facing the contempt of all loyal citizens, Frank refused to take any part in the war.

The letter he'd written to his German friends is brief, barely half a page. In a novel, surely, even this short note would be heavy with importance, somewhere between Alle Menschen werden Brüder and, in 1910, Anglo-German and Portugese plans for asset stripping on the Baghdad railway. Instead, it's almost absurdly trivial, just a friendly note, accompanying photos of their recent holiday together. Hopefully, next year's will be just as good. This is the complete text :

8, Emsworth Road,

Mossley Hill,

Liverpool,

den 19 Juli, 1910

Liebe Freunde,

Wir hoffen dasz Sie diese Bilde interessanten finden werden, und dasz sie angenehme Erinnerungen erwecken mögen. Auszer den Bilden von Hayfield, haben wir einige von Liverpool, London, unden anderen von den Deutschern besuchten Orten eingeschlossen.

Dasz wir alle eine ebenso fröliche Woche nächstes Jahres haben mögen.

Auf Wiedersehen, F.R. & G Bourne.

(Dear Friends,

We hope you'll find these photos interesting, and that you'll enjoy the pleasant memories they awake. As well as the photos of Hayfield, we have some of Liverpool, London, and others, which we took of the German visitors. Let's hope we all enjoy an equally happy week next year ! See you,)[9]

But who were these friends ? And how long had Frank known them ?

The reference to Hayfield, a small town on the northern edge of the Peak District, indicates that the Bourne brothers had spent time with their German friends at Park Hall, a small country house, which had been leased as a C.H.A. hostel since 1902. Rents for such houses were low. Long before WWI, big houses, especially in rural areas, couldn't easily source or keep staff.[10] C.H.A. records confirm that many young Germans stayed at Park Hall in the summer of 1910. On July 2nd, 1910, four parties from Frankfurt's Ferienheimgesellschaft arrived in Britain. Accommodation had been arranged for them in university hostels, with host families, and at C.H.A. centres all over the UK. According to which tour they chose, the visitors could explore the UK from Beachy Head to the Scottish glens and Arran. In Wales, the energetic could climb Snowdon with Arthur Leonard. In Scotland, there were ascents of Ben Ime and Ben Lomond. [11]

Frank's letter indicates that he was one of the C.H.A. hosts for the second party. Exploring first historic London, then Oxford, then Stratford, the first week appears conventional enough, ostensibly similar to other touring holidays of this period, but the status of their hosts and lecturers is striking. Fusing education with adventure and music, Arthur Leonard had always recruited the ablest people he could find, no matter how demanding their other commitments. Dr Alex Hill, Master of Downing and the distinguished churchman, Canon Rawnsley, founder of the National Trust and vicar of a busy parish were clearly ideal.[12] Exploring historic London, the party's guide was the distinguished architect, Phillips Figgis. The Paton family connection continued, Mr Figgis was Lewis Paton's brother in law. In Oxford, where they stayed at a boarding house on Iffley Road, their host was the professor of German, Hermann Fiedler. In Stratford, they were received by the actor-manager Frank Benson, Director of the Shakespeare Memorial Theatre.[13] Apart from a day trip to Liverpool and Port Sunlight, the party spent most of their second week in the Peak District, hillwalking and visiting stately homes. Frank's letter refers to photos taken in London, Hayfield and Liverpool, which he was forwarding to Germany. In a photo taken in Hayfield on July 9th, 1910, Frank, who had joined them for the second week, is standing in the back row. Several members of the group are young men in their early twenties and late teens. That same summer, over fifty members of the Deutsche Freie Studentenschaft stayed in Oxford, and the German flag flew over the university press. [14] When war broke out, they'd be ordered to fight for their country. In Germany, conscientious objection was never an option.

Staying at mountain huts would have been considerably cheaper than the Hotel Taunusblick, but the German idea of simplicity was more spartan and adventurous than anything the C.H.A. had yet dared to offer its English members.[16] Frank would have no problem at all. On the flyleaf of another collection of photos, he quotes Stevenson :

' Discomfort, when it is honestly uncomfortable, makes no nauseous pretensions to the contrary, and is a vastly humorous business. People who sleep stupefied in the open air are in good vein for laughter.' [17]

Backpacking in France, in the cold and rainswept summer of 1912, Frank and his friends knew all about chosen discomfort, laughed at their daily drenchings and the routine thunderstorms.

The most intriguing aspect of the 1910 visit is the time they spent at Port Sunlight. Two of the Ferienheimgesellschaft parties spent a day at this garden city. Intelligent town planning is, of course, vital for the health and well being of all urban communities. As a holiday diversion, the subject seems curiously unappealing, especially for people in their teens and early twenties. Why would so many young people spend a whole day studying a company town where people made soap ? Why not stay longer in Oxford or Stratford, enjoying Britain at its best ? The timing of their visit gives part of the answer. Students visiting garden cities might not remember the ravages of cholera and typhoid. Their parents certainly would. T.B. was still a killer. In Britain, in Germany, and throughout the world, the Garden City movement was an important and valuable development. The movement wasn't without its critics. Priestley, in his English Journey, would ridicule the controlled world of Bournville, but he didn't volunteer to live in the back streets of Salford or any other of the classic slums. In its infancy, western industrialisation had spawned vile rookeries and cellars, back to back houses and foetid tenements, first in Britain, then across Northern Europe. The slums of Manchester became an international byword for the disease and misery of industrialisation, inspiring a gamut of political treatises and harrowing novels. Tourists could read all about the condition of the working class in England, their very hard times, the gulf that divided two nations, the other worlds of North and South. Travelling by rail to enjoy Derbyshire, the Lake District and Scotland, tourists could see more than enough of the dark and disease-ridden northern cities from the train.

Industrialists learned, slowly, that a sick, stunted and strife-ridden workforce isn't cost effective. In 1887, founding their 'garden village' of Port Sunlight, Lever Brothers established the highest possible standard of living for their workforce. Paying unfeasibly modest rents for the village's picturesque cottages and generous allotments, employees enjoyed their own schools, hospital, public baths, park, bowling greens and sports fields. In strictly financial terms, the cost to Lever Brothers made no economic sense. As an investment in their employees, the return was incalculable.[18] In the same year, arriving to work in another company town, twenty-three year old Arthur Leonard confronted the 'rough, tough and insanitary ' urban wilderness of Barrow in Furness, where industry had allowed an unplanned but substantial town to happen, with little or no thought for the health, let alone the happiness of the workforce. Barrow isn't listed in any of the Ferienheimgesellschaft itineraries. They'd know what to expect. The recipe for slums, sickness and social breakdown had been known for decades.

On websites and on the high street, travel agents don't offer city breaks in Peterlee, Skelmersdale, or even Milton Keynes. In the first decade of the twentieth century, visitors crossed continents to visit Port Sunlight. Lever Brothers' visitors' books include names from Australia, Canada, Ceylon, Japan, Russia, South Africa and New Zealand.[19] In 1909, there were over fifty thousand visitors, including hundreds of German members of the Garden City Movement. Port Sunlight's worldwide reputation attracted finance ministers, former prime ministers, engineers, doctors and of course, a plethora of architects. On the eve of the first global war, the financiers, planners, consuls and medical officers of health were all studying the art of living well, creating good environments for work and leisure.[20] It's safe to assume that few, if any, of these distinguished visitors would be interrupting a week of backpacking in the Peak District. Most would be safely beyond military age. In July 1910, the visitors from Frankfurt experienced the very best Britain could offer, from the historic sights of London and the university of Oxford, to the mountains and glens of Scotland. Arthur Leonard and his friends in the Ferienheimgesellschaft thought they should see Port Sunlight too.

Years before the arrival of these organised parties, German students had already discovered the attractions of C.H.A. holidays. Among Leonard's own papers is Franz Crämer's 1903 review of 'Ein Studienaufenthalt in England', by the linguist, Adolf Reusch. Crämer himself was a historian and teacher from the Eifel, who would later attend key C.H.A. meetings in Northern England.[21] Reusch's engaging account of a C.H.A. holiday in Whitby begins by challenging Iago's cynical 'Put money in thy purse'. In a German educational journal, his readers were, of course, expected to recognise and understand the quotation from Othello. Iago, true to form, was manipulating and exploiting Roderigo. Supported by willing contributors like Frank, Leonard's cooperative movement took a different approach to funding travel.[22] Supporting the genuinely disadvantaged was voluntary. Moving swiftly from Othello to the seventh century poet, Caedmon of Whitby, 'Ein Studienaufenthalt in England' celebrates an exhilarating and unusual holiday. Leonard aimed to bring young people of all incomes and backgrounds together. At Whitby, he seems to have succeeded. Reusch recognised accents from all parts of Britain, from Cockney to Scottish. The mixed sex hostelling scandalised many townspeople, who had, apparently, forgotten the history of their ancient abbey, where Abbess Hild of Whitby had been the head of a foundation for men and women. (As a serious scholar, Reusch doesn't, of course, mention Count Dracula's recent visit to the town.)

In the spartan Abbey House, bedrooms were shared and so were household chores. They cleaned, not their own but each other's muddy boots. (an important distinction) On the North Yorkshire coast, sandcastles were built. Studying geology, botany and the coal industry was just as important as the energetic walks. Even their approach to music was democratic and versatile. Reusch seems mystified by the ease with which his British companions move from singing a Bach chorale to the latest popular hits. Like the Nomads in France, the young guests didn't want to be mere tourists. Climbing the arduous 199 steps up to the Abbey was their only concession to tourism. Professionally, Reusch recognised a superb environment in which to master a language, enjoy an outdoor centre, and make many new friends. Both he and Crämer supplied Leonard's address, advising readers to send for a C.H.A. brochure.[23]

According to Leonard, German groups begin to join C.H.A. holidays the following year.[24] By the time of Frank's 1910 holiday with his German friends, the programme of student exchange visits and shared holidays for young people was firmly established. In Britain and Germany, the project was welcomed and supported by political leaders, academics and many schoolteachers. Speaking the languages of Europe was vital, not just for unwilling schoolboys but for young workers planning holidays abroad. Published in Manchester, the C.H.A. journal, Comradeship, delivers this message in almost every issue. Travelling to other countries should never be an end in itself. Mastering, or even struggling with a new language is part of the adventure, an essential skill in forming real friendships. Advertisements for British summer staff specify that they should be able to speak German or French, and ideally both.[25]

Two years after Franz Crämer and Adolf Reusch reported on Leonard's project, Dr Max Walter, gave lectures in London and at Oxford on modern language teaching. At Cambridge, in the same year, Dr Walter of the Musterschule and Dr Reinhardt, of the Goethe Gymnasium, visited the linguist, Dr Karl Breul, who would later become the university's first professor of German. As a linguist, Breul's career had been dedicated to promoting the study of German and German literature in Britain, and in both countries, understanding of each other's culture.[26] At Manchester Grammar School, Lewis Paton was promoting modern language skills, stressing the importance of beginning early, certainly before the age of fourteen.[27] Their shared commitment to language teaching extended far beyond the tutorial or classroom. Anticipating the multilingual community of Europe, these linguists recognised the crucial value of learning each others' language and experiencing every aspect of another culture. French was, as the realists in Germany recognised, the current lingua franca of diplomacy. (Only the Vatican still conducted its business in Latin.)

Dr Walter and Dr Reinhardt encouraged their students to study mathematics, sciences and modern languages, rather than the Latin and Greek still favoured by most English public schools. Like the travelling scholars of earlier centuries, German students, speaking two or more modern languages could move between the ancient universities of Europe. In that first decade of the twentieth century, it was natural enough for students from Germany to spend time studying at Oxford and Cambridge.[28] Frank Bourne's thoroughly modern education at Christ's Hospital School had equipped him equally well. In 1910, he was well qualified to serve as one of the Ferienheimgesellschaft's C.H.A. hosts. In July, 1913, walking in the Chilterns, Frank enjoyed another holiday with German friends. More photos were taken and shared. In 1916, rather than deny his conscience and betray that friendship, he chose disgrace, facing the harshest punishment the state could impose.

Designed by Lutyens, the Thiepval Memorial commemorates 72,090 men.

Alec describes the conditions at 'Clapham Junction' on September 26th 1917.

Chateau Wood, boarded track, October 1917, as described by Alec.

Alec Westmore   Embarkation Photo 1915

Copyright Norman Westmore

The Story of the 63rd Field Ambulance

(2/2 West Lancashire Field Ambulance T.F.)

1914 - 1919

————

By

A. W. WESTMORE.
M. THOMSON.
J. E. ALLISON, B.A.

————

Printed for the 63rd Field Ambulance Association.

Hon. Secretary—A. W. WESTMORE,
23 Roxburgh Avenue,
Higher Tranmere.

Passchendaele, Battle of Pickem Ridge, 1917.

PROGRAMME

Selection........	The Smithy in the Estaminet.	THE BAND.
Song............	Another little Drink won't do us any Harm.	O.C.
Recital.........	Oh! let me see thy Foot prints.	Pte MOSS.
Clarinette Solo.	The Snake Charmer.	Pte MEEK.
Song...........	"Marching, marching, marching, Always.........marching".	S.Sgt. MOORE.
Stump Speech...	Iodoform, its use and abuse.	Sgt. MASSEY.
Song...........	If those lips could only speak !	Pte T.G. WILLIAMS
Concerted Item.	Pay ! Pay !! Pay !!!	THE CLERKS.

During the Interval, S. Sgt. Major MANNING, and his Gun Team will give an Exhibition of Marksmanship.

(NOTE.- Rifle Pattern 1799, Mark 606 only will be used in this performance.)

Chorus..........	Dixie Land.	THE COOKS.
Song....	Where does Daddy go when he goes out ?	Lt. Q.M. PRICE.
Humorous Song.	I wonder why ?	M. CRETIN.
Recitation.......	The Rear Admiral.	Pte WHALLEY.
Song...........	Work, for the night is coming !	Sgt. ARNOTT.
Cornet Solo.....	Cherry Blossom.	Dr COLLINS.
Monologue......	It's a way they have in the Army.	Pte BLAIR.
Sketch..........	Box & Cox.	L.Cpl. THIRSLEY. Sgt. BROYARD. and No 1 Coy.

GOD SAVE THE KING

Menu & Programme.
Xomas, 1916.

63RD FIELD AMBULANCE
(W.La.&Cs. I.F.)

B.E.F. FRANCE.

Motor Ambulances collecting wounded in the ruined village of Mametz, July, 1916. (63rd Field Ambulance).

I.W.M. Photo. Copyright Reserved).

Captains : W. F. Young, C. Brennan, J. D. Adamson, O. D. Price, M. Cretin (Interpreter).

Rev. B. Marshall, C.F., Major R. Storrs, Capt. J. H. Mather, Capt. J. R. Thierens.

L'Institution St. Jude, Armentieres, December 1915

Roll of Honour

"Their Name Liveth for Evermore."

Rank	Name		Cause	Date
Private	JOHN BENNETT BOOTH	...	D-of-w	20 Dec., 1917
Sgt.-Maj.	WILFRED BROOKE, D.C.M., M.M., C., de G.	...	D	26 July, 1920
Private	ALBERT BURROWS	...	K-in-a	21 March, 1918
Private	DAVID COPLAND	...	D-of-w	29 April, 1918
Private	GILBERT SOMERVILLE COMRIE	...		6 Oct., 1918
Private	SYDNEY LEO CURL	...	K-in-a	21 March, 1918
Private	ALEXANDER CAMERON ELLACOTT		K-in-a	6 Oct., 1917
Captain	CLAUDE HENRY FISCHEL	...	K-in-a	14 Sept., 1918
Private	HAROLD HALE	...	K-in-a	25 April, 1918
Bugler	GEORGE W. HALES	...	D	23 Nov., 1918
Private	ALFRED HORNBY HARTER	...	D-of-w	11 Oct., 1917
Major	ROBERT CHARLES IRVINE	...	D	10 Nov., 1918
Sgt.-Maj.	GEORGE W. ISAAC	...	D	22 Nov., 1918
Corporal	FRANK DUNCAN JEFFREYS	...		5 March, 1916
Private	WALTER EDWIN KNIGHT	...	K-in-a	26 Aug., 1918
Private	FRED LAMB	...	D	30 Nov., 1918
Private	GEORGE WILLIAM LEATHER	...	D-of-w	27 Oct., 1917
Private	E. LEWIS	...	D	28 Nov., 1918
Private	FRED LORD	...	D-of-w	9 July, 1916
Private	WILLIAM MARTINDALE	...	K-in-a	6 Oct., 1917
Private	WILLIAM NOWELL	...	K-in-a	15 Aug., 1918
Private	THOMAS RIMMER	...	K-in-a	9 April, 1917
Private	HERBERT ROBINSON	...	D	5 March, 1916
Private	JOHN ARTHUR STRUGNELL	...	D-of-w	26 March, 1918
Private	HAROLD CELLIS WALKDEN	...	D-of-w	9 Oct., 1918
Driver	JOSEPH MOON, A.S.C.	...	K-in-a	3 July, 1918
Private	SIDNEY NIGHTINGALE, M.T.	...	K-in-a	1 June, 1918
Corporal	W. WISEMAN, M.T.	...	D-of-w	Oct., 1917

"They shall not grow old, as we that are left grow old;
Age shall not weary, nor the years condemn,
At the going down of the sun, and in the morning,
We will remember them."

LAWRENCE BINYON.

WANTED

SPLENDID OFFER!

CAPABLE MANAGER

for recently constructed

FAT-PLANT

Applicants must have experience in control of

MACONOCHIES

Apply "LU. LU."
BOX-RESPIRATOR.

AN OVEN FOR A PENNY.

FOR 3 YEARS OR DURATION ONLY!

FREE SAMPLE OVEN

Write at once, enclosing a penny stamp for carriage

TELEGRAPHIC ADDRESS:—
"MALONEY."

'Tis not in Mortals to command Success. "But we do more, deserve it".

TESTIMONIALS FROM ALL PRINCIPAL H.Qs!

BRICKLAYERS, BOOTMAKERS, CARPENTERS, CYCLISTS, CINEMA OPERATORS, CLERKS, COOKS, CHEFS, CHEMISTS, CHIROPODISTS, DECORATORS, DISPENSERS, DRAUGHTSMEN, DENTISTS, ELECTRICIANS, FARRIERS, FINERS, MINERS, MUSICIANS, PAINTERS, POST-IRONMONGRFR, ROAD-MAKERS, TINSMITHS, TYPISTS, VALETS, WASHERMEN, etc.

Supplied at an hours notice **Moderate Fees!**

APPLY E J KAVANAGH CO. BEF

ALEXANDER'S RAG-TIME BAND

HAVE YOU HEARD IT? IF SO, WHY NOT?

PERFORMANCES DAILY

Conductor. Herr Von UZZELL, F.L.A.T. (Fellow Liverpool Ass'n Trombonists)

Patronise DARKIE'S COSY KITCHEN!

Pommes de Terre frites. Œufs et Café au Lait.

Tres beans. Quatre sous!

Always open! Always Ready!! Always Gay!

ALLEMAN NO BON!

N.B.—Owing to an undoubted testimonial from a well-known personage temporarily suspended during structural alterations.

WHITE, WASH, & Co.

We undertake all branches of structural alterations.

CHATEAUX A SPECIALITY

CELLARS CONVERTED INTO CASTLES

DUG-OUTS MADE DRAWING ROOMS

Proximity to Trenches no object

TELEPHONE F.A. 63.

G. Baker. J. Rotherham. D. Rimmer. Sgt. H. Watson. G. Meek. S. Leech. J. Fennett. F. Lamb.
W. Clemas. W. Butterworth. Sgt. D. Conway. G. Hales. R. Greenwood. W. E. Kneale. J. Micklewright. J. Owens. J. Leech.
S. Cheetham. J. Challinor. H. Gayton. W. Bidston. Sgt. Uzzell. P. Collins. J. Booth. H. Walkden. R. Howard.
A. D. Thorne. H. Hodgkinson.

Independent Labour Party, Dartmoor Prison Branch, September 1917.

PLEASE READ FIRST THE PERSONAL NOTES ON THE OTHER SIDE

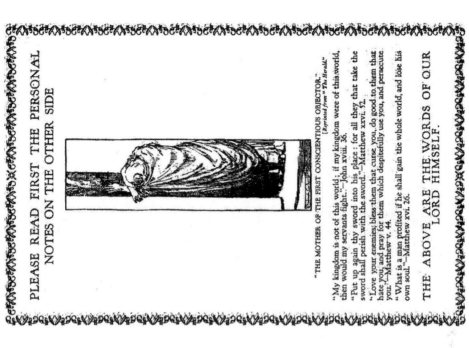

"THE MOTHER OF THE FIRST CONSCIENTIOUS OBJECTOR."
[Reprinted from "The Herald."]

"My kingdom is not of this world; if my kingdom were of this world, then would my servants fight."—John xviii. 36.

"Put up again thy sword into his place : for all they that take the sword shall perish with the sword."—Matthew xxvi. 52.

"Love your enemies; bless them that curse you, do good to them that hate you, and pray for them which despitefully use you, and persecute you."—Matthew v. 44.

"What is a man profited if he shall gain the whole world, and lose his own soul."—Matthew xvi. 26.

THE ABOVE ARE THE WORDS OF OUR LORD HIMSELF.

A young member of the

WELSH TABERNACLE
KING'S CROSS

IS SUFFERING PERSECUTION FOR CONSCIENCE' SAKE

HIS NAME is JOHN RICHARD REYNOLDS of 87 East Street Buildings, Manchester Square, W. He was arrested on March 5th, remanded for a week, and yesterday (March 13th) delivered over to the Military. He is nineteen years old.

HIS OFFENCE is that he takes literally the words of Christ, and wishes to follow what he believes to be His teaching. He is a conscientious objector to military service. He is anxious to do any work of national importance that is not part of the machine for killing.

THE TRIBUNAL acknowledged the sincerity of his convictions, but gave him no relief. The so-called "non-combatant" corps to which he was ordered is as integral a portion of the Army as the Army Service Corps or the Royal Engineers. Reynolds will not himself shed blood, and this means to a conscientious man that he will not help any one else to shed blood—he will not kill by proxy.

MANY conscientious objectors are now in irons, in solitary confinement in dark cells, under the absolute and secret control of the Military. Their crime, like Reynolds', is that they have stood to their consciences.

ARE YOU CONTENT (whether you yourself are a pacifist does not matter) THAT THIS SHALL BE THE FATE OF ONE OF YOUR MEMBERS?

P.T.O.

WHY I STILL RESIST

BY CLIFFORD ALLEN

CHAIRMAN OF THE NO-CONSCRIPTION FELLOWSHIP

The text of this leaflet is the Defence made by Clifford Allen on 25th May, 1917, at Parkhouse Camp, Salisbury Plain, before his third Court-Martial. He had then already served two sentences of Hard Labour, "amounting to nine months' actual imprisonment," on the completion of each term having been returned immediately to his military unit and again put under arrest within 48 hours. The sentence of the third Court-Martial had not been announced before this leaflet went to press.

A S this is my third trial by Court-Martial for the same offence of refusing to obey military orders, I do not propose to take up the time of the Court by a lengthy repetition of my general views on war and militarism.

In order, however, to comply with the provisions of Army Order X, dated May 25th, 1916, I claim the right to explain why I continue my refusal to acknowledge military authority; I need hardly say that no personal discourtesy or lack of respect to the officers in command is intended by my decision.

A CRIMELESS CRIMINAL

May I remind the Court that there has never been any question about the genuineness of my opinions since the date, over a year ago, when the Statutory Appeal Tribunal unanimously exempted me from all kinds of military service, combatant and non-combatant. My only offence now consists in my declining the repeated attractive offers of the Government to release me if only I will become a party to the Conscription Acts by under-taking some form of civil work imposed as a condition of my exemption or release. I have chosen to serve sentence after sentence of Hard Labour rather than secure my discharge from

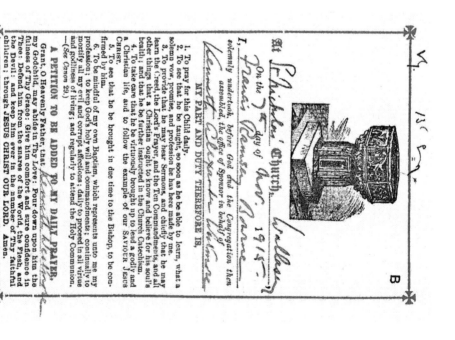

At St Philips' Church.
On the 5th day of Nov. 1915.
I, Francis Clements Browne
solemnly understood, before God did the Congregation then assembled, the office of Sponsor in behalf of
Kenneth Alexander Wilmore

MY PART AND DUTY THEREFORE IS,

1. To pray for this Child daily.
2. To see that he be taught, so soon as he be able to learn, what a solemn vow, promise, and profession he has here made by me.
3. To provide that he may hear Sermons, and chiefly that he may learn the Creed, the Lord's Prayer, and the Ten Commandments, and all other things that a Christian ought to know and believe for his soul's health; and that he be further instructed in the Church Catechism.
4. To take care that he be virtuously brought up to lead a godly and a Christian life, and to follow the example of our SAVIOUR JESUS CHRIST.
5. To see that he be brought in due time to the Bishop, to be con-firmed by him.
6. To be mindful of my own Baptism, which represents unto me my profession; to keep God's holy will and commandments; continually to mortify all my evil and corrupt affections; daily to proceed in all virtue and godliness of living; and regularly to attend the Holy Communion. —(*See Canon* 29.)

A PETITION TO BE ADDED TO MY DAILY PRAYER.

Grant, O Heavenly Father, that Kenneth Alexander my Godchild, may abide in Thy Love: Pour down upon him the fulness of Thy Grace: Give him comfort and sure confidence in Thee: Defend him from the snares of the World, the Flesh, and the Devil: and keep him ever in the number of Thy faithful children: through JESUS CHRIST OUR LORD. Amen.

[TURN OVER.

S.P.C.K., No. 1681.

Chapter Fourteen
Liebe Freunde

On a June morning in 1909, just over a year before Frank Bourne's holiday with his German friends, a party of British walkers arrived at Frankfurt station. Catching an early train, they'd travelled from Kelkheim, which was their base for exploring the Taunus. The timing was no accident. Tension between the 'cousin nations' was mounting rapidly, inflamed, according to Ramsay Macdonald, by powerful press barons with their own agenda.[1] Asquith's government, which had initially halted the building of warships, was planning eight more Dreadnoughts for Britain's already powerful navy. Under threat, Germany was, inevitably, expanding her own fleet.[2]

Meeting at Frankfurt station, German hosts and British guests knew this only too well. A few days earlier, the British visitors' arrival in Kelkheim hadn't gone unnoticed. Greeted by the Bürgermeister, Herr Phillipp Kremer, they were expected and welcome guests. In Frankfurt, the welcoming party included Dr Max Walter, Direktor of the Musterschule, Dr August Lorey, and the city architect, Dr Julius Hülsen. The man who'd planned their ambitious visit to Germany was Arthur Leonard. Leonard believed still that it was possible to heal Britain's damaged relationship with Germany. In 1909, many of his friends in the emerging Labour Party shared this determined optimism. School exchange visits were already proving successful. Travelling during the Whitsun holiday, when students and school pupils would be taking examinations, the group Leonard had brought to Frankfurt were older. Surviving photos in Kelkheim and in the C.H.A. records show young people who appear to be in their early twenties, together with some older adults.

In Frankfurt, the British party might have been visiting royalty. At the Cathedral, they enjoyed an organ recital in their honour. At the Rathhaus, they were welcomed by OberBürgermeister Franz Adickes, one of the founders of Frankfurt's university. Adickes' long career had directed the city's transformation.[3] No British mayor or Lord Mayor from this period could match his international status, politically or academically. Franz Adickes and Frankfurt's leading schools evidently wanted this project to succeed. Years before the first C.H.A. visit to Frankfurt, teachers and pupils at the Musterschule had been working closely with Lewis Paton and his pupils at Manchester Grammar School. In 1909, the High Master and his pupils were still committed to the Anglo-German enterprise. Exchange visits were planned with great care, introducing pupils to their host families and often continuing the relationship long after the original visits ended. Several boys accepted the invitation to stay longer. The reasoning was simple. Alice, at the Looking Glass banquet, learned that it isn't etiquette to cut any one you've been introduced to. In Frankfurt, welcoming their English guests, the Deutsche Englishchen Verstandigungs Komite declared their commitment to peace :

'We know of no possible ground of a serious quarrel between the two countries. On the contrary, we find in their history, their common faith and long friendship, their mutual interest in literature, science and art the strongest reasons for the maintenance of cordial and friendly relations'.[4]

In the city's council chambers, speech after speech celebrated the British 'invasion'. Visits such as this would undoubtedly correct any misunderstandings between nations. German and British photos both refer to the 'invaders'. All day long, Leonard's party explored the city, visiting the Stadel Art Gallery, the museum, and the new concert hall. Invited to sing for their hosts, the rucksack diplomats obliged. Armed with their songbook, widely known as le petit livre vert, their repertoire was already international, including Tannenbaum, Gruss den Walde, Die Lorelei and many traditional songs from other European countries.[5] Perhaps some of the British party enjoyed the lecture on the use of local taxation to fund municipal improvement ? Perhaps the finer points were lost in translation? Knowing Franz Adickes' worldwide reputation, academically and as the administrator of a great city, Arthur Leonard would surely listen attentively. Nearly ten years earlier, his own passion for living well in a life-enhancing environment had inspired his approach to Patrick Geddes, who had welcomed the vacation use of Edinburgh university accommodation and at the Outlook Tower introduced some of the earliest C.H.A. parties to his radical vision of mankind's place in the world. A 1901 report in the Edinburgh Globe confirms the very modest cost of accommodation, 32s 6d, for a week's board and lodging in halls of residence, with an additional fee of 5s to take part in lectures and excursions. Based at the 'Outlook Tower', C.H.A. students worked with many distinguished academics from Edinburgh and other universities.[6]

The merits of local taxation and town planning might be a minority interest, especially for younger visitors. International friendship was the great goal, encouraging young people to share holidays in the British and German countryside. Enabling those with very little money to take part was important. In Frankfurt, the Ferienheimgesellschaft was founded later that year. Berlin quickly followed suit, forming the Vereinigung der C.H.A. Freunde.[7] Mountaineering and hillwalking had long been a privilege reserved for an international elite, educated at the ancient universities. Founded in London in 1857, the Austrian, British and German climbers of the Alpine Club claimed the rarified world of the high Alps. A network of high altitude mountain huts offered access to the highest peaks and dramatic ridges. At twenty-seven, Leonard dared to invade an equally rarified world of upper-class and intellectual privilege, bringing his Lancashire millworkers - the despised 'toiling millions' - to the gentler hills of the English Lake District. Now forty-five, his attitude to hostility between nations was equally direct and very far from naive. As the British government poured money into the Dreadnought programme, Leonard and his friends in Frankfurt were refining their plans for shared holidays, the surest route to international friendship.[8]

At the heart of every iconoclastic enterprise was Leonard's increasingly radical faith, inseparable from his equally radical politics. Many found his faith dangerously unconventional and his politics subversive. In his early career, he had tried, admittedly with only moderate success, to overcome Britain's class barriers. His response to the mounting suspicion and fear of Germany was characteristically optimistic. Militarism in Britain and Germany threatened the whole of Europe. Mutual hostility and suspicion was a recent development. Britain's former relationship with Germany had been unsettled by the shifting ententes and alliances of the early twentieth century. Leonard's consciously diplomatic C.H.A. project and the school exchanges were exactly contemporary with William Beveridge's research visits to Germany, studying the structured German approach to unemployment [9]

The high profile welcome in Frankfurt followed months of careful preparation. In September, 1908, Leonard travelled to the city to visit Dr Walter and Auguste Lorey.[10] He wanted to explain exactly what the C.H.A. was trying to achieve, how the project had begun among the mill-workers of Lancashire, and how he hoped it might develop internationally. Leonard's own account of this mission emphasises that securing practical support for the Kelkheim project was secondary. Educated in Heidelberg, he'd have no problem arranging accommodation and transport. Leonard hoped that Dr Walter and Dr Lorey would help the British visitors to meet local people. An outline of this project had been submitted to the Deutsche Englischen Verstandigungs Komite. Months before the first British travellers arrived, Leonard also wrote to the newspapers in Frankfurt and Cologne, explaining that this was a deliberate bid to encourage friendship between the young people of England and Germany. Next summer, when the British arrived in force, they hoped local people would join them.

Dr Walter and Lewis Paton had already suggested that German boys visiting Britain might stay at C.H.A centres, exploring the countryside by day, and taking part in the evening programme of lectures and music.[11] Lewis Paton's friendship with Arthur Leonard and both men's positive memories of their schooldays in Germany kindled a response far more focused than mere enthusiasm. In Berlin, Frankfurt and in the cities of Northern England, teachers, youth leaders and some church groups recognised the power of shared experiences. At the end of the twentieth century, Westminster and Stormont staged the theatrical 'Good Friday Agreement'. Real peace wasn't achieved by lip-trembling political histrionics, Protestant or Catholic. In their daily lives, many politicians and private citizens courageously chose to transcend the sectarian hatreds, which had torn their communities apart. Shared holidays for a few of the religiously segregated children of Northern Ireland allowed friendships to grow, but segregation and outbreaks of sectarian violence continue.

The first Musterschule group to visit Britain under the aegis of the C.H.A. planned a five week stay. Only part of the time would be spent at hostels. Appeals in 'Comradeship' and at the AGM stress the need for host families. Manchester Grammar School could source its own host families, but the idea had now spread to other schools in the North of England, including Bradford Grammar School, Brighouse School, and schools in the Colne valley and in Scotland. Evidence in the C.H.A. archives and in Colne, the town to which Leonard often returned, indicates that many German schoolboys spent time with families in Northern England, visiting the Yorkshire moors, the Peak District and the Lake District. Walking in the Black Forest and Borrowdale, bog-trotting on Kinder Scout, climbing to the mountain huts of the Taunus, staying in Kelkheim and Keswick or simply living as members of their host families, boys shared each others' daily lives. British boys visiting Germany would stay with school sourced host families, and hostel with the Bibelkranzchen.[12]

Leonard's enthusiastic account of the first Kelkheim summer suggests unusual fluency in the British party; German hosts and British guests apparently speaking both languages. (his optimism was incurable.) At the Palmgarten in Frankfurt, where they'd been invited to tea, the visitors were welcomed by Baron von Siebold, president of the Anglo-German friendship association. The British consul, Sir Francis Oppenheimer, also took part. Next day, the arduous tour continued. Advertised as 'Summer Holidays in the Taunus', the Anglo-German adventures demanded total commitment and boundless energy. By day, the Taunus experience offered miles of high level mountain walking. For British walkers, used to the tradition of getting lost and confrontations with angry gamekeepers, coloured waymarked routes were a fascinating novelty. So were family friendly beer-gardens. There were visits to archaeological sites, including the reconstructed Roman camp at Saalburg, to Heidelberg, Epstein, Homburg and every other destination recommended by Drs Walter and Lorey.

'Guests' were reminded to behave at all times as ambassadors for their country, remembering that their visit wasn't merely a holiday.[13] On a Cook's package tour, holidaymakers travelled through a landscape, admired fine buildings and works of art, stayed in rooms with a view. The ethos of a C.H.A. holiday was totally different, resembling, in many respects, exchange visits between twenty-first century twin towns. In the Taunus, responding to Leonard's invitations, published in the Frankfurt and Cologne press, local people did join their visitors on mountain walks. In the evenings, by way of relaxation, there were lectures on German history, culture, music and philosophy. In German or English ? Mancunian travellers would have little excuse. The C.H.A. headquarters were now in Brunswick St, Manchester, in the heart of the university area. Leonard and his colleagues, including Joseph Findlay, Manchester's Professor of Education, believed that encouraging the study of languages was crucial to the international movement. In Germany, all the prime movers in the schools project were linguists. At College House, the original women's college of Manchester university, and in the city centre, evening classes in French and German were available throughout the autumn and winter. Publishing articles in German, the C.H.A. journal, 'Comradeship' evidently assumes that enough members could read this material.[14]

Before the move to Kelkheim, C.H.A parties had spent two summers in the Eifel. The idea of creating a dedicated centre in the Taunus region had developed in tandem with the school exchanges. Lewis Paton, Arthur Leonard and Dr Walter became a triumvirate, introducing the young people in their charge to life in another country, not merely as holidaymakers, but as welcome guests. The 1910 'trek' from Manchester was led by Lewis Paton, who delivered a gift of books to the Musterschule. After the official school trip, some of the Manchester boys remained with their host families for another fortnight. C.H.A. minutes record donations to churches, schools and youth centres in Frankfurt. On January 6th, 1912, the C.H.A. meeting in Manchester was attended by Rektor Könzack of Frankfurt, who also attended a meeting in Bradford. With Rektor Könzack was Franz Crämar, the historian who had so enthusiastically endorsed Adolf Reusch's account of a C.H.A holiday.[15]

Cultural links with Frankfurt weren't limited to the C.H.A and the school exchange project. Through Charles Hallé, founder of the orchestra, which still bears his name, Manchester already had strong musical links with Germany. In June 1911, a Manchester choir performed the Deutches Requiem before a Frankfurt audience. According to the Manchester Guardian's correspondent, these singers from the alleged 'Land without Music' gave a strong performance. Both their singing and their pronunciation of German were praised. (Northerners pronounce final consonants; an advantage when speaking or singing in German).[16]

Two elite schools had led the way. Teachers active in the C.H.A. had approached other German schools, inviting contact. Throughout the immediate pre-war years, articles in Comradeship stress the importance of maintaining a good relationship with Germany and the key role of teachers in counteracting prejudice and hostility. According to reports in Comradeship, half a dozen schools in Frankfurt and others in Berlin were interested in exchange visits. In Germany, no material from these schools has survived WWII bombing, but some German records of the school exchange project, the C.H.A and the Ferienheimgesellschaft are held in British record offices.[17] The German venture was proving so successful, Leonard wondered, cautiously, whether something like this might be attempted in France. France was unfamiliar, and he had few, if any, personal links with the country. The Belgian residents of his childhood home in London had Flemish names.

Reports in 'Comradeship', in the Manchester Guardian, the Yorkshire Observer and the Frankfurter Allgemeine claim widespread support for the Anglo-German project. Welcoming a student from another country is always an experience shared by the whole family. Writing to Comradeship, British and German parents insist that the friendship created between their sons would surely be lifelong. Schoolboys describe, in very good English, how much they've valued their time in England, especially the friendships they've made.[18] Language skills were an important tool in their policy of direct and regular communication with like-minded people in Germany, but as the linguist Ernest Breul recognised, this was only one aspect of the project. In his 1910 article, published in Modern Language Teaching, Ernest Breul defined the ethical mission of both the C.H.A. and its sister movement in Frankfurt. Members of both associations were encouraged to move beyond differences of sex, creed, political opinion and status. Ernest had first hand experience of working at the C.H.A. centre in Dinan.[19]

Throughout the intensifying difficulties of 1911, the C.H.A. peace project was pursued with even greater determination. Blaming Germany for increasing her own expenditure, the Admiralty now wanted thirty Dreadnoughts. At every level of society, from working people in the industrial North to the Duke of Argyll, (one of Queen Victoria's sons in law), the banker Lord Avebury, and the diplomat Sir Frank Lascelles, pragmatists warned of the likely outcome. The ruinous expenditure on armaments would mean lower wages, higher prices, and harder work for both England and Germany.[20] The Admiralty, of course, got its Dreadnoughts.

In July 1911, with Germany and France at loggerheads in Morocco, Arthur Leonard and Ernest Breul were the joint promoters of an academic mission to Westminster. A party of seventy or more German professors and teachers visited the House of Commons, ostensibly to study British parliamentary democracy. Their host was Ramsay Macdonald. Days later, on July 15th, 1911, in a speech delivered in his Leicester constituency, Macdonald referred to this visit, and again emphasised the key role of the school exchange visits in promoting friendship between the two countries. Later, in a letter which was published in Comradeship, he expressed his conviction that ' the mass of English people desire nothing but the most friendly co-operation, and that the sections which seek to stir up strife between us, if rich and influential because they own the Press, are nevertheless small in numbers, and can easily be overcome by a friendly and intelligent democracy, on both sides of the North Sea.'[21]

Friendly and intelligent democracy was failing rapidly now. Macdonald's speech to his constituents had paid tribute to the C. H A.'s political role, and the spirit of internationalism. Politically, this was becoming a dangerous position for Leonard and his colleagues, and, of course, for Macdonald too. Under Leonard's leadership, the C.H.A. was deliberately encouraging and celebrating 'German invasions', claiming that this was in the cause of international peace. Macdonald's suggestion that most British people desired friendship with Germany seriously underestimates the bogeyman effect of syndicated serials. Newspaper readers might routinely ignore international and even local news, but they'd turn, eagerly, to the latest tale of dastardly German spies. The C.H.A.'s internationalist policy was heading for very serious trouble.

Leonard and his closest supporters wanted to believe in the success of their German project, but, almost from the beginning, the bid for friendship with Germany was challenged and opposed. Gifts to Frankfurt were questioned, and there are repeated claims that the German boys are in some way 'unsuitable'. The objections are never specific and none of the offending youngsters are named. Presumably the boys' real crime was their nationality, rather than their no doubt lively behaviour during the excitement of a school trip. It was agreed, reluctantly, that in future, no more than two boys from the 'East' would be allowed to stay in each hostel. Like the boys' alleged unsuitability, the 'East' is never defined. Such caution was vital. In the Coronation summer of 1911, attacks on 'unsuitable' visitors had to steer well clear of lese-majesty. Britain was welcoming many visitors from the 'East', including, of course, the Kaiser, and almost every other crowned head in Europe.[22]

Inevitably, the hostility recorded at C.H.A. meetings expresses the views of adults rather than those of the young people themselves. No schoolboys spoke at meetings, and it is highly unlikely that any would be invited. Editorially, 'Comradeship' appears unchanged, despite the increasing acrimony over Germany. Early in 1912, the journal's regular book recommendations include two works by Norman Angell, suggesting still, a liberal, internationalist, and solidly anti-war readership. Though the MGS exchange visits had come to end in December, 1911, to be replaced with serious Officer Training Corps exercises, other British visitors to the Kelkheim centre still found their hosts welcoming, seeking not war but friendship. In the words of one Comradeship contributor, identified only by the initials 'F.B.S.' : 'Without any seeking after it, the C.H.A and the individual members of it have been put in the position of being able to do something for international peace. Not to talk, but to do .'[23] Following the success of Kelkheim, the Black Forest's Wolfach centre had become popular too. Together, in the mountains, young men and women, British and German, still 'went hunting wild / After the wildest beauty in the world'.[24] Ernest Breul's 1910 prose comes poignantly close to Owen's 1918 poem : 'Comradeship, simplicity, reverence may perhaps be regarded as the watch-words of our movement... We train our eyes to see the beauties and our hearts to feel the wonder of the world we live in.'[25]

In their own specialised territory, liberal internationalists and members of the ethical movement had enjoyed considerable success. Like-minded young people from all over Europe had enjoyed adventures together, and the most successful links had been with Germany. The so-called 'cousin nations' always have understood, perhaps better than some of their neighbours, the peculiar attraction of punishing hill walks in equally punishing weather. The enthusiasm for exhausting and often uncomfortable outdoor exercise is impossible to explain.[26]

When the Liverpool Nomads set sail for adventures in France, the society Leonard had founded was already in turmoil, reflecting the increasingly fraught international situation. At the end of 1912, the C.H.A. and its founder parted company. Like almost every divorce, the separation was bitter, though the hostility is markedly one-sided. Early in 1913, Leonard became the manager of a new organisation, to be known as the 'Holiday Fellowship'. Later accounts of the regime change and Leonard's own 1934 book are tactful, indicating that his core of simple 'Fellowship' hostels chose to reflect the movement's democratic and internationalist origins. Most of the centres he'd opened would continue to be managed by the C.H.A., supposedly catering for 'guests requiring greater comfort and the company of their own class.' In fact, the middle-class takeover and preference for 'their own sort' was only minor aspect of the real story. Documents in the Manchester and Colne archives reveal a far more complicated and intensely political agenda, driven by a cohort of members who object repeatedly to the continuing relationship with Germany, to the visiting German pupils, to Ernest Breul's role in the C.H.A, and to Leonard's relationship with notorious and far from popular Labour party politicians, including the ' rascally, unpatriotic, pro-German scoundrel', Ramsay Macdonald.[27]

On November 17th, 1911, in the uneasy aftermath of the Morocco crisis, Leonard warned an audience in Colne that war was nearer than any of them imagined. Newly returned from a visit to Germany, he had been alarmed by the change in even his closest friends there. They no longer trusted England, and looked for a 'real, practical move' from the English Government. Leonard insisted that the Germans were in favour of peace. The German people he knew as friends wanted to stop the race for armaments, and they were willing to come to some arrangement whereby this could be done. According to the Nelson and Colne reporter, Leonard argued that 'the blame for hostility did not lay (sic) as much with Germany as with England.' Leonard then suggested to his audience that miners and railwaymen in Britain and Germany could unite in strike action, to prevent war between their countries. That this speech was well received in Colne is hardly surprising.[28] The local newspaper report is supportive. Philip Snowden, then representing Blackburn, but later becoming the MP for Colne Valley, may well have been present. He and Leonard were friends and exact contemporaries. On a later important occasion, Snowden and Macdonald certainly stayed with Leonard at his house in Conwy, and the Macdonald family also visited the Leonards independently.[29]

Almost a fortnight later, addressing an audience which could hardly be more different (a meeting of the Primrose League in his Portsmouth constituency), Admiral and Conservative M.P. Lord Charles Beresford was more explicit, and, given his status, impeccably authoritative. Beresford had been

Commander in Chief of the Channel Fleet. He had just 'retired'. According to the Manchester Guardian report, Admiral Beresford said that : ' The feeling in Germany had originated through our own fault. We began by threatening Germany with Dreadnoughts, saying that one ship could sink her entire fleet, and much of what has happened and been said was due to our attitude to that country.'[30] The Admiral too was applauded. Traditional accounts of Beresford's dispute with Admiral 'Jackie' Fisher and his opposition to aspects of the massive Dreadnought programme favour Fisher, the First Sea Lord who had risen from supposedly humble origins to become 'one of the greatest administrators in the history of the Royal Navy.'[31] Beresford's Portsmouth speech is perfectly clear. Beresford recognised that Britain had nothing to gain from a conflict with Germany.The Conservative M.P and naval leader's assessment of the situation was remarkably similar to that of Arthur Leonard, whose political affiliations were so very different.

In his 1916 reflections on this period, Prince Lichnowsky (German ambassador to Britain, 1912 - 1914) reached a very similar conclusion, apparently admitting to Germany's diplomatic shortcomings. ' In spite of former mistakes, all might still have been put right in July, 1912. An agreement with England had been arrived at. We ought to have sent a representative. We wanted only treaties that would safeguard us and others, and secure our economic development.[32]

On January 12th, 1912, Leonard was back in Colne, delivering another intensely political speech. To loud applause, he spoke about socialist opposition to war and the waste of money on armaments, which could be spent on education and the relief of poverty. Like his exasperation with mindless dissipation in Blackpool, the theme is wearily familiar. The speech concludes on a more positive note, with an account of the C. H. A's years of work promoting international goodwill, literally bringing the people of Europe nearer together, staying in each other's homes. ' This intermingling of the peoples of various countries, especially the cousin nations, will do as much to create fraternal feeling amongst nations and help to lessen the probability of a war between Germany and this country.'[33]

Finally, in January, 1914, after he'd 'resigned' from the C.H.A., and launched his small group of 'Holiday Fellowship' hostels, Leonard was charged with serious financial impropriety.[34] The charge was rejected, and his integrity strenuously defended by his supporters, including the C.H.A. Treasurer, the Midland Bank director, Sir Drummond Fraser. Public accusations were, at Sir Drummond's insistence, publicly refuted, but the damage was done. Mud sticks. Only two committee members resigned on his behalf.[35] In many quarters, it was no longer safe to court friendship with Germany. Leonard fought to remain responsible for running the Kelkheim centre, but the new C.H.A. board insisted on vetting all arrangements involving Germany. He was to be allowed a long-term loan to purchase Newlands, at a modest price, but when war broke out, this loan was immediately called in.

Leonard's real offence was, of course, like that of his political friends, his determination to continue seeking 'a good understanding with Germany'. His only book was published eventually in 1934, by the Holiday Fellowship, with a foreword by Lewis Paton.[36] Leonard's own introduction is intriguingly circumspect. The answer to one question 'must be left to the discernment of the

170

reader'. There are cryptic references to 'widening its scope', and 'the inclusion of material that had not at first appeared suitable'.[37] He never refers, specifically, to the bitterness which ended his leadership of the C.H.A. Nor does he mention the hostility he encountered and the serious legal action which was threatened, when in 1929, he began to write a history of 'the people's holiday movement'. Throughout the autumn of 1929, urgent exchanges of letters between C.H.A. officers and their solicitors insist that his plans to publish a history must be checked. By December, there were plans to serve an injunction, preventing the publication or distribution of such a book. It was feared that 'a great deal of damage might be done to the association'. The best way to deal with Leonard would be to forestall him. He would, of course, be denied access to all material filed in the C.H.A. office, including, obviously, the minutes of all meetings.[38]

Initially, Leonard had hoped for C.H.A. support, which he actively sought, courteously approaching people who had explicitly opposed the links with Germany and the visits made by German schoolboys and students. A typescript draft written by Leonard is undated, but filed amongst other letters and papers dated 1929 - 30. [39] The text is markedly different from the book which was eventually published. Specific information has been omitted, so specific, any need for further research in his part can be ruled out. In 1929, Leonard would know the names of the Prime Minister, the Chancellor and the Home Secretary. He'd known them all well for years, as friends, and at his home in Conwy, as welcome guests. He does refer briefly to Bernhard Seib, formerly of the Musterschule, who became assistant secretary (i.e., junior warden) of Newlands, the Derwentwater hostel.

Adventures in Holidaymaking has no index. Leonard really needed a firm editor. The lack of access to any C.H.A. records was a serious constraint. Aspects of some key events are scattered throughout the text, which needs to be read and referenced like a chaotic box of letters, every one of which might have been written by a distinguished statesman, scholar or musician. In the seventh chapter, there is a tantalising reference to 'rumours' about Macdonald and a wartime search of Leonard's house by armed officers. Leonard, his wife, and their surviving child, Jessie, were living at Bryn Corach, the Holiday Fellowship hostel and headquarters in Conwy. Here, he doesn't give enough information to confirm the status of such rumours. Later, in the fourteenth chapter, there's a far longer account of the same incident. Macdonald was certainly at Bryn Corach. With him were over thirty members of the Labour party, all of whom could be accommodated at the hostel. According to this second and more detailed version, Macdonald held a wartime Labour party conference at Bryn Corach. Most of the people who would hold Cabinet office in his first and second administrations were present.[40] An energetic hillwalker, Macdonald also visited the Leonards privately, with his children, spending some weeks of the winter with them in Snowdonia.

Leonard was also welcoming 'peace lovers who suffered for their principles', by which he can only mean conscientious objectors. Including Frank Bourne ? Possibly... Until his forced resignation, it was Leonard himself who managed the funding of 'Goodwill Holidays' for the poor. He would have logged Frank's contributions from sales of photographs.[41] Leonard's M. P , Lloyd George, still the Secretary of State for War, but soon to become Prime Minister, could hardly ignore the presence of so much sedition on his own doorstep. Whether Lloyd George instigated the armed searches of Bryn Corach is hard to determine, but there were many reasons why Leonard could have been under surveillance. An early U-boat target, the North Wales coast was a restricted area. Leonard's extensive pre-war connections with Germany, his known support for 'peacelovers' (his own preferred word, given that 'pacifism' had been robbed of its literal meaning) and his close relationship with politicians of the left identified him as an unpatriotic troublemaker. He and many of his friends had done everything in their power to maintain peace. Throughout the war, many of those who had experienced holidays in Germany remained in contact with their friends.[42] In his account of the war years at Bryn Corach, Leonard acknowledges that most of the 'Holiday Fellowship' were convinced pacifists. Many absolutist conscientious objectors from the North of England were imprisoned in North Wales. A high proportion of these were certainly Nonconformists.[43]

Even in the first and obviously constrained draft of his book, Leonard had to include Bernhard Seib. In his brief life, this young man from Frankfurt seems to have epitomised everything Leonard had hoped to achieve. Bernhard and the other boys who came to Britain through the schools' exchange project would be close to the age of Leonard's own son, who had been killed in a rail accident at the age of twelve. Publishing at last in 1934, Leonard was able to say more. Originally, as part of the exchange project with Manchester Grammar School, Seib had come to Newlands with five other senior boys from the Musterschule; Ruhl, Weber, Büge, Schweib and Georgi. Returning to school in September 1909, they gave an account of their holiday to parents and fellow pupils, displaying many of the photos they'd taken during their visit to England.[44] Seib and his Danish friend 'Mick' Michaelsen, who became the C.H.A. Wasdale hostel warden, first met at Newlands. Traditional Danish-German hostilities ruled, until Leonard himself urged the young men to consider a truce, just for the holidays. They became close friends. Leonard would never forget either of them.[45]

In the summer of 1913, boys from Frankfurt were once more based at the hostel, accompanied by some of their teachers. Acquiring the old mill had been one of Leonard's most successful ventures, though its location and strenuous activities sometimes led to conflict with town bred guests.[46] Newlands remained, as he'd hoped, classless and internationalist, and Cumberland, as it then was, had centuries old links with Germany.[47] The spicy, coiled and distinctly Germanic 'Cumberland' sausage is a legacy from a group of highly skilled and actively sought economic migrants who arrived in the sixteenth century. Close to Newlands, there are ancient and extensive lead workings. Invited by Elizabeth I, the German mining expert Daniel Hechstetter came to Keswick to investigate the prospects. As there were very few experienced local miners, Hechstetter persuaded many more German miners to come over. 'Goldscope', the local name for the richest of these mines, is a corruption of Göttes gabe . German mining experts also prospected and guided copper mining in the Coniston area. Specialising in the extraction of lead and copper, many other miners came to settle in Cumbria, where their descendants live to this day.[48]

Summoned to fight for his country, Bernhard Seib was at first based near Rheims. He pleaded that he couldn't shoot his English friends. Germany had made no official provision for conscientious objectors, but Bernhard's wishes were respected. He was allowed to move to the eastern front. His last letter to C.H.A. friends has survived : ' Vergessen werde ich nie, was ich während langer Jahre von ihnen all an treuer Freundschaft und Liebe erfahren habe meh kann icht nicht tun. Sie seien nicht am Krieg und all dem elend Schuld, so sagen sie auf ihrer Insel. Und unsere tapferem Männer, Söhne und Brüder, deren lieben nun trauernhaben sie den krieg gewollt ? Trotz allem, grusse Sie bitte, von mir und wenn dies mein letzter Gruss an dich sein sollte... '.[49] Bernhard and Mick both died in the war.

At Manchester Grammar School, the WWI Roll of Honour includes the name of one young German who had taught at the school. Frank Bourne's papers, letters and photographs had revealed, at last, the key connection between the Liverpool Nomads, their adventures in France, and Arthur Leonard's hopes for 'the company of youth'. Like his friend Ramsay Macdonald, Leonard believed that international friendship, especially between young people, would be the key to international peace. As the political leaders of Europe prepared for war, internationalists suggested a very different version of the future. Reporting on the peaceful 'German invasion' of 1911, Hubert Beaumont claimed to recognise the immense economic advantages of peace, envisaging a world in which international finance would become a potent factor in achieving that end. Beaumont argued that ultimately, humanity would recognise the economic futility of war, but why wait for 'the forces of sordid materialism' ?

The 'silken cords of friendship and brotherhood' didn't prevent Beaumont from enlisting and serving as a Captain during WWI. Lewis Paton, who had encouraged many Manchester Grammar School boys to share his love of Germany and welcome German boys as guests, promoted recruitment for the Public Schools Battalion. In 1911 and again in 1912, giving his lectures in Colne, Arthur Leonard, the man who believed so passionately in the power of friendship, had identified the prosaic but effective unifying power of coal, steel, and transport. In the very long term, dreamers and realists were both right, though the dreamers expected too much of human nature, including their own. The 'International Brotherhood of Man' was a romantic and ill-defined ideal. The League of Nations failed to prevent the rise of Hitler and WWII. In July 1952, the European Coal and Steel Community linked the six founding nations of the EU.

Arthur Leonard never held political office. His radical vision and practical policies were valued by the statesmen, scholars and social reformers who were among his closest friends. In August 1912, six of the young people whom he'd inspired raised a toast in sparkling Normandy cider. Celebrating their own journey towards peace and reconciliation, they drank to 'better friendship, long life, and happy, happy days.' The leaders of armed Europe arranged a different future, for them and for the whole twentieth century.

Source Notes

Introduction

1   Rosemary Hardern at the Museum of Costume in Bath and Dr Miles Lambert, of Platt Fields, Manchester.

2   Dr Jacques Gury, Rennes (latest publication, 2008, editor of Les Grands Voyageurs racontent Les Iïes Britanniiques, Readers' Digest) .

Chapter One

  ' We dreamt of showing the earth to the company of youth. '

1   Captain J. Bagot, M.P., addressing constituents, reported in the Westmorland Gazette, April 29th, 1911.

2   Lancaster Guardian, agricultural reports, Sept 1911.

3   Westmorland Gazette, December 30th, 1911

4   After the Coronation of George V, celebrations continued for weeks. Prince Henry / Heinrich finished second. But for the death of his mother in law, the prizes would have been presented by Lord Derby, who would serve as Minister for War.

5   Westmorland Gazette, December 30th, 1911

6   Ibid. 'Anything said against Britain in is received by the populace with tumultuous applause'. The Crown Prince, the future Emperor, went to a debate in the Reichstag, and clapped his hands at utterances against Britain. His august father reproved him, and put him on water and toast for four days'

7   Manchester Guardian, year-end editorial, December 30th 1911.

8   Keswick Convention, 1912, vol 38. One optimistic speaker was Canon Barnes Lawrence, reporting that the Germans he'd met while visiting the country were nothing like the Germans as portrayed in English newspapers. C.R.O. Carlisle

9   Six Nomads in Normandy' MCMXII, Ch VIII p 61

10 Sept 16th, 1914   Becoming a Red Cross hospital for wounded French soldiers, the Villa St Charles was exempt from taxes. B/CHA/ADM/1/4, Greater Manchester County Record Office.

11 Approximately twenty-five per cent of Blackpool' s town council made their living in branches of the drink industry. J.A.R. Pimlott, The Englishman's Holiday, Chapter II.

12 Pimlott, ibid.

13 Bryn Trescatheric, Barrow Town Hall, 1887 - 1987 Titus Wilson, Kendal 1987

14 Bryn Trescatheric, How Barrow was built... Hougenai Press... 1985 Barrow's high death rate and the prevalence of infectious disease could account for Leonard's approach to Dr Alexander Hill, as a pioneer of environmental medicine.

15 Nelson and Colne Times, August 7th, 1890, reporting a speech by TAL.

16 Quarry Bank Mill, Styal, Cheshire, (National Trust) and Wigan Pier both offer the experience, explaining that mill workers communicated by sign-language. The combination of high humidity and lint-polluted atmosphere are associated with several serious respiratory disease, including asthma, bronchitis, oral cancers, and byssyniosis, from dust inhalation. Even when masks were provided, workers proved reluctant to wear them. In the high humidity, masks added to existing discomfort. Various sources, including HMSO publications on industrial diseases, National Trust and English Heritage industrial heritage presentations.

17 Minutes, Colne Congregational Church, May 1890, CUCO 7/1 Lancashire Record Office , Preston.

18 Independent Church, Colne, letter to Arthur Leonard, November, 1894 Leonard family papers.

19 Textile districts like Colne were becoming hotbeds of working class politics. In the 1890's, Leonard's increasingly controversial and political Congregational ministry was matched by that of his contemporary and near neighbour, Philip Snowden. Ordained minister and journalist/editor, both were passionate campaigners against war, and for a new moral order. See David James, 1987, ' Our Philip', The Bradford Antiquary, Vol 3, pp 39 - 47

20 Mark Bevin, ' Labour Churches and Ethical Socialism,' History Today, Vol 47, April, 1997

21 Arthur Leonard, Adventures in Holidaymaking, 1936, pp 24 - 25

22 Lewis Paton 's and Leonard's own schooldays in Germany are cited as inspiring both men to introduce urban boys to the countryside and long-distance hillwalking. Rural workers, especially miners, habitually walked long distances to their work. Government initiatives, seeking to achieve ethnic balance in access to National Parks, have resulted in the withdrawal of services such as guided walks, judged to be ethnically unrepresentative, despite the fact that some groups from low-lying countries such as Bangladesh don't yet have a tradition of hill-walking.

23 The Ambleside Railway Bill, Select Committee Enquiry, 1887

24 Offered, almost verbatim, to A level history students and undergraduates, the vituperative letters and articles are invariably assumed to refer to immigrants from Pakistan or Bangladesh.

25 John Ruskin, 1885 - 1887, letters to the Westmorland Gazette, the Times, and others, objecting to working class visitors.

26 T.Arthur Leonard, Adventures in Holidaymaking, 1936, pp 24 - 25

27 Leonard's young millworkers are not impoverished, certainly not to the same degree as the families studied by Maud Pember Reeves, in her Fabian inspired ' Round About A Pound A Week' (1911)

28 Nelson and Colne Times, September, 1890

29 T.A.Leonard, personal papers, B/CHA/HIS/16/11 GMCRO

30 Professor Peter Sandiford, University of Toronto, quoted in T. Arthur Leonard, Adventures on Holidaymaking, p 37

31 Norman Angell, (1872 - 1967) educated St Omer and Geneva, publicist, writer, editor, League of Nations pioneer, Labour MP, 1929 - 31, Nobel Peace Prize, 1933. (Dictionary of Natonal Bigraphy, OUP)   In 'The Foundations of International Policy', a collection of Angell's lectures to various audiences, delivered in Oxford, Cambridge, France and Germany, and London, Angell 's lecture on ' The Influence of Credit on International Relations' is just as valid in the 21st century.

32 Letter to Professor (Sir) Patrick Geddes, from Arthur Leonard, August 8th, 1900 (Strathclyde University Archives), also, University of Dundee, School of Town and Regional Planning, and The Geddes Institute., Dundee. Edinburgh Globe, ' An Educational Experiment,', June 1901 B/CHA/HIS/16

33 Papers of Charlotte Mason, Box CM 15, The Armitt Library, Ambleside

34 Dominic Hibberd, Wilfred Owen, A New Biography, Ch 14, pp 256 - 7. Weidenfeld & Nicholson, 2002

35 The former mill, known as Newlands, was leased from 1905, and later bought, for £1270. T. Arthur Leonard, Adventures in Holidaymaking, Holiday Fellowship, 1936, pp 40 - 42 Canon Rawnsley sometimes revised his opinion on social and political issues. Opposing the construction of Thirlmere reservoir, he wrote a passionate ode in defence of the existing scenery and soon to be evicted residents. When the first Lakeland water reached Manchester, he was ready with equally passionate verses in praise of this engineering triumph. Written for Newlands, his ode to 'A Stair Rest House' is free from such controversy.

36 T. Arthur Leonard, Adventures in Holidaymaking, Holiday Fellowship 136

37 Ibid, p 93 - 95

38 From the earliest days of the war, recruiting posters reassured men that they would be able to serve ' in the company of their own friends and business acquaintances.'   Liverpool Courier, August 25th, 1914

Chapter Two

Sac à dos

1 Dr et Madame Jamaux, St Malo Traditionally, every Breton was expected to take a walk of over 400 miles, visiting each of the seven cathedrals of Brittany. If the walk was not taken in life, the threat was that the Breton soul must take it after death, advancing along the route by one coffin length every seven years. Judy Smith Holiday Walks in Brittany ISBN 1-85058-733-7 2001

2 Six Nomads in Normandy, Ch VIII

3 Liverpool Courier, advertisement, 20th July, 1912

4 Antony Trollope, The Warden Chapter XVI, 1855

5 Guide books the Nomads could have used include Spencer Musson, La Côte d'Emeraude, 1912 , D.B.W Brittany for Britons, 1896. both published by A & C Black

6 Oxford Dictionary of Quotations

7 M. Phillippe Lanoe, Institut Culturel de Bretagne, by e-mail

8 National Railway Museum Research Centre, York; Bradshaw, July, 1912

9 In 1915, a sharp-eyed antiquarian in Ambleside spotted two leather-bound eighteenth century guidebooks to the Lake District in a pile of ' waste paper', unpatriotically rescuing them for a historic library. (The Armitt Library, Ambleside, Cumbria)

10 Martin Jarvis, profile, Sunday Times, April 9th, 2006

11 www.nationalarchives. gov. uk Also ancestry.co.uk

12 Entitlement to a week's holiday with pay became law in Britain only in 1939.

13 In the late 19th century, when the young Nomads were primary school children, over 100, 00 0 boys and girls worked as half-timers mostly in the cotton-mills of Lancashire. See www.rochdale.gov. uk

14 The sequence of devastating reports didn't, at first, achieve real social change, implemented by government. (Henry Mayhew, London Life and the London Poor, 1850s, Seebohm Rowntree, Poverty: A Study of Town Life, London, 1889 - 7, and Charles Booth, Life and Labour in London, Macmillan, 1903

15 Like white and green papers, Blue Books, i.e. reports on nineteenth century social issues by Royal Commissions were so called simply because of the colour of their binding.

16 At Lanhydrock, in Cornwall, (National Trust) a board is still on display, instructing servants that they must never make eye-contact with any members of the family. www.nationaltrust.org.uk

17 Maud Pember Reeves, Round About A Pound A Week, G Bell & Sons, 1913, reissued by Virago, 1979. Pember Reeves specifically did not select the most destitute for her study, but typical working families.

18 Round About a Pound a Week, Ch VI

Chapter Three

I can trace my ancestry back to a protoplasmal primordial atomic globule.

W. S. Gilbert, The Mikado, 1885

1 Mrs Gaskell, Wives and Daughters, 1864, Ch VI. Squire Hamley's London born wife 'couldn't tell her great-grandfather from Adam'

2 www.bbc.co.uk/history

3 Like many illegitimate children, novelist Catherine Cookson , born in 1906, believed for years that her birth mother was her sister.

4   Searching Victorian census returns for just six people, I encountered a host of mistranscriptions, mostly misread forenames, but also more serious inaccuracies. Online sites, such as ancestry. co. uk, continue such errors. Although the original census entry records Fred Pulford's father as Thomas, ancestry.co .uk lists him as Homer.

5   Lost Voices of the Edwardians, Harper Collins, 2006

6   In 1901, Ada Gleave had been a second year B. Sc student at Edge Hill College, graduating in 1902. Emma Louise Gleave also graduated from Edge Hill, gaining her B.Sc. in 1911 and her M.Sc three years later.

7   Though the paper tax was abolished in 1860, the text of newspapers, books and magazines remained small., and the use of magnifying glasses was common.

8   Before the war, 75% of children left school by the age of fourteen. For the impact of war on education, see ' Blighty', Gerard J. De Groot, Ch. 10, Houses, Homes and Health Longman, 1996

9   Some employers did keep very detailed records of even their most junior employees. The archives of HSBC and Unilever record their employees career and salaries from entry to retirement.

10   Six Nomads in Normandy, Chapter IV

11   www. statistics. gov. uk , 2004, reporting on the 2001 census.

12   Fiona A.Montgomery. Edge Hill University College A History 1885 - 1997 Phillimore & Co Ltd, 1997

13   Gladys passed her B. A. Part One exams in Latin, English and History, but failed her finals. (Liverpool university archives)

14   FOI Act, Department for Constitutional Affairs,. www. foi. gov. uk

15   Births, Marriages and Deaths since 1837 are available at www. stcaths. com, and on microfiche at record offices and many major libraries.

16   Liverpool Courier, advertisement, July 20th, 1912

Chapter Four

' Lord Kitchener has sanctioned my endeavours to raise a battalion, which would be composed entirely of the classes mentioned, and in which a man could be certain that he would be amongst friends.'

Lord Derby, Liverpool, 26th August, 1914

1   In October, 1915, only months before conscription became law, the War Office couldn't accommodate or equip all ' attested' men who were ready to serve. They could be billeted at home, at the rate of 3s per day. In the same month, a Southport man who refused to accept billeted soldiers was fined £2. In January, 1916, Caernarfon Town Council objected to the billeting of soldiers.

2   At the Congregational Church in Kendal, the ladies decided, reluctantly, to defer the annual Christmas Sale of Work until after the war. They agreed on a new date; March 25th, 1915.

3   King's Liverpool Regiment archives

4   Burnt Series. www.nationalarchives.gov.uk WO 363

5   www. 1914-1918. net. Also known as The Long, Long Trail.

6   Lancaster City Museum. Great War Wheel of Fortune., statistics of WWI

7   The most comprehensive source for information on soldiers blinded in the Great War is held by St Dunstan's. (www.st-dunstans.org.uk)

8   www.cwgc.com

9   Personal history; all of this happened in my own family.

10 Graham Maddocks, ' Liverpool Pals' Leo Cooper, London, 1991, Appendix. This is still the most complete record of Pals killed.

    WWI casualty records remain incomplete. The CWGC continues to correct and amend data.

11 Census of England and Wales, 1911, General Report, HMSO, London, 1917, Census of England and Wales, 1921, General Report with Tables, HMSO, London, 1925.

12 Lieutenant Wrayford Willmer, 17th Bn, KLR, GS 1753, Liddle Collection, Brotherton Library, University of Leeds.

13 Gordon Corrigan ' Mud, Blood and Poppycock', Table 4,   p 56. Cassell, 2003

14 WO 364, National Archives

15 HSBC Group Archives ref : 0274/06

16 J. Robertson, editor of the Liverpool Courier. (Minutes of the Liverpool Stock Exchange, 25 th August, 1914) Liverpool Record Office

17 Lord Derby's speech at St George's Hall, reported in the Liverpool Courier, August, 1914, also quoted in Maddocks, ' Liverpool Pals', Ch I, p 24

18 Gordon Corrigan ' Mud, Blood and Poppycock' Cassell, 2003, Ch 2 ' The Lost Generation', pp 69 - 74

19 Most of the British press reported Edith Cavell's execution at great length. In the Liverpool Courier, the first accounts filled two broadsheet pages, with additional comment and letters also focusing on Nurse Cavell.

20 King's Liverpool Regiment exhibition, Museum of Liverpool Life, Pier Head, Liverpool.   No formal counselling or support was available for bereaved families. For the Liverpool press and WWI, see Mike Finn, The Realities of War, History Today, August 2002   KLR archives, liverpoolmuseums.org.uk ; KLR exhibition, Museum of Liverpool Life.

21 John Keegan 'The First World War', Pimlico, 1999, Ch I ' A European Tragedy'

22 The Stock Exchange called a boardroom meeting to agree on this. (minutes of the Liverpool Stock Exchange, August, 1914, Liverpool Record Office. In ' Liverpool Pals' Ch I, p 26 , Graham Maddocks simply reports that the young men assembled at their places of work. The boardroom records confirm how carefully this was orchestrated. For a detailed account of the arrangements in St George's Hall on August 31st, 1914, see Peter Simkins, 'Kitchener's Army' The Raising of the New Armies, 1914 - 1916, Pen & Sword, 1988, 2007, Ch 3, pp 84-5

23 This first published work of George Orwell's appeared in the Henley and South Oxford Standard, in October, 1914. Writing under his real name, the patriotic Master Blair made this appeal :

' Awake, oh you young men of England

For if, when your country's in need

You do not enlist by the thousand,

You truly are cowards indeed. '

Quoted in ' George Orwell' by Gordon Bowker, Little, Brown, 2003

24 William Le Queaux's thrillers were syndicated nationally and in many local papers, including the Liverpool Courier.

25 John William Waterhouse's ' La Belle Dame Sans Merci ' is a classic example. of a genre that still stocks civic galleries.

26 Roberts, ' Minds at War', pp 28 - 29 See also John Ramsden Don't Mention The War, The British and the Germans since 1890. Little, Brown, 2006, Ch I, pp 1 - 55 ' An amiable, kindly and unselfish people'

27 Lord Derby's wartime correspondence with Asquith, Lloyd George and Douglas Haig frequently indicates the difficult relationship with French commanders. Off the record, and using his personal rather than official stationery, Douglas Haig warned Derby about corruption among French munitions workers. According to Haig's sources, for all Russian orders given to French munition makers, an extra 20% was paid over/above the price paid for the same articles when ordered by the French government,to induce them to quote still lower terms. The French, allegedly, insisted on the Russians signing contracts for large amounts of material, on the understanding that only a comparatively small portion will be delivered - e.g, of 400 items ordered, only 12 were to be delivered. Haig warned Derby that 50% of Renault employees were in uniform - i.e, judged fit for combat. 920/DER/ 17/27/4 Liverpool Record Office.

28 A.N. Wilson ' The Victorians' , Hutchinson, 2002, Chapter 41, pp 611 - 13, and Pl 63, showing emaciated Boer children in camps. In August, 1902, Ramsay Macdonald and his wife travelled to South Africa, investigating the aftermath of that war. See David Marquand, Ramsay Macdonald, Jonathan Cape, 1977, Chapter 5, pp 76 - 77, quoting from What I saw in South Africa, 1902

29 Sue Townsend, ' The Growing Pains of Adrian Mole', 1983 Adrian's father, shocked by news of the invasion, thinks the Falklands are near Scotland. Mr Mole wasn't alone.

30 Kendal, in Cumbria, takes its motto ' pannis mihi panis' - wool is my bread - from the local wool trade. In the aftermath of the Falklands, traders in the town patriotically promoted the Falkland product, rather than wool produced in Cumbria.

31 HSBC Group Archives ref : 0274/065

32 www.statistics.gov.uk./census

33 KLR archives, facsimile, 17th Battalion diary, liverpoolmuseums.org.

Chapter Five

In the ranks of death you'll find him...

Thomas Moore, The Minstrel Boy

1 Gordon Corrigan, Mud, Blood and Poppycock. Ch 1, p 14 , explains the military position, ' An army exists to fight wars, when and if these occur. A war is not a moral crusade, whatever the propagandists at the time might say; it is a trial of strength., with each army striving to destroy the other, by all means open to them.'

2 Lieutenant Wrayford Willmer , 17th Battalion, KLR, GS1753, Liddle Collection, Brotherton Library, University of Leeds.

3 King's Liverpool Regiment, 17th Battalion diary, transcript www.liverpoolmuseums.co.uk Suicide was still a crime; Ryder isn't included in the 17th's casualty lists. Suicide before conscription or a return to the front was reported regularly, but the individuals are rarely named.

4 Iona and Peter Opie (eds) The Oxford Dictionary of Nursery Rhymes, Oxford University Press, p 442. -443. The rhyme could date back to even earlier weary marching.

5 Pte Tongue, 17th Battalion, GS 1613, Liddle Collection, Brotherton Library, University of Leeds.

6 Commentating on the German offer of peace in ' Nation', Professor Hemmel challenged Britain's indiscriminate use of mines. ' Therefore, the conscience of everyone who has retained a spark of chivalry in the 20th century feels for the German plan not withstanding its manifold objections. It is not clear why England should be allowed to sow mines in the North sea, mines which make no difference between Germans and neutrals. D/Mar/4/1, C.R.O., Carlisle

7 Reports from GHQ in France appeared regularly in British newspapers, presenting the official version of the Allies position. See Niall Ferguson, 'The Pity of War', Penguin, 1998, Ch I The Myths of Militarism, pp 1 - 11 See also David Roberts (ed.) 'Minds at War', Ch 1, Fiction and Press Propaganda. Saxon Books, 1196, 2003

8 Many editorials from December, 1915 and January, 1916 are staunchly patriotic., reflecting the spirit of their readership and their proprietors.

Exceptions can be found, in areas less committed to the war, and a British victory. On January 7th 1916, the Caernarfon and Denbigh Herald anticipated carnage rather than glorious victory. ' We live in momentous times. This year opens with the sun rising on a blood red world. How will it set on December 31st 1916 ? ' In the far north of England, the independently owned Cumberland and Westmorland Herald regularly published dissent from approved patriotism. and occasionally, published extracts from the German press.

9   Lieutenant Aidan Chavasse, GS 0298, Liddle Collection, University of Leeds

10   Richard Holmes ' Tommy'   Harper Collins, 2004   pp 680 - 684, Abbreviations and Glossary

11   Richard Van Emden The Trench, Corgi, 2003, Chapter Four, p 97, Based on the BBC series.

12   Personal experience, excavating in winter conditions, Northumbria and other UK sites. One director relented bonly after a student was admitted to hospital in Newcastle, suffering from hypothermia.

13   Private W.L.P. Dunn, 17th Bn, KLR, GS 0481, Liddle Collection, University of Leeds. Dunn later visited the dead man's family, giving them his first-hand account of the death. The family gave him a silver watch.

14   Lieutenant Wrayford Willmer, 17th Bn, KLR, GS 1753 and Lieutenant Lewis Roberts, 17th Bn, KLR, RUS 140, Liddle Collection, University of Leeds.

15   KLR 17th Battalion diary, May 1916. www.liverpoolmuseums.co.uk

16   Graham Maddocks, Liverpool Pals ,

17   Pte W. L.P.Dunn, 17th Bn, KLR, GS 0481, Liddle Collection

18   KLR, 17th Bn diary and Maddocks, ' Liverpool Pals' , Appendix II See Ch Four, above, n 27 Lord Derby's wartime correspondence with Asquith, Lloyd George and Douglas Haig frequently indicates the difficult relationship with French commanders. Off the record, and using his personal rather than official stationery, Douglas Haig warned Derby about corruption among French munitions workers. According to Haig's sources, for all Russian orders given to French munition makers, an extra 20% was paid over/above the price paid for the same articles when ordered by the French government,to induce them to quote still lower terms. The French, allegedly, insisted on the Russians signing contracts for large amounts of material, on the understanding that only a comparatively small portion will be delivered - e.g, of 400 items ordered, only 12 were to be delivered. Haig warned Derby that 50% of Renault employees were in uniform - i.e, judged fit for combat. See : 920/DER/ 17/27/4 Liverpool City Archives.

19   Lieutenant Aidan Chavasse, 17th Bn, KLR, Liddle Collection, University of Leeds.

20   KLR, 17th Bn diary,

21   KLR, 17th Bn diary

22 Pte. W. L. P. Dunn, 17th Bn, KLR, GS0481, Liddle Collection

23 KLR, 17th Bn diary

24 KLR, 17th Bn diary.

25 KLR, 17th Bn diary.

26 Pte. W. L. P. Dunn, 17th Bn, KLR, GS0481, Liddle Collection

27 Martin Gilbert, First World War. The total population of the Allies was 779 millions., that of and the Central powers, 154 millions. (Niewe Rotterdamsche Courant, 14/2/1915) See also The Financial Cost of the First World War, www.spartacus.schoolnet.co.uk

28 KLR, 17th Bn diary

29 The official record remains imperfect. Graham Maddocks, in ' Liverpool Pals' Appendix II, pp 227 - 229 offers the best calculation, to date, of Liverpool's casualties.

30 Lieutenant (later Rev) Lewis Roberts, 17th Bn, KLR, RUS 140, Liddle Collection. From his parish of Sheepwash, in Devon, Rev Roberts expressed his thoughts on the 50th anniversary of the Somme. ' It would seem therefore that our prayerful thoughts of regret for the untimely deaths of millions of people, most of them the cream of the young men of a generation, are woefully lacking in the ability to translate prayers into practical thoughts and actions, and, as we are confronted with the menacing possibility of a third and probably world war, it is clear that our prayers and elaborate services of commemoration year after year on Remembrance Day are so much futile, superficial outbursts of sentimentality having no relevance or meaning so far as the intelligent translation of prayers into action - in the field of politics and economics is concerned - by the abandonment of the personal pursuit of material wealth arising from the simple basic vice of greed.'

Chapter Six

> They told me, Heraclitus, they told me you were dead
>
> They brought me bitter news to hear, and bitter tears to shed.
>
> I wept as I remembered how often you and I
>
> had tired the sun with talking, and sent him down the sky.

William Cory, 1823 - 1892

1 Many complained that money spent on the Thiepval Memorial to the Missing of the Somme should have been spent on survivors. See www.FIRSTWORLDWAR.com

2 www.kingsregiment.org Offered only ' Ross', the website offered several candidates. None matched the exacting Nomad profile.

3 ' During an attack he tended the wounded in the open all day, under heavy fire, frequently in view of the enemy. During the ensuing night, he searched for the wounded on the ground in front of the enemy's lines, for four hours. Next day, he took one stretcher-bearer to the advanced trenches, and under

heavy shell fire, carried an urgent case for 500 yards.' Mortally wounded on the battlefield, August 2nd, 1917, Chavasse died two days later. Chavasse papers, GS 0298, Liddle Collection, Brotherton Library, University of Leeds.

4   Chavasse himself reported the heavy toll on bearers. ' I have had 4 stretcher bearers killed and one wounded, and one had to go home with a stressed heart, and another, because his nerves gave way after very bad shelling.' Captain Noel Chavasse, VC. July 5th, 1915,   GS 0298, Liddle Collection, University of Leeds.

5   Over 50% of UK doctors served during WWI. See the Army Medical Services website, army.mod.uk/medical/ams.museum.   See also Richard Holmes' ' Tommy',   ' Woeful Crimson', pp 266 - 285, and Richard Van Emden, ' The Trench', Ch 11, ' Wounds and Medics', pp 251 - 268.

6   www.1914 - 18.net.

7   A. W. Westmore and others, The Story of the 63rd Field Ambulance, 1928

8   www. 1914 -1918 .net. How to Read a Medal Card

9   Gerard J.DeGroot, ' Blighty ' British Society in the Era of the Great War, Longman, 1996, Ch 5, pp 92 - 95

10   The antiseptic properties of sphagnum had been known for centuries, possibly millennia. See ' Sphagnum cybifolium' in 'A Modern Herbal', Grieve, Mrs M, www.botanical.com, peatlands. ni. gov. uk, and www. dartmoor. npa. gov. uk , for accounts of WWI and WWII harvesting.

11   Richard Van Emden, The Trench, Ch 11, Wounds and Medics, p 251 - 268, Bantam, 2002

12   Richard Holmes, Tommy', p 414.

13   ' Burnt Series', WO 364, Attestation and pension records, national archives,

14. www.st-dunstans.org.uk

15   Holmes, ' Tommy ',   introd, p xxiv   www.1914 -1918. net

16   Rogers' extensive notes on water purifying include the following instructions: Pass water through several pieces of blanket or canvas, strewn with wood ashes from camp fire. Also, add alum to water before passing through strainer. The alum forms gelatinous particles in the water and on the straining surface, which entangle and hold back the suspended matter. Alt : Permanganate of Potash - Purifies water moderately, but not very dirty water. Alt : Acid Sulphate of Soda, or Iodine, or Bromine. Rogers, A.F., 439157   63rd Field Ambulance B section. GS 1378 Liddle Collection, University of Leeds

17   Noel Chavasse, July 1915, Liddle Collection, GS 0298, University of Leeds Even in the last bitter months of the war, Alec Westmore and his colleagues report occasions when bearers and wounded were not fired on, though obviously within rifle range.

18   Erich Maria Remarque Im Westen nichts Neues, 1929,

19   Frank Dunham, The Long Carry' London, 1970

Chapter Seven

The pity of it !

1   Frank J. Gordon, ' Liberal German Churchmen and the First World War', German Studies Review, Vol 4, No. 1 (Feb 1981) pp 39 - 62

2   Richard van Emden,   The Trench

3   Rogers, A.F.,   439157   63rd Field Ambulance   B section. GS 1378 Liddle Collection, University of Leeds

4   Peter Ardern, When Matron Ruled Robert Hale 2003

5   Westmore, Ch 1

6   Westmore, Ch 1

7   Westmore Ch 2, p 19

8   Westmore et al., Ch 2, p 21

9   The Last Tommies   Channel 4, 2006

10 Westmore, Ch 2, p 22

11 Westmore, Ch 2, p 23

12 Richard Curtis and Ben Elton, Blackadder Goes Forth. 'General Hospital', 1987

13 Cassell's Household Guide, The Waverley Book Company, London, 1912, Vol II, pp 439 - 442, ' Domestic Hygiene'

14 Peacock, A.D. The Louse problem on the Western Front, Journal of the Royal Army Medical Corps: 27, pp 36 - 60

15 Westmore, Ch III, pp 26 - 27 16

16 Westmore, Ch III

17 Westmore ,   Ch III

18 Many versions of this WWI song exist. Few would be have been acceptable on the home front. See Gerald Browne Soldiers Songs of the Great War. www.westernfront.co.uk

20 Westmore, Ch III, p 31

21 Westmore, p 32

22 Dr David Payne The RAMC and the Great War, www.westernfront.co.uk

23 Westmore, Ch III, p 32

24 Dr David Payne   'The   Great War and the pandemic of 1918' www.westernfront.co.uk

25 Westmore, The Somme, p 36

26 Westmore, Ch IV, p 36

27 Westmore, Ch IV, p 37

28 Westmore, Ch IV, p 38

29 Westmore, Ch IV, p 38

30 Westmore, Ch IV   p 38

31 Westmore, Ch IV, p 39

32 Westmore, Ch IV, The Somme p 41

33 Most British dug-outs didn't instal electricity before 1917.

34 Westmore, Ch IV, p 42. Understanding of shell-shock developed as the war progressed. See : contactus@ combatstress.org.uk

35 Westmore, Ch IV, p 44

36 Ilana R.bet-El, ' Conscripts ' Sutton, 1999, Ch 5 ' Living in War', pp 109 - 120.

37 Maud Pember Reeves

38 Westmore, Ch IV, p 47

39 Corrigan, ' Mud, Blood and Poppycock', Ch 10, ' A needless slaughter', pp 298 - 299.

40 Westmore, Ch IV , p 49

Chapter Eight

I fell,

Into the bottomless mud, and lost the light

(Siegfried Sassoon, Memorial Tablet,, 1918)

1   St Cyprian's Church records, Liverpool Record Office

2   Lord Derby to Douglas Haig. 920/DER/17/27/4 L. R. O.

3   Westmore, Ch V, p 52

4   www.army.mod.uk/medical/ams.museum,   Kendal Mountain Rescue., also personal experience, training in Snowdonia.

5   Westmore, Ch V, pp 52 - 53

6   Lord Derby to Maj. Philip Sassoon. 920/DER/27/4/ L. R. O.

7   Westmore, Ch V, p 55

8   Westmore, The Arras Offensive, p 57

9   Lord Derby to Maj. Philip Sassoon, 920/ DER /17/27/4 , L. R. O.

10 Westmore, Ch VI p 63

11 Westmore, Ch VI p 64

12 Westmore, Ch VI, p 64

13 Westmore, Ch VI

14 Lord Derby to Douglas Haig, 920DER/ 17/27/4, L. R. O.

15 Lord Derby to Douglas Haig, 920/DER/17/27/4, L. R.O.

16 Cork Examiner, 1916 . M I 7 investigations into German propaganda can be found in 46. W.O. 3405. (Watergate House, September, 1916). The report

details two German methods of exercising censorship. 1: The police seem adept at seizing before they are on general sale newspapers, which have published objectionable articles. 2: A paper may be put into ' preventive censorship'. Although greater latitude is now allowed than formerly, for the discussion of economics and war news, still, the absence of genuine critics remains a leading character of German policy. ' This remarkable document was produced when Britain's Defence of the Realm Act could forbid the distribution of such dangerous propaganda as ' Blessed are the peacemakers.'

17 Lord Derby to Douglas Haig, 920/DER/ 17/27/4, L . R. O.

18 Westmore, Ch VII, p 71

19 Westmore, ChVII , p 72

20 Westmore, Ch VII, p 73-4

21 Douglas Haig, to Lord Derby 920/DER/27 /4 , L. R. O.

22 Lord Derby to Lloyd George 920/ DER/17/27/1, L. R. O.

23 Lord Derby to Douglas Haig, 920/DER/17/27/4, November 10th, 1918. L.R.O.

24 Derby's assessment of Foch's desire to continue the war seems accurate enough. Haig, in Lidell-Hart's words, had become a realist. For Foch's role at the Paris Conference, see Margaret Macmillan, 'PEACEMAKERS' , especially Ch 14, ' Keeping Down', John Murray, 2001

25 Lidell-Hart, B, Foch, Man of Orleans, Penguin, 1937 Lidell-Hart considers the deliberate significance of Foch's name, and, at least equally important, that of his father, Napoleon Foch, b 1803. Religious migrants from one border region, to another, Alsace to the Pyrenees, the Fochs emphasised their patriotism.

25 Liverpool Courier, November 12th, 1918.

Chapter Nine

War's annals will cloud into night...

Ere their story die

(Thomas Hardy, 'In Time of The Breaking of Nations ')

1 When the Swallows and Amazons climb ' Kanchenjunga,', they find, hidden at the summit, a message from three earlier young climbers, the Amazon's mother and uncle, and ' Bob Blackett'.

' Who is Bob Blackett', asked Susan

' He was father'. said Nancy. Nobody said anything for a minute. (Arthur Ransome, Swallowdale, Jonathan Cape, 1931) Ransome's young readers would understand the situation well enough, including the minute's silence. A few years earlier, the motherless Bastable Treasure Seekers are equally reticent, and Mary Lennox, suddenly orphaned by cholera and shipped to England, is represented as a self-centred monster rather than tragic orphan.

2 Pickering : Have you no morals, man ?

Doolittle : Can't afford them, Governor. (George Bernard Shaw, Pygmalion, 1912)

3. Jane Cox, (ed) A Singular Marriage...' Afterword' by Sheila Lochhead, p 377 Harrap, 1988. (Ramsay Macdonald's youngest daughter)

4 Versions of this research appeared in various publications, including Local Population Studies, Cumbria, and The Westmorland Gazette

5 Elizabeth Roberts. A Woman's Place. An oral history of working class life. Blackwells, 1984, 1996

6 Peter Taylor Whifen. Shot at Dawn bbc.co.uk/history/war/wwone. Some of the men who were shot as cowards were actually underage boys.

7 Dr David Payne ' The Great War and the Influenza Pandemic of 1918' www.westernfront.co.uk

8 Six Nomads in Normandy, Ch 1

9 The Red Cross Hospital at Netley has been demolished. There is a comprehensive history of Netley at http:// www.southernlife.org.uk

10 David Payne, The RAMC in the Great War. www.westernfront.co.uk

11 Regular advertisements offering payment for salvaged paper appeared in the press, including the Liverpool Courier.

12 In July, 1916, the Liverpool Courier reported that wood pulp for paper production was now being imported from Canada. Manufacturers hoped that this would become a permanent arrangement. Traditionally, wood pulp had been imported from Sweden. Like the Baltic timber, Germany now blocked this trade.

13 Margaret Lane, The Tale of Beatrix Potter

14 Pember Reeves, Round About a Pound a Week, Ch I

15 www.westernfront.co.uk

16 www.cwgc.org

17 One pupil had been born in Brazil, another in India. In 1901, England was well stocked with boarding schools of this type. In Wuthering Heights', Emily Brontë suggests that the previously uncouth Heathcliff had improved himself as a ' sizar', or pupil teacher. At Cambridge, Patrick Brontë was a sizar.

18 J.M.Winter The Great War and the British People. Ch 2, part IV, Medical Fitness and Military Service, Palgrave, 2003, pp 48 - 64

The incidence of gastric ulcers diagnosed in recruits was unusually high. The condition is uncommon in men under fifty. Surviving pension records identify the high incidence of chronic sickness found in men who had been passed fit on recruitment, and the Army's profound reluctance to support such men. (WO 364, National Archives.)

Chapter Ten

' Let every soldier hew himself a bough'

1   King's Liverpool Regiment ref

2   Six Nomads in Normandy, Chapter IV

3   In the tapestry, felling and shipbuilding appear in the same scenes.

4   Six Nomads in Normandy

5   Inspecting 1870's building projects, the County Surveyor for Westmorland routinely rejected a whole consignment of timber if one piece showed too many knots. (Rigmayden papers, C.R.O., Kendal)

6   Institute of Wood Science, Liverpool

7   Timber Town - The History of the Liverpool Timber Trade. (monograph) Frank Latham, 1967, pub Institute of Wood Science.

8   www.national archives WO 364   Attestation and pension records

9   WO 364   One Tyneside steelworker was released at last by the Army when he was identified as a key worker on a government contract, supplying the War Office.

10   Noel Chavasse, VC, G.S. 1753, Liddle Collection, University of Leeds.

11   Wirecutters were one of the items urgently requested by Lieutenant Wrayford Willmer. G.S. 1753, Liddle Collection, University of Leeds.

12   Army Council Instruction 730., 1917   The Imperial War Museum was able to supply this information, but they have no copy of the directive.

13   Appeals Tribunal, referred from Wales. Liverpool, January 1916 , defendant not named, case reported in the Liverpool Courier

14   ' I think it will be necessary to entirely prohibit the import of timber, in which case, you would not have to be dependent on timber cut in France.' 920/DER/17/27/1   Derby to Lloyd George, 1916 - 18, L.R.O.

15   ' As we are able to tranship coloured labour to France,   the situation will become eased here, but at the present moment, we have a large amount of coloured labour in all parts of the globe, waiting for shipment. As timber cutting in France is relatively more important than it is in this country, - as shipping across the channel is saved, we are sending to France the Canadians now in this country. 920/DER/17/27/1   Derby to Lloyd George, L.R.O.

16   In my own area (southern Cumbria) felling and the sale of large quantities of timber from rural estates increased rapidly. Lots were advertised as usual in the local press, but the Goverrnment had first call on all such timber.

17   G.H.Barker & Sons, Newby Bridge,   est 1858, Accounts, 1914 - 1918 The company still operates in Newby Bridge, Cumbria. By the autumn of 1914, the impact of wartime demand is obvious, including a major contract with the Navy.

18   Military records - as in the case of Liuetenant Ross Irving - are often more flexible, clearly indicating which forename is actually used. 21st C identity

controls insist on first given names. Banks, Building Societies and government departments also insist on the use of the first given forename.

19 Telfer/Irving family records, www.ancestry.co.uk and personal communication.

20 See Colin Poole, Living in Liverpool, pp 191 - 256. Liverpool 800, Culture, character and history, ed John Belderne. pub City of Liverpool and University of Liverpool, 2006

21 www.national-archives.gov.uk BT 27, passenger lists 1890 - 1960

22 This system, including the meagre £20 p.a. income didn't change until 1918. Once a young man qualified, he could become a salesman, earning perhaps £85 p.a.

23 One huge walnut specimen, cut in Italy in 1767, was used as a grape press - brought to Liverpool, sold in 1902.

24 Timber Town, Frank Latham., 1967

25 Timber and Plywood, August 21st, 1952

26 Timber Town, Frank Latham. Ulverston, then in North Lancashire, became a major wartime timber yard.

27 Karl Zuckerman 's Merseyside factory produced plywood panels. Under Government control throughout WWII, his specialist materials were used for both aeroplane construction and also the dummy installations. Latham, as above, Timber Town, and personal communication from Mr Latham, and the Telfer family.

28 Astute Roman Catholic teachers taught their pupils the approved (Protestant) alphabet. ' Haitch' was strongly discouraged.

Chapter Eleven

Dishonour not your mothers

1 The ' order of the white feather' , indicating cowardice, was created in the first days of the war by Admiral Charles Fitzgerald.

2 Joanna Trollope , Britannia's Daughters : Women of the British Empire, Pimlico, 2006

3 Maddocks, Liverpool Pals, 1991, Ch 1, p 27 6. For recruiting posters, see the IWM website. Examples are also displayed at many regimental museums.

4 Lewis Ewan Roberts, RUS 140, Liddle Collection, University of Leeds.

5 Pension and discharge records include the cases of many underage boys WO 364 National Archives.

6 Philip Snowden, The Living Wage, Hodder and Stoughton, 1912

7 Corrigan, Mud, Blood and Poppycock, 2003, Ch 8, p 245. A 2006 'Timewatch' broadcast investigated the discovery of the remains of a 1917 US casualty, well under five feet tall. (February 24th, '06) In 1914. Army rations offered significantly more calories and better overall nutrition than

the average working   class diet. Men used to a   life of poverty and monotonous drudgery were a positive asset to the army .

8   ' There is a serious issue of recruiting, now that Tribunals have given exemptions on trivial grounds. Doctors in Scotland are exempting more than 50% on medical grounds. The retention as badged men, of so many men of military age , especially young ones., is another serious matter.' 920/DER/17/27/1, L.R.O.

9   After declaring their loyalty, many local authorities swiftly voted to support claims for exemption. In Brough, Westmorland, they applied, successfully, on behalf of the local doctor. Coniston, then in Lancashire, sought exemption for their Overseer of the Poor. Council Minutes, 1916, C.R.O., Kendal.

10   The British Journal Alamanac Advertisements, 1912 , p 196   The same firm's 'Imperial' promoted as ' The leading low-priced set ' started at 67/6 for the quarter-plate model, i.e., £3. 2p, or, for many young men, three week's wages, out of which married men would be expected to support a family. A basic tripod cost at least 9s.

11   The distinctive crimson paper for Remembrance Day poppies is made in Cumbria, by James Cropper, plc of Burneside, near Kendal. Produced all the year round, it yields approximately 36 million poppies. Croppers also produce the laurel green paper for the wreaths.

12   John Keegan, The First World War , Chapter One ' A European Tragedy ' p.3, Pimlico, 1999

13   AQA, English Literature A-level syllabus, which includes the poetry popular during WWI.

14   Fortunately, between the wars, hundreds of regimmental histories had been written. Archives stored in Munich and Stuttgart survived. Jack Sheldon, The German Army on the Somme, introduction, pp 8 - 10, Pen & Sword, 2005

15   Council minute books from the Eden Valley and the Northern Lakes record many resignations from tribunals. As in the Llyn peninsula, in North Wales, tribunals in Eden were remarkably lenient to those who appealed against conscription.   Minute books,   C.R.O., Carlisle., and   tribunal reports, Cumberland & Westmorland Herald.

16   Beavis was sentenced to ten years. His case is reported in the NCF archive, D/Mar/4/13, C.R.O.

17   Fenner Brockway, Towards Tomorrow, Hart-Davis MacGibbon, 1977, Ch 4, pp 34 - 42 Articulate and mentally robust, Lord Brockway had secured many books for his month in solitary, on bread and water, but questioned the effect on his sanity.

18   One Welsh Tabernacle Church example of confiscated ' sedition' shows a woman at the foot of a cross, and four extracts from the New Testament.

19   Unilever file on F.R.Bourne. archives@unilever.com

20 ' It is my hope, and my brother's hope, some day to build houses in which our work people will be able to live and be comfortable, semi-detached houses, with gardens back and front, in which they will be able to know more about the science of living than in a back slum, and in which they will learn there is more enjoyment in life than the mere going to and coming from work' www.unilever.com .also www.mersey-gateway.org.

21 www.ancestry.co.uk

22 Michael Anderson, Approaches to the History of the Western Family, Macmillan, 1980, pp 30 - 31

23 Personal communications; interviews with the families of WWI and WWII conscientious objectors, including the family of one Richmond Castle prisoner.

24 Christ's Hospital School archives

25 Minutes of the Liverpool Stock Exchange, 25th August, 1914 L.R. O. See Ch One.

26 D/Mar/4/9 August 2, 1916, C.R.O.Carlisle.

27 Details of the new arrangements for enlisting and reserved occupations were published in national and local newspapers. Liverpool Courier, 1/11/15 Report from the War Office.' Starred men' not to be enlisted at present. Dockers and Railwaymen - Placed on Reserve Government Badges - munitions workers etc Khaki armlets in process of manufacture, will be issued to the following categories :

1) Men who enlist and are placed in groups awaiting a call to join the colours.

2) Men who offer themselves for enlistment, and are found to be medically unfit.

3) Men who have been invalided out of the service with good character or have been discharged ' not likely to become efficient' on medical grounds.

Grand Total - (period October 23rd, 1915 to December 15th, 1915)

Men of military age...	5,011,441
Total of men attested, enlisted, rejected :	2,829,263
Remainder	1,182,178
Married men not yet enlisted etc	1,152,947
Single men	1,029,231

In all, 59.23% of married men had enlisted or attested.
52.88% single

In Liverpool alone, over 13,000 single men had failed to attest.

28 Minutes of Liverpool City Council , 1915

29 War is the result of viewing wrongly ones duty to God and to ones neighbour. God was meant to rule not only innocent earth and stainless heaven, but to dwell in and rule the hearts of mankind. ' Canon Rawnsley, sermon, given during the service of intercession, Crosthwaite Church, January 2nd, 1916, Cumberland & Westmorland Herald, January, 1916

30 North Wales Pioneer, September 2nd 1915.

31 Caernarfon Council Minutes, 14th January, 1916. Archifdy Caernarfon, Gwynedd, also reported in the Caernarfon and Denbigh Herald, January 14th 1916.

32 Lloyd George himself had favoured self-interest rather than patriotism. Before the war, his majority was small. On December 22nd, 1911, the North Wales Pioneer reported that he was considering a move to the safe seat of Bordesley, Birmingham.

33 William Lloyd George , reported in the Caernarfon & Denbigh Herald, September 6th, 1918.

34 T. Arthur Leonard, Adventures in Holidaymaking, 1934, pp 59 - 60 and p 113

Chapter Twelve

' Blessed are the peacemakers, for they shall be called the children of God...'

1   Industrial workers often refused to work with C.O's See D/Mar/4/4/ C.R.O. Carlisle.

2   Survey of the religious and political affiliation of absolutists, June, 1916, D/Mar/ 4/7 , C.R.O. Carlisle. See also Andrew Thompson, Logical Nonconformity ? Conscientious Objectors in the Cambridge Free Churches After 1914. Journal or the United Reformed Church History Society, Vol 5, No 9, Nov 1996

3   Newspaper reports, September/October, 1915, Liverpool Courier and Liverpool Echo, December, 1915, Cumberland and Westmorland Herald. Just before conscription became law, the Bishop of Carlisle questioned, once more whether the church should encourage anyone to enlist.

4   Lord Derby and Douglas Haig, 1916 - 18 920 DER /17 /27/2 Liverpool Record Office

5   Reports from Wandsworth, June, 1916 D/Mar/4/7, C.R.O. Carlisle.

6   Ilana Bet-El, Conscripts, Sutton, 1999, Introduction, p 2.

7   Peter Simkins Kitchener's Army Ch 4 Recruiting in decline, October 1914 - May 1915, Pen & Sword, 1988, 2007

8   ' Sermon on the Mount ' not to be taken literally'. Report, Caernarfon and Denbigh Herald, May 17th, 1916

9   The No Conscription Fellowship archive includes several reports from penal 'work camps'   D/Mar/4/22,   C.R.O.Carlisle   Despite his own commitment to the war, Lewis Paton supported Mr Leyton . (Personal communication, from Professor Clyde Binfield.) In 1915, Joseph Hacking and his wife were among those to resign at Colne. CUCO 7/1, Lancashire Record Office

10 Published in the Sunday Herald, Mr Davies's letter is included in a collection of anti-conscription newspaper reports, in English and Welsh, hand-copied into an exercise book. XD/36/61/7.Archidfy Caernarfon

11 Munster News, January, 1916 (precise date obscured on a damaged copy) Archidfy Caernarfon

12 Lord Derby identified agitation against conscripting Russians as a serious problem, directed by Russian socialists, some groups within the Lanour party, and some newspapers, notably his own bête-noire, the Manchester Guardian. The Russian issue seems to have been something of a red herring. In 1916, of the 30,000 or so military age Russians resident in Britain, only seventy had enlisted. 920 DER/17/27/13 Liverpool Record Office

13 NCF survey of the religious affiliation of absolutists, June, 1916,. D/Mar/ 4/7 , C.R.O. Carlisle

14' The War in the Diocese' H 283 .9. CHA L. R.O. As part of the war effort, Bishop Chavasse also favoured a high-maintenance approach to clerical dress

15 Canon Thomas Irving, Hawkshead, quoted in 'Barbara Crossley, ' The Other Ambleside' self-published, 2000 copied

16 Canon Thomas Irving, report on his Armistice sermon, Hawkshead parish magazine, November, 1918, C.R.O. Kendal

17 Military Tribunal Report, April   1916, Liverpool Courier. As the lay minister isn't named, it wasn't possible to investigate his case.

18 Report from Philip Snowden, in a letter to the NCF, 10th August, 1917, concerning C.O. Macpherson, then on a punishment diet of bread and water, who suffered two major seizures during five visits. D/Mar/4/22, C.R.O. Carlisle

19 www.ppu.org.uk

20 Personal communication, from archive staff, Liverpool Record Office, who were aware of this document.

21 Fenner Brockway, Towards Tomorrow, Chs 5 & 6 Hart-Davis Macgibbon, London, 1977

22 In August, 1916, civil and military authorities descended on Sefton Park, Liverpool, rounding up any young men not in uniform. Reports, Liverpool Courier, August 28th, 1916, Westmorland Gazette, September 1st, 1916

23 Statistics on conscientious objectors, www.ppu.org.uk

24 Report from Birkenhead to NCF, August 29th, 1916 D / Mar / 4/ 10 , C.R.O., Carlisle

25 ' C.O's and Perpetual Hard Labour' G.Bernard Shaw, Manchester Guardian, June 12th, 1917 Reprinted as NCF Leaflet 8.

26 These and several similar cases were tried in April, 1916 D/Mar/4/4/, C.R.O. , Carlisle.

27 Labour Leader, March 16th, 1916, quoted in David Marquand, Ramsay Macdonald, Ch 9, p 185, Jonathan Cape, 1977

28 Labour Leader, as above

29 Lord Derby to Lloyd George 920. DER /17 /27/15 , Liverpool Record Office. Also, Ausgust, 1916, D/ Mar/4/4, recognising Derby's ob jection to the arrests of married men.

30 Accounts of the problems faced by discharged men can be found in WO 364, National Archives.

31 A letter from her friend, Emma Bartsch , reached Catherine in March 1915. D/Mar/2/33, 1915. In the summer, the NCF received the following statement issued in Sweden on Women's Peace Sunday, ' We can never forget that during these days young and vigorous men have been slaughtered, in thousands, women and children have been driven out of their wrecked homes, to succumb to hunger, sickness and outrage. We can never forget that where the battle raged, not only women became childless, but the whole province, because young children cannot endure the severe hardships of war. We know that the harvest the products of the future, were sacrificed, that irreplaceable treasures of culture were lost, and the fathers' inheritance which should have been the children's We know that the intellectual collaboration of nations, the group sympathy and confidence, the result of building up of international law, all these were damned and given as sacrifices to war.' On May 16th, 1917, a packet of letters from international conscientious objectors reached the NCF D/Mar/4/4, C.R.O., Carlisle

32 Already an experienced campaigner, Catherine was initially reluctant to take a leading role. Replying to Dr Ethel Williams, who had invited her to speak against the war, Catherine wrote : ' I am not yet qualified to speak on any of the subjects you suggest. I have a horror of people who undertake to talk about subjects which they have not carefully studied. 30th November, 1914, D/Mar/4/1. C.R. O. Carlisle.

33 Jo Vellacott, Bertrand Russell and the Pacifists of the First World War, Harvester Press, New York, Macmillan, 1980. See also additional texts, now added to The Collected Papers of Bertrand Russell., and Vellacott's paper on ' An Open Letter to Some Would-Be Friends of the Conscientious Objector.' Journal of Bertrand Russell Studies, McMaster University Press, winter 1999-2000 copied

34 Following a prison visit to Clifford Allen, Catherine wrote to the commanding officer : ' I shall always think of the Tort as a place where you put prisoners in barbarous dungeons, and then treat them with utmost consideration and courtesy.' CM to Maj.Dow, D/Mar/4/22, C.R.O., Carlisle

35 Fenner Brockway.' Towards Tomorrow' Ch Five, p 45   Hart-Davis, MacGibbon, 1977

36 The invitation from Lloyd George was signed by Frances Stevenson., April 10th, 1916 D/Mar/4/ 53. C.R.O., Carlisle.

37 Norman Angell to CM, undated, written on League of Nations Society paper, evidently early 1916 , D/Mar/4/9 C.R.O.Carlisle

38 Report, Liverpool Courier, April 1916.

39 Extract from Report, xxxix The statement may have provided by Charles Dukes, at Gamblin's Camp, near Birkenhead D/Mar.4/8, C.R.O., Carlisle

40 Fred Crowsley , to the NCF, D/Mar.4/7, C.R.O. Carlisle.

41 Absolutist C.N. Norman, reporting on his own experiences in Wandsworth, D/Mar/4/7 C.R.O., Carlisle

42 23rd May, 1916, D/Mar/ 4/4 C.R.O. , Carlisle

43 'Refused to sign. An obstinate recruit' Liverpool Courier, 27th March, 1916.

44 Private T Thacker, Aug 9th, 1917, letter to his mother on prison paper, loaned to the NCF, never returned, D/Mar/4/22 C.R.O. Carlisle.

45 6th July, 1916 D/Mar/4/8   C.R.O., Carlisle

46 22nd Nov.1916 D/Mar/4/37 C.R.O., Carlisle

47 Reported in the Sunday Chronicle, May 31st, 1916   The Richmond abuse is extensively documented, and now includes the English Heritage presentation at the castle. www.english-heritage.gov. uk See also NCF reports from May - July, 1916 D/Mar/ 4/7 C.R.O., Carlisle

48 Sylvia Pankhurst to NCF, June, 1916, D/Mar/4/8

49 29/8/1916 D/Mar/4/37 C.R.O. Carlisle

50 At Llandreusant, men working on the reservoir slept in wet bedding. According to a report made on March 24th, 1917, some were tubercular. D/Mar/4/ 22 C.R.O.Carlisle

51 23rd May, 1916. D/Mar/4/4, C.R.O., Carlisle. Professor Murray had opposed conscription as an assault on British liberty. His preface to Prince Lichnowsky's Revelations of the last German ambassador to England. My mission to London, 1912 - 1914, Cassell, 1918, presents a complex and somewhat inconsistent interpretation of Lichnowsky's paper. Identifying the 'murderous and corrupting power of the organised lie.' Murray focuses on the evil of German propaganda and, in the early months of the war, German atrocities.   His analysis could be applied equally to British propaganda. Writing in 1918, Professor Murray envisaged a future in which Sir Edward Grey's pre-war policies would come to fruition, with the Entente Cordiale extended, ' by gradual steps, to all nations who would come into it, and to bring the two groups of Europe nearer - this was the right policy, whether it succeeded or failed, and it will, in spirit at least, some day be the right policy again.

52 The War Office brought this correspondence to a curtly written end on October 14th. Russell had refused to give ' an honourable undertaking' to

confine his lectures to the expression of a general philosophy, or to abstain from using them as a vehicle for propaganda that contravenes the Defence of the Realm regulations. As he explained to the General, : ' I cannot undertake to avoid expressing respect for the ethical teachings of Christ, but I am quite uncertain whether, in dolng so, I shall be breaking the law. Bertrand Russell to General Cockerill, 29th September, 1916.

53 June, 1916, D/Mar/4/5, C.R.O., Carlisle.

54 March, 1917, letters between CM & BR.

55 Catherine had described Wakefield prison as his 'funkhole'. D/Mar/4/17 C.R.O. Carlisle.

56 'Why I Still Resist' Clifford Allen, Text of his self-defence, 25th May 1917, NCF, Leaflet No. 5 , C.R.O. Carlisle

57 ' The Archbishop is, I think, inclined to take some action on their behalf, but I am a little afraid of this. Unless parallel pressure is brought to bear on behalf of those who are suffering as moral as distinct from religious grounds. We must look to the Nonconformists to help hereI think, to uphold the principle of respect for freedom of conscience, whatever form each individual conscience may take'. 2nd September 1916 D/Mar / 4/ 13 C.R.O., Carlisle

58 Accepting 'work of national importance' often came after periods of imprisonment and work camp labour. Aged eighteen, the Seventh Day Adventist E.A. Beavon was sent first to Wormwood Scrubs, and then to Dartmoor. In his notebooks, he wrote ' In the name of Christ, I must defy all the pagan armies of Europe.' After year or so of prison and deliberately pointless labour , Beavon had become cynical, seeking a way to early release. He became a Seventh Day pastor in the U.S A. C.O. 007, Liddle Collection, Brotherton Library, University of Leeds.

59 Letter from Bertrand Russell to Catherine Marshall, 11/4/1916 D/Mar4/4 C.R.O., Carlisle

60 The NCF archive includes many reports of such raids. To the patriotic 'Westmorland Gazette', Miss Wilson was 'a pacifist'. The independent Cumberland and Westmorland Herald published her work. See also Fenner Brockway, ' Towards Tomorrow' Ch Five.

61 23rd May, 1916 D / Mar /4/4 C.R.O. Carlisle

62 19th May, 1916. Letter to CM from C. P. Scott, editor, Manchester Guardian. D/Mar /4/4 C.R.O. Carlisle

63 August, 1917, Private Moss to NCF D/ Mar/4/18 C.R.O., Carlisle Men like Alec, who had already served abroad, remained exempt from bearing arms.

64 www.national-archives.gov.uk (MH 47) and national-archives, Scotland, HH 30

65 On December 1st 1916, investigating an attempted suicide, Catherine learned that the man was the father of a severely disabled child. Suffering from influenza himself, he went to see his own doctor. Remembering that his

patient was a conscientious objector, the doctor then tore up his prescription and refused to do anything for him. D/Mar/4/13, C.R.O., Carlisle.

67   Bertrand Russell & The War Office. A Personal Statement, pub September, 1916, after the War Office order had been served on him, forbidding him to enter any prohibited area without permission in writing from the competent Military Authority. Russell refers to Latimer and Ridley, martyred in Oxford because they had broken the law imposed by Mary Tudor.

68   Dr Alan Billings, University of Lancaster, BBC Radio 4, April 2006

69   www.unilever.com/archives

70   £9. 16s per week was a moderately good income. In 1950, UK agricultural wages were fixed at £5. 8s 1 1/2 d (www.wirksworth.org.uk)

71   www.unilever.com/archives

Chapter Thirteen

The better course ?

1   Voltaire, Candide, 1759, Chapter III

2   Personal communication, interviews with the families of WWII conscientious objectors and the children of WWI c.o's

3   Commenced 20th September, 1915. See Westmore, The History of the 63rd Field Ambulance, Ch II copied into text

4   Bourne family papers.

5   Several serving soldiers wrote to the NCF, reporting the abuse of conscientious objectors. See, for example, June 8th, 1916, D / Mar/ 4/22 C.R.O.

6   www.nationalarchives.gov.uk/catalogue HO 214, internees, 1940 - 1949

7   A.W.Westmore, The History of the 63rd Field Ambulance, Ch III, pp 29 - 31

8   Francis Ramsey Bourne, personal papers, information to purchasers of his photographs. From its earliest days, the C.H.A. made grants to children's holiday funds. In 1903, grants were made to support children in Leeds, Birmingham, Oldham, Rochdale, London, Liverpool and Sheffield. B/CHA/ADM/1/3 Greater Manchester Record Office In Comradeship, spring 1909 , T.A.Leonard acknowledges many donations to the holiday fund, including, from one photographer, 22/- Even after WWII, many children in Birmingham had never seen the sea.

9   Liebe Freunde... Francis Ramsey Bourne, 1910, copy of a letter sent to his German friends, after a holiday in May, 1910. Bourne family papers.

10   Tramping through a foot of snow from Hayfield station, with Sir Drummond Fraser, Arthur and within easy reach of Manchester , Leonard had explored the deserted building by matchlight. A modest country house, the Hall was close to Hayfield station, the moors around Kinder Scout. (T.Arthur Leonard, Adventures in Holidaymaking, p 35)

11 The visit of the Ferienheimgesellschaft, a/ Main to some Centres of the Cooperative Holidays Association, July 1910. Arriving in London on July 2nd, the first two groups spent four days exploring central and outer London. The first party remained in the south, the second group travelling on to Oxford, Stratford, the Peak District, and Port Sunlight, which was also an all-day venue for the third group, who spent most of their time in the Peak District and Snowdonia. Led by Ernest Breul, elder son of Professor Karl Breul, the energetic fourth group spent a week in North Yorkshire, and a fortnight at Rhu, Ardenconnel. B/CHA/ PUB/5/2 , GMCRO B/CHA/PUB/6/1/2, GMCRO

12 C.H.A. summer programmes list all participating guides, lecturers, and other staff. In 1909, summer staff at Newlands included Canon Rawnsley, Lewis Paton, A.W. Rumney, of Keswick, Dr Barraclough, of Sheffield, and Mr Fred Marquis, of Liverpool, better known by his later title, Lord Woolton. Other summer staff included Dr Alex Hill, of Downing , and at Ardenconnell, in 1911, Alex M.Hill, M.A. B/CHA/PUB/5/2, GMCRO.

13 Ferienheimgesellschaft, Party 2, London, Oxford, Stratford, Hayfield, July 1st - 16th 1910, B/CHA/GMCRO.

14 ' Our Friends ' The Enemy', Elite Education in Britain and Germany before WWI. Thomas Weber, Stanford University Press, Stanford, California, 2008, B/CHA/PHT/3/16, 1910 - 1911, GMCRO Hayfield, July 9th, 1910,

15 B/CHA/PHT/3/16, photo albums, 1910 - 1911, GMCRO

16 Lewis Paton extolled the (supposed) character building virtues of primitive conditions, sharing every hardship with his pupils. One Manchester Grammar School partry stayed at Keld, the C.H.A's starkest hostel, eight miles from the nearest station, and without running water. The revered headmaster sat on the ground peeling buckets of potatoes.

17 Robert Louis Stevenson. An Inland Voyage, 1876. Quoted by Frank Bourne, on the flyleaf of a photographic collection. Stevenson is describing a sometimes uncomfortable journey along the Willebroek canal in Belgium.

18 The Town Planning Exhibition at the Royal Academy, Patrick Abercrombie, in ' Progress', Vol 10, pp 16 - 18, Lever Brothers' capital outlay on Port Sunlight amounted to over £500,000. Annual rents for the cottages and allotments amounted to nearly £9,000. At the current interest rate of 5%, the company was, in theory, ' losing' £25,000 per annum., but creating a world famous model community .archives@unilver.com

19 'Progress', Jan, 1910, p 12. archives@unilver.com

20 In October, 1910, a group of Belgian, Canadian, Dutch and German architects and planners attending the Royal Academy exhibition travelled to Port Sunlight together. In July, 1911, another group of over sixty Austrians, Belgians and Germans from the Garden City Association visited the town. 'Visit from German Garden City Friends' , Sir William Lever, ' Progress', Vol 11, pp 150 - 153. Some of Sir William's observations on Chinese and Indian competitors reflect prevalent contemporary attitudes to perceived racial differences. archives@unilever.com

21 Franz Crämer, 1860 - 1923, historian, taught in Munster, published works on Roman place names in Germany.

22 Othello, Act 1, Sc 3. Lying and manipulative, Iago bullied the gullible Roderigo in to funding his journey to Cyprus. Socially advantaged C.H.A. members were encouraged to help even the poorest to enjoy 'recreative and educative holidays, at the lowest possible cost' Franz Crämer, review of 'Ein Studienaufenthalt in England', by Adolf Reusch, 1903 B/CHA/HIS/16 GMCRO

23 Ibid.

24 The first CHA groups travelled to the Eifel., staying at the Gasthaus Meyer for two summers, 1907 - 8 B/CHA/HIS/16/GMCRO

25 Advertisements for summer staff at European centres stipulate that applicants should speak German or French fluently. 'Comradeship', February, 1913, B/CHA/Pub/1/1 GMCRO

26 Born in Hanover, Karl Breul (1860 - 1932) was educated at the Lyceum II Gymnasium, where the headmaster , a Schiller scholar, believed in the compulsory teaching of foreign languages. Breul later studied at the universities of Tübingen, Berlin, and Paris. In 1884, he was appointed as the first lecturer in Germanic language and literature at Cambridge. In 1886, he was elected a fellow of King's College, and in 1897, he was one of the co-founders of the ' Modern Languages Quarterly'. In 1910, he was appointed as the first Schröder Professor of German at Cambridge. Professor Breul was also President of the English Goethe Society. (Institute of Germanic Studies, home page) See Ch 14.

27 Letters from Karl Breul to Oscar Browning, 1905 - 1908 King's College Cambridge, OB/1/208/ C In October, 1904, Dr Breul questioned the accuracy of an article by Lewis Paton. Nevertheless, in 1911, Paton became the president of the Modern Languages Association, a post he held until 1933.

28 Karl Breul to Oscar Browning, as above, November 23rd, 1908. OB/1/208/C

Chapter Fourteen

Liebe Freunde

1 Ramsay Macdonald's letter on this subject is published in full in Comradeship, Autumn issue, 1911, pp 37-38 B/CHA/5/2 GMCRO. Press barons can change their opinions and party allegiance overnight, denouncing the very policies they had eagerly promoted. In June, 1916, The Times and the Daily Mail were removed from public libraries in Wales., because of their newly unpatriotic attitude to conscription. Report, June10th, North Wales Pioneer.

2 Massive expenditure in Britain encouraged Germany to increase her own spending on armaments. See Gerard De Groot, ' The First World War', Palgrave, 2001, Chapter 4, 'The War at Sea. See also '1905 - 1914; 'The Dreadnought Race' http://www.worldwar.com.Punch cartoons were published in the national and regional press. On July 4th, 1914, ' The Price

of Admiralty' recorded the following dialogue between Mr Punch and Britannia.

Mr Punch : You seem a little anxious, Madam.

Britannia : I'm waiting to know whether I can lay down the ships I want.

3   Franz Adickes 1848 - 1915 See Liberalism and the city in 19th century, James J Sheehan, Past and Present, Vo 51, pp 116 -137, 1971

4   Address to British guests, quoted in ' Summer Holidays in the Taunus, 1911' B/CHA/5/2, GMCRO

5   Two years earlier, at an AGM held in Manchester, some CHA members urged that the more warlike national songs should be removed. They weren't. In fact, apart from the British national anthem, ' le petit livre vert' included only one song of a warlike nature; La Marseilleise In 1919, during the postwar occupation of Germany, British soldiers heard local children singing ' Do you ken John Peel ? ' They, or their parents, had learned the Cumbrian ballad from C.H.A. visitors. When the war began, the British Army had no appropriate collection of music available for the troops. At the suggestion of the YMCA, many soldiers marching to the Western Front carried ' le petit livre vert', the original C.H.A songbook which had served for years almost as a passport for young people travelling to European hostels. Though the separation was supposedly honourable, the name of Leonard's politically suspect ' Holiday Fellowship' wasn't allowed to appear on the cover.

6   See Ch One, n 25, Letter to Professor (Sir) Patrick Geddes, from Arthur Leonard, August 8th, 1900 (Strathclyde University Archives)

7   Comradeship, 1909, B/CHA/PUB/131, also B/CHA/1/2, GMCRO

8   T.A.Leonard, In the Taunus, pp 3 - 5 Comradeship, 1909   GMCRO

9   Beveridge on Unemployment, 1909 Atsushi Komine, Journal of Economic Literature, revised March 2001. Despite the political crisis, Anglo-German engagements continued in the UK. Report, Westmorland Gazette, .July 1911. In Windermere, Prince Henry stayed with the Managing D irector of the Daimler' s UK headquarters. At the last minute, following the death of his mother in law, Lord Derby was obliged to withdraw from his role as judge.

10   Articles and letters written from are published in German. Those from Berlin are in English.

11   The new committee and Leonard's letters to newspapers achieved results. British visitors were , as they'd hoped, regularly joined by local people. Frankfurter Allgemeine etc

12   Nelson and Colne Times, report, November 17th 1911

13   T. Arthur Leonard, Adventures in Holidaymaking, pp 44 - 45. In his 1909 article for Comradeship, Leonard details the preparation which preceded the

Kelkheim project. Surviving programmes for the Taunus holidays record meticulously planned days. Breakfast could be at 6 or 7 a.m, and a typical day's activities included nine or ten miles of hillwalking, followed or preceded by visits to archaeological sites, theatres, galleries, cathedrals and civic buildings. Almost every day, local residents and civic office holders offer hospitality. B/CHA/5/2, GMCRO

14 See August Lory, Ferienheimgesellschaft,, A/M, Comradeship, spring 1911, pp 73 - 74, B/CHA/5/2, GMCRO

15 On January 4th, 1910 , a gift of £ 5 was voted to the funds of the Taunus church, and £5 to the local branch of the Taunus club,in Kelkheim. Gifts became reciprocal. B/CHA/ADM/1/3, GMCRO.

16 Reported in the Manchester Guardian, June 10th, 1911.

17 Comradeship, various short items, 1909 - 1913. The journal also reprinted articles from the regional press, reporting many initiatives designed to continue the educational links between Britain and Germany. In Brighouse, Yorkshire, every teacher in the area, together with the Mayor and the chairman of the Education Committee signed a goodwill message. B/CHA/ADM, GMCRO

18 One enthusiastic father sent the following message of support :

' The friendship which I am sure has been created between our charming guest Ludwig and our boy cannot fail to be continued through life, and through them, between the respective parents.' A German boy was equally appreciative : ' I have learned to like, and esteem the English people just as if they were my own countrymen. I have met with so much kindness which I never really expected in a foreign country .' Comradeship, November, 1911, B/CHA/ 5/2, GMCRO

19 Ernest Breul ' The Co-operative Holidays Association', Modern Language Teaching, Vol VI, 1910. Ernest was Professor Karl Breul's elder son, and Assistant General Secretary of the C.H.A. In 1909, he worked at the Villa St Charles, Dinan. A year later, he led the Ferienheimgesellschaft groups based at Rhu, near Ardenconnell,. and in the summer of 1911, he and Auguste Lorey were working at the Abbey House centre, Whitby. B/CHA/PUB/5/2

20 May 6th, 1911, meeting of the Anglo-German Friendship Society, Sir Frank Lascelles in the chair, Duke of Argyll president. Report, Manchester Guardian, Westmorland Gazette, , etc, May 7th, 1911.

21 Hubert Beaumont, (1883 - 1948) Cooperative employee, graduate of Ruskin College Oxford, where he was sponsored by the Coop, later studied at the Central Labour College. Labour MP, 1931 - 1948 (See Dictionary of National Biography) copy Beaumont's article, ' International Friendship through Holidays,', includes Macdonald's letter , published in full, identifying the C.H.A's political role. Comradeship, Autumn issue, 1911, pp 37-38 GMCRO.

22 On September 6th, 1911, in Manchester, a Mr Renshaw notified the meeting that he intended to raise the issue of the German boys, 'some of

whom are unsuitable.' Subsequently, on October 11th, he drew attention to the irregular conduct of certain members of this party, and it was agreed that representation should be made, with a view to securing safeguards to the proper selection of the boys, and to keep the size of visiting groups within manageable limits. Minute Book, 1911 - 21, B/CHA/ADM/1/4 GMCRO

23   'F.B.S' Our German Guests, Comradeship, 1912, B/CHA/.Pub/GMCRO

24   Wilfred Owen, ' Strange Meeting,' July, 1918

It seemed that out of battle I escaped,

Down some profound dull tunnel long since scooped

Through granite which titanic wars had groined

Yet also there encumbered sleepers groaned

To fast in thought or death to be bestirred

Then, as I probed them, one sprang up and stared

Lifting distressful hands, as if to bless

And by his smile, I knew that sullen hall

By his dead smile, I knew we stood in Hell...

With a thousand pains that vision's face was grained

Yet no blood reached there from the upper ground

And no guns thumped, or down the flues made moan

" Strange friend", I said, " here is no cause to mourn."

" None.", said the other, " save the undone years.

The hopelessness. Whatever hope is yours.

as my life also. I went hunting wild

After the wildest beauty in the world

.....

I am the enemy you killed, my friend.

25   Ernest Breul, in Modern Language Teaching, as above.

26   Professor Findlay of Manchester University attempts a contemporary analysis. Anglo-German Understanding, Victoria University. B/CHA/ADM/1/4   GMCRO

27   See above, Hubert Beaumont, n 19. Ramsay Macdonald,'s speech given in his Leicester constituency, July 15th, 1911, is quoted in Beaumont's article in Comradeship. Leonard's friendship with Macdonald appears to have been personal as well as political. During the war, Macdonald and his younger children would stay with the Leonards in North Wales. T.Arthur Leonard, Adventures in Holidaymaking, p 113

28   Nelson and Colne Times,   political speeches given by T.A.Leonard, reported November 17th, 1911, and January 12th, 1912 .

29   TAL, Adventures in Holidaymaking, p 113

30   Admiral Beresford's speech is reported in the Manchester Guardian, Nov 23rd, 1911. See also McDonough, Frank, The ConservativeParty and Anglo-German Relations, 1905 – 1914, Palgrave, 2007

31   Admiral ' Jackie' Fisher - Dictionary of National Biography

32   Prince Lichnowsky Revelations of the last German ambassador to England. My mission to London, 1912 - 1914, preface by Professor Gilbert Murray, Cassell, 1918, p 38   Lichnowsky served in Prussian army, 1885, attached to the German Embassy, 1885. Councillor of the Embassy in Vienna, 1899 - 1904, employed in German foreign office, 1904 - 1912, retired to his estates in Silesia, 1912, appointed Ambassador in London, on the death of Baron Marschal von Bieberstein. Lichnowsky did much to diminish the friction that had arisen during the time that Prince Bulow was Chancellor.

33   Nelson and Colne Times, 1911, 1912

34   On January 2nd, 1914, Leonard was accused of deliberate and continuous dishonesty. In Leonard's defence, others spoke of his twenty-one years of service, ' marked with unswerving industry and integrity'. Sir Drummond Fraser issued the followeing statement : ' Rumours constituting a specific charge of deliberate and continuous dishonesty on his part, and may do injury to the new Holiday Fellowship, with which he is now identified with. We desire to publicly state that Mr Leonard's retirement was due to his own in intiativeand his reasons were in the highest degree honourable.' B/CHA/ADM/1/4 GMCRO

35   The two committee members who resigned were Professor Charles Weiss and C.H.Smith.   It's possible that in private, others did support Leonard. In public, supporting an unpopular cause isn't easy, being more difficult still without the protection of a secret ballot. B/CHA/ADM/4 GMCRO.

36   Lewis Paton's introduction recognises the need to ' learn a wider fellowship with our fellow men', Adventures in Holidaymaking , Introit, pp 13 - 16

37   Adventures in Holidaymaking, p 9

38   Herbert Ibberson, Solicitor, 5th December, 1929, regarding plans to obstruct Leonard's intended publication. B/CHA/HIS/16/1,   GMCRO

39   Arthur Leonard's undated typescript, filed with many other papers from evidently 1929/30, B/CHA/HIS/16/1,   GMCRO

40   Adventures in Holidaymaking, p 60 and pp 112 - 113

41   Many photos survive, with the addresses of those who had ordered copies, and confirmation that all proceeds would be directed to the holiday charity. Francis Ramsey Bourne, personal papers.

41   According to Betrand Russell, Lloyd George ' would prosecute a reprint of the Sermon on the Mount if it interfered with the supply of munitions'. (a statement later hotly denied by Lloyd George. Letters exchanged between

Bertrand Russell and General Cockerill, 29th September - 12th October, 1916, D/Mar/4, C.R.O. Carlisle.

42 As reported in the Liverpool papers, the scale of exemptions was remarkable. In April, 1916, the Llanrwst tribunal had exempted all but nine out of 260 applicants. Many didn't bother to apply, confident of support in their local community. Caernarfon and Denbigh Herald, April 4th, 1916, also, personal information in North Wales

43 Reverend D.Evans, quoted at length in the Caernarfonshire and Denbigh Herald, March 17th, 1916 Other ministers explained, often, that young men needed to have the correct meaning of the New Testament explained to them.

44 Stuart Beavis, who had lived and worked as a teacher in Germany was sentenced to ten years. His case is reported in the NCF archive, D/Mar/4/13, C.R.O. Carlisle The records of many conscientious objectors can be read in the extensive Marshall papers of the No Conscription Fellowship, held in the C.R.O., Carlisle, and in the Liddle Collection, Brotherton Library, University of Leeds

45 In 1916, a survey of absolutists undertaken by the No Conscription Fellowship identifies the majority of Christian ' conchies' as members of the different Methodist churches. There were as many Congregationalists as Anglicans, but (see above) by no means all Comgregationalists opposed the war or conscription.

46 The participation of Seib and other members of the Musterschule/CHA project is referred to in the newspapers of September, 1909. See B/CHA/HIS/16/1, GMCRO

47 TAL, Adventures in Holidaymaking, pp 94 - 96 A surviving Newlands summer programme for 1911 identifies Seib as the assistant hostel manager. See B/CHA/5/2, GMCRO

48 Leonard's pragmatism can be startling. Newlands was several miles from the nearest plumber, and wasn't on the mains. Horrifying many middle class members, he favoured earth closets, rather than flushing lavatories, an arrangement which works well in the highest Alpine climbing huts. In the 21st century, thousands of Lake District properties still aren't connected to the mains. During a recent drought, households barely three miles from the largest lake in England struggled without water for weeks. His programme notes for intending hillwakers include warnings about litter, respect for wildlife, and the paramount importance of closing gates. The guidelines also include practical advice on answering calls of nature where there are no lavatories. There is no problem. The party should separate, men and women allowing each other fifteen minutes.

49 W. T.Shaw, Mining in the Lake Counties, pp 7 - 9, Dalesman Publishing Company, Third Edition, 1975 See also www.rock-site.co.uk The Coniston based artist and writer W.G. Collingwood studied the German ancestry of many Cumbrian families. See Collingwood family papers, C.R.O., Kendal & Marshall papers, esp. D/Mar/2/33, C.R.O., Carlisle

50 Leonard supplies his own translation : ' I shall never forget all the true friendship and love I experienced during the years I have been with you. I

cannot say more. You in your island say you are not responsible for this war and all the sorrow it has brought. What of the brave men, sons and brothers whome we loved and mourn ? Did they wish for the war ? Despite all, however, I send you my greetings, and if this should be my last greeting...

Key Source and associated documents

'Six Nomads in Normandy'   Bound typescript, 1912, unpublished

Letters and papers of the 17th Earl of Derby

Francis Ramsey Bourne Photographic archive, papers,and letters.

Telfer family papers and photos

Westmore family papers and photos

Leonard/Green family papers and photos

The National Archives.

Medal Rolls, 1914 - 1918

WO 363 and WO 364 'Burnt Series'

BT 27 passenger lists 1890 - 1960

Census returns, 1871 - 1901

Commonwealth War Graves Commission

Printed records and microfiches, copies of original documents in the National Archives.

King's Liverpool Regiment, 17th battalion diaries, 1915 - 16. (official transcript) KLR archives, Maritime Museum, Pier Head, Liverpool)

Other Primary Sources

Downing College, Cambridge

Dr Alex Hill's papers.

King's College, Cambridge

Karl Breul's papers, including letters on modern language teaching to Oscar Browning, OB/1/208/C.

Caernarfon Record Office

Oral history record of meetings with Arthur Leonard.

Press cuttings and manuscript records of conscientious objectors in Caernarfon borough.

Minutes of Caernarfon boroughs

Minutes of Caernarfon Labour council. (Working men, not the Labour Party.)

Christ's Hospital School archives.

Colne Local History Library

Papers of the C.H.A. and Holiday Fellowship.

Cumbria Record Offices,

       Barrow : Records of X Congregational Church, 1887 - 1890,

       Carlisle : Records of the Keswick Convention, 1911 & 1912,

            The papers of Catherine Marshall, No Conscription Fellowship,

            Council Minute Books for Carlisle and Keswick, 1914 - 1918

       Kendal : Council Minute Books for Appleby, Coniston and Kendal, 1914 - 1918.

            Records of the Congregational Church and the Friends' Meeting House, 1914 - 1918

Greater Manchester Record Office, Co-operative (later 'Countrywide') Holidays Association archives, papers of T.Arthur Leonard.

Liddle Collection, Brotherton Library, University of Leeds, ms of Lieutenant Wrayford Willmer, 17th Bn, KLR, GS 1753, Noel Chavasse,V.C., RAMC, GS 0298, Pte Tongue, GS 1613, Lieutenant Roberts, RUS 140, Pte Rogers, GS 1378, 63rd Field Ambulance, E.A.Beavon, C.O. 007, J.H. Todd and other conscientious objectors.

Liverpool Record Office and Local History Library : Records of Blackburne House school, the Collegiate School and the Liverpool Institute, Lord Derby's private correspondence with Asquith, Lloyd George, Douglas Haig and Philip Sassoon, 1914 - 1918, Records of St Cyprian's Church, West Derby, Street

Directories and Poll Books for Liverpool and Birkenhead, Liverpool Courier, Liverpool Echo,

Central Library, Manchester, Council Minutes, 1909 - 1913

Manchester Grammar School Archives

Newlands Outdoor Centre, Keswick, documents, printed papers and photographs

Company archives

G.H.Barker Ltd

James Cropper plc

HSBC

Unilever

Printed Records and microfiches, copies of original documents.

King's Liverpool Regiment, 17th battalion, diary, 1915 - 16. (official transcript) KLR archives, Maritime Museum, Pier Head, Liverpool)

Liverpool Customs Rolls, 1820 – 1939, Liverpool Record Office

Newspapers 1905 - 1918

Caernarfon and Denbigh Herald

Cork Examiner

Crosby Herald

Cumberland and Westmorland Herald

Daily Mail

Frankfurter Allgemeine

Liverpool Courier

Liverpool Echo

Manchester City News

Manchester Guardian

Nelson & Colne Times

North Wales Weekly News

Städtische Nachrichten

The Times

Westmorland Gazette

Westmorland Mercury

Journals and Trade Papers

Bradshaw, 1912

The British Journal Almanac, Advertisements, 1912 (photographic)

Church & Co, Export Price List of Men's Boots & Shoes etc, 1912

Clark, C & J, Street, Somerset, stock & price list, 1910

'Comradeship' - journal of the Cooperative Holidays Association, 1908 - 1914

Die Neue Zeitung, 1903

Railway News, 1912

Railway Times.1912

Timber and Plywood

Bibliography

Books

Anderson, Michael, Approaches to the History of the Western Family.
Macmillan, 1980

Annals of Cartmel

Arden, Peter, When Matron Ruled, Robert Hale, 2002

Army & Navy Stores Catalogue, 1907, facsimile edition, David & Charles,
1980,

Arthur, Max, Lost Voices of the Edwardians, Harper Collins, 2006

Baker, Dr Robert, Epidemic, Vision Paperback, 2007

Barker, Bernard, Ramsay Macdonald's Political Writings, Allen Lane, Penguin,
1972

Bennett, Alan, The History Boys : The Film, faber and faber, 2006

Bowker, Gordon, George Orwell, Little, Brown, 2003

Bet-El, Ilana, Conscripts, Sutton, 1999

Booth, Charles, Life and Labour in London, Macmillan, 1903

Brockway, Fenner, Towards Tomorrow, Hart Davis MacGibbon, 1977

Brown, Malcolm, ed, Letters of T. E. Lawrence OUP, 1991

Brown, Malcolm, Hislop, Ian, The Wipers Times Little Books, 2006

Burall, Simon, Donnelly, Brendan, Weir, Stuart, (editors) Not in Our Name,
Democracy and Foreign Policy in the UK, Politico's, 2006

Cannadine, David, Class in Britain, Yale University Press, 1998

Carroll, Andrew, Behind the Lines, Revealing and Uncensored Letters from our war-torn world,

Ebury Press, Random House, 2005

Cassell's Household Guide, The Waverley Book Company, London, 1912

Census of England and Wales, 1911, General Report, HMSO, London, 1917,

Census of England and Wales, 1921, General Report with Tables, HMSO, London, 1925

Clark, Alan, The Donkeys, Hutchinson, 1961

Corrigan, Gordon, Mud, Blood and Poppycock, Cassell, 2003

Curtis, Richard, and Elton, Ben, Blackadder Goes Forth,

Crossley, Barbara, The Other Ambleside self-published, 2000

Darlow, Stephen, D-day Bombers, The Veterans' Story, Grub Street, 2004

Deary, Terry, The Frightful First World War, Hippo, 1998

De Groot, Gerald J., Blighty, Longman, 1996

The First World War, Palgrave, 2001

Duffy, Christopher Through German Eyes : The British & the Somme, 1916,Weidenfeld & Nicholson, 2006

Dunham, Frank, The Long Carry London, 1970

Emsworth-Jones, Will, We Will Not Fight The Untold Story of World War One's Conscientious Objectors, Aurum Press, 2008

Ferguson, Niall, The Pity of War, Penguin, 1998

Ferro, Marc, Brown, Malcolm, Cazals, Remy, Mueller, Olaf, Meetings in No Man's Land, Christmas, 1914, and Fraternisation in the Great War. Constable & Robinson, 2007

Goldstein, Joshua S. War and Gender, C.U.P. 2001.

Goodall, Felicity, A Question of Conscience. Conscientious Objection in the two world wars, Sutton, 1977

Graves, Robert, Goodbye to All That, Jonathan cape, 1929

Grigg, John, Lloyd George, From Peace to War, 1912 - 1916 Eyre Methuen, 1985, Penguin, 2002

Hargreaves, Claire, Normandy, Cadogan, 2004

Harrison, A. Women's Industries in Liverpool, Liverpool University Press, 1904

Hibbard, Dominic, Wilfred Owen, Weidenfeld, 2002

Holmes, Richard, Tommy, Harper Collins, 2004

Johnson, James Turner, Morality and Contemporary Warfare, Yale University Press, 1999

Keegan, John, The First World War, Pimlico, 1999

Latham, Frank, Timber Town,

Lane, Margaret, The Tale of Beatrix Potter

Laussucq, Catherine, (ed) Brittany, DK, 2005

Liddell-Hart, B, Foch : Man of Orleans, Penguin, 2 vols, 1937

Macdonald, Lyn, They Called it Passchendaele, Penguin, 1978

    To the Last Man, Spring 1918, Viking, 1998

Macmillan, Margaret, Peacemakers The Paris Conference of 1919 and its
attempts to end war.

John Murray, 2001

Maddocks, Graham, Liverpool Pals, Leo Cooper, Pen and Sword, 1991

Marquand, David, Ramsay MacDonald, Joanathan Cape, 1977

Marlow, Joyce (ed) The Virago Book of Women of the Great War, Virago, 1998

Massie, Robert, Dreadnought, Ballantine, 1991

Mayhew, Henry, London Life and the London Poor, 1850s

MacArthur, Brian (ed) For King and Country, Little, Brown, 2008

McDonough, Frank, The Conservative Party and Anglo-German Relations

1905 – 1914, Palgarve, 2007

McKenna, Michael, Le Notre's Gardens.

McKintosh, Soil and Soul,

Miles, David, The Tribes of Britain, Who Are We ? And Where Do We Come
From? Weidenfeld and Nicholson, 2005

Mombauer, Annika, The Origins of the First World War, Longman

Montgomery, Fiona M. Edge Hill University College - A History 1885 - 1997
Phillimore & Co Ltd, 1997

Mulgan, Geoff, Good and Bad Power, The Ideals and Betrayals of Government,
Allen Lane, 2006

Musson, Spencer C. La Côte d'Emeraude, A & C Black, 1912

Nicholson, Virginia, Singled Out, Viking, 2007

Osborne, Peter, The Rise of Political Lying, The Free Press, 2005

O' Mara, Pat, Autobiography of a Liverpool Slummy, London, 1934.

Opie, Iona and Peter (eds) The Oxford Dictionary of Nursery Rhymes, Oxford
University Press

Oborne, Peter, The Rise of Political Lying, The Free Press, 2006

Pember Reeves, Maud, Round About A Pound A Week, G. Bell & Sons, 1913,
Virago, 1979

Ramsden, John, Don't Mention the War, The British and the Germans since 1890
Little, Brown, 2006

Porter, Roy, London. A Social History, Hamish Hamilton, 1994

Ransome, Arthur, Swallowdale, Jonathan Cape, 1931

Remarque, Erich Maria , All Quiet on the Western Front, 1929

Roberts, David (ed) Minds at War The Poetry and Experience of the First World War Saxon, 2003

Roberts, Elizabeth, A Woman's Place. An oral history of working class life. Blackwells, 1984, 1996

Rowntree, Seebohm, Poverty: A Study of Town Life, London, 1889 - 7

Samuel, A War Imagined, The First World War and British Culture. London, 1990.

Sassoon, Siegfried, Collected Poems, 1947

Shannon, Richard, Gladstone, Heroic Minister, 1869 - 98 Allen Lane, The Penguin Press, 1999

Simkins, Peter, Kitchener's Army, Pen and Sword, 2007

Sheldon, Jack, The German Army on the Somme, 1914 - 1916, Pen & Sword, 2005

Sheppard, David, and Worlock, Derek, Better Together, 1988

Sladen, D. B. W Brittany for Britons, A & C Black, 1896

Smith, Col.F. A Short History of the Army Medical Corps. Aldershot, Gale and Polden, 1929

Smith, Judy, Holiday Walks in Brittany ISBN 1-85058-733-7 2001

Steel, Nigel and Hart, Peter, Passchendaele - The Sacrificial Ground, Cassell Military Paperbacks, 2000

Stallworthy, Jon, (ed) Wilfred Owen, The War Poems, Chatto & Windus, 1994

Stevenson, Robert Louis Virginibis Puerisque, 1881.

Stevenson. Robert Louis An Inland Voyage, 1876

Strachan, Huw, Oxford Illustrated History of the First World War, O.U.O. 1998

Thomson, C.L. ed, A Book of Ballads, 1904

Todman, Dan The Great War, Myth and Memory, Hambledon & London, 2005

Toye, Richard Lloyd George & Churchill Rivals for Greatness, Macmillan, 2007

Van Emden, Richard, The Trench, Corgi, 2002

Boy Soldiers of the Great War, Headline, 2005

Vellacott, Bertrand Russell and the Pacifists of the First World War, Harvester Press, New York

Macmillan, 1980.

Vellacott, Jo, From Liberal to Labour with Women's Suffrage, The Story of Catherine Marshall,

McGill-Queen's University Press, 1993

Voltaire, Candide, 1759

Waller, P. J. ' A Political and Social history of Liverpool, 1868 - 1939,

Warren, W. L. King John, Peregrine, 1961

Weber, Thomas, Our Friends ' The Enemy ', Elite Education in Brtain and Germany before WWI, Stanford University Press, 2008

Westmore, A. W. and others The Story of the 63rd Field Ambulance, 1928

White, Michael, The Fruits of War, Simon and Schuster, 2005

Wilson, A. N. The Victorians , Hutchinson, 2002

Winter, J.M The Great War and the British People, Palgrave Macmillan, 2003

Woods, Abigail, A Manufactured Plague, 2004

Articles

Abercrombie, Patrick, The Town Planning Exhibition at the Royal Academy, ' Progress' pp 16 - 18, Jan, 1911

Allen, Clifford, ' Why I Still Resist' Text of his self-defence, 25th May, 1917, NCF, Leaflet No. 5

Beveridge, William Public Labour in Germany, 1908, Economic Journal

Beveridge on Unemployment, 1909, Atsushi Komine, Journal of Economic Literature, revised March 2001

Bevin, Mark, ' Labour Churches and Ethical Socialism,' History Today, Vol 47, April, 1997

Beaumont, Hubert, ' International Friendship Through Holidays', Comradeship, pp 37 - 38, Nov 1911

Breul, Ernest, The Co-operative Holidays Association,Modern Language Teaching, Vol V1, 1910

Gerald Browne Soldiers Songs of the Great War. www.westernfront.co.uk

Cochrane, Robert, ' Our Friends the Germans', Comradeship, pp 67 - 71,

Crämer, Franz, Ein StudienAufenthalt in England,   1903

Finn, Mike, The Realities of War, History Today, August 2002

Gillon, J K, Patrick Geddes and the Outlook Tower, Geddes Institute, Town and Regional Planning, University of Dundee, 2006

Gordon, Frank J, ' Liberal German Churchmen and the First World War', German Studies Review,

Vol 4, No. 1 (Feb 1981) pp 39 - 62

Graham, John W, Mr Norman Angell's New Book, in ' Comradeship', pp 68 - 69, April, 1911

Grieve, Mrs M, ' Sphagnum cybifolium' in 'A Modern Herbal',
www.botanical.com, peatlands. ni.

gov. uk

Hayward, Dr John A.. A Casualty Clearing Station 7 pp, Memoirs and Diaries,
First World War.com

Hindley, J.M.J, Whitsuntide in Germany, Comradeship, pp 71 - 73, autumn 1909

James, David, ' The Foundations of International Polity',1987, 'Our Philip', The
Bradford Antiquary, Vol 3, pp 39 - 47

Latham, Frank, Timber Town - The History of the Liverpool Timber Trade.
(monograph) 1967, pub

Institute of Wood Science.

Lever, Sir William, Visit from German Garden City Friends, Business versus
Philanthropy, ' Progress',

Vol 11, No 104, October, 1911 pp 15 - 153,

Prince Lichnowsky's Revelations of the last German ambassador to England. My
mission to London, 1912 - 1914, Cassell, 1918

Lory, August, ' Ferienheimgesellschaft, Frankfurt A/M, Comradeship, pp 73 - 74,
April, 1911

Macdonald, Ramsay, What I saw in South Africa, 1902 , quoted in David
Marquand, Ramsay

Macdonald, Jonathan Cape, 1977, Chapter 5, pp 76 - 77

Payne, Dr David, The Great War and the Influenza pandemic of 1918
www.westernfront.co.uk

The RAMC and the Great War, www.westernfront.co.uk

The Dreadnoughts and the Western Front, revided ed, May 2009,
www westernfrontassociation

Peacock, A.D. The Louse problem on the Western Front, Journal of the Royal
ArmyMedicalCorps.Vol. 27, pp 36 - 60

Pugh, Martin, The People's Budget, Causes and Consequences New Perspective,
1995

Russell, Bertrand, A Personal Statement, pub September, 1916

'An Open Letter to Some Would-Be Friends of the Conscientious
Objector.' ed. Jo Vellacott, Journal of Bertrand Russell Studies,
McMaster University Press, winter 1999-2000

Correspondence with General Cockerill, 1916

Autobiography, 3 vols, Allen and Unwin, 1967 - 69

Shaw, G Bernard, ' C.O's and Perpetual Hard Labour' Manchester Guardian,
June 12th, 1917 Reprinted as NCF Leaflet 8.

Strachan, Hew, The Entente Cordiale, War and Empire, Journal of the Royal
United Services, April 2004

Walter, Dr Max, Die Reform des Neusprachlichen Unterrichts auf Schule und Universitat. 2nd ed, Marburg, 1912.

Westmore, A. W, articles on the 63rd Field Ambulance, published in the Liverpool Courier, 1919

Websites

www.army.mod.uk/medical/ams.museum

www.bbc.co.uk/history,www.botanical.com

www.1901census-nationalarchives.gov.uk

www.english-heritage.gov.uk

www.francetourism.com

www.gmcro.co.uk

www.iwm.org.uk

www.jerseyheritagetrust.org

www.mersey-gateway.org

www.nationaltrust.org.uk

www.naturtrek.co.uk

www.normandy-tourism.org

www.peatlandsni.gov.uk

www.ppu.org.uk

www.rochdale.gov.uk

www.stcaths.com

www.waramps.ca

www.westernfront.co.uk

Acknowledgements

On the title page of their 1912 book, the authors of 'Six Nomads in Normandy' do not give their names, recording only that it was written 'By Themselves'. Analysis of the text and photographs achieved, eventually, four complete names, one unnamed woman, and 'Ross'. Identifying all six 'Nomads' was only possible because supportive editors in Cumbria, in Liverpool and on the Wirral agreed to publish articles and photographs about the ' Nomads' and their journey. Magazine and newspaper articles reached many descendants, who contacted me, offering invaluable material, including four more copies of the Nomads' book, many other photographs and the documents, which led eventually, to the international movement inspired by Arthur Leonard.

Without the information provided by all these descendants, little of my research would have been possible, and this book could not have been written. My thanks to Elizabeth Griffiths, née Bourne, Frank's daughter, John Bourne, Frank's son, Brian Griffiths, Frank's grandson, Martin Gleave, nephew of Gladys Gleave, Nancy Green, great-granddaughter of T. Arthur Leonard, Mary Slack, granddaughter of Emma Irving, Hedy Telfer, daughter in law of Ross, Mark Telfer, grandson of Ross, Susan Dunigan, née Telfer, granddaughter of Ross, Enid Beech, Diane Meade, Telfer cousins, Norman and Gwyneth Westmore, son and daughter in law of Alec.

Beginning my research in the Liverpool Record Office, I was able to read the WWI letters and papers of the 17th Earl of Derby My thanks to the Earl of Derby, who has allowed me to quote from his great-grandfather's letters, especially the personal correspondence with Douglas Haig.

I would like to thank every single person who has helped with this book, including Phil Atkins, Archivist, National Railway Museum, Lydia Bartlett, Abbott Hall, Kendal, Debbie Beament, Newlands Outdoor Centre, Derwentwater, Roger Beckwith, Steve Beinder, Director, Newlands, Professor Stefan Berger, University of Manchester, Professor Clyde Binfield, University of Sheffield, Frank Bland, Christine Bradley, Local History Library, Colne, David Bowcock, Carlisle Record Office, Michael Brian, Liverpool History Society, Danita Chisholm, Canadian Association of War Amputees. Tom Clark, Jeff Cowton, The Wordsworth Trust, Jacqueline Cox, University Archives, Cambridge, Benedicte Crebessac, Frankfurt A/M, Barbara Crossley, Joyce Culling,Richard Davies, special collections, University of Leeds, Joseph Dawson, Neil Dixon, Timber Trade Journal, English Heritage staff, Richmond Castle, Elizabeth Ennions, archivist, King's College, Cambridge, Lois Evans, Society of Friends, Liverpool, Paul Evans, Royal Artillery Museum, Mark Featherstone-Witty, Principal, L.I.P.A., Jan Flamman, HM Prison, Liverpool, Jan Fullman, Holiday Fellowship, Alison Gill, Greater Manchester Record Office, Susan Grant, Newlands, Richard Grisenthwaite, Cumbria Record Office, Kendal, Dr Jacques Gury, Rennes, Jane Haase, Hilary Haig, John Hamilton, Rosemary Harden, Museum of Costume, Bath, Rev David Harkisson, United Reformed Church, Kendal, Christopher Hayes, Institute of Romance and Germanic Studies, Roberta Hazan, St Dunstan's, Peter Hillebrecht, Kelkheim, Ruth Hobbins, Liverpool Record Office, John Highfield, Society of Friends, Liverpool, Joe Hodgson,editor, Western Front Newsletter,Professor Richard Holmes, Cranfield University Roger Hull, Liverpool Record Office, David and Sheila Iley, Dr et MMe Alfred Jameaux, Saint-Malo, Angharad Jones, Caernarfon Record Office, Bill Jones, Granada Television, Clifford Jones, Christ's Hospital School, Gary Jones, Conwy Record Office, Dr Miles Lambert, Gallery of Costume, Manchester, Philippe Lanoë, Institut Culturel de Bretagne, Frank Latham, Anja Schiffler-Laue, Frankfurt A/M, Alice Leach, Reverend David Lewis, St Cyprian's Church, Liverpool, Jo McCann, Liverpool History Society, Carol Mee, Liddle Collection, Tina Myles, HSBC archives, Alex Miller Unilever Archives, Professor Fiona Montgomery, Bath Spa University, Sue Mullally, Diocese of Liverpool, Mark Naylor, Queen's Lancashire Regiment, Joan Nicholson, Karen O'Rourke, King's Liverpool Regiment Archives, Professor Nigel Palmer, University of Oxford, Rev Dr Pope, University of Bangor, Daniel Pressler, Edge Hill University College, Rev Dr Dan Rees, Cedric Robinson, Queen's Guide, Tony Richards, Imperial War Museum,

Dorothy Ridley, Rebecca Shawcross, Northampton Shoe Museum, Peter Simm, John Snelson, Liverpool Institute,Ellie Somers, Museum of Costume, Bath, Capt. P.H. Starling, Army Medical Services Museum, Dr Rainer Stephan, Frankfurt, June Swann, Consultant, History of Shoemaking, Janet Targett, Clarks, Street, Somerset, D.R. Thompson, Governor, HM Prison, Wakefield, Margaret Thompson, Westminster College, Cambridge, Lesley Toll, Bryn Trecatheric, Jean-Paul Le Trionnaire, Andy Tucker, Naturetre, Chris Walker, Managing Editor, Liverpool Echo.

Every effort has been made to trace all copyright holders and seek their permission to quote from relevant documents.

Afterword

Everybody who reads Emma Irving's confident 1912 toast to ' long life and happy days' wants to know what really happened. At first, answering that question seemed impossible. My husband, son and daughters have supported and sometimes endured the years of research which led me from a junkshop discovery to the Western Front, Fred Pulford's death on the Somme, Alec Westmore's years as a stretcher bearer and his work as an early WWI historian. Pre-war, the six young backpackers had enjoyed outdoor adventures in the C.H.A. Research in Colne, Cumbria and Manchester identified its founder, Arthur Leonard as a charismatic social reformer and pioneer of outdoor education, with many friends in the emerging Labour party and in the universities. There the story might have ended. Two of the four young men had become bone fide heroes.

Norman Westmore's revelation that his godfather Frank Bourne 'wasn't in the war' took the Nomads' story in a new direction. Frank's 1910 letter to his friends in Frankfurt's Ferienheimgesellschaft led, eventually, to Arthur Leonard's important political role before and during the war, and to the many statesmen, scholars and social reformers of all political parties in Britain and Germany who were among his closest friends. Informally, I call them the ' Stop WWI Coalition '. Like the 'Stop the War' coalition which hoped to prevent the invasion of Iraq in 2003, the peace campaigners of the early twentieth century didn't succeed. Edmund Burke's much-quoted observation on the triumph of evil is merely a truism. Across Europe, good men and women were doing everything in their power to prevent the 'Great War'.

SIX NOMADS IN NORMANDY

Chapter I

"Mr.Pulford's party" was now 'en train', and the journey up to London was very pleasant, plans and projects being freely discussed, while Fred gave us chemical experiments on the capture of the cold germ. Arrived at London, we dived into labyrinthine tubes, coming up for a breather at Charing Cross, and incidentally to feed the 'Lions'. It was a short walk to the Tate Collection where we spent the afternoon, many of us making a first acquaintance of some of the finest masterpieces of modern art. Leaving the Tate we made our way to the Abbey and spent a quiet half-hour there.

It was now time to make our way to Waterloo, and on arrival we found a special carriage reserved for "Mr. Pulford's party", which we instantly commandeered. We had a very jolly journey to Southampton; conversation never flagged, and jokes, and stories held the audience, except for occasional surrenders to side show attractions on the platform on the part of certain members who shall be nameless. Southampton reached, a short walk brought us to the Docks, where the good ship "Hantonia" awaited our arrival.

We were all very tired and soon sought our berths, to sleep if that were possible. But what with the babel of French tongues, Fred's monologues, and the vibration of the screws, sleep was out of the question. We were early on deck, and although it was chilly the sun shone encouragingly upon the sea, telling us that he only tarried out of deference to the moon. Away on the horizon a solitary fishing smack caught the first glow on its sails, reminding us that "they that go down to the sea in ships .... these see the wonders of the deep."

Slowly we entered the harbour of Le Havre (if this is not tautological) and out of the slight mist emerged the lighthouse, and, gradually, the houses and the quay. A rather motley collection of porters, relieved by the bright uniforms of the gendarmes, awaited our arrival, and after the ship's papers had been delivered we scrambled ashore up a steep gangway, but we did not repeat William I' s little piece of stage play, although the circumstances were propitious. The old lady who presided at the Douane was not a very formidable 'eye of the law', as she only winked at our portmanteaux, and contented herself with supplying us with a little French chalk gratis.

The environs of the quay are not very salubrious, so we made for the more fashionable quarter. Having discovered a very nice open air cafe we had our first acquaintance of French waiters - who are invariably attentive and polite - and French coffee and rolls, to say nothing of eggs ' à la coq'. (sic) We found everything very good, and despite our sleepiness felt on very much better terms with the world in general and France in particular. It was still quite early, and it seemed very strange to be promenading the streets at 7.30 a.m. on Sunday morning, so we repaired to the pretty gardens in front of the Hotel de Ville. Ross meanwhile looked up an old friend - a young Frenchman who had spent some years in England - and while we waited we saw all the 'pères de familles' in their Sunday attire, bringing home their carrots etc. from market!

Our young friend duly appeared and very kindly offered to show us round the town. A service was being held at the Church of Notre Dame so we could not properly examine the building, but some parts of the exterior seemed very old. The church was crowded, and the ritual seemed spectacular to an Anglican, but the music was very impressive.

We now boarded a car running along the 'plage' to St. Adresse. There were no outside seats, but we stood round the driver and thus obtained the maximum of air at the minimum of cost, which seemed to be the fashion. St. Adresse is a modern sea-side suburb, and there were some very pretty chalets on the hillside overlooking the sea. The Post Office people here were very obliging, as although it was closed they gave us stamps through the window (Is this Sunday trading?) and we had just time to write some post-cards before our tram returned to Havre. It was now time to go for the boat, so after provisioning, which occasioned some juggling with kilogrammes, we boarded the river boat.

Accommodation was rather limited, to say the least, and whenever we attempted to sit down we were informed we were impeding navigation. However, when we were once off we went 'forard', and getting some deck stools from the hold made ourselves comfortable. The sun blazed down on us as we laboured across the broad estuary of the Seine, passing in the distance Honfleur and Trouville, and whilst some of the party had a nap, the more energetic sat on the prow and cheered passing motor launches. We now headed inland for the mouth of the Orne, and called at Ouistreham, a pretty little poplar-fringed village. Here the river and canal journey side by side, so entering the latter we lazily made our way between broad fields dotted here and there with poplars, and finally came in sight of the noble spires of Caen.

Without much difficulty we found the Hotel de Normandie, where Madame welcomed us in the courtyard. We were a little dejected when we found we had about two hours to wait for dinner, but waited as patiently as we could in the 'salle à manger'. Meanwhile we started Madame on the subject of churches, and if we could only have followed half the good lady told us a guide book would have been superfluous. At last the dinner bell clanged out, and one would have thought that all Caen were coming by the vigorous onslaught of the bellman. But beyond a separate table of 'pensionnaires', our fellow diners were limited to two, and as we had not yet stood the trial of the French cuisine we were not sorry. However our smiling garcon soon adjusted any maladroit table etiquette, and we gradually learnt when to cling to our knives and forks and when to surrender them. This was our first taste of Normandy cider, and although it was a little tart we soon found that it improved on further acquaintance (ce n'est que le premier verre qui coute).

We now sallied forth to see the town, first directing our steps to the church of St. Pierre. It is a fine old Norman church with a beautiful tower, and the elaborate decorative work on the abside is a marvel of mediaeval workmanship. Continuing our peregrinations up the rue de Saint Pierre, we passed many old timbered houses to delight the antiquarian's heart, and we were struck by the Frenchman's love of the open air, everybody being at the door or in the street.

Returning to our hotel we retired to rest, promising ourselves much to see on the morrow. And what curious beds they were! High four posters that almost required a ladder to reach them, with a huge cushion reposing on the top, which we promptly relegated to the floor. But we slept soundly enough and were awake betimes, Frank, indefatigable as ever, snapping the beds (only the camera) and courtyard.

It was a very quaint inn, and much more spacious than its exterior promised. Passing the estaminet and bureau you entered a square courtyard with bedrooms on three sides with a bell for each. An open gallery ran along each side reached by a flight of steps, and on the right was the 'salle à manger'. Whilst the early birds were looking for photographic worms, two heads appeared at an upper window (telling of shaving operations still proceeding) and were instantly snapped.

Breakfast in the 'estaminet' was not a very elaborate affair, and Ross's persevering enterprise on the subject of 'miel' deserved better success. However, we got 'confiture'.

We now resumed our sight seeing, visiting the Abbaye aux Dames, which has two very fine square towers. It was founded by Queen Matilde, as the Abbaye aux Hommes was by William, as a pious offering to the Pope, to appease his Holiness and obtain condonement for marrying within the limits of consanguinity. We only regretted that our time was so limited that it prevented us lingering in these monuments of craftsmanship and giving them the study they deserved.

Returning to our hotel we put on our war paint and bade adieu to our kindly hostess, who suggested that we would want three legs for our enterprise.

Background to Chapter I

On July 20th, 1912, six young people caught the early morning train from Lime Street, paused, for an energetic speed-tour of London, crossed the Channel, and headed west. For one idyllic fortnight, France was theirs. Reading their book, they sprang to life at once, intensely and vividly real. Why they decided to tramp across Normandy and Brittany is never explained, but, wandering through the French countryside, they might be twenty-first century backpackers. Preparing for this kind of adventure is a science. Every single item in a rucksack must earn its place. Five miles down the road, everything weighs at least twice as much. Trekking around the Arctic Circle and climbing in the Alps, I learned the ruthless balloon-basket test. Today, there's a huge and high-tech global industry in travel goods, offering everything from pocket GPS to in-flight stockings, all ultra light weight. In their leather and canvas rucksacks, what would 1912 backpackers carry ? How much would it all cost ?

Like for like, comparing the Nomads' equipment and other expenses with modern equivalents isn't always possible. The real cost of so many everyday items has been slashed, especially food and clothing. Throughout their journey, the yardstick for their adventure has to be the ordinary family budget, the everyday cost of living in 1912. In Liverpool, of course, they'd have access to city department stores, but, for convenience and consistency, I sourced most of their holiday kit in the facsimile of the Army and Navy Catalogue for 1907. For busy young workers, the Army & Navy would have been an invaluable one-stop source.[1]

In some respects, they were luckier than modern travellers. Without biometric passports and platoons of armed guards, they could move casually between England and France. Before terrorism, sending luggage ahead was so much simpler, so long as you could afford the fees. At Le Havre, they take three portmanteaux through customs, don't see this heavy luggage again till they reach Granville, a week later. But for many of their contemporaries, even their luggage itself would be an impossible luxury, let alone the contents, and the holiday itself. At 89/- (£4. 45p) the cheapest portmanteau cost four times more than the average working man's wage. Arriving in London, they don't seem to be hampered by heavy luggage. It would make sense to send everything directly from their homes to Southampton docks.[2]

Leaving Caen next morning, the rucksacks they're carrying closely resemble Army and Navy models costing from 16s 3d to 21s 3d. For many families, this would be a week's income.[3] Born into a very different world, the Nomads needed proper equipment for their adventure. If they were to achieve their goal of walking to Brittany, they couldn't afford to skimp. Backpacking, a comfortable rucksack's essential. Travelling every day, they'd need all the usual toiletries. Tins of toothpowder cost around 10d. So did shaving sticks. A basic toothbrush was 6d, and a guard, converting it into a travel toothbrush, added another 4 ½ d. Early 20th century travellers carried impregnated soap sheets, at 4d a book. For women, there were tightly compressed sanitary towels at 1s 6d per dozen. Contemporary advertisements stress discretion, but at least, long before the advent of tampons, manufacturers recognised that women were travelling and catered for them. Beards being out of favour, men needed a shaving kit. A traveling mirror cost 3s 3d. At 21s, the newly fashionable Gillette safety razors were far from cheap. A basic travel first aid kit cost 10s 6d - more than most working families could allow for food, and a travelling ink bottle was 2s 3d. Perhaps they'd use pencil ? Planning to write about their adventures, taking notes en route would be essential. Pencils were cheap enough, at 9d per dozen for the kind with a rubber at the tip.[4] For the same money, a Lambeth family struggling to feed six children could buy a week's a week's supply of potatoes.[5]

Until the discovery of George Mallory's body on Everest, in 1999, modern outdoor clothing designers scorned the natural fibres worn by earlier adventurers. Not any more... Recent research has proved that silk, tweed, fine wool and cotton, as worn by Mallory, can match and even outperform twenty-first century hi-tech sports wear.[6] Around the time of their journey, Army and Navy cotton shirts for ladies started at 4s 9d. Light and cool in summer heat, silk underwear was, inevitably, quite expensive, 6s 4d for a man's spun-silk vest, 10s 9d for ladies' silk knickerbockers. (underwear) Cheaper longcloth or flannel knickers started at 2s 3d . Cotton socks for men were 1s 3d a pair; sturdy cycling socks 4s. 0d. The book mentions mackintoshes. Worn over the rucksacks, as described in their sodden arrival at St Aubyn's, these must have been loose. A motor cyclist's waterproof poncho cost 39s 6d, or nearly two pounds. A lady's showerproof summer coat cost 14s 9d, and the man's version 17s. Perhaps the enterprising Nomads made their own ? Showerproof twill cost 3s 3d a yard.[7]

Shaving kits and silk knickers are expendable... On the road, every day, sometimes for twenty miles and more, strong, comfortable shoes are vital. Most Edwardian shoes were neither. Setting an Edwardian scene, costume museums usually display ladies' shoes and boots in delicate brocades and glacé kid, the Manolos and Jimmy Choos of their day, unlikely to last one mile, let alone twenty on unmade roads. Since the 1880's, high fashion styles for men, women and children had been a podiatrist's nightmare. Impossibly narrow and viciously pointed, they crippled and distorted the feet of anyone who could afford shoes.[8] Barefoot or in clogs, the children of the poor fared better, or at least, their chilblained toes were straight. Working class parents struggled to provide their children with boots, often paying between 6d - 1s a week into a boot club.[9] Footwear prices remained high until cheaper imports reached Britain during the 1950's. As ' tramps' in France, the Nomads would need something far sturdier than brocade or kid, and preferably, not in the least fashionable. Book photos don't give a clear view of their feet, but in a photo taken at Hayfield, in the Peak District, they've achieved an inspired compromise, magnificent hats, but on their feet, both sexes are wearing serviceable shoes. In 1914, the K shoes factory at Netherfield, in Kendal, secured a War Office contract for thousands of army boots. Demand was so overwhelming that work on civilian footwear had to stop.[10]

Sensibly shod or not, leaving Liverpool on July 20th, they had an excellent train service. The 8.0 a.m. from Lime Street was timetabled to reach Euston by midday. The 9.45 express was only marginally faster, arriving at 1.40 p.m.[11] Even the later train allowed plenty of time for the Tate, Trafalgar Square and the Abbey, before boarding the boat train.[12] Rail journeys were priced per mile, rather than the current bewildering lottery. Their one-way journey from Waterloo to Le Havre cost 24s 6d. Returning from St Malo to London, two weeks later, they'd pay 35s 10d for first class, and 25s 10d for a second class passage. Built by Camell Laird, their ship, the Hantonia was owned by the railway company, which also owned their own quay at Le Havre, and another, at St Malo. Long before the EU, trading practicality was uniting Europe.[13]

Overnight, on board, they were kept awake by Fred's monologues, and the vibration of the Hantonia's engine. As they'd spent the train journey laughing and joking, presumably Fred entertained them with popular comic monologues, such as Milton Hayes' 1911 classic, The Green Eye of the Yellow God, rather than more serious recitations.[14]

' There's a one-eyed yellow idol to the north of Khatmandu

There's a little marble grave above the town...'

Works such as Browning's sardonic ' Soliloquy in a Spanish Cloister ' and the sinister ' My Last Duchess' were available from Edison, and in 1912, on both sides of the Atlantic, even passionate suffragette speeches sold well, the podcasts of their day.[15] Delivering course-work, and allowed to take set texts into their modular exams, schoolchildren and students no longer need heroic memories. Working in film and TV, actors can avoid the painful business of mastering a complete script. Autocues protect stand-up comedians from sudden death. Fred, as a late Victorian child, would have to master the art of memorising long poems, just as he'd learn his tables and verses of scripture. Before ubiquitous 24/7 multichannel broadcasting, DVDs and Ipods, reciting, singing and playing for friends and family was open to all, not just embryo professionals.[16]

At dawn on July 21st, the sea was smooth as a pond, but they reached the French coast in heavy mist.[17] The book quotes from Psalm 107. According to the Book of Common Prayer, this would be said as part of morning prayers. As practising Christians, all the Nomads would be familiar with the psalms, just as they'd know the traditions of English history. The reference to William the Conqueror's ' piece of stage play' refers to his tripping and falling on the beach at Pevensey. According to legend, or William's spin doctors, he then seized a handful of sand, claiming his right to the whole country. Multicultural and democratic, English primary schools no longer teach children to list the Kings and Queens of England back to the Conquest, let alone back to Alfred.

Like all the best travel writers, the Nomads celebrate the gloriously unexpected. Arriving at Le Havre, on a Sunday morning, they're fascinated by what was, for them, two equally extraordinary sights; hatless women, buying bread, and grown men, actually shopping for vegetables. In 1912 Liverpool men of any class would sooner starve than be caught doing any kind of ' women's work'. Anywhere in Britain, nobody would be shopping, with or without hats, because the Lord's Day Act of 1906 had forbidden Sunday trading. Three years later, Lloyd George sharply curtailed pub opening hours. Allegedly, long working hours and round the clock drinking were at the root of so many social problems, family breakdown, violence and child abuse. Obviously, the government had to intervene. The Nomads' world is often eerily familiar.[18]

Using public transport with confidence, they never waste a moment. Leaving their heavy luggage at the Caen boat, the tram they caught to St Adresse cost half a franc inside, but only ten sous, if you stood on the platform, by the driver.[19] Heading for the beach, perhaps they knew what to expect ? Manet's paintings of St Adresse are ubiquitous now, on calendars, mouse-mats, and the kind of tote bags sold by museums and galleries. By three o'clock, after lunching on cake, they were back at Le Havre. From the river boat to Caen, they looked on, as a motorboat chased harbour porpoises. For a week, the Nomads would explore 'lovely pastoral Normandy'. So much of the Normandy they knew suffered grievously in 1944. Leaving the Seine estuary to enter the canal, they were now in the heart of what would become, in 1944, the D-Day battlegrounds. Reaching Caen, surely exhausted by two days of constant travelling and a sleepless night, they were fascinated by the hotel's high beds, and immense duvet-style feather cushions. After the first cautious taste, they approved of Normandy's famous cider. ' Ce n' est que le premier verre qui coute.' is their twist on Mme Du Deffand's famous comment on the legend of St Denis.[20]

Sadly, very little remains of the picturesque Norman town where the Nomads spent the night of July 21st, 1912. In the Allied bombardment of June, 1944, almost all the pretty half-timbered houses of mediaeval Caen were destroyed. Caen's famous churches were luckier. On June 9th, 1944, the church of St Pierre lost a spire, but miraculously the twin abbeys built by William of Normandy and his wife Matilda were almost unscathed. William's Abbaye aux Hommes and his wife's Abbaye aux Dames were built to appease the Pope, because their marriage had broken the arcane and for the papacy, highly lucrative rules of consanguinity.[21] Modern Caen is almost another city. Like Le Havre, it was rebuilt, but not recreated. The Mémorial de Caen challenges visitors with the causes of war and peace.[22]

Chapter II

We were now actually on the road - sac à dos - boats and trains were things of the past, and conveyances anathema. Our road lay along the broad route nationale to Bayeux; so far so good, but as our objective was Creully, we knew we must shortly make a digression. At the first turning we enquired the way of an old lady and got quite a torrent of directions, from which we gleaned that we could take the side road and look out for a cemetery. It was little more than a country lane, and eventually ended in a mere cart track. To make matters worse, the path forked, and either way might equally have led to a cemetery or anywhere! However we hazarded one path, but after following it a short time it seemed inclined to double back, so forsaking it we made a bee line across the fields in the opposite direction and regained the other path.

It was now about one o'clock, and our café complet was getting ancient history, so calling a halt we demolished some chocolate. Once more shouldering our knapsacks we trudged on, passing what appeared to be an abbey approached by a fine avenue of chestnut trees; and to our joy an old lady appeared in sight walking towards us. We enquired if we were going in the direction of Creully, and after answering in the affirmative the good lady asked us if we had seen the abbey, which she said everybody went to see. As we retraced our steps our guide kept up a perfect volley of information, from which we gathered that the abbey was 'très ancienne' and that the patron saint was still feted. The men might also, she said, ascend the tower, but she evidently did not know English ladies. The abbey was a fine specimen of Norman architecture, but had evidently fallen on evil days, for it was full of hay, carts and ploughs, although garlands were still hanging on the walls, evidently left over from the festival. The ladies did ascend the tower, and we had a fine view of the surrounding country.

A sharp shower had now come on, so we sheltered in the tithe barn, but as there was nothing eatable to be had we shortly made our way to a small village and entered a 'débit de boissons'.

Madame was at first very chary of offering hospitality to so many. "Of course you are not in the town, and in the country ... " (French shrugs can be very expressive). However, we suggested omelette and bread and cheese, and by degrees all were forthcoming, to say nothing of the indispensable cider. We were very glad to be relieved of our baggage, and while the omelette was in preparation we made overtures to Young France. Happily our school French seemed to have been designed for such a meeting; "What is your name?" and "How old are you?" being quite apropos. Jacques Bonhomme, who now entered and called for a drink, seemed very much amused with one of the ladies' hats, drying on the table. Madame informed him of its ownership, and thereupon he was profuse with apologies. The omelette was very good, as also the cider, and we now cheerily took the road again, Young France waving adieu.

At the cross roads there was a very fine Calvary, and here we rejoined the Route Nationale, which even a blind man might follow. But it was not without interest to English eyes. The road itself was very wide, and then there was as much greensward separating it from the fields. These stretched away as far as one could see to the poplar-fringed horizon, not a vestige of a hedge or wall intervening. The cattle too looked very strange, chained up in the fields, but of course the absence of hedges renders this imperative. Lanes of poppies made the fields of corn and barley very gay, and the white flower of the buckwheat is also very pretty.

An old woman washing clothes in a stream next engaged our attention, and, at the request of our photographer, posed for a snap. It was very nearly time for dinner when we arrived at Creully, and we were quite ready to show our appreciation of French cookery.

Background to Chapter II

As young Edwardians, they'd grown accustomed to long hot summers. Planning their walking holiday, they surely hoped for dry weather. Conditions in 1912 were often atrocious, cold, wet, and stormy, across the Northern Hemisphere.[1] Throughout their energetic fortnight of tramping, the Nomads became accustomed to incredulity too. Why did they plan to walk so far, especially when there was perfectly good public transport available ? Working near Arromanches as a student, I met with the same mystified reaction. As in 1912, explanations were probably a waste of time.[2] In Normandy, the Nomads are using a map, and often walk on footpaths, suggesting they had access to a specialist map shop, such as Stanfords'. Later, in Brittany, no map is mentioned, and they're walking along the busy Routes Nationales. In Britain, especially in the South, access to the countryside was bitterly contested, and had been since enclosure. Until the mid-twentieth century, landowners and their gamekeepers threatened ramblers with man-traps, prosecution, and even shotguns.[3]

Leaving Caen, and heading for Creully, they quickly became lost. Eventually, an old lady put them on the right road. As a bonus, she told them how to find the Abbaye d'Ardennes, and delivered a high-speed account of its history. Frank notes, on the back of a photo, that she was one of the fastest speakers they met. They found this thirteenth century abbey in a sorry state, being used as a farm store, a fate shared by so many English abbeys, including Fountains, Rievaulx and Byland, until their twentieth century rescue by the heritage industry. Sheltering in the tithe barn from a typical 1912 downpour, they had time to calculate its size, about 50 metres by 50. Creully, so tranquil in 1912 became a key military centre for the Allies during the battle for Normandy. Landing at Juno beach, this area was liberated by the Canadians. Here, in 1944, in the abbey ruins, Canadian officers of the Sherbrook Fusiliers were killed after being 'interrogated' by the Germans. Legally, they were prisoners of war, and subsequently, the SS officer who ordered their deaths was tried for war crimes.[4]

The roadside Calvary admired by the writer of this chapter is typical of thousands erected across Europe to create local centres for pilgrims, a practice which began after the loss of Jerusalem in 1243. The majority of Calvary scenes were created during the sixteenth century Catholic backlash, known as the 'Counter-Reformation'. The example photographed near Creully shows only Christ crucified. Many Calvaries are of the traditional Crucifixion scene, Christ in the centre, with his mother Mary on one side, and St John the Evangelist on the other. [5]

Protestantism rejected all imagery, even that of Christ on the Cross, regarding it as idolatrous, removing all statues, carvings and paintings from churches, limewashing over wallpaintings, and using only a plain cross with no figure on the communion table.

In the hedgeless open countryside of Normandy, the Nomads thought tethered cattle looked odd, but, city-bred, assumed this was essential. On the contrary, sheep, cattle, and semi-wild ponies still graze the unfenced and hedgeless uplands of England, but only horses belonging to Romany and other travellers are tethered. Long before mandatory ear-tags and chips, British farmers marked their animals, either with dye or by notching ears or horns, so the owner could be identified when they were rounded up for sale or shearing. Across Europe, attitudes to animal welfare differ. Until recently, tethered cattle were still a common sight in France, and other parts of mainland Europe. Under new EU regulations, tethering of cattle will be illegal by 2010.[6]

Admiring the bright poppies, in 1912, only pretty flowers in a cornfield, they also noticed buckwheat. Rarely grown in England, buckwheat is a useful crop, for all kinds of reasons, including the burgeoning market for special diet foods. One of its French names, sarassin, indicates that it was brought from the Middle East, allegedly by the Crusaders, but its origins are even further away, in southwest Asia. A useful pollinator, it's often cultivated in or close to orchards, and thrives on poor soils. Sometimes called ' blé noir', it isn't actually wheat at all. Unlike most cereals, it isn't a grass. In Normandy, they would see the cultivated variety, fagopyrum esculentum.[7] Used to make the popular galettes and crêpes of the region, the naturally gluten-free sarassin is often included in recipes for people with coeliac disease. In Normandy, the condition is common. The Normans - or 'Norsemen' were Vikings, arriving in France from Scandinavia, and, incidentally, bringing with them coeliac disease, caused by the inability to digest gluten. Other Norsemen carried the condition to Ireland, especially around Dublin, and on the west coast.[8]

Wandering through rural Normandy, the Nomads would see flourishing family farms, on a scale rarely found in England, even in 1912. Across the channel, strict primogeniture inheritance consolidated properties in the hands of one heir. The Napoleonic code rejects this winner takes all approach to land ownership. The English, as the first industrial nation, had all but lost their connection with the land, and, to this day, can't understand the politics and passion of French agriculture. Admiring the productive small farms of Normandy, a 1912 English guide book laments this state of affairs :

' When one sees the multitude of trim little homesteads, each with its own croft, orchard and kaleyard, one reflects, regretfully, how comparatively few Englishmen own a rood of England '[9]

Chapter III

The good people whom we informed, earlier on in the day, that we proposed to walk to Creully, were very astonished at our having the hardihood to attempt such a thing, but here we are in good time at our destination. There, right in front of us, is the inn at which we hope to secure our night's lodging, so without wasting any time we march up to the door and prepare to "parlez-vous". Our arrival has evidently been noticed by the inn-keeper, who comes out to meet us, and we enquire, in carefully prepared phrases, raising our hats and bowing in the approved style, whether he can receive us for the night. So far so good, but when he replies by firing off a volley of phrases which we have not had an opportunity of learning in advance it is another matter altogether. However, by concentrating all our attention, we are able, between us, to collect sufficient of the rapidly falling words to gather that he can give us the accommodation we require and will be pleased to show us the rooms if we will follow him upstairs. So a torch-light procession is formed up the staircase, which our host informs us is rather dark, and which in fact we find might safely be used as a photographic dark room. We take possession of our quarters forthwith, gentlemen tossing up for rooms (heads stay here, tails down the passage), and proceed to make ourselves look as respectable as circumstances will permit - and it is no use worrying too much about your appearance when you have got to carry all your wardrobe on your back. However, as we generally found to be the case, there is no lack of water, so after a refreshing wash, and having opened wide the windows (to which they do not appear to be accustomed) we cautiously grope our way downstairs, very ready to make the closer acquaintance of the savoury odours which greet us from the kitchen.

A fair was visiting the town, and in an open space in front of the hotel was a roundabout, the sight of which raised doubts in our minds - quite groundless as it turned out - with regard to our night's repose. During dinner it started operations, and to our surprise there fell on our ears the familiar strains of "Yip-I-addy-I-ay". The music soon brought forth the inhabitants, and as we watched the passing groups through the open door of the dining room, with the quaint shops and houses across the way in the background, we almost imagined we were watching a scene in a play.

After dauntlessly going through the long programme of courses of which a French dinner consists, we sallied forth ourselves to see the fun. All the village seemed to be assembled, and the competition for places on the roundabout was of a nature to delight the showman's heart. No up-to-date steam-driven machine was this, equipped with all the ingenious appliances required to satisfy the town-dwellers' appetite for thrills. The motive power was supplied by a horse which trudged patiently round and round, while the music was ground out by a man who was energetically turning the handle of the organ. But if it was only one "horse-power" it was capable of affording no less amusement than the more blatant machines, and we did not flee from it as we probably should at ordinary times, but even joined in the scramble for seats in the rocking boat. This was the most exciting and the most popular feature of the roundabout, and we were unable to get possession of it until later on in the evening when the people were beginning to go home. Meanwhile we amused ourselves in various directions, Ross going to the Post Office to buy stamps, and practise his French on the lady in charge. Oh! if we could only have heard this conversation, wonderful reports of which were related to us afterwards. The rest of us explored the village and we all met at the roundabout later on.

When we had had enough of the fun of the fair we all went for a stroll down the now deserted village street, past the Church, and out into the country beyond. How delightful is a night walk! We quite forget that we ought to be tired, so exhilarating is the cool air. We find that while we are the only human beings abroad we are far from alone. The roadside seems to be alive with insects, whose merry chirrupping betrays their presence. Bats flit about in their peculiar fashion. And, like a subdued accompaniment to Nature's music, we hear around us in all directions the sweet-sounding liquid notes of the cattle-bells.

A short stop, and then back to bed, where we slept as walking tourists ought to sleep, until we were awakened at 4.30 A.M. by the clattering sabots and chattering tongues of passers-by. Then the Church bell rang for service at 5 o'clock, and the day had begun in this little Norman town, where apparently the rule of "early to bed and early to rise" is observed. Breakfast, as usual, consisted of coffee with rolls and butter, and as usual we did ample justice to it, for our next meal was hidden among clouds of uncertainty.

While we were waiting till the rest of the party were ready to start, a funeral procession came along the road on its way to the Church, preceded by the Cross, and the priests and acolytes, chanting an they marched along at a fairly brisk pace. It seemed, however, to lack some of the solemnity associated with a similar scene in England.

We were to go in the same direction as we had taken for our nocturnal ramble, along the street, and past the old castle of Creully. This, unfortunately, is only open for inspection on another day of the week so we had to be content with what we could see from the road. Then the Church, with its grotesque gargoyles, attracted our notice, but here again we had to be content with the exterior, for the funeral service was then going on.

Having got clear of the town, we took our instructions from the map and a signpost, and set out to see what fresh experiences this day had in store for us. We were supposed to be making, in the first instance, for the Priory of St. Gabriel, some ruins which the inn-keeper had advised us to visit. However, not seeing any sign of the ruins when our legs were beginning to tell us we had walked far enough to get there, we enquired at a cottage as to our whereabouts. We were informed that we were at Brecy, and that close by was an old chateau which was worth a visit. So in search of the Chateau we went. Sure enough, it was close at hand, and we soon found ourselves at the entrance, which was of quite imposing appearance. The buildings appeared to be now used as a farm, and as we had not obtained from the old lady at the cottage a very clear idea as to what there was to see, we were in some doubt as to whether we ought to penetrate further, or whether this handsome gateway was the objective. However, we did not want to risk missing anything, so a deputation wan sent to make enquiries, or rather - since we did not know what to ask for - to ascertain diplomatically if there was anything else which was shown to visitors. The dogs on either side of the entrance seemed to view our intrusion with very great resentment - in fact their language was extremely uncivil even for Norman watchdogs, which is saying a good deal. The clamour brought out the lady of the house, and as I suppose she had no difficulty in guessing from our appearance what we were and why we had come, she immediately invited us to go through and see the garden at the back. The garden! Of course that was what we had come to see! In the days of its prime this must have been a beautiful garden, and we peopled it in imagination with the lords and ladies of a bygone age, strolling as we were doing, perhaps, from terrace to terrace, and resting at the top to enjoy the view of the chateau and the neighbouring church, now ivy-covered and in ruins, nestling among the trees.

Leaving the Chateau at length, we returned to the main road and continued our walk towards Bayeux. After a time the sky became clouded and the shower - which we soon learned to regard as a daily occurrence -commenced. It began rather suddenly, and four of us scrambled (which the French dictionary informs you is to proceed with the aid of the hands and feet) up the bank and sheltered under the trees on one side of the road, while Ross and Fred scuttled to a similar refuge on the other side. They, with characteristic enterprise, got into conversation with some peasants who had been working in the fields and were also taking shelter. There being no such facilities for linguistic exercise on our side we had to be content with watching their performance, which proved highly entertaining. What the conversation was about I cannot tell, but it seemed to go on swimmingly. We had already heard accounts of our friends' ingenuity at circumlocution, and now we were treated to an exhibition of their resourcefulness. If language failed gestures were called to their aid; points were driven home with the camera stand, used as a baton, and when, after the rain had stopped, we crossed over and rejoined them, we found that such progress had been made that they had secured a promise from the peasants to sing us the "Marseillaise", and had invited them to pose for a photograph. They were delighted at this idea, and fetching their implements quickly formed quite a picturesque group, which was duly bagged - and one more anxiety was added to the photographer's ever-increasing load, for we promised to send them copies.

Forward once more, and by this time our thoughts were beginning to turn to the subject of lunch, but there was no sign so far of any break in the clouds of uncertainty by which that meal was enshrouded. At length, after a stretch of hot field-path, followed by a pleasantly cool, tree-shaded road, we came to a row of cottages where we decided to try our luck. One of them proclaimed itself to be a "Débit de Boissons", and to that we turned our attention. But while the good lady was quite willing to give us cider, she explained that she did not supply meals, and that being so far out in the country it was difficult to get things.

However, as there did not seem to be any other chance of lunch within a reasonable distance, we conveniently did not quite understand, and asked for bread and cheese, and anything else we could think of the name for. At length the clouds of uncertainty were dissipated by the appearance of some substantial fare of this description, together with plenty of cider, and thus importunity was once again rewarded. Half a loaf is better than no bread anywhere, but half a Norman loaf would feed a squad of soldiers, so we were in no immediate danger of starvation.

Most of the remainder of the way to Bayeux lay along the "Route Nationale", which in this case was a fine avenue of large trees, separated by grassy margins from the adjoining fields, and we reached that town without further incident beyond another shower, from which we found shelter under the trees. Before entering the town a halt was called in order that hats - more particularly the gentlemen's - might be put straight, for had we not to meet the critical gaze of more than 7000 inhabitants?

The first thing that interested us was the sight of several people washing clothes in the river, and they were promptly 'snapped'. The town we found rather quaint, but it seemed to have somewhat too much of a 'touristy' flavour to please us altogether. Before tea we visited the Cathedral, meeting on the way two ladies who asked us in English where the Tapestry was - the first chance of speaking English to a stranger!

The next item on the programme was tea, and, after wavering between a very old timbered house and an up to date café, we decided on the latter, and got tea for five, and chocolate for one "tea-totaller", and some French pastries (in their native land). Thus refreshed we felt equal to the Tapestry and accordingly presented ourselves at the Museum. The "gardienne" however informed us that they close at four - and it was considerably past that hour. Was our tea to cost us the sight of the world-famed Tapestry? Apparently the look of disappointment on our faces was effective, and we were told that we might enter, thus having the place to ourselves. Enclosed in a long glass case, the Tapestry is excellently arranged for inspection, and following the various scenes and puzzling out the Latin descriptions provided a good deal of entertainment, the latter, I understand, being found to lend themselves to particularly diverting misinterpretations.

The next stage of our journey was to be a ride in the "tram" to Balleroy, and after ascertaining the time this left we sat in a square and wrote picture-postcards, our usual occupation in spare moments. The tram, a diminutive train consisting of engine and four or five carriages, runs through the streets of the town and along the country roads. The lines are of a very narrow gauge, but the engines and carriages are of the usual width, that is to say that - as we found by experiment - it is just possible for six people to sit on a seat. The guard comes along the foot-board to take the fares, and he collects the tickets when you get out. We were taken through some beautiful country, and the ride was very novel and interesting, but rather chilly - hence the over-crowding above referred to - and in due course we arrived at Balleroy.

Background to Chapter III

When in Rome.... Exuberantly unconventional, the Nomads often admit that they look like tramps, distance themselves from conventional tourists, fashionably dressed, and travelling by car. Celebrating the Entente Cordiale, chatting with their hosts, persuading villagers to pose for photos, or sell them a little food, they were (usually) well-behaved tramps, keen to conform in matters of etiquette. Eavesdropping in Jersey, they're amused to hear themselves described as 'a disreputable looking party'. Living out of rucksacks, backpackers never aim for haute couture, but the Nomads understood, perfectly, the difference between eccentricity and bad manners. In Creully, arriving at the Hotel Martin, they wanted to make a good impression, raising and doffing hats ' in the approved style'. First mentioned when they land at Le Havre, the wearing of hats is a leit-motif throughout their adventures. Should they or shouldn't they ? Can hats been safely abandoned, or should they be worn even indoors ? In August, 1914, all over England, young men in straw boaters queued to fight for King and Country. Working men wear flat caps. Nobody is bareheaded. Ragged, frequently, but to be hatless was unthinkable. Training in Sefton Park, Liverpool, in September, 1914, the 19th Battalion of Liverpool Pals wear their boaters still.[1]

At half-past four in the morning, the church bells and clattering sabots of Creully startled the urban Nomads. Perhaps they didn't understand that late July is harvest time. Every minute of daylight is precious, doubly so during the cold and sodden summer of 1912. Twenty-first century farmers get the crops in under arc lights, usually one man and his Ipod, on a combine harvester, but even combines can't compete with serious flooding. Technology couldn't save the crops of 2007. The early morning funeral and its lack of English solemnity disconcerted the Nomads. Decent English Protestants buried their dead quietly. In 1912, hostility between Catholic and Protestant Liverpool was savage.[2] Carefully insulated from their fellow citizens' Catholic excesses, the Nomads wouldn't know the glorious irreverence of an Irish wake, frequently attended by the deceased, dressed in their best, and propped up in the coffin.

At Creully, in 1944, the BBC established a recording studio in a tower of the castle.[3] Montgomery's official headquarters were also in the castle, though in practice, he preferred to use his unofficial and carefully camouflaged headquarters in the grounds.[4] Denied both the castle and the church at Creully, the Nomads settled for Brécy, and its own castle. Designed by Le Notre, later to be Louis XIV's gardener at Versailles, the gardens at Brécy, neglected for generations, have now been wonderfully restored. In 1912, the Nomads could only imagine a bygone age.[5] And then, heading for Bayeux, dodging the daily downpour, they met the peasants, who were also sheltering. The Marseilleise photo is superb. Ten 'peasants', men, women and a girl old enough to be useful line up with their implements. Some of the tools are familiar scythes and sickles. Others are more unusual. Whether the harvesters ever received their promised photo isn't recorded.

In Normandy, Bayeux and the tapestry were more or less compulsory. Definitely travellers, not tourists, the Nomads didn't linger here, and don't, of course, describe the tapestry. On handsets, modern audio tours are available in a plethora of languages. Left to their own devices, the Nomads could attempt their own mischievous translations of the text. Frank certainly knew Latin, and, as a Liverpool University student, so did Gladys. Conventional tourism didn't really appeal to the party, and they didn't linger here. They bought postcards of the cathedral, but the only photos actually taken in Bayeux are of closely-observed washerwomen, by the river. Frank notes that they began by immersing dirty items in hot water, then stirred them vigorously, with a big thick stick. 6 His photo of the washing place shows tubs, on the river bank. On July 23rd, 1912, Bayeux meant 1066, Hastings, a handsome cathedral, and, already, too many tourists. There was no Bataille de Normandie museum, no stark and poignant war graves.[7] When the Nomads came to Normandy, most of the men who died here in the summer of 1944 weren't even born.

Chapter IV

When we were originally mapping out our route, Balleroy was the place as to whose ability to entertain us we felt most doubtful. Now that the tour is a thing of the past we treasure the memory of our stay there as one of our pleasantest recollections. Its name is on our lips more frequently than any other; when we meet it is to Balleroy that we tell one another we must pay another visit. And yet I think we might find it difficult to explain to a sceptical hearer the precise grounds of our infatuation. I think it was one of those places, your enjoyment of which depends as much on what you bring to them as on what they have to offer. You must be in tune with them; otherwise their charms will awaken no sympathetic vibrations in your mind, and you will probably be merely bored.

To attempt to describe the place from the brief glimpse we had as we walked through it from the station, when our eyes were mainly occupied in searching for our prospective hotel, and a large part of our thoughts was busily wondering what we should get to eat, it being well past the usual dinner time, is out of the question. Repeated meditations and memory-probings have only conjured up a more or less hazy picture of a very long, very wide, straight street, with a row of plain houses on each side. Coming from Bayeux, where there were notice boards in the streets to inform tourists what places they ought to "do", stock-taking sales, and similar evidences of civilization, I think it was the uncommercial, old-world atmosphere of Balleroy which particularly appealed to us. It was so entirely different from any other place we had seen that our interest was at once awakened, and as we marched along the street, exchanging salutations with several of the natives, who seemed to take considerable interest in our appearance and equipment, our spirits were rising "wisibly", until they reached high water mark in the kindly welcome we received at the Hotel de la Place. The description of the hotel and its surroundings will have to wait till the morning; there was other more pressing business to be attended to. Dinner was over, of course, but Madame said she would see what could be done, and her efforts were very successful, for the "potage" - which here consisted of bread and milk - was on the table before we were ready.

There was a lady staying at the hotel who spoke English quite well. She had been sitting outside while we were interviewing the landlady and had very kindly facilitated the conversation, and she now came to see that we were well looked after in the direction of refreshment. She was "sick in her eyes" she told us and was staying with her daughter at Balleroy - ideal place for the purpose - for a rest. It was in America that she had learned her English, and though she had never been in England she liked the English people very much. Unfortunately the farewell had to follow close upon the introduction, as these ladies were retiring early and would not be down before our departure next morning, but brief as the acquaintance had been it was enough to give one member of our party a severe attack of "mal au coeur".

The dining room was adorned with implements and trophies of the chase, and we learned from Madame that hunting was carried on a grand scale in the neighbouring forest. Our hostess tendered apologies -quite uncalled for, be it said - for the "indifferent service", due to the untimely hour of our arrival, but, as we told her, we had really had an excellent meal, and it was surprising how well and quickly it had been prepared. The only shortcoming was in regard to the number of courses, which was not quite so formidable as usual, but this was a fault which we were very ready to forgive.

After dinner we went out for a stroll. Again it was a fine night, pleasantly cool, and with a beautiful moon. We wandered along the road until we came to a bridge over a little stream, on which we sat and warbled sweet and low, to the music of the rippling water, until our peace of mind was rudely disturbed by somebody discovering that the stone on which we were sitting was damp, whereupon we returned to the hotel, and after singing "Good Night" (No. 95) as a final serenade, we sought our beds and were very soon in the land of dreams, and there is nothing more to record until the next morning.

One of my earliest impressions on waking was of the beauty of the chimes at the Church. These bells, like everything else in this delightful place, were quite out of the ordinary, and I remember looking forward to hearing them again at each quarter hour. And if the bells were pleasant to the ear, the view from the bed-room window was no less attractive to the eye. The road along which we had come from the station led straight up to the gates of the Chateau, in front of which it broadened out into an open space. On one side of this was the Hotel, and from the window I could see the Chateau, a fine, though rather severe-looking building, and, at its entrance, the little Church peeping out from among the trees. The plate on which this view was recorded unfortunately did not survive its subsequent travels, and came home in three pieces. Hinc illae lachrymae.

We breakfasted in great style - jam, by request, and plates, as a consequence of the jam, for plates are by no means a matter of course at "petit déjeuner", as we had already discovered.

Now there appeared signs of mutiny in the camp, and certain members of the party announced their intention of going on strike. Programme or no programme, they were going to stop at Balleroy a little longer. Additional force was given to their arguments by the fact that the Chateau would be open to visitors at 12 o'clock. (Moreover M'lle X. would appear later on in the morning). However, unless we wanted to make our next night's lodging extremely problematical - St. Lo, our destination, was 13 miles away, and there was no place in between at which there seemed any chance of putting up - it was necessary that we should start in fairly good time, so with a heroic sacrifice of personal inclinations we prepared once more for the road.

Before we left, the hotel people were persuaded to face the camera, and - conditionally - promised copies of the result, which reminds me that I have said hardly anything yet about these good people. The old gentleman in the photograph was the "patron", though he did not appear to take any active part in the management. This was in the hands of his wife, a state of things which we found to exist at other places which we visited. We gathered that he had lived there as long as the house had been built - 40 years. Now he had retired from active service, and appeared to spend most of his time sitting out in front of the hotel. Madame was a most kindhearted, motherly woman, who did her best to make us feel at home. When the time came for settling the bill, which was really ridiculously low, she explained - and she had to write it down before we could grasp it - that she made a special reduction for tourists.

At length all was ready for our departure, so saying "au revoir" - and I think in this case we really meant it - to our kind friends, we proceeded to the Chateau. We could of course only go as far as the gates, but from there we had a good view of the building, with the fine, but rather stiff and formal-looking gardens in front. A photograph from the gates, then a parting snapshot of the "Place" and the village street, and we turned our backs on Balleroy, bearing with us a stock of pleasant recollections which it will take a long tine to efface from our minds.

Before long we came to a place where no less than seven roads met, and we improved the occasion by selecting the wrong one. The first kilometre stone aroused our suspicions, and from a glance at the map it appeared that we were going in altogether the wrong direction. To economise the collective store of energy, it was decided to send out a scout to reconnoitre, and Alec undertook this duty while the rest of us reclined on the grass at the side of the road, and Fred taught Ross how to sell timber! We were soon signalled to go back, however, and found that Alec had discovered the right road, and had also sighted wild animals passing through the forest. Lest any apprehension should be aroused in the mind of the reader, I hasten to explain that they were in a travelling menagerie.

Our road for a considerable distance lay through the Forest of Cerisy, but as it was, as usual, very wide, and bordered with wide grassy margins, there was no shade for pedestrians, and the males were soon obliged to ask permission to carry their coats in an unorthodox manner. Wild flowers were growing in grcat variety along the roadside; occasionally a modest strawberry was spied out in its leafy hiding-place and transferred to some thirsty mouth; hundreds of beautiful butterflies, flitting from flower to flower, gave life and animation to the scene, and once or twice we noticed the glint of the sunlight on the elegant form of a dragon-fly, in its brilliant uniform of blue and black, hovering at one spot and then passing like a flash to another. On the road itself numbers of beetles were crawling solemnly hither and thither, and we could not help wondering what led them to forsake the grass for the hot dusty road, where they were in constant danger of extinction. Still, ignorance is bliss, and I suppose a beetle crosses the road for the same reason as the proverbial chicken.

The weather was magnificent, but very thirst-provoking, and soon we were all eyes for a "débit de boissons". We looked in vain, however for human habitations were few and far between. When at last we did come to a pretty little house on the edge of the forest we made enquiries and learned that there was an "Auberge" a little further on, at which we mentally resolved to secure our lunch. The lady brought us some water, but accompanied it with warnings of dreadful consequences of imbibing it, so we used it "comme les soldats", as Fred told her, rather to her mystification.

Another kilometre or so brought us to the Auberge, and we were very soon seated round the table, regarding with satisfaction a plentiful supply of bread and jam, and various bottles of cidre and vin rouge An ordinary knife proving a poor weapon to attack the immense loaf, Madame came to the rescue with a kind of sickle which appeared very effective. The light in the cottage being quite good, I determined to attempt a photo, and our hostesses seemed quite pleased when we asked permission to include them in it.

Thus refreshed we proceeded once more, and as we had plenty of time we decided to indulge in a siesta. The fine weather, however, was becoming exhausted, and our first attempt to settle down was vetoed by the first drops of the daily shower. We found a more sheltered spot under some trees just off the road, and there, enveloping ourselves in our mackintoshes, we reclined - and waited. Fred had some doubts as to the ground floor being flooded out, and went en haut, where he tried with his usual want of success to get comfortable. Here we stopped for a considerable time, doing nothing more energetic than eat chocolate - all except Fred, who was up above, nursing a sick heart and a sore heel, and whose meanderings brought down on our heads little avalanches of burs, interspersed with laments at leaving Balleroy, and shafts of humour which kept our spirits at all events from getting damped. After a time the rain permitted us to go forward, only to resume its performance when we were just in sight of a débit de boissons- an obvious hint which was duly taken.

After these little interludes we made good progress, and soon found ourselves in the neighbourhood of St. Lo, which town was reached in good time, and without any further incidents of an exciting nature.

Background to Chapter IV

Progress is, of course, a myth. Twenty-first century guidebooks for this area insist that to enjoy all it has to offer, visitors must have their own transport. The Nomads narrow-gauge train that carried them from Bayeux no longer exists.[1] Their delight in Balleroy is almost impossible to define. It's easy enough to download hundreds of more-or less identical travelogues on Venice, Prague, or the English Lakes. The affection for Balleroy rings true. All real travellers know a Balleroy of their own, somewhere in the world, ' one of those places your enjoyment of which depends as much on what you bring to them as on what they have to offer.'[2]

Collaboration can be dangerous. Six very different Nomads travelled to France together. Perhaps all six wanted to tell their story, but didn't actually put pen to paper. The book records the experiences, interests, and contradictions of six individuals. They didn't share the same prejudices, or literary ability. In this reflective chapter, the writer, Frank, knows he's attempting the impossible. This is why he succeeds and why he fails. As John Stuart Mill famously warned, ask yourself why you're happy, and you cease to be so. Frank's Balleroy is almost elegiac in its effort to recapture their idyll, understand exactly why they were so happy. It was, definitely, love at first sight, as he wrote on the back of one Balleroy photo. Love defies analysis. In the photos, Balleroy doesn't seem in any way special. So very little happens, a warm welcome from their hosts, Madame being most definitely in charge, rather than the alleged ' patron'. The food she served was excellent. Later, on a bridge, by moonlight, they sang popular hits, ending with ' No 95' as a final serenade. They could enjoy all that in any 18 - 30 resort today, though the recipe would probably include far too much alcohol and, for the women, very little clothing. In 1912, did the early-to-bed residents of Balleroy appreciate late night music, sung by noisy tourists ?

The photos and postcards record only the bare facts, handsome houses, a wide street, the 'fine, though rather severe-looking Chateau' In 1912, there was no hot-air balloon museum to attract visitors.[3]   A sensitive ear for music recalls rippling water, and the beauty of church bells, a photographer's eye recognises the right balance of light and shade. Taken from the hotel window, Frank's photograph of the church didn't survive the journey home. Glass plates are fragile. In rural Normandy, he'd be lucky to find any more. (Hinc illae lacrymae... Hence these tears)[4]

Leaving Balleroy, they faced a fifteen mile walk to St Lo, mainly through the Forest of Cerisy. A hundred years later, visitors still come here, many of them English, many more from other Allied countries. Sixty years and more after D-Day, few veterans are still alive, but other generations come to visit the museums, cemeteries, and ghosts of old battlegrounds.[5] In the Forest, descendants of the 1912 variety of wayside flowers the Nomads admired still provide a perfect habitat for many species of butterflies. Cerisy is now a popular centre for wildlife holidays. During July, they'd probably see the dark green fritillary, the Queen of Spain fritillary, the Mallow Skipper, Clouded Yellow, the Purple Emperor, and a host of others. The black and blue dragonfly they saw might have been the Emperor; or, possibly, a rare blue-tailed damsel fly. The details hardly matter. In Cerisy, the Nomads could still enjoy the butterflies, and wild strawberries too.[6] Frank, who had no cine camera, asked his friends to walk slowly.[7] For a still photo, it succeeds remarkably. Later, chez Mme Veuve Maupas, he decided the light was good enough for an interior shot, five Nomads and their hosts.[8]

Chapter V

We reached St. Lo at about 8 p.m. in a weary and dusty condition. We put up at an Hotel which had a show at the back of it, whirligigs and music resounded incessantly, and we sighed as we thought of the coming night, for the music did not sound the soothing lullaby type.

We had dinner in a large room which was filled with visitors. It seems the fashion for the French town women to wear hats always, just as it seems customary for the peasants to dispense with them almost altogether. All the ladies wore hats except our party, who preferred the peasant fashion. Then we all went out, one part in search of a remedy for a cold; the wickeder portion discovering, as usual, a Débit de Boissons.

We started our journey again next morning after breakfasting in an evil-looking estaminet, where, judging from the combined odours of tobacco and spirits, many "revelled long o'nights".

We visited, as was our pious custom, the Cathedral of the town, of the inside of which I have not the vaguest recollection. Any who are curious as to its outside may here consult a picture postcard.

Then we bought p.p.c's, loitered round (also a morning custom), and of course had to make a wild dash for the train. As we were in the first week of the tour we travelled 2nd class. The luxury of removing knapsacks and leaning against the comfortably cushioned carriage did much to restore our amiability, which we had somehow mislaid while sprinting for the train, the aforementioned exercise on a very hot day not being the best specific for the temper. We left the train at Cametours and started to walk to Coutances.

On the roadside we called a halt and ate cherries, while the strenuous member of the party, who usually rested by despatching postcards at the rate of sixty an hour, went in search of cider. At a little house near he procured cider from a man who had once lived in the Channel Islands and could speak broken English, in which he gave us many directions regarding where to stay in the next town. He was so delighted to meet English speaking people that he would not charge for the cider. Although this was the only time we had cider gratis, the friendly spirit and kindliness he showed seemed typical of the French peasantry.

At noon we had lunch at Belval, where we were photographed, as usual, eating. We had proceeded a little along the road when a heavy thunderstorm came on. We took refuge in a shed which luckily happened to be near. The indefatigable workers seized this opportunity to write more post cards. After about half an hour of the heaviest rain I have ever seen, the sky cleared and we set off once more.

At Coutances we refreshed our physical needs on chocolate, and our non-bodily requirements (I don't know whether a psychologist would class them as mental or moral) by a visit to the Cathedral. This was really a refreshing spectacle. The building was of white stone inside, and had none of the usual tawdry decoration to detract from the beauty and dignity of the workmanship; the austerity of the style of architecture, the whiteness of the stone, and the cold light which streamed through the beautiful green windows, together with the rest and quiet it afforded, suggested purity and sanctity to a far greater degree than did any of the more ornate buildings we visited.

Reshouldering our baggage we marched through country which was much more undulating than our first view of Normandy. Occasional glimpses of the sea when we reached higher ground were very welcome, as we had been walking inland since leaving Caen. Some ideas were entertained of bathing before breakfast next morning, but none were surprised that thought was fatal to action.

We reached Montmartin-sur-Mer that evening in our usual condition, rather weary, dusty, and very hungry. The Hotel Robillard was truly rural; its hostess wore a white muslin cap, a rather short black dress, and was of homely and cheerful appearance. We had the luxury of a room all to ourselves, and we duly appreciated it.

It might here be noted that we drank water for the first time since entering France. I do not attribute the hilarity of our evening meal to this fact, as it is well known that stolid Britishers do not enthuse on cold water. Another reason I might incidentally mention to support the belief that water was not responsible for our mirth at dinner, was that we did not drink the aforesaid water till bed time, when the spirits of the party were not in any degree noticeable.

In the interim - it would hardly be kind to call it a lucid interval - between the cider and water drinking, we explored the road to the sea. We here encountered scores of glow worms and grasshoppers, both of which proved so interesting that we did not reach the sea at all that night.

Next morning after café, which we drank from bowls with no handles to them, our hostess presented us with a large tome in which she requested us to write. This book began by asking your name, and not content with that, demanded age, occupation, and address, none of which we were very anxious to be reminded of on a tramp holiday. However, after doing a little mental arithmetic and reviewing our work-a-day lives, which we had happily forgotten, we obliged the good lady with the required information and set off for Granville. Here the country became much quainter and more picturesque, and also, alas! more poverty stricken. The land holdings here seemed very much smaller than in the country we saw during the first few days march, a comparatively small field containing corn, 'sarassin', a plot of grass where a cow and goat were tethered, and several apple trees.

Through this picturesque and undulating medley, always in views of the sea, we marched till lunch time. Then we enquired at a rather large house, where we could obtain lunch. The owner of the house directed us in English to a cafe a little further along the road. We had just ordered lunch when he came into the cafe to ensure us being well catered for. He was very interesting and communicative, and told us he had a son in the States, and a daughter who had married an Englishman and lived in London. One of us remarking on the friendly feeling the French apparently had for the English, he said, "None more than I. In my garden fly three flags, the Union Jack, the American flag, and the French flag." We bade a very friendly goodbye to the old gentleman, and had to march in real earnest to reach Granville in time for the Jersey boat.

We arrived at Granville much worn, but in good time, and drank lemonade at the first Débit de Boissons, afterwards hiring a rickety 'voiture' drawn by a lively horse, to the boat.

Background to Chapter V

Perhaps Fred still had a cold ? Or had he passed it on to one of his friends ? And, at St Lo, which of the ' weary and dusty' Nomads formed the 'wickeder party', who headed for the nearest ' Débit de Bossons ' ? Did the chapel-going contingent try to disapprove of so much cider and red wine ?[1]   They wouldn't recognise St Lo now. In 1944, it was virtually annihilated, and over five hundred civilians were killed.

By day, the Nomads lived off the land, tracking down food and drink wherever they could find it, but don't seem to have carried any liquids, even on their longest walks, though light weight camping bottles were available.[2] Before ubiquitous plastic bottles and EU regulated purity, cautious travellers would avoid all unboiled water. In the hotel at Montmartin sur Mer, five days after leaving England, the party drank water for the first time, apparently without ill-effects. Here, too, they were asked to supply their names, UK address, and occupation. Hotel registers are expendable, the record hasn't survived. The 'strenuous member of the party' who set off in search of cider while the rest ate cherries could be either Ross, blessed with a ' superabundance of energy' or the 'indefatigable' Frank On the way to Coutances, they experience, according to the writer, the heaviest rain they'd ever known. Since the date was July 25th, 1912, this is almost certainly true. On the 25th and 26th, thunderstorms and torrential rain swept over much of Northern Europe. August 1912 was also memorably wet and unseasonably cold.

It's not easy to work out which of the party wrote this chapter. It could well be a joint effort by two or three of the men, reporting with amusement the women's decision to go hatless, peasant fashion. At Coutances, they approve of the cathedral's austerity, the clear light, white stone, and lack of ' the usual tawdry decoration'. As Protestants, all the Nomads were distinctly wary of Catholicism, and they were unfamiliar with the bright colours of statues and stained glass windows found in most Catholic churches. Since the late twentieth century, many English churches and cathedrals have repainted and regilded their interiors, removing Puritan limewash to expose highly coloured mediaeval wallpaintings. At York Minster, after the 1984 lightning-strike fire, new roof bosses, some of them designed by children, are, like the mediaeval originals, a riot of colour.[3] Guides to ruined abbeys such as Fountains now remind visitors that the exteriors would have been limewashed a dazzling white, and the interiors richly painted.

Leaving Montmartin, heading towards Granville, they realise that the countryside is changing. Landholdings are smaller, the farming barely subsistence.[4] Arriving in Granville just in time to catch the Jersey boat, they have little to say about the place. Described as ' an old-fashioned little grey town ' the photo taken in Granville on their return from Jersey betrays a clear family resemblance to Kendal, also of Viking origin.[5]

Granville once liked to call itself ' The Monaco of the North', and in 1912, its usual clientele didn't include 'trampish' backpackers. In the contemporary guide-book, La Côte d'Emeraude, the author offers a precise description of what the Jersey-bound Nomads would have seen.

'Built on a rocky promontory that juts westward into the Channel, Granville is almost separated from the main plateau by a great cleft known as the Tranchée des Anglais. Nearby on an apex of rock is its church of Notre Dame, a severe, sombre edifice in granite, which almost seems hewn out of the rock it stands on. The grey, storm-beaten cliffs are draped with ivy, wallflower, pinks and other rock plants. On the south side, three artificial basins make a port. Under the cool north side nestles the Casino, by a long beach of sand, which in summer is crowded with bathers, idlers, and happy little people having the grandest time that ever was, engrossed in the hundred industries and adventures that sand, sea and rocks furnish in the golden age of life'[6]   Casinos, sandcastles and paddling... Conventional seaside Granville wouldn't do at all for the disreputable Nomads.

Chapter VI

Even if the sea trip to Jersey was uneventful, our arrival there was certainly not so. In France, throughout the previous week, we had always been kindly received, but we got a very damp reception at St. Heliers. The weather had looked black for some time, but just as we landed it seemed that the floodgates of heaven were opened, and we were treated to one of the heaviest possible showers of rain, accompanied by thunder and lightning. There seemed nothing for it but to put our best foot forward and find shelter, and so the party of six, laden now with three portmanteaux in addition to our knapsacks, trudged along the quay-side until we came to what seemed like the entrance to a stable, and there we waited to shake ourselves and allow the water to run off our hats and down our necks. On arrival at St. Heliers it had been our intention to make straight to the station, and take train to St. Aubyns, this place being known to one of the party as being select and quiet, and just the spot where we could meditate and listen to the music of the rain-drops falling from the trees. In view of the heavy rain we hailed a passing carriage, which I honestly believe was made for only two persons, and into this the whole party of six tried to get. It was a memorable ride, and has often since been the cause of a hearty laugh. Although all of the party were there, I do not think that anyone could give a truly correct account of how we arrived at the station. Two or three were sitting on seats, and I think two more were sitting on somebody's knees or feet, whilst Fred seemed to be held in by his arms, his legs being quite outside the carriage, and getting the full benefit of the rain. Fortunately (or shall I say unfortunately, seeing that we were almost in one another's arms!) the drive was only a short one, and in due course we disentangled ourselves at the station. After making enquiries regarding trains, we had tea at the station restaurant, the lady in charge going to a good deal of trouble to make us comfortable in a small private room, and finally earning our good wishes by charging us the modest sum of sixpence each, whereas we would willingly have paid double for the luxury of English tea and a shelter from the rain. During preparations for the meal two gentlemen members of the party proceeded to wrap pages of the "Daily Mail" inside their trousers to keep off the effects of the wetting. This was in fact the only occasion during our holiday when we really got very wet, and in this instance it did not matter so much, as we had with us a change of raiment - truly a boon, I can assure you.

One thing worth mentioning is, that on our arrival at Jersey from France we had no Customs formalities to go through with, which was to my mind a great advantage. Upon the two occasions when we entered France and also on our return to England, we were compelled to line up and declare whether or not we had any dutiable goods in our possession. Taxes in Jersey, however, are very light. On the one hand they have no poor to keep, and on the other no expensive officialdom to pay for.

One other fact I should also like to mention in connection with our arrival, and that is the persistence of a certain tout who wished us to accompany him to a certain Mrs. Somebody's (I don't think we should advertise the place) boarding house. In rural Normandy during the previous week we had encountered no touts, but this person seemed to be an expert in the art, and was so persistent that I think he must have been meeting the steamers for years, and has doubtless become quite an institution in the Island.

Another institution, however, this time a national one, was of more interest to us, and at the Post Office we found about six or eight letters awaiting us, these being practically the only news we had from home whilst on our holiday. The most unlooked-for, unasked-for, uncalled-for letter was a request (fruitless as it turned out) from Mr. Lloyd George for one of our members to subscribe to the nation's upkeep. Why can't we live in Jersey, where the taxes are so extremely light ?

The train landed us at St. Aubyns in a few minutes, and here Fred kindly consented to do sentry duty and guard the baggage whilst other members sallied forth to seek for apartments. We were extremely fortunate in finding a suitable house without much trouble. After making our mission known to the lady, she immediately informed us that her hours for meals were 9 a.m., 1 p.m., 6.30 p.m., and on Sundays 9 a.m., 1 p.m., and 8.30 for supper; if visitors went out for their mid-day meal, she packed something up for them, and that her inclusive terms were so much per day. This, however, did not frighten us, and we asked forthwith to see the rooms. It seemed to me that the lady was very loth to go further, but she finally secured candles, and led us upstairs, and in less time than it takes to tell we were duly installed in our new quarters, and after bringing up the luggage, were soon removing our wet clothes and getting into something dry. A day or two later we learnt that we were described as "a rather disreputable looking party", and that may perhaps account for the hesitation on the part of the lady to accept us. You will quite understand this when I tell you that everyone was very wet; some had collars turned up and hats pulled down, and some knapsacks were underneath the mackintoshes, giving one the impression of a camel - perhaps some of us already had the hump!

After a light supper and a chat, we retired for the night, and on Saturday morning rose to find the sun shining, and every prospect of a very fine day.

At breakfast we met a most charming man, brother of the hostess, and we were all greatly taken with his account of life in India. About 10.30 a.m. we set off for a walk, intending to go to La Corbière, and on this occasion we put a knapsack to a new use, viz. to carry our lunch. We had a very pleasant walk through footpaths and nicely wooded roads, until we came to a field from which we had a splendid view of St. Brelade's Bay. Here we rested for quite a long time, the gentleman having removed their coats owing to the heat. It was a most delightful morning, and we just lazed away the time. To the front and to the right of us stretched the green fields, where the Jersey cattle grazed peacefully, entirely oblivious of the fact that we shared the field with them. The Jersey cows are a special feature of these Islands. They are smaller animals than one usually sees in England, they seemed to be of a neater shape, and we understand they are valuable animals. The Islands have never yet suffered from any cattle scourge (such as at present time in England), and consequently they are very careful not to import any cattle whatever. Away to our left we saw the golden sands of St. Brelade's Bay, and the calm sea, with the sun transforming it into a silvery sea. One of the party had thoughtfully brought a book -"Kidnapped" - and we took it in turns to read a chapter. Then we had lunch in real alfresco style, reclining on the grass like the five thousand of old. Our good landlady had sent along a supply of sandwiches cakes, fruit, etc., the only thing missing from the commissariat department being cider. (For all details and full information re Cider, see French section - reference Débit de Boissons!) In due course we moved from that camping ground, and having drunk to the health of a certain Frenchman who lived near Granville, made our way down to St. Brelade's Bay. The coast of Jersey is very rocky, and doubtless very dangerous, owing to the fact that at high tide many huge pieces of rook are entirely covered by only a small depth of water, whilst at low tide the coast is strewn with dozens of jagged boulders pushing their heads Just out of the sea. We walked right across from the Eastern to the Western end of this Bay, and here the gentlemen of the party decided to bathe, which they did, Fred easily taking the prize for long distance swimming, his companions keeping for the most part in fairly shallow water, or what might be called 'the 5 ft. end'. After a race across the shore, and a hasty dressing, we all repaired to the Hotel verandah, where a cup of tea soon cleared any feelings of sickness or headache which had followed the bathing. Just at this time it was raining heavily, but we dodged along between the showers, and arrived back at our abode, just in time to wash for dinner.

Our hostess was a very interesting lady, who had always lived in the Channel Islands, and who could trace her ancestry through a number of generations. At meal times we were always interested in her conversation regarding the people and their ways. She told us how, although most of the inhabitants were originally of French extraction, they were loyal subjects of Britain; how that nowadays almost everyone spoke English in the Islands, and that English was taught in the schools. A great number of the folk are bi-lingual, and our good lady was of the number. It was a very common thing for her to address us at dinner saying "Monsieur X. voulez-vous du boeuf?" to which we replied "Oui, s'il vous plait, Madame." Almost invariably Madame would then switch off into English, and ask if you would have some potatoes or vegetables, and if you merely said "Yes, please," you would hear your good lady say "Avez-vous fait une bonne promenade?" Thus our meals were always interesting, and generally we were provided with a fund of good stories regarding foreign gentlemen who had stayed in the house, and who sometimes got mixed in their English.

I do not doubt but that the disreputable looking party of six tramps will be the means of creating a laugh or two on some occasion, and why not? Pourquoi pas!! During the three days in Jersey meals were the most important thing, and we never forgot the hours - it was a case of "Once more unto the breach, dear friends." But then we were recuperating our shattered frames, taking it easy, so to speak.

During the evening of Saturday our guide and interpreter, Frank, appeared in a new role, viz: that of entertainer, and delighted us with a few recitations, and selections on the piano.

Sunday morning was bright and fine, and promptly at nine o'clock Madame took her seat at the head of the table, and greeted us with the usual "Bon jour, Messieurs et Mesdames," informing us shortly afterwards that she had received a post card from Paris announcing the safe arrival of Alice in that gay city at 24 o'clock on the previous day, and here we must say something about Alice. Such a history as this would be incomplete without it, as, although the aforesaid Alice was little more than a myth to all of us, yet during the remaining part of the holiday she occupied a much greater portion of our thoughts (especially the gentlemen's thoughts) than any other person whom we had met en route. Yet we had never seen her. She lived in our imagination only, each one doubtless having a different vision of what she was really like, our whole ideas being based on the facts, figures and photos given by Madame, our Hostess? It was at mealtimes we generally heard of this young lady - she was the niece of Madame, had been born in India, was being educated in England, and worst of all (to the exceeding sorrow of the men folk) would return to the former place one month after our visit. Her father was a charming man, who interested us greatly with his stories of life in India, and for this reason, if for no other, we think kindly of his daughter, who had gone over to France for a few days. We were assured that she would have been delighted to entertain us; that she many times complained to her aunt that she "never had any young men here," and that she herself was quite willing and able, to entertain them. "Auntie" wrote to Alice saying that she had a party of 2 ladies and 4 gentlemen staying with her, and expected that Alice would return immediately, and finding we had departed, say "It isn't fair, Auntie, you never have any gentlemen when I'm here." Perhaps for the peace of mind of the gentlemen it was as well Alice wasn't there - as it is, she lives in their hearts as some lovely vision beyond reach, clothed in the unutterable charm of the unobtainable; otherwise, how might it have been? She couldn't favour all, result, severed friendships, broken heads, and worst of all, broken hearts! It is a dispensation of Providence that they can each sigh out the ever unanswered query - "Alice, where art thou?" until Alice the Myth is succeeded by Alice the Reality!.

Madame told us, confidentially of course, she had hoped Alice would find a husband in England, and by settling down here, be the means of bringing her mother and father to this country when the latter retired. We think the lady had designs on one of our gentlemen, and we think too he "was willin'," because he was very loth to leave St. Aubyns when the time came!

After breakfast the party went to church and chapel, meeting again at dinner. During the meal, which was served in "the summer wing" of the house, the usual daily thunderstorm commenced, and in a few minutes we were almost flooded out, the rain running down the walls and across the floor. Shortly afterwards the sun shone forth brilliantly, and we settled ourselves comfortably on the verandah overlooking the bay, to be disturbed in less than ten minutes with another downpour of rain, which necessitated our taking refuge in the conservatory, where we spent the remainder of the afternoon, various members reading a chapter each of "Kidnapped," whilst the others demolished "chocs" and other confections.

At six o'clock four of us went out for a walk, and as far as possible we went right ahead, turning neither to the right nor to the left for almost five miles, and passing through some delightfully wooded lanes, up hill and down dale, where one could commune with nature without fear of being disturbed by the noise of a motor horn or other product of civilisation. This was about the prettiest walk of the holiday, and everything looked so very fresh after the rain. Finally we asked of a passer-by (in English if you please) another route to St. Aubyns, and were surprised to find that he could not understand us. He told us the way in French, and in due course we arrived at St. Aubyns, and after a pleasant evening in the company of Madame, we retired for the night.

On Monday we left St. Aubyns early by train, and spent the morning in the town of St. Heliers, afterwards going to Gorée, where we lunched on the red granite rocks, below the Mont Orgueil Castle. A warship came near to the coast, and having made certain that we were not a party of German spies, turned round and went off at full speed. By the way, we had the vessel under observation for quite a long time, our military expert suggesting that possibly it was a forerunner of the German invasion. 8 In this connection the two over-energetic or restless members of the party climbed the heights of the castle wall, but were unable to obtain an entrance here, as they were like the thief and the robber who desireth not to enter the fold by the door, but seeketh to come in some other way.

We walked back to St. Heliers, the road for most of the way being very pretty, but we had little opportunity to look round, owing to two or three very heavy showers, and on one occasion when under the trees, we were invited into a house to shelter, which surely testifies that on this occasion at least we did not look a disreputable party.

During dinner Madame said how sorry she was that we were going, and how much more sorry Alice would be that she had missed us all. Our hostess told us that her house very often accommodated honeymoon couples, was indeed famous for them, and she looked forward to the day when all of us would come there and do likewise. After dinner we were introduced to a lady, specially brought from the other side of the Island, who told us our fortunes from tea leaves! We do not intend to let the public know what the Fates have in store for us, but without giving away secrets can faithfully tell you that some of us will get married, some of us might not, some were to get money (wages probably), whilst others would find letters awaiting them; then one had to beware of a dark gentleman who would come between her and another! But on the great and much debated question as to who would marry Alice, not a word! Finding, therefore, that the Fates had decided against us, we bade the good lady and her friends "good-bye", promising to add another song to those which we had sung in the moonlight the previous week on the banks of the rippling streams, viz: "Alice where art thou?"

The train, entirely oblivious of the emotions which dwelt with some of us, quickly hurried us from St.Aubyns and landed us at St.Heliers.

As one might expect, it was raining heavily, and we wandered round in pitch darkness for some minutes, eventually taking a wrong turning, and on discovering that we were on the wrong track, accosted a small native, who directed us to our steamer, which we boarded without further mishap.

Thus ended our three days' holiday in Jersey, and we carried away pleasant memories of our sojourn there, of Madame herself and her brother from India, and lastly of the "adorable Alice" whom we had never seen.

Background to Chapter VI

Jersey proved even wetter than Normandy, but here they could at least change out of rain-sodden clothes. On the back of a photo, Frank's wry comment assesses the island weather.

' On our arrival in Jersey, the heavens wept for (joy/sorrow)

When we left, they shed tears of (sorrow/joy) Take your choice ! [1]

In Jersey, where they buy the Daily Mail and collect their post, including a tax demand, they were in grave danger of becoming mere tourists.[2] Staying at a St Aubyn's guest house, drinking English tea, never walking much more than five miles, they're relaxed to the point of laziness. Their carefree Déjeuner sur l'herbe near St Brelade's Bay sounds almost indecently idyllic. Reading the page again, and remembering the date, history intervenes. In the green pastures just beyond the shore, pretty little Jersey cattle graze peacefully.[3] Across the Channel, there was Foot and Mouth disease.

Protected by strict import controls, Jersey's cattle had never suffered from FMD. They escaped the English outbreak of 1912.[4] In Britain, infected cattle were shot. During the 2001 outbreak, the carcasses of a slaughtered herd were frequently left where they'd fallen for days. Very soon, they stank of death. In 1912, they'd be thrown into pits, then covered with quicklime, which was still the practice during the 1967 outbreak. Then the mass grave would be filled in. The regulations have changed since then. In 2001, cattle and sheep were burned on massive pyres, the sweet foul stench giving way to other smells, just as vile, burning flesh, bones and hair.[5] Finding the Nomads' story in Cumbria, only a few years after the 2001 Foot and Mouth epidemic, the memories of brutal mass slaughter in muddy fields were still hideous.[6] These who die as cattle ? On the

Western Front, where more than five hundred thousand men died, thousands were covered with quicklime, buried in mass graves. Thousands more in no grave at all.

Once shattered, the illusion of a golden age never really recovers. Carefree still, the Nomads are recording their 1912 adventure. Jersey seems almost mundane and definitely too English. Politics and too much reality intrude. In St Heliers, at the post office, they complain about a tax demand, and it's Lloyd George's fault. His People's Budget of 1909 was modest enough by twenty-first century standards. Those eligible for tax paid a mere 9d in the pound. In other words, income tax was under 5%. Those earning more than £2,000 p.a. paid 1s, i.e. 5p in the pound. Most working men, who wouldn't earn anything like the £156 tax threshold, escaped entirely.[7] Twenty-something, single and childfree still, the Nomads weren't interested in taxes, claiming to approve of Jersey, where taxes were even lighter, and there weren't any poor people to worry about. Callous and privileged Edwardian Tory yuppies ? It's a pose, yet another of their private jokes. Reality was very different. At home on Merseyside, Gladys, working as a very modestly paid elementary school teacher, was sacrificing her weekends to teaching voluntary classes at a ' Ragged School '.[8] At twenty-three, Frank Bourne was selling his photos, not for profit, but to provide free holidays for the poor.[9]

The next skull in this Arcadian landscape is brutal, perhaps more so, because the Nomads seem so casual, almost flippant. Approaching the Jersey coast, near Mont Orgueil Castle, the warshipthey've spotted ' made certain that we were not a party of German spies' They've almost a week of holiday left, days of wandering through Brittany, but from now on, the shadow of war is ever present.[10] In 1905, the Entente Cordiale between Britain and France had begun almost as a marriage of convenience. It suited both countries to agree which areas of North Africa they would control. Like the EU, what started as a business agreement developed into an increasing close relationship between traditional enemies.[11] The international situation remained tense. How much were the six Nomads aware of relations between Britain, France and Germany ? Liverpool didn't build Dreadnoughts or airships, but, living in a maritime city, they'd understand the international situation better than most. Frank spoke French confidently. Alec Westmore and Gladys were good linguists too. Ross was always determined to make himself understood. Fred worked for a bank. Alec and Frank worked in finance too. Backpacking today, they'd pick up news on their phones, watch Sky on their hotel TVs, but the role of newspapers was very different then. Throughout the day, they'd publish breaking news. The text of papers now classed as tabloids was far denser and their vocabulary far more demanding than most twenty-first century broadsheet journalism. Even papers serving rural areas published serious international news and comment. In theory, Britain had won the undeclared arms race. At Westminster, few ministers were really expecting Germany to invade England. 1911's Morocco crisis was history. On this very weekend, the Liverpool Courier published an optimistic report on a future of, as they put it 'amity with the Germans.' [12] Picnicking by the seaside, seeing their warship, the Nomads had, allegedly, a military expert on hand to assess the situation. Which of them might this be ? Military service wasn't compulsory in Britain, though at many public schools, boys were expected to serve in the Officer Training Corps. One of the men might be a serving officer or a member of the Territorials... Fred, perhaps ? Hot and thirsty in Normandy, warned that the only water available isn't safe to drink, Fred splashed it all over himself ' comme les soldats '. During the Boer War, (1899 - 1902) they were all approaching adolescence, quite old enough to form strong opinions, for or against jingoism, pro-Boer or patriots.

Chapter VII

It was about 5 o'clock on the morning of the memorable Tuesday July 30th when I awoke, turned out of my bunk, proceeded to dress as speedily as the motion of the boat would permit, and ascended, to find all hands on deck preparing to weigh anchor and steam off. The weather was dull and threatening; large banks of black clouds drifted across the sky under the influence of a strong S.E. wind.

None of our little party seemed very anxious to leave the beautiful Island of Jersey, where we had spent such a jolly time in spite of the unsettled weather we had experienced. I think we all entertained a lingering desire to see it under more favourable conditions. However our guide was inexorable, and having decided to resume our walk through Normandy, the sooner we landed at Granville the better.

Passing out of the shelter of St. Heliers harbour, a scene of wonderful peacefulness, our noble craft launched forth to face the elements. Once outside the harbour walls any hope of a calm passage was dispelled; an ugly swell (the after effects of the storm of the previous day) caused the vessel to roll unpleasantly, with the result that a number of the passengers were prostrated with mal de mer. This was my first experience of a rough sea, but I quite enjoyed it. All of us remained on deck except Ross (who wisely remained in his bunk) but none felt in the humour for continued conversation.

Standing on the forecastle in the teeth of the gale, watching the boat roll from side to side in the trough of the waves, I felt how insignificant she was in the presence of the mighty forces of nature, and yet the captain stood on his bridge, quite unperturbed, confident in his ability to navigate her safely to her destination. What can be more exhilarating than being buffeted by a strong sea breeze, every muscle and nerve tingling with health and vigour.

About 6.30 a.m. the French coast came in sight. As we approached the land the sea became calmer and the temperature rose a little. About 8 a.m. we entered Granville harbour and prepared to disembark. Fortunately we were not detained long by the Customs Officials who, attired in red pantaloons and blue blouses, slouched about with their long sabres nearly reaching the ground, appearing to have little to do but gaze about them. We submitted to the usual procedure with our usual indifference and eagerly sought out a cafe near to the harbour walls to obtain breakfast.

Being very hungry and a little tired we were not inclined to be fastidious; otherwise we might have complained at the fare placed before us. The coffee was hardly as good as usual, and the butter, well, least said the better. Having rested and refreshed ourselves, we proceeded on our way, passing through the main thoroughfare of Granville - not a very imposing street.

There is a certain similarity about Norman streets; usually narrow, well paved, flanked with rows of old houses of very varied styles of architecture.

As the morning progressed, the sun came out, scattering the mists of early dawn. Our road led us along the coast, fairly elevated, overlooking the sea. Occasionally a glimpse of fine cliffs and a sandy shore were seen. I noticed a greater variety in the scenery than any we had seen in the first week. Beautiful stretches of undulating and well wooded country lay before us. At Granville the air appeared to be somewhat relaxing, but when nearing Carolles, crossing a fine expanse of common land between the hills and the shore, a delightful sea breeze braced us up and gave us a good appetite for our lunch.

Having been informed that we should be too late to cross to Mont St. Michel that afternoon, as originally arranged, we decided to take matters easy, so after an excellent déjeuner at the Hotel de la Plage under a pretty verandah, the party retired to a neighbouring field and enjoyed a rest, basking full length in the sun. Our general appearance caused considerable amusement to passers by, the majority of whom were fashionably dressed, in contrast to our trampish attire. A little dog approached us in a very friendly manner, and further enhanced our opinion of French cordiality.

Ross with his usual super-abundance of energy, reconnoitered the locality, and returned with the report that Carolles possessed an excellent shore with numerous bathing vans. Of the inhabitants, not a word, but it is my firm belief that part of his mission was to see the fairer sex at their holiday amusements.

Leaving Carolles we ascended a fairly steep hill, and after a mile or two walking through pretty lanes we arrived at the top of a fine plateau. Stretching before us lay a magnificent panorama of land and sea, and almost on the horizon Mont St. Michel reared majestically above the surrounding sands, for the tide had not yet filled the bay. A beautiful blue sky, the atmosphere wonderfully clear, scarcely a sound disturbed the solitude of our environment. With the sun shining on the golden corn waving in the gentle summer breeze, and the glittering of the waves of the incoming tide, all conduced to make a picture of exquisite loveliness.

Descending towards the shore, we entered the picturesque little village of St. Jean le Thomas, where we obtained an excellent tea, after which we crossed the sandhills and gained the shore. The evening became very fresh and our walk exceedingly invigorating, putting us all in the best of spirits. What promised to be a glorious sunset was spoiled by a concentration of small clouds on the horizon. Just before dusk we come in sight of Genets. Skirting a temporary race-course on the sands, and safely passing a squadron of geese gathered in martial array to give us a warm reception, we entered the village, where the touts of the Hotel des Voyageurs clustered around us, and with noisy clamourings and wild gesticulations persuaded us to put up for the night at their hospitable premises.

The party had to separate at night owing to lack of accommodation at the Hotel itself for so large a party. Certain members of the party were a bit suspicious of the place, but everything passed off all right, even if our quarters were not as comfortable as those we had become accustomed to. Frank, Ross and I were rather amused at our bedrooms in an outhouse converted into an annexe of the Hotel. The furniture, of splendid oak, seemed rather out of place, and the mantelpiece was covered with tawdry ornaments, crucifixes and other superstitious relics.

As usual, after supper, we had our evening stroll. All was quiet when we passed along the village street, the majority of the villagers having retired to sleep. The next morning we noticed that many of the houses were in a dilapidated state, and a general appearance of poverty characterised the place. The village church, a plain stone structure, we visited after breakfast; its internal decorations were exceedingly dirty and tawdry, and I could scarcely conceal my disgust at the signs of superstition and ignorance of these priest-ridden people. Wednesday morning was wet and dismal, but we were informed that as the day advanced it would turn out very fine, an assurance that proved to be well founded.

We were not a little amused at the reception accorded to a party of Manchester people consisting of two gentlemen and three ladies, who had travelled from Granville by train that morning. The proprietress and her staff gathered round them and repeated the previous evening's performance. As spectators we enjoyed it immensely.

About 12 o'clock two traps drove up; our party together with the Manchester gentlemen occupied one, and the other ladies followed in the other. Bidding farewell to our hospitable friends (who, as I understood afterwards, had an idea that a sovereign was only worth 20 francs -certainly an error on the right side from their point of view) we set forth on our adventurous journey, considerable zest being added to it by the knowledge of hidden quicksands, possibly right in our path. A guide, barelegged, wearing a mackintosh, led the way, holding in his hand a kind of trident with which from time to time he prodded the sand and threw up small mounds which we surmised were to assist them on their return journey. He was accompanied by a dog, similar to our sheep dog, which showed extraordinary intelligence and appreciation of its morning run.

As we drew near the famous island city all eyes were on the alert. From the North it presents a magnificent spectacle; the massive rocks, covered with trees, rise almost precipitously from the sandy plain, and towering above stands the ancient Abbey, a splendid stone structure flanked with countless artistic buttresses. From the centre rears a lofty spire, on the apex of which stands a figure of Saint Michael Archangel, nearly six hundred feet above the bay. Passing round the West side under the shadow of the city walls we came to an embankment connecting the island with the mainland. Here we were photographed in the conveyance, but the result we found out later was very disappointing, due no doubt to our bedraggled appearance.

Entering the city through a gateway in the South wall, we passed into a narrow street possessing very quaint old buildings. After making a few purchases at a fancy shop, we entered a cafe (the famous Poulard) and procured an excellent lunch, and thus fortified proceeded to see the sights. Leaving the narrow winding street we ascended the walls (about 150 feet high) from the summit of which an expansive view of the bay and surrounding country was obtained. Gazing from the mighty battlements one realised what a wonderful strength the place must have possessed as a fortress in mediaeval times. Many attempts by the neighbouring nobles to capture it have been frustrated by its heroic defenders. From the walls we ascended a flight of steps to the main entrance to the Abbey, known I believe as the Grand Degre. It would require the talents of poet, architect and antiquarian combined to do full justice to the wonders of this historic edifice; not possessing these, I can but attempt to give my poor impressions.

Together with a small party of sightseers of different nationalities, we were conducted through the Abbey and adjacent buildings by a typical French official, who by his appearance led me to believe he had held a commission in the French army. His descriptions of the various things of interest were no doubt very eloquent, but being recited in his native tongue I was little the wiser, although I attempted to appear greatly interested. First we were shown, the old barracks constructed for the troops in charge of the political prisoners incarcerated by the French Government in the early part of the 19th century. Then passing through a labyrinth of subterranean passages and rooms supported by massive stone pillars with arched roofs, we visited the Refectory, a chamber of 13th century architecture, long and lofty, with a circular roof, and flanked on either side by arched recesses containing Gothic windows giving an admirable light to the place. At one end was large hole in the side of the wall through which the provisions for the Monastic banquets were hauled. The Church is neither as large nor yet as beautiful architecturally as Westminster, but nevertheless a handsome edifice with fine transepts and choir. From the Church we ascended by a small spiral staircase on to the roof, and from this lofty position we gained a magnificent panoramic view. The cloister, part of which Frank photographed, is in a good state of preservation and is one of the finest of its kind in Europe. A number of pillars have been renovated with new stone which can easily be distinguished from the old on close observation. Descending again to the subterranean vaults, the dungeons next occupied our attention. One of these, entered by a narrow doorway cut in the thick stone walls, hardly high enough to stand erect in, was pitch dark within. By means of a lighted match we examined it, and it was a horrible sight with its chains fastened to the wall in one corner. One could readily conjure up vivid pictures of despairing prisoners, crouching on the cold stone floors, longing for death to relieve then of their long drawn agonies.

An amusing incident occurred in one of those dungeons. The light suddenly went out, and a female voice cried out in real cockney accent "Strike another light, please!" We also saw a huge wooden wheel near an aperture in the outer wall, through which provisions were hoisted for the Abbey when it was used as a prison. In parts of the buildings renovations were going on at the time of our visit.

Well, by the time our guide had showed us all he intended, we were all feeling somewhat fatigued, and glad to return to the cafe for tea. As this is not a customary meal on the Continent, we could seldom obtain it as we wished. Bread, butter and confiture, with a liquid concoction supposed to be tea, formed our repast. During tea we were surprised by a visit from the enterprising photographer, desirous of selling us copies of the photograph he had taken of us before entering the town. Refreshed by our tea we prepared to take leave of our charming surroundings. Before taking the train that crosses the embankment to Pontorson we went on to the sands to watch the incoming tide - a wonderful sight. It enters a narrow channel at a remarkable speed with an incessant hissing noise, and some idea of the force of the current can be obtained by the fact that some boats at anchor were nearly wrested from their anchorage. From the windows of the train we saw vast stretches of reclaimed land, which appears to be very fertile.

Arrived at Pontorson we decided to train to La Boussac, and it was here that the first serious mishap threatened us, as Ross, engaged in a foraging expedition, was very nearly left behind. There was a breathless suspense, but at the last moment Ross appeared, unperturbed, chronometer in hand, declaring he had two seconds to spare. Explanations were deferred until we were in motion, and all excitement had subsided by the time we reached La Boussac, ready to negotiate the six miles which lay between us and bed.

Background to Chapter VII

Un jour Coesnon

En sa folie

A mit le Mont

En Normandie [1]

Like the Bayeux tapestry, their visit to Mont St Michel was nonnegotiable. Crossing quicksands anywhere is a matter of expert knowledge and timing. At Mont St Michel, and at Morecambe Bay, in the north west of England, where the Nomads' story was found, the quicksand guides are legendary, their craft mysterious.[2] The technique seems identical, learned, perhaps, when the old Celtic language was spoken in both areas. Shifting sands and hidden channels are lethal. Conditions can become deadly in minutes, or even seconds. Even a brief heavy shower can affect the strength of freshwater streams, flowing into the estuaries. If the guide decides to turn back, his word is law.[3]

Their visit to the Mont is described in loving detail. They admire the superb architecture, observe the unique geography of the Bay, smile when they hear a Cockney accent. Their extravagant lunch at Poulard's was 'excellent'.[4] Tracked down by a determined freelance, they paid for a photograph of their horse and trap journey. Approaching an island by causeway is awesome. Studying tide tables, watching the sea surge in at Morecambe Bay, Lindisfarne or St Michael's Mount, even the smallest child understands the proverbs and poems. Watching the incoming tide, before catching their train to Pontorson, the Nomads could see for themselves its deadly force, at least six m.p.h. Crossing the viaduct, they could see, too, all the fertile reclaimed land. Saltmarsh lamb is a local delicacy. This reclamation has been a decidedly mixed blessing. Since the embankment of the Coesnon, and extensive reclamation, the bay has been silting up. Without intervention, the Mont could soon become attached to the mainland. But which ? Brittany or Normandy ?

Why isn't Mont St Michel in Brittany ? An accident, surely, as the old rhyme suggests. Exactly like visitors to its Cornish twin, travellers can arrive by boat or splash across the causeway, barefoot, paying about six euros to their guide for the privilege. Only a real island for a couple of hours at high tide, in 1979, the Mont became one of the first World Heritage Sites.[5] On their way to Pontorson and La Boussac, the Nomads never mention the Coesnon, only that Ross nearly missed the train. Costing anything from £1 17s to £8, the chronometer Ross produces to confirm that he has two seconds spare was an expensive gadget.[6] Possibly, they didn't realise the river's significance. Like the Tamar, the Tweed and the Solway, the Coesnon forms an ancient boundary between kingdoms. From Liverpool, the Nomads had often visited Snowdonia. Surely they realised Brittany was a Celtic country, with its own unique language and culture ? Perhaps not... English and Protestant, the Nomads didn't really understand Brittany. How could they ? They'd grown up in an age when Britannia really did rule the waves. Britain was Top Nation.[7]   Without a trace of irony, every confident Edwardian child knew this, especially if that child was male, middle class and a member of the Established Church.

In the early twentieth century, the prosperous middle-classes of England knew - or thought they knew, the kind of Brittany they wanted, a summer playground, well stocked with casinos and luxury hotels, serving the tourist market. Paying as little as three or four francs a day for their board, the British enjoyed a bargain. In 1906, a few days before his eighteenth birthday, T. E. Lawrence set off on a cycling tour of France, discovering that, including all other expenses, he could live very well for under eight francs a day. Two years later, on another cycling tour, he's again spending about 7f a day.[8] Affordable pleasure-grounds were highly desirable, so long as they knew their place. On both sides of the channel, ancient kingdoms and their equally ancient languages were rigorously discouraged. There were no bilingual road signs, official forms, or TV channels. In Wales, place-names were anglicised. Welsh children were still punished at school for speaking their own language. Scots Gaelic was a remote Highland peculiarity, and Britain ruled the whole of Ireland. A hundred years later, all the Celtic languages enjoy EU support. Most guidebooks to Brittany now include Breton glossaries, road signs are in Breton and French. My Breton born cousins speak Breton, French and English. At school, they study the language and culture of Brittany. As in Wales, this is the result of a hard-won battle.[9]

In every practical detail, the Nomads had planned their days in Brittany meticulously, including their journey by horse and trap, from Genêts to Mont St Michel. In this chapter, the writer appears to be seriously distressed by the intensity of Breton worship, even claiming to feel physically sick. Distaste for 'superstition and ignorance' jars in our politically correct twenty-first century. Bretons are alien and 'priest-ridden'. All Protestants, the Nomads had come to France from a city where religious hatred often led to violence and even death. Four days in Brittany was nowhere near long enough for a complete change of hearts and minds. Meeting and socialising with Breton Catholics was a significant move.

Urban and salaried, the Nomads couldn't be expected to understand the fragility of Breton life, let alone the psychological and spiritual impact of such vulnerability. Poverty distressed them. Still in Normandy, and approaching Granville, they'd seen dilapidated buildings, tiny impoverished smallholdings. Brittany was poorer still. Inevitably, given their background, they connect economic deprivation with Catholicism. They certainly couldn't understand rural and maritime poverty, or faith.[10]   Like modern city children who know that food comes from supermarkets, most of the group had little connection with failed harvests or rough seas. In Liverpool, the docks were for ocean liners and vast merchant ships, not tiny fishing boats, out after mackerel.

For some of the party, their stormy return from Jersey was their first experience of a rough crossing. Protestant travellers wouldn't think of praying to Ste Anne d'Auray, mother of the Virgin Mary, patron saint of Brittany and her fishermen. Yet they clearly love Brittany. Travelling through 'scenes of surpassing beauty and constant change', they treasure every moment. Meeting local women, they admire exquisite lace, graceful headdresses. At their hotel, the food's wonderful, their hosts warm and welcoming. Down at the docks, in St Malo, they're fascinated by shipbuilders at work. But they don't really understand the intangibles, the intensity of a faith never kept for Sunday best. As Spencer Musson explains, ' Everywhere, you recognise that you are among a God-fearing folk, whose faith keeps to the ancient ways, and whose life is hedged with reminders of the unseen. Its hidden foundations lie too deep to be shaken by reason, or sapped by knowledge. In all the ways of worldly life are reminders that man is compassed about with benign influences that prompt to good and shield from harm; the crucifix raises its tragic appeal on hill tops, at cross-roads, or in wayside groves. Everywhere are shrines, in cottage and garden walls, on the stone canopies of wells, or in the trunks of ancient oaks.[11]

Bank clerks and teachers could believe they were in control of their world. Fishermen and peasant farmers knew better. The Nomads don't seem to have experienced one of the celebrated Breton 'pardons', the colourful festivals which originated in penitence for sins, still enjoyed today by locals and tourists alike.[12] Perhaps it's just as well. Disconcerted in Normandy by a less than sombre funeral, disapproving of crucifixes and other 'superstitions', they probably wouldn't appreciate a traditional Breton 'pardon'. In England, since the Reformation did away with bawdy irreverent Mystery Plays, the boundaries between sacred and secular had been strictly drawn. The Protestant God of the early twentieth century expected sobriety, even at weddings.[13] No processions, no crucifixes, and, until the Oxford Movement of Victorian times, definitely no smells or bells.

In Catholic Brittany, things were very different : ' Long before daybreak, the whole population gathers before the church. The streets have been strewn with flowers and rushes, the recesses of doorways and windows have been made into little floral shrines, where tapers burn before sacred images. At seven o'clock, the crowd forms into a procession... Singing the Ave Maris Stella, the procession goes along the narrow promontory. Here, looking out on the infinite sea, the home and tomb of so many of their people, a canticle is chanted to the Mater Dolorosa....'[14] At home in Liverpool, and throughout Northern England, the Nomads could have watched very similar festivities. Until the Sixties, rival Catholic and Anglican street processions attracted huge crowds. Town and city centre shops closed for the day. Catholic men carried flower-decked statues of Jesus and Mary. Anglican schoolchildren held out texts, such as 'God is Love', spelled out in flowers. Anglican or Catholic, every church had a richly coloured silk banner for its patron saint. So did the Trade Unions, parading the icons of socialism. Through the streets of Northern England, schoolgirls dressed like brides, all in white, with flowers in their hair.

Chapter VIII

A lovely, glowing evening. The sun, ere parting, flinging with prodigal hand floods of rose and gold over the sky; a breeze laden with the scent of many flowers, and freshened by the sweet, damp earth. In front a straight, good road, hedged for the most part by ripening apple trees. Quietness supreme - too early for the grasshoppers, too late for the birds!

"Combien y-a-t'il d'ici a Dol, Monsieur?" we enquire of the Station Master at La Boussac. "Huit kilometres," he replies. "Merci, bon soir, Monsieur," and we are off at a good pace, accompanied by two fine young Frenchmen, who too were journeying to Dol. They, were friendly and talkative, and walked with us some distance, leaving us to partake of refreshment at a small wayside cafe, the inmates of which greeted them with a friendly welcome. On we pressed, the pace rather increasing than diminishing, the kilos flashing past like white spectres in the now darkening evening. We passed on the way a nun, and a few peasants - no one else; evidently no one but ourselves was labouring for Dol as the only place on the map! The last kilo gone, and now a few lights were to be seen, and we knew our toil for the day was nearly over.

We were greeted here by electric light in the open! An uncommon luxury of late - but Dol is a fairly large place, sufficiently so, according to the code of The Party, to demand hats on at the correct angle, and the most conventional appearance possible! We found our night's quarters - an imposing hotel, and were soon seated at our evening meal, washed and in our right minds! A party of English motorists were dining at another table. We had only asked for supper, but as course succeeded course we began to realise that we were having a fully fledged dinner, and at last the bravest had to give in! We entreated the waiter (a gentleman who spared neither our nerves nor the dishes) to somewhat curtail the meal, and bring us some wholesome fruit, which he did, with the result that we rose from the table more refreshed, and more comfortably, than we might otherwise have done!! After our repast we took a walk, though the darkness was so intense that we couldn't see anything, only the trees standing like huge, black sentinels, and here and there a light showing human habitation. A shower made us beat a hasty retreat, and finally, candles in hand, we climbed the stairs, and sought our apartments. When a day has been spent for the most part in the open, and the mind has been free to take flights where it will - when, in other words, both the body and soul have their intended scope; one has no fear of sleeplessness! It is as if health and happiness are not enough - nature must crown all with that gift of gifts - sleep!

Thursday. Morning saw us all down in good time. We were speaking to an old English gentleman, who, poor soul, was suffering from gout, and the astonishment he evinced at our walking was quite sufficient to verify his statement that his feet weren't in the best of order! Our café-au-lait was served outside. A very chilly morning, but fine and bright. The waiter of deft hands and noisy habits attended to us, and, at our request, brought us some jam, which was evidently made of tomatoes - it went down, as most things did! After breakfast we set out to look round the town. There was a fine cathedral here, dating back to the thirteenth century, which we visited, and where we also saw our hotel friends of the previous night, the motorists. The cathedral was very handsome, and possessed of a large, richly carved porch. The town was pretty, and clean, and there seemed many trees about. Our time was rather short, so after some hurried purchases for our mid-day meal, we shouldered baggage, and again took the road.

A lovely sunny morning, and again a good road, and the knowledge that this was to be one of our record walks as regards distance - our destination Dinan. The way was very pretty, though there wasn't anything very remarkable about it. We were besieged with motors, this being one of the principal highways in Brittany, and I think many of us had a secret longing for the unfrequented ways of the previous week in lovely pastoral Normandy! How the kilos passed! Strange beings! Enjoying things to the full, and yet straining every nerve to shorten the distance between France and home! Stern necessity! Why this is Thursday, and Saturday must find us all in England! We called a halt at mid-day, and sought the shelter of a spreading (not chestnut) pear tree, where we ate our lunch - plain sponge cake, some small jam tarts, pears and grapes. And after we had a quiet rest, all of us fairly silent, feeling that untold joy of leisure worked for, without the nagging of conscience that we ought to have been doing something else! By and by, from some unknown source, crept a feeling in the camp that it was time to be moving - Oh! cruel fate! Must it ever be thus - that one no sooner grasps to the full a gracious pleasure, than some uncomfortable element comes along, and ere one barely tastes, the cup is dashed away! With sundry expressions, all good-tempered, we scrambled to our feet, left the pear-tree and the field, and set our faces for Dinan.

The afternoon was lovely, and the road now very pretty; fields, green dells, and lovely trees, hedges of blackberries, from which we refreshed ourselves from time to time. "On for ever," like "The Brook." "Another kilo!" Magic words, like a battle drum to spur one on, or sweet music to lull a tired mind! By the middle of the afternoon, having dined but sparsely, and entirely without liquor, we were feeling the need of a little refreshment, so sent a faithful ambassador on in front to discover a place. We came on behind, and in no great lapse of time were hailed by the said ambassador, the tone of whose voice, regardless of words, proclaimed to the oncoming thirsty toilers that he had found a cafe where we could obtain our customary "cidre!" Such a nice place too, - a fairly large room, a long wooden table without a cloth, rows of bottles, whose floral labels told of "vins" of different kinds. And a nice old lady, be-capped, as is the custom, in a lace head-dress. She set us down to cups of clear, pale cider, then brought what she had of fruit, plums and pears, talking all the while, and making us feel at home. Such nice little interludes, these, in the march - unlooked for and unsought; the rest so welcome, and the people so interesting. We said our adieux cordially, and again set off. With the dwindling of the kilometres we again called a halt, and sat by the roadside to consume chocolate. A party of motorists enquired the way to Dol, expressing the greatest astonishment at our walking! No doubt too slow for them!

When we came in sight of Dinan, all the labour was forgotten - it was without doubt one of the most beautifully situated places we had yet seen. It is difficult to describe exactly how it lies. Part seems in a lovely, wooded hollow, with the river winding through, and part on wooded hills; but as it first burst on the view it looked a perfect whole, and infinitely lovely. We circled the town, bisected it, indeed absolutely traversed it, in search of the C.H.A. Centre, which we knew was somewhere; but like many good things it proved elusive, and we had to abandon the search until later. We had tea in a nice cafe - the real actual beverage tea, and some most deadly looking cakes! After tea we divided, Mr. Bourne, Ross and Mr. Pulford going in search of the C.H.A. again, while the rest of us sat in a lovely little park. They soon returned with news of success, and the name of a good Hotel - Hotel de la Poste - to which we speedily repaired, and which proved on the whole the nicest place we came across. A very nice lady took us to our rooms, most anxious to make us comfortable, and we were downstairs, and crossing the large courtyard to the dining-room, before one could say the proverbial "Jack Robinson!" Oh! what a dinner! How memories like this stand out! The chinking glasses, and the red wine! The potage, the cotelettes, and the haricots verts!! One can picture the lovely town, with its ancient gates surmounted with shrines; the wooded slopes, and the winding river; and yet, well to the forefront of memory, stands out such a mundane recollection as one's dinner!!!! After dinner we went out, and made for the C.H.A. house, where we had been invited. The party scattered - Mr. Pulford and Ross thinking they would like to get a boat on the river. We four remaining went to visit the C.H.A. where we received such a cordial welcome, and had a nice chat with the host, Mr. Hinchcliff, and his wife. From the dining-room came the buzz of many tongues, and much laughter. We were asked to remain for the games and music, but didn't do so, I scarcely know why, unless we felt our clothing hardly suitable. We came away with a promise to renew our friendship on the morrow, by a sail down the river to St. Malo, and I think we all felt refreshed by the nice welcome from our own people.

It was a lovely night, a clear, starry sky, and very peaceful. We attempted to find the river, by descending as far as possible into the valley, but didn't succeed. It was very dark, and one could scarcely discern anything, and not a breath stirred even the leaves. We sat for a while on a low wall, and had a short lecture on the stars by Mr. Bourne, and then reluctantly tore ourselves away. This was to be our last night in France, and I've no doubt this thought occupied the mind of each of us, and brought in its train various emotions - a glad anticipation of home, and yet a vague regret at the passing of this happy time! We got back to the hotel, intending to wait until our party was complete, but I was promptly presented with a candle, as much as to say "Go to bed, it's quite time!" It was only about 9.45, and four of our people were yet absent, but I had to go!! We should many times have valued a sitting-room, to talk over the day's incidents, and chat a little before going aloft, but this was always lacking. I suppose the others were soon all in, and as promptly presented with candles as I was! Thus ended a day crammed from start to finish, without a wasted moment. We had walked over twenty miles, and on the strength of this we felt entitled to be favoured with a good night's rest, which I think we all had.

Friday morning. Sunny, with a fresh breeze. Our café-au-lait was served in the salle a manger, and we were the first in to the meal. We went round the town again, visited the church, purchased post cards, etc. The shops in Dinan were very nice, and there was some lovely lace displayed in various windows. We were to meet our C.H.A. friends at 9.45, so finally took our way down to the river, through the quaintest, oldest street I've ever seen, the houses being after the style of some of the oldest in Chester. We had a little wait, but soon our friends joined us, and we boarded the gaily be-flagged boat, and cast off for what proved to be a wonderful sail down the River Rance. We were told that this river is held to be finer on the whole than the Rhine. The sail took about 2 ½ hours, and for the whole of this time we passed through scenes of surpassing beauty and constant change. Little villages, each with its church spire; well wooded slopes; handsome chateaux; rocks, and greensward, so varied, and so indescribably beautiful. The river broadened in places to a tremendous width, and as we proceeded, took the appearance of a sea. At one point we were stuck in a lock for quite a time. Just here a gentleman was fishing, his wife with him, a patient onlooker! A man in a boat was also fishing, by means of a curious net, let down by a kind of pulley arrangement (I understand sardines are caught here); he too seemed to be learning patience, as we all must in different schools! Our friends left us at a point some distance from our destination, and we six gave them a hearty cheer as they disappeared with waving hands into the shades of a lovely wood.

We arrived at St. Malo shortly after mid-day, and sought a place to dine, one having been recommended by Mr. Hinchcliff. We had our lunch literally in the street! The place was very crowded, and the types of people most varied, but all apparently French. During lunch a squadron of Boy Scouts, with the French Flag and Union Jack unfurled, passed, to the tatoo of the drum one knows so well! The entente cordiale! As usual, after supper, we had our evening stroll. All was quiet when we passed along the village street, the majority of the villagers having retired to sleep. The next morning we noticed that many of the houses were in a dilapidated state, and a general appearance of poverty characterised the place. The village church, a plain stone structure, we visited after breakfast; its internal decorations were exceedingly dirty and tawdry, and I could scarcely conceal my disgust at the signs of superstition and ignorance of these priest-ridden people... Then we made some purchases at a shop which bore the inviting announcement "English spoken," and a very nice lady it was who spoke English, as my companion could doubtless testify in better terms than myself! (Give a dog a bad name!) We finally all met for tea, and in spite of impending departure, made a good meal. Miss Gleave and I repaired to a pretty park, quite close to the Casino and sea, while the others went to ascend the church tower, from whence a very good view of the town was to be had. By and by we all met again, and while three of us stayed with the traps, the other three went for the luggage. An eye-witness of this scene should have recorded it, for speaking from hearsay only a lot must be lost; but I suppose the difficulties to obtain our luggage were fairly unspeakable! It was after hours, and the officials absolutely refused to deliver it up, and the indignation of the three was evidently a thing to be remembered! Not the least trouble was the inability to find sufficiently strong terms in French to express their feelings (French, as is well known, is a language which admits of little impoliteness!), and I understand the greatest stroke of resistance against this officialdom was a defiant protest which ran, interpreted, "Not at all!" However, British persistence conquered, and they returned victorious!

Nine o'clock saw us all on board, the gangways being taken in, and hands waving farewell from the shore. We stood and watched the lights of St. Malo fade, and the coast of France, black now, but ever bright in memory, die away in the shades of the night. The sea was calm, and the sky clear. We presently took a little refreshment, and then sat on deck in a sheltered spot until about 10.30 p.m., when we sought our bunks. There was scarcely any motion; the boat plodded on at a good pace, and soon I think there were few eyes open but those of the captain and crew, to whose watchful care we trusted ourselves without a thought!

Saturday - morning, and England in sight. A rosy dawn, and from the sea, soft silvery mists. How seldom we see the beauty of the rising sun - the imperceptible giving way of the purple curtains of night, to the all-conquering glory of a fresh day! Only on such rare occasions as this. The English coast looked lovely in this early light, with its white cliffs lapped by the sea, while the green slopes of the Isle of Wight reflected lights and shades from the sun and the mist. A scene in which nature alone had the voice, without the inharmonious effects so often produced by man.

We arrived at Southampton about 6 a.m. or thereabouts, were soon ashore, but had to wait an unconscionable time for the Customs. We got through alright, only one bag being searched, and the last stage of our journey with the party complete was from Southampton to London - a pleasant journey, but not so enthusiastic as that same distance traversed in the opposite direction! Well, that wasn't a very strange coincidence; the previous journey was the beginning of our holiday, now we were ending it! We reached London in good time, and were soon at breakfast, which was a real "breakfast," for we had been fasting practically from teatime the night before!

And now we had to part, three remaining in London, while three returned to Liverpool. A hearty send-off from the station, a waving of hands, promises of renewed friendship - then the whistle of the engine, and we were off, and after straining for the last glimpse of our erstwhile companions, we three journeying to Liverpool leant back on the carriage cushions, and gave ourselves up to reflection!

And it is quite possible, indeed very probable, that we will all carry reflections of that fortnight in France right through our lives. Experiences like this do not vanish. How can one forget the unfailing courtesy of the French people, standing out above all we saw, and casting a sense of happiness and comradeship over everything? We will remember this when perhaps the actual scenes we have walked through will have faded from the memory! And how can one forget the untold joy of ACHIEVEMENT! The setting out with an object in view, and by the dint of one's own labour accomplishing that object!

Was ever holiday crammed with so much? Writing now, when pages have been turned, and those days rank with others in the past, a halo of romance seems over it all. The days so full of pleasure and variety, the constant interest kept up by the constant change; the interludes with people different from ourselves in race and tongue, and yet possessing the one touch of nature that made us all akin! Happy time - as close to Nature as any of us will ever get!

Come! let us raise a glass of sparkling cider, reminiscent of alfresco meals, laughter and jokes, and pledge with real sincerity those to whom we owe this happy time! Real thanks to them, and blessings on the day the thought was first conceived. There must have been much thought and care bestowed on a tour so excellently mapped out, and so capable of achievement.

And once again raise the glass - refill it to the brim, and with clinkings and deep draughts, each pledge each, to better friendship, long life, and happy, happy days, as full of good as was Our Holiday in France!!

Background to Chapter VIII

The final chapter was also written by Emma Irving. In Cold Comfort Farm, her innocently romantic purple prose would surely earn three asterisks.[1] Sunsets in particular are best avoided by anyone in fear of a critic's scorn.[2] Emma's linguistic extravagance is easily forgiven. Backpacking, she had no paint or canvas, and in 1912, no cheap digital camera. Arriving at Dol after dark, to find the luxury of street lighting, their carefree 'trampish existence' has reached injury time. Next morning, their brief stay in the town barely allows time to appreciate the cathedral, or remark on why it dates back to the thirteenth century, but not earlier.[3] Leaving Dol de Bretagne on August 1st, they faced one of their most gruelling walks, twenty miles, and entirely by road. ' Beseiged by motors' or not, walking along a main highway is anything but relaxing, at any time of the year, yet they never stray onto footpaths. Perhaps, once again, they were anxious about trespass, or they simply didn't know of a better route.[4] In August, and carrying nothing to drink, twenty miles would be punishing. Tackling this heroic walk, they passed a resolution not to eat any of their rations until they'd passed the halfway mark.[5] Despite the picnic, and the hedges of blackberries, the journey is a weary business, but they ' managed to abstain from cider until well into the afternoon.'[6]

Their reward was Dinan, ' a perfect whole, and infinitely lovely.' Musson's 1912 guidebook describes the approach to Dinan rather more precisely : 'The long Rue du Petit Port winds up hence to the Porte de Jersual. The broad low-browed doorways, the wide granite sills of the windows on the ground floor, the massive beams and corbels by which storey projects beyond storey over the street, the leaning gables above, the glimpses of dark panelled interiors below, and finally, the great gothic gateway with arch groined behind arch, framing the steep, twisting Rue de Jersual, with its sixteenth century houses form a characteristic entrance to the most picturesque city of that region.'[7]

In Dinan, at the CHA guesthouse, the Villa St Charles, the host and his wife were English, but the 'buzz of many tongues' might indicate an international clientele. The property was substantial, and entirely suitable for young middle-class holiday makers. By the summer of 1912, the organisation founded to enable young working class people to take adventurous holidays was about to splinter.[8] How many grocer's boys or millhands from Northern England travelled to Brittany, stayed at the C.H.A in Dinan ? Backpacking for almost a fortnight, the Nomads weren't dressed for polite company. Next morning, sailing down the Rance to St Malo, they relaxed again, delighted by 'scenes of surpassing beauty'; the journey, according to the locals, finer than the Rhine.[9] In 1912, the river that at times 'took on the appearance of a sea' was navigable as far as Dinan by ships up to 100 tons.[10]

In St Malo, the London and South Western Railway Company had its own pier. Arriving only in time for lunch, and boarding their ship for Southampton at 9 pm, they had little enough time to explore. A popular centre for French family holidays, in the early twentieth century, accommodation could be cheerfully basic.[11] Regrettably, pressed for time, preoccupied with luggage and last minute shopping, the last chapter says little about the St Malo of 1912, and there are only three photos. The best of these records shipbuilding, which was, apart from fishing, St Malo's main industry. The cathedral is merely 'a vast place, and very handsome ' By August 2nd, even the wary Emma had become used to Catholic churches, where they'd find people praying, at any hour of the day. Severely damaged in 1944, the Cathédrale de Saint Vincent has since been restored. Very little of the ancient city survived the 1944 bombing, but the restoration has been sympathetic. Unfortunately, the photo Frank took from a church tower is badly foxed. Then, in the way of all wonderful holidays, time kicks the accelerator, they're boarding the ship, heading for England with all the usual mixed feelings of returning travellers. Three of them stayed on in London, while the other three, including Emma, returned to Liverpool.[12]

How soon was the story of their adventures written, typed, and bound? The last chapter suggests that 'many pages have been turned', but the date on the flyleaf is still 1912, or rather, MCMXII. Very soon, wartime paper shortages would severely constrain the production of anything so expendable as a private travel book, let alone several copies. During the war, almost any blank paper or card would be used for letters, including end papers torn from books.[13] Presumably Emma, as a professional typist, would edit any handwritten contributions. In this final chapter, despite her instinctive disapproval of Catholics, the tribute to their Norman and Breton hosts is graceful and unreserved. ' How can one forget the unfailing courtesy of the French people, standing out above all we saw, and casting a sense of happiness and comradeship over everything ? We will remember this when perhaps the actual scenes we have walked through will have faded from the memory!'

The impact of their time in Normandy and Brittany is almost tangible. As Protestants, they were unlikely to meet a Catholic at school, at work, or socially. They would certainly never worship together. Catholicism was suspect, too closely linked to poverty and immigration. Catholics were at least equally wary of contacts with Protestants. The Scouts and the Girl Guides were officially nondenominational, but as recently as the 1970's, young Catholics were barred by their own communities from joining such organisations. Parents who sent their children to ' Non-Catholic' schools were severely censured. Until the late 1960's, following the second Vatican Council, Catholics were not permitted to attend 'ecumenical' services, where members of the different Christian traditions worship together. More than fifty years earlier, celebrating their own 'entente cordiale', the Nomads learned to move beyond religious prejudice and national stereotyping, recognising ' the one touch of nature that made us all akin' [14]

They'd achieved so much. Translating a possibly crazy idea into a real-time journey is never easy. In 1912, they could have settled for a package tour of Brittany or Normandy. For 32s 6d, the London and South Western Railway Company offered a 528 mile rail and sea trip to Rouen, ' through beautiful scenery equalled only by the Rhine' 15 Package tourists, then and now, can, if they wish, avoid all contact with their hosts, and inconvenient people who can't speak English. For 25s 6d, the L & SWR could give them a ' delightful sea passage' to St Malo. No need whatsoever for weary miles on foot, heavy rucksacks, daily drenchings, anxious searches for a night's lodging, or even, when lost, the challenge of asking for directions and understanding the reply.

Reading the story of their French idyll, seeing that date, the final toast is unbearably poignant. Better friendship, long life, and happy, happy days ?

Footnotes for the Nomad's Diary

Chapter I

1   ' Yesterday's Shopping' The Army & Navy Catalogue, 1907, facsimile reprint, David and Charles, 1969, 1980.

2   Bradshaw, July, 1912, pp 498 - 499 (National Railway Museum archives, York)

3   Maud Pember Reeves, Round About A Pound A Week, Chapter I, Bell, 1913, and Virago, 1979

    (This Fabian Society source book was chosen because it is almost exactly contemporary with the Nomads' journey)

4   Yesterday's Shopping, No 5, Stationery

5   Pember Reeves, Ch X

6   John Angus, Programme Leader for Textiles, University of Derby, has proved that Mallory's clothing was suitable for Everest. www.derby.ac.uk

7   ' Yesterday's Shopping,' No 9, Household Linen etc.

8   The History of Shoes and Shoemaking Museum, Northampton, and shoe consultant, Janet Targett, of Clark's,

9   Pember Reeves, Ch VI.

10 'K' Heritage Centre, Kendal, Cumbria

11 Bradshaw, July 12, London and South Western Railway, p 987. (NRM, York)

12 In July, 1912, the Tate offered two exhibitions, on Alphonse Legros, and James McNeill Whistler.

13 In WWII, the L & SWR vessel Hantonia became a troop ship.

14 ' There's a one-eyed yellow idol to the north of Katmandu...' J. Milton Hayes, 1911.

15 Many online sites offer early 20th century Edison recordings.

16 In 1904, the Board of Education prescribed the analysis, and then learning by heart of many traditional ballads such as Chevy Chase, Barbara Allan, and longer poems by Byron, Browning, Longfellow, Macaulay and Tennyson. (C.L. Thomson, ed, A Book of Ballads, 1904)

17 Francis Ramsey Bourne, photographic archive

18 Martin Pugh, ' The People's Budget, Causes and Consequences New Perspective, Vol 1, No 1, September 1995

19 Francis Ramsey Bourne, photographic archive. (in private hands)

20 Commenting on the legend that St Denis walked two leagues after his head was cut off, Mme Duffand said : ' La distance n'y fait rien, il n'y a que le

premier pas qui coûte.' - (The distance is nothing, it's only the first step that's difficult) (Oxford Dictionary of Quotations.)

21   ' Consanguinity' was, for church lawyers, Popes, and many mediaeval rulers, a flexible concept. Properly negotiated, annulment could be arranged to suit the parties concerned, as in the case of Louis VII of France, Henry II of England, and the woman both men married, Eleanor of Aquitaine.

22   www.memorial - caen . f r.   Clare Hargreaves, Normandy...The D-Day Coast, pp 231 - 2. More than a war museum, a harrowing and unforgettable experience.

Chapter II

1   In the summer of 1912, rainfall records were broken across the whole Northern Hemisphere. Some rainfall records were exceeded in 2007, but 1912 was also exceptionally cold. (bbc.co.uk/weather   See also earthobservatory.nasa.gov.newsroom)

2   Dr Jacques Gury, of the Société Archéologique et Historique D'Ille et Vilaine, remains mystified, and has supplied a detailed transport map of the region. Of course, they had no need to walk. Normandy and Brittany had excellent public transport.

3   Francis Ramsey Bourne, photographic archive.

4   Murder of Canadian Prisoners of War. The trial of Kurt Meyer, 12th SS Panzers, P. Whitney Lackerbauer. There are several Canadian websites linked to units who served in Normandy. www.waramps.ca includes many reports on action around Creully and the Abbaye d'Ardennes.

5   Colin Morris ' The Sepulchre of Christ in the Mediaeval West' O.U.P 2005

6   An EU directive should end the tethering of cattle by 2010. Compassion in World Farming offers a more intelligible version ciwf.org.uk

7   http://en.wikipedia.org/wiki/Buckwheat

8   The coeliac condition, caused by the inability to digest gluten, travelled with the Vikings/Norsemen/Normans. Dr Joe West, of Nottingham University, is researching the epidemiology of this condition. research.nottingham.ac.uk

9   Spencer C Musson, La Côte d'Emeraude,   A & C Black,1912

Chapter III

1   Graham Maddocks, ' Liverpool Pals', Chapter One.

2   In May, 1911, a Catholic speaker in Birkenhead was attacked by a mob of several thousands. Placed under police protection, the man was advised to withdraw. For a profile of early twentieth sectarian violence on Merseyside, see Pat O'Mara, Autobiography of a Liverpool Slummy, London, 1934.

3   Clare Hargreaves, Normandy, The D-Day Coast, pp 240 - 241, Cadogan Guides, 2004

4   www.normandy/battlefields.com   Later, the British press revealed this location in such detail, the Field Marshall had to move to Blay, near Bayeux

5   The chateau gardens at Brécy were designed by Le Notre, who later became Louis XIV's gardener at Versailles. Seriously neglected when the Nomads visited, they have now been superbly restored. See Michael McKenna, Le Notre's Gardens.

6   Francis Ramsey Bourne, photographic archive.

7   Musée -Mémorial de la Bataille de Normandie, Boulevard Fabian Ware, Bayeux The British war graves are nearby, and also, the memorial to those who have no known grave. www. normandybattlefields.com

Chapter IV

1   Hargreaves, Normandy, The D-Day coast, pp 258 - 259

2   Six Nomads in Normandy, Ch IV.

3   Balleroy, bought in the 1970's by an American multi-millionaire friend of the Reagans, is now a popular ballooning centre. (www.chateau-balleroy.com)

4   The quotation is from Terence, 190 - 159 B.C. Public school educated, Frank would know his Latin poets.

5   As they headed west from Le Havre, much of the Nomads' route is haunted by D-Day and the battle for Normandy. Many battleground tours include some of their 1912 journey. www.normandy-battlefields.com.

6   naturetrek.co.uk offers specialist wildlife holidays, including tours based around Cerisy, observing the butterflies

7   Frank has recorded this instruction on the reverse of the Cerisy photo.

8   The photograph reveals that Mme Veuve Maupas didn't provide her guests with plates, but the jugs of vin rouge and cidre look generous.

Chapter V

1   In the late 19th century, the Nonconformist churches recognised the abuse of alcohol as a terrible social scourge, and promoted temperance, even offering fruit cordial rather than wine at their communion services. Notices posted in early 20th century C.H.A. hostels reminded guests that 'cider is an intoxicant'. Brandy was kept at centres, for medicinal purposes only, but 'only sal volatile could be permitted for excursions'.

2   Débits de Boissons - these small bars did not usually supply food, but the party relied on them for refreshment. On most of their long walks, they carried food, but not liquids. Thermos flasks were available, but fairly expensive, 21/0 for the pint size. Aluminium water bottles with straps cost

from 12s 6d for the quart size; (just over a litre) (Army & Navy Stores, p 284)

3   Restoration is based on traces of the original pigment. For instance, in York Minster, the 1346 tomb of Prince William, son of Edward III, has been painted its original strong crimson and gold.

4   Six Nomads in Normandy, Ch V.

5   Many guide books to Normandy observe that the Vikings/Norsemen don't favour urban life, siting the few towns they have close to the sea.

6   Musson, La Côte d'Emeraude, 1912

Chapter VI

1   Francis Ramsey Bourne, photographic archive,

2   No political significance need be attached to their choice of paper. On Jersey, it might have been the easiest paper to obtain ? In WWII, the Daily Mail was the first British newspaper to reach the liberated Channel Islands, the day after V.E. day. (www.jerseyheritagetrust.org)

3   The History of FMD in Britain ww.defra.gov.uk

4   Abigail Woods, A Manufactured Plague, Earthscan, 2004

5   Cumbria Foot and Mouth Disease 2001, Inquiry Report, pp 41 - 46, Cumbria County Council, 2002

6   Personal experience, Cumbria, 2001.

7   Martin Pugh, The People's Budget.New Perspective, Vol 1, No 1 September 1995

8   Personal communication, from Norman Westmore.

9   Francis Ramsey Bourne, private papers. Frank's photography was sold to raise money for the C.H.A. ' Goodwill Holidays'.

10   David Payne, 'The Dreadnoughts and the Western Front' www.westernfront.co.uk

11   Professor Hew Strachan, ' The Entente Cordiale, War and Empire. ' Journal of the Royal United Services, April, 2004

12   Liverpool Courier, 27th July, 1912

Chapter VII

1   Quoted in La Côte d'Emeraude. According to Breton tradition, it is only through a freak of the turbulent little stream that the famous shrine of the Archangel is not Breton.

2   Traversée de la Baie du Mont St Michel à pied... http://fliot.free.fr/traversee
     At Morecambe Bay and at Mont St Michel, information on crossing the
     sands is virtually identical, as are the graphic hazard warnings.

3   www.projetmontsaintmichel.fr

4   Poulard's is still considered the best hotel on Mont St Michel. Ridiculed in
     'Punch' cartoons as ' the sick man of Europe' the franc was weak. Like
     T.E.Lawrence, the Nomads enjoyed a very good exchange rate. (See below,
     n.8)

5   www.worldheritagesite.org/site/montsaintmichel.

6   Yesterday's Shopping,, p 573 and 1073.

7   Sellars and Yeatman, 1066 and All That

8   Writing to his mother, in August, 1906, Lawrence, like all cautious travellers,
     expects to be cheated, but like the Nomads, knew the official exchange rate.
     ' There is no doubt that people would cheat you if possible. When we did not
     get an accurate statement of accounts, we got huge bills, (this only happened
     twice) I thus spent some 61 francs in the eight days and this includes repairs,
     5 francs, (to his bike) and postcards with stamps, a gigantic item. ' Two
     years later, he reports : ' I'm afraid I'll be short later on. In fact, I am rather
     disgusted with my costs to date. The hotels all charge 2f for bed, and at least
     2 for dinner. (I don't like going to any but fairly decent places, alone, with
     money) I had really hoped to do it cheaper. 6/- a day is absurd for one.'
     (Letters of T.E.Lawrence, selected and edited by Malcolm Brown, OUP,
     1991, ISBN 0-19- 282796 - 0

9   In 1912, Spencer Musson believed that Breton and other Celtic languages
     couldn't survive. ' soon, the realm of the Celt will be not in land or
     language, but in the thought and nature of the peoples that have absorbed and
     effaced them' (La Côte d'Emeraude, introd.) Fortunately, Musson was
     wrong. The French government don't conduct linguistic censuses, but as in
     Wales, Breton children can now study their language and heritage at school.
     (www.bbc.co.uk/languages , and my own Breton born cousins)

10   Liverpool's social and economic history was powerfully influenced by the
     high numbers of immigrants arriving in the city. See ' A political and social
     history of Liverpool, 1868 - 1939', P. J. Waller, L.U.P., 1981.

11   Musson, La Côte d'Emeraude . In France, the shrine of Ste Anne d'Auray is
     second only to Lourdes as a place of pilgrimage, and was visited by Pope
     John Paul II.

12   These colourful celebrations are still very popular with both Bretons and
     tourists. Eyewitness Travel Guides, Brittany, pp 32-33. DK, 2005. For
     dates and times, see www.brittanytourism.com

13   As stipulated in the Solemnization of Matrimony. (Book of Common
     Prayer)

14   Musson La Côte d'Emeraude

Chapter VIII

1   Stella Gibbons, Cold Comfort Farm, introduction, parodying the extravagantly descriptive of writers such as D .H. Lawrence and Mary Webb.

2   ' Nobody of any real culture, for instance, ever talks nowadays about the beauty of sunsets. ' Oscar Wilde, 1891.

3   The original cathedral was razed to the ground in 1203, by King John / Sans Terre., murderer, among countless other crimes, of Prince Arthur of Brittany.

4   They could have taken the train from La Boussac to Dol. Although most transport ephemera was lost to paper salvage, Dr Jacques Gury of Rennes located a map of the public transport network as it was in the early twentieth century.

5   Francis Ramsey Bourne, photographic records

6   Francis Ramsey Bourne, photographic records

7   La Côte d'Emeraude

8   By 1912, the main faction of the CHA had distanced itself from the political and social policies of its founder, forcing Arthur Leonard's resignation in December that year. At the Villa St Charles, English visitors complained that the French menu was unsuitable for English digestions. See Chapter 14, Liebe Freunde

9   The Rhine is cited in every rail and sea advertisement, and in every guidebook.

10   Musson, La Côte d'Emeraude

11   Spencer Musson suggests a robust disregard for health and safety: ' The number of members of a family that can make one bedroom do on such occasions is surprising. Centuries of similar experience have evolved a sturdy bourgeoisy (sic) that is immune from the trifles about which modern hygiene makes such a fuss.' La Côte d'Emeraude, p 53 '

12   Frank Bourne's own final photo of the journey was taken in Lombard Street. Fred Pulford worked for the London City and Midland Bank, but didn't transfer from Liverpool to Threadneedle St until shortly before the outbreak of war. Ross Telfer presumably had business at Vincent Murphy's London dock, managing softwood imports from Germany or Scandinavia. Unfortunately, WWII bombing of docks around the UK destroyed many records, including those for Vincent Murphy. See Chs Five and Ten.

13   During the war, wood which could have been used for paper production was required for military purposes, including documents and the lining of shellcases. In Carlisle, the Marshall archive of the No Conscription Fellowship includes letters written on the end papers of books and cardboard packaging.

14   David Sheppard and Derek Worlock ' Better Together'

15   The Railway News, p 74, July 6, 1912 (NRM, York)